Programming Language Processors

Prentice Hall International Series in Computer Science

C. A. R. Hoare, Series Editor

BACKHOUSE, R. C., *Program Construction and Verification*
DEBAKKER, J. W., *Mathematical Theory of Program Correctness*
BARR, M. and WELLS, C., *Category Theory for Computing Science*
BEN-ARI, M., *Principles of Concurrent and Distributed Programming*
BIRD, R. and WADLER, P., *Introduction to Functional Programming*
BORNAT, R., *Programming from First Principles*
BUSTARD, D., ELDER, J. and WELSH, J., *Concurrent Program Structures*
CLARK, K. and McCABE, F. G., *Micro-Prolog: Programming in Logic*
CROOKES, D., *Introduction to Programming in Prolog*
DAHL, O.-J., *Verifiable Programming*
DROMEY, R. G., *How to Solve it by Computer*
DUNCAN, E., *Microprocessor Programming and Software Development*
ELDER, J., *Construction of Data Processing Software*
ELLIOTT, R. J. and HOARE, C. A. R. (eds), *Scientific Applications of Multiprocessors*
FREEMAN, T. L. and PHILLIPS, R. C., *Parallel Numerical Algorithms*
GOLDSCHLAGER, L. and LISTER, A., *Computer Science: A modern introduction (2nd edn)*
GORDON, M. J. C., *Programming Language Theory and its Implementation*
GRAY, P. M. D., KULKARNI, K. G. and PATON, N. W., *Object-Oriented Databases*
HAYES, I. (ed), *Specification Case Studies*
HEHNER, E. C. R., *The Logic of Programming*
HENDERSON, P., *Functional Programming: Application and implementation*
HOARE, C. A. R., *Communicating Sequential Processes*
HOARE, C. A. R. and GORDON, M. J. C. (eds), *Mechanized Reasoning and Hardware Design*
HOARE, C. A. R. and JONES, C. B. (eds), *Essays in Computing Science*
HOARE, C. A. R. and SHEPHERDSON, J. C. (eds), *Mathematical Logic and Programming Languages*
HUGHES, J. G., *Database Technology: a software engineering approach*
HUGHES, J. G., *Object-oriented Databases*
INMOS LTD, *Occam 2 Reference Manual*
JACKSON, M. A., *System Development*
JOHNSTON, H., *Learning to Program*
JONES, C. B., *Systematic Software Development using VDM (2nd edn)*
JONES, C. B. and SHAW, R. C. F. (eds), *Case Studies in Systematic Software Development*
JONES, G., *Programming in occam*
JONES, G. and GOLDSMITH, M., *Programming in occam 2*
JOSEPH, M., PRASAD, V. R. and NATARAJAN, N., *A Multiprocessor Operating System*
KALDEWAIJ, A., *Programming: The Derivation of Algorithms*
KING, P. J. B., *Computer and Communications Systems Performance Modelling*
LEW, A., *Computer Science: A mathematical introduction*
MARTIN, J. J., *Data Types and Data Structures*
McCABE, F. G., *High-Level Programmer's Guide to the 68000*
MEYER, B., *Introduction to the Theory of Programming Languages*
MEYER, B., *Object-oriented Software Construction*
MILNER, R., *Communication and Concurrency*
MITCHELL, R., *Abstract Data Types and Modula 2*
MORGAN, C., *Programming from Specifications*
PEYTON JONES, S. L., *The Implementation of Functional Programming Languages*
PEYTON JONES, S. and LESTER, D., *Implementing Function Languages*
POMBERGER, G., *Software Engineering and Modula-2*
POTTER, B., SINCLAIR, J. and TILL, D., *An introduction to Formal Specification and Z*
REYNOLDS, J. C., *The Craft of Programming*
RYDEHEARD, D. E. and BURSTALL, R. M., *Computational Category Theory*
SLOMAN, M. and KRAMER, J., *Distributed Systems and Computer Networks*
SPIVEY, J. M., *The Z Notation: A reference manual (second edition)*
TENNENT, R. D., *Principles of Programming Languages*
TENNENT, R. D., *Semantics of Programming Languages*
WATT, D. A., *Programming Language Concepts and Paradigms*
WATT, D. A., WICHMANN, B. A. and FINDLAY, W., *ADA: language and methodology*
WELSH, J. and ELDER, J., *Introduction to Modula 2*
WELSH, J. and ELDER, J., *Introduction to Pascal (3rd edn)*
WELSH, J., ELDER, J. and BUSTARD, D., *Sequential Program Structures*
WELSH, J. and HAY, A., *A Model Implementation of Standard Pascal*
WELSH, J. and McKEAG, M., *Structured System Programming*
WIKSTRÖM, Å., *Functional Programming using Standard ML*

Programming Language Processors

Compilers and Interpreters

David A. Watt
University of Glasgow, UK

Prentice Hall

New York   London   Toronto   Sydney   Tokyo   Singapore

First published 1993 by
Prentice Hall International (UK) Ltd
Campus 400, Maylands Avenue
Hemel Hempstead
Hertfordshire, HP2 7EZ
A division of
Simon & Schuster International Group
© Prentice Hall International (UK) Ltd, 1993

Unix is a registered trademark of AT&T Bell Laboratories.

THINK Pascal is a registered trademark of Symantec Corporation

Ada is a registered trademark of the United States Department of Defense
(Ada Joint Program Office).

Apple and Macintosh are trademarks of Apple Computers, Inc.

Printed and bound in Great Britain at the University Press, Cambridge

Library of Congress Cataloging-in-Publication Data

Watt, David A. (David Anthony)
    Programming language processors: compilers and interpreters /
David A. Watt.
    p.   cm. — (Prentice Hall International series in computer
science)
    Includes bibliographical references and index.
    ISBN 0-13-720137-0 : — ISBN 0-13-720129-X (pbk.)
    1. Programming languages (Electronic computers)   2. Compilers
(Computer programs)   3. Translators (Computer programs)   I. Title.
II. Series.
QA76.7.W398   1993
005.4'5—dc20   92-30999
                                                                    CIP

British Library Cataloguing in Publication Data

A catalogue record for this book is available from
the British Library

ISBN 0-13-720129-X (pbk)

2 3 4 5   97 96 95 94 93

Contents

Preface

I first studied computer science in 1968, on a graduate course at Glasgow University. At that time computer science was hardly an academic discipline worthy of the name; rather, it was a disjointed collection of topics, connected only by a sometimes slender relationship with computer programming. Many of these topics are no longer regarded as central to computer science. But one topic was and still is of central importance, and that is the study of programming languages. This topic caught my interest then, and remains my favorite today.

Part of my first job as a programmer at Glasgow University's computer center was to maintain the Algol and Fortran compilers. Both compilers were written in assembly language (like nearly all system software at the time). Each compiler consisted of about 100,000 instructions. Not surprisingly, I never did thoroughly master these compilers, even with the help of the documentation. Still, it was very satisfying to achieve sufficient mastery to make local modifications and to see them work!

Next I joined a Glasgow University project to design and construct an Algol-W compiler for a new minicomputer. In order to make the compiler portable (we thought), we chose to write it in Fortran! Perhaps we were all crazy – if not at the beginning, then certainly by the end of the project. At about the same time Niklaus Wirth chose Fortran as the implementation language for his first Pascal compiler at ETH Zürich; but the Glasgow team could claim independent discovery of this brilliant idea.

Wirth wisely scrapped his first compiler, and rewrote the compiler in Pascal itself. The new compiler was one of the first widely known applications of the technique of bootstrapping. This compiler generated CDC 6600 machine code. Jim Welsh then adapted the compiler to generate ICL 1900 machine code, and moved it to Queen's University, Belfast. This was another application of bootstrapping.

Later, Belfast and Glasgow collaborated on a re-engineered version of the Belfast Pascal compiler. For me (affected as I was by exposure to compilers written in assembly language and Fortran), reading the Belfast compiler was a revelation. Written in Pascal itself, it was beautifully crafted, and could be clearly understood at every level of decomposition. Moreover, it generated efficient machine code, smoothly overcoming the obstacles that the ICL 1900 architecture placed in the way of the compiler writer. Bill Findlay and I were able rather easily to retrofit the compiler and run-time system with a symbolic diagnostic facility, although this was not anticipated when the compiler was first designed. You can judge the quality of this compiler for yourself, for it became the basis of a model implementation of Pascal, published in book form by Welsh and Hay (1986).

Nowadays, methods for implementing programming languages are very well understood. An experienced compiler writer can implement a simple programming language about as fast as he or she can type. The basic methods are quite simple yet effective, and can be lucidly presented to students. Once the methods have been mastered, building a compiler from scratch is essentially an exercise in software engineering.

A textbook example of a compiler is likely to be the first complete program of its size seen by computer science students. Such an example should therefore be an exemplar of good software engineering principles. Regrettably, many compiler textbooks offend these principles. In this textbook, based on about fifteen years' teaching experience, I have done my very best to promote good principles.

A programming languages trilogy

This is the third of a series of three books on programming languages:

- *Programming Language Concepts and Paradigms*
- *Programming Language Syntax and Semantics*
- *Programming Language Processors*

Programming Language Concepts and Paradigms studies the concepts underlying programming languages, and the major language paradigms that use these concepts in different ways; in other words, it is about language design. *Programming Language Syntax and Semantics* shows how we can formally specify the syntax (form) and semantics (meaning) of programming languages. *Programming Language Processors* studies the implementation of programming languages, examining language processors such as compilers and interpreters.

In these three books I am attempting something that has not previously been achieved, as far as I know: a broad study of all aspects of programming languages, using consistent terminology, and emphasizing connections likely to be missed by books that deal with these aspects separately. For example, the concepts incorporated in a language must be defined precisely in the language's semantic specification. Conversely, a study of semantics helps us to discover and refine elegant and powerful new concepts, which can be incorporated in future language designs. A language's syntax underlies analysis of source programs by language processors; its semantics underlies object code generation and interpretation. Implementation is an important consideration for the language designer, since a language that cannot be implemented with acceptable efficiency will not be used.

The three books are designed to be read as a series. However, each book is sufficiently self-contained to be read on its own, if the reader prefers.

Content of this book

Chapter 1 introduces the subject of the book. It reviews the concepts of high-level programming languages, and their syntax, contextual constraints, and semantics. It explains what a language processor is, drawing examples from well-known programming systems.

Chapter 2 introduces the basic terminology of language processors: translators, compilers, interpreters, source and target languages, and real and abstract machines. It goes on to study interesting ways of using language processors: interpretive compilers, portable compilers, and bootstrapping. In this chapter we view language processors as 'black boxes'. In the following chapters we look inside these black boxes.

Chapter 3 looks inside compilers. It shows how compilation can be decomposed into three principal phases: syntactic analysis, contextual analysis, and code generation. It also compares different ways of structuring compilers, leading to single-pass and multi-pass compilation.

Chapter 4 studies syntactic analysis in detail. It decomposes syntactic analysis into scanning, parsing, and abstract syntax tree construction. It introduces the recursive-descent parsing method, and shows how a parser and scanner can be systematically constructed from the source language's syntactic specification.

Chapter 5 studies contextual analysis in detail, assuming that the source language exhibits static bindings and is statically typed. The main topics are identification, which is related to the language's scope rules, and type checking, which is related to the language's type rules.

Chapter 6 prepares for code generation by discussing the relationship between the source language and the target machine. It shows how target machine instructions and storage must be marshalled to support the higher-level concepts of the source language. The topics covered include data representation, expression evaluation, storage allocation, routines and their arguments, and garbage collection.

Chapter 7 studies code generation in detail. It shows how to organize the translation from source language to object code. It relates the selection of object code to the semantics of the source language. As this is an introductory textbook, only code generation for a stack-based target machine is covered. (The more difficult topics of code generation for a register-based machine, and code transformations, are left to more advanced textbooks.)

Chapter 8 looks inside interpreters. It gives examples of interpreters for both low-level and high-level languages. It also relates interpretation to the semantics of the source language.

Chapter 9 concludes the book. It places the implementation of a programming language in the context of the language's life cycle, along with design and specification. It also discusses quality issues, namely error reporting and efficiency.

There are several possible orders for studying the main topics of this book. The chapter on interpretation can be read independently of the chapters on compilation. Within the latter, the chapters on syntactic analysis, contextual analysis, and code generation can be read in any order. The following diagram summarizes the dependencies between chapters.

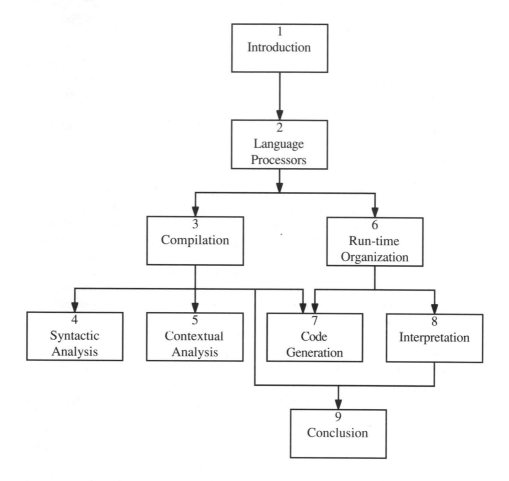

Examples and case studies

The methods described in this textbook are freely illustrated by examples. In Chapter 2, the examples are of language processors for real programming languages. In the remaining chapters, most examples are based on smaller languages, in order that the essential points can be conveyed without the reader getting lost in detail.

A complete programming language is a synthesis of numerous concepts, which often interact with one another in quite complicated ways. It is important that the reader understands how we cope with these complications in implementing a complete programming language. For this purpose we use the programming language Δ as a case study. An overview of Δ is given in Section 1.4. A reader already familiar with a Pascal-like language should have no trouble in reading Δ programs. A complete specification of Δ is given in Appendix B; this includes a formal specification of its syntax, but is otherwise informal. A compiler for Δ is listed in Appendix E. This compiler generates code for an abstract machine, TAM; an interpreter for TAM is listed in Appendix D.

A complete integrated Δ language processor, incorporating an editor, the Δ compiler, and the TAM interpreter, is available for educational use in conjunction with this textbook. The Δ language processor is written entirely in Pascal, and will run on any Apple Macintosh with at least 1MB memory. Moreover, it can easily be modified to run on another computer. You can obtain a copy by remote anonymous FTP from `ftp.cs.glasgow.ac.uk`; after logging in, change to directory `pub/triangle`, and read the instructions you find there.

I designed Δ for two specific purposes: to illustrate how a programming language can be formally specified (in the companion textbook *Programming Language Syntax and Semantics*), and to illustrate how a programming language can be implemented. Ideally a real programming language such as Pascal should be used for these purposes. In practice, however, real languages are excessively complicated. They contain numerous features that are tedious but unilluminating to specify and to implement. Although Δ is a model language, it is large enough to do realistic programming. (Indeed, it includes useful constructs missing from Pascal.) It is also large enough to illustrate basic methods of specification and implementation. Finally, it can readily be extended in various ways (such as adding new types, new control structures, or packages), and such extensions are a basis for a variety of projects.

Exercises and projects

Each chapter of this book is followed by a number of relevant exercises. These vary from short exercises, through longer ones (marked *), up to truly demanding ones (marked **) that could be treated as projects.

A typical exercise is to apply the methods of the chapter to a very small toy language, or a minor extension of Δ.

A typical project is to implement some substantial extension to Δ. Most of the projects are gathered together at the end of Chapter 9; they require modifications to several parts of the Δ compiler, and should be undertaken only after reading up to Chapter 7 at least.

Readership

This book and its two companions are aimed at junior, senior, and graduate students of computer science and information technology, all of whom need some understanding of the fundamentals of programming languages. The books should also be of interest to professional software engineers, especially project leaders responsible for language evaluation and selection, designers and implementors of language processors, and designers of new languages and extensions to existing languages.

The basic prerequisites for this textbook are a second-level course in programming and data structures, and a course in programming languages that covers concepts, syntax, and semantics. The reader should be familiar with Pascal, and preferably at least one other high-level language, since in studying implementation of programming languages it is important not to be unduly influenced by the idiosyncrasies of a particular language. All the algorithms in this textbook are expressed in Pascal.

Ability to read a programming language specification critically is an essential skill. A programming language implementor is forced to explore the entire language, including its darker corners. (The ordinary programmer can wisely avoid these dark corners!) The reader of this textbook will need a good knowledge of syntax and at least a little knowledge of semantics; these topics are briefly reviewed in Chapter 1 for the benefit of readers who might lack such knowledge. Familiarity with BNF and EBNF (which are commonly used, even in informal language specifications) is essential, because in Chapter 4 I show how to exploit them in syntactic analysis. I have not assumed detailed knowledge of formal semantics, but in Chapters 7 and 8 I demonstrate how code generation and interpretation are based on semantics, and the reader will need some knowledge of semantics to benefit from these insights.

The reader should be comfortable with some elementary concepts from discrete mathematics – sets and recursive functions – as these help to sharpen understanding of, for example, parsing algorithms. The mathematics are essential for a deeper understanding of compilation theory; however, only a minimum of theory is presented in this book.

The three books together attempt to cover all the most important aspects of a large subject. Where necessary, depth has been sacrificed for breadth. Thus the really serious student will need to follow up with more advanced studies. Each book has an extensive bibliography, and each chapter closes with pointers to further reading on the topics covered by the chapter.

Acknowledgments

Most of the methods described in this textbook have long since passed into compiler folklore, and are almost impossible to acknowledge to individuals. Instead, I shall mention three persons who have particularly influenced me personally.

John Patterson, as my teacher and Ph.D. supervisor, was the person who first interested me in programming languages and their implementation. I well remember being mystified by his lectures on bootstrapping. He was also the leader of the Glasgow Algol-W compiler project mentioned earlier. Perhaps affected by this experience, he subsequently moved away to computer graphics and animation.

Frank DeRemer has been another major influence on me. Our numerous discussions over the years have ranged from the minutiæ of parsing algorithms to high-level issues of language design and compiler structure. In 1982 he recruited me to teach his semantics and compiler courses at the University of California, and he will recognize in this book the considerable influence he has had on my thinking.

Peter Mosses invited me in 1984 to collaborate with him on the development of action semantics. This work nicely complemented my previous interest in language processors, and has led me to study the relationships among semantics, code generation, and interpretation of programming languages. In this textbook I have attempted to convey to readers an insight into these fascinating relationships.

For providing a stimulating environment in which to think about programming language issues, I am grateful to colleagues in the Computing Science Department of

Glasgow University, in particular Malcolm Atkinson, Kieran Clenaghan, Bill Findlay, John Hughes, John Launchbury, Simon Peyton Jones, Muffy Thomas, Phil Trinder, and Phil Wadler. My research students Deryck Brown and Hermano Moura have a beneficial influence on me, forcing me to think and explain myself more clearly! I have also been strongly influenced, in many different ways, by the work of Luca Cardelli, Edsger Dijkstra, Tony Hoare, Jean Ichbiah, Mehdi Jazayeri, Robin Milner, Bob Tennent, Jim Welsh, and Niklaus Wirth.

I wish to thank Deryck Brown, Hermano Moura, and the Prentice Hall reviewers for reading and providing valuable comments on an earlier draft of the book. Two generations of undergraduate students taking the *Programming Languages 3* module at Glasgow University made an involuntary but essential contribution by class-testing the Δ language processor. One of them, Nick Cropper, has completely redesigned the editor and user interface of the Δ language processor, and I am pleased to acknowledge his contribution.

I am particularly grateful to Tony Hoare, editor of the Prentice Hall International Series in Computer Science, for his encouragement and advice, freely and generously offered when I was still planning this book. If this book is more than just another compiler textbook, that is partly due to his suggestion to emphasize the connections between compilation, interpretation, and semantics. Helen Martin, Editorial Director of Prentice Hall International, guided this book smoothly from initial planning through to production.

Finally, the patience of my family deserves to be acknowledged above all. They have had to tolerate my closeting myself for hours at a time drafting, polishing, and repolishing the text, and (worse still) monopolizing the home computer. To them I dedicate this book.

Glasgow   D.A.W.
July, 1992

CHAPTER ONE

Introduction

In this introductory chapter we start by reviewing the distinction between low-level and high-level programming languages. We then see what is meant by a programming language processor, and look at examples from different programming systems. We review the specification of programming languages, including notations for specifying syntax and semantics. Finally, we look at Δ, a programming language that will be used as a case study throughout this book.

1.1 Levels of programming language

Programming languages are the basic tools of all programmers. A programming language is a formal notation for expressing algorithms. Now, an algorithm is an abstract concept, and has an existence independent of any particular notation in which it might be expressed. Without a notation, however, we cannot (precisely) express an algorithm, nor communicate it to others, nor reason about its correctness.

Practising programmers, of course, are concerned not only with expressing and analyzing algorithms, but also with constructing software that instructs machines to perform useful tasks. For this purpose programmers need facilities to enter, edit, translate, and interpret programs on machines. Tools that perform these tasks are called *programming language processors*, and are the subject of this book.

Machines are driven by programs expressed in ***machine code*** (or *machine language*). A machine-code program is a sequence of *instructions*, where each instruction is just a bit string that is interpreted by the machine to perform some defined operation. Typical machine-code instructions perform primitive operations like the following:

- Load an item of data from memory address 366.
- Add two numbers held in registers 1 and 2.
- Jump to instruction 13 if the result of the previous operation was zero.

In the very early days of computing, programs were written directly in machine code. The above instructions might be written, respectively, as follows:

1

- 0000 0001 0110 1110
- 0100 0000 0001 0010
- 1100 0000 0000 1101

Once written, a program could simply be loaded into the machine and run.

Clearly, machine-code programs are extremely difficult to write and modify, and almost impossible to understand. The programmer must keep track of the exact address of each item of data and each instruction in storage, and must encode every single instruction as a bit string. For small programs (consisting of thousands of instructions) this task is onerous; for larger programs the task is practically infeasible.

Programmers soon began to invent symbolic notations to make programs easier to write and to edit. The above instructions might be written, respectively, as follows:

- `LOAD x`
- `ADD R1 R2`
- `JUMPZ h`

where `LOAD`, `ADD`, and `JUMPZ` are symbolic names for operations, `R1` and `R2` are symbolic names for registers, `x` is a symbolic name for the address of a particular item of data, and `h` is a symbolic name for the address of a particular instruction. Having written a program like this on paper, the programmer would prepare it to be run by manually translating each instruction into machine code. This process was called *assembling* the program.

The obvious next step was to make the machine itself assemble the program. For this process to work, it is necessary to standardize the symbolic names for operations and registers. (However, the programmer should still be free to choose symbolic names for data and instruction addresses.) Thus the symbolic notation is formalized, and can now be termed an ***assembly language***.

Even when writing programs in an assembly language, the programmer is still working in terms of the machine's instruction set. A program consists of a large number of very primitive instructions. The instructions must be written individually, and put together in the correct sequence. The algorithm in the mind of the programmer tends to be swamped by details of registers, jumps, and so on. To take a very simple example, consider computing the area of a triangle with sides a, b, and c, using the formula:

$$\sqrt{(s \times (s - a) \times (s - b) \times (s - c))}$$
where $s = (a + b + c) / 2$

Written in assembly language, the program must be expressed in terms of individual arithmetic operations, and in terms of the registers that contain intermediate results:

```
LOAD R1 a;   ADD R1 b;   ADD R1 c;   DIV R1 #2;
LOAD R2 R1;
LOAD R3 R1;   SUB R3 a;   MULT R2 R3;
LOAD R3 R1;   SUB R3 b;   MULT R2 R3;
LOAD R3 R1;   SUB R3 c;   MULT R2 R3;
LOAD R0 R2;   CALL sqrt
```

Programming is made very much easier if we can use notation similar to the familiar mathematical notation:

```
let s = (a+b+c)/2
in sqrt(s*(s-a)*(s-b)*(s-c))
```

Today the vast majority of programs are written in programming languages of this kind. These are called ***high-level languages***, by contrast with machine languages and assembly languages which are ***low-level languages***. Low-level languages are so called because they force algorithms to be expressed in terms of primitive instructions, of the kind that can be performed directly by electronic hardware. High-level languages are so called because they allow algorithms to be expressed in terms that are closer to the way in which we conceptualize these algorithms in our heads. The following are typical of concepts that are supported by high-level languages, but are supported only in a rudimentary form or not at all by low-level languages:

- *Expressions*
  An expression is a rule for computing a value. The high-level language programmer can write expressions similar to ordinary mathematical notation, using operators such as '+', '−', '*', and '/'.

- *Data types*
  Programs manipulate data of many types: primitive types such as truth values, characters, and integers, and composite types such as records and arrays. The high-level language programmer can explicitly define such types, and declare constants, variables, functions, and parameters of these types.

- *Control structures*
  Control structures allow the high-level language programmer to program selective computation (e.g., by if- and case-commands) and iterative computation (e.g., by while- and for-commands).

- *Declarations*
  Declarations allow the high-level language programmer to introduce identifiers to denote entities such as constant values, variables, procedures, functions, and types.

- *Abstraction*
  An essential mental tool of the programmer is abstraction, or separation of concerns: separating the notion of *what* computation is to be performed from the details of *how* it is to be performed. The programmer can emphasize this separation by use of named procedures and functions. Moreover, these can be parameterized with respect to the entities on which they operate.

Section 1.5 suggests further reading on the concepts of high-level programming languages.

1.2   Programming language processors

A *programming language processor* is any system that manipulates programs expressed in some particular programming language. With the help of language processors we can run programs, or prepare them to be run.

This definition of language processors is very general. It encompasses a variety of systems, including the following:

* *Editors*. An editor allows a program text to be entered, modified, and saved in a file. The simplest kind is an ordinary text editor, which lets us edit any textual document (not necessarily a program text). A more sophisticated kind of editor is one tailored to edit programs expressed in a particular language.

* *Translators and compilers*. A translator translates a text from one language to another. In particular, a compiler translates a program from a high-level language to a low-level language, thus preparing it to be run on a machine. Prior to performing this translation, a compiler checks the program for syntactic and contextual errors.

* *Interpreters*. An interpreter takes a program expressed in a particular language, and runs it immediately. This mode of execution, omitting a compilation stage in favor of immediate response, is preferred in an interactive environment. Database query languages and operating system command languages are usually interpreted.

In practice, we use all the above kinds of language processor in program development. In a conventional programming system, these language processors are usually separate tools. This is the 'software tools' philosophy. However, there is currently a trend towards integrated language processors, in which editing, compilation, and interpretation are just options within a single system. The following examples contrast these two approaches.

Example 1.1
The 'software tools' philosophy is well exemplified by the Unix operating system. Indeed, this philosophy was fundamental to the system's design.

Consider a Unix user developing a chess-playing program in Pascal. The user invokes an editor, such as the screen editor `vi`, to enter and store the program text in a file named (say) `chess.p`:

```
vi chess.p
```

Then the user invokes the Pascal compiler, `pc`, to translate the stored program into machine code, and store the latter in a file named (say) `chess`:

```
pc chess.p -o chess
```

Then the user tests the machine-code program by running it:

```
chess
```

If the program fails to compile, or misbehaves when run, the user reinvokes the editor to modify the program; then reinvokes the compiler; and so on. Thus program development is an edit–compile–run cycle.

There is no direct communication among the language processors involved. If the program fails to compile, the compiler will generate one or more error reports, each indicating the position of the error. The user must make a note of these error reports, and on reinvoking the editor must find the errors and correct them. This is very inconvenient, especially in the early stages of program development when errors are numerous.   □

The essence of the 'software tools' philosophy is to provide a small number of common and simple tools, which can be used in various combinations to perform a large variety of tasks. Thus only a single editor need be provided, one that can be used to edit programs in a variety of languages, and indeed other textual documents too.

What we have described is the 'software tools' philosophy in its purest form. In practice, the philosophy is compromized in order to make program development easier. The editor has a facility that allows the user to compile the program (or indeed issue any system command) without leaving the editor. Some compilers go further: if the program fails to compile, the editor is automatically reinvoked and positioned at the first error.

These are *ad hoc* solutions. A fresh approach seems preferable: a fully integrated language processor, designed specifically to support the edit–compile–run cycle.

Example 1.2

THINK Pascal is a fully integrated language processor, consisting of an editor, a compiler, and other facilities. The user issues commands to open, edit, compile, and run the program. These commands may be selected from pull-down menus, or from the keyboard.

The editor is tailored to Pascal. It decides the program layout automatically, using indentation, thus relieving the user of a tedious chore. Moreover, if the user introduces a syntactic error while editing, the editor detects and highlights it immediately.

The compiler is integrated with the editor. When the user issues the 'compile' command, and the program is found to contain a compile-time error, the erroneous phrase is highlighted, ready for immediate editing. (If the program contains several errors, the compiler will highlight only the first of these. Thus the user will be informed of errors one at a time. This might seem tedious, but is actually less tedious than working through a long list of error reports! Furthermore, a compiler that simply halts on detecting the first error is significantly simpler and even a little faster than a compiler that attempts error recovery.)

The object program is also integrated with the editor. If the program fails at run-time, the failing phrase is highlighted. (Of course, this phrase is not necessarily the one that contains the logical error. But it would be unreasonable to expect the language processor to debug the program automatically!)   □

1.3 Specification of programming languages

Several groups of people have a direct interest in a programming language: the *designer* who invented the language in the first place; the *implementors*, whose task it is to write language processors; and the much larger community of ordinary *programmers*. All these people must rely on a common understanding of the language, for which they must refer to an agreed **specification** of the language.

Several aspects of a programming language need to be specified:

- *Syntax* is concerned with the form of programs. A language's syntax defines what tokens (symbols) are used in programs, and how phrases are composed from tokens and subphrases. Examples of phrases are commands, expressions, declarations, and complete programs.

- **Contextual constraints** (sometimes called *static semantics*) are rules such as the following. *Scope rules* determine the scope of each declaration, and allow us to locate the declaration of each identifier. *Type rules* allow us to infer the type of each expression, and thus to ensure that each operation is supplied with operands of the correct types. Contextual constraints are so called because whether a phrase such as an expression is well-formed depends on its context.

- *Semantics* is concerned with the meanings of programs. There are various points of view on how we should specify semantics. From one point of view, we can take the meaning of a program to be a mathematical function, mapping the program's inputs to its outputs. (This is the basis of *denotational semantics*.) From another point of view, we can take the meaning of a program to be its behavior when it is run on a machine. (This is the basis of *operational semantics*.) Since this book is about language processors, i.e., systems that run programs or prepare them to be run, we shall prefer the operational point of view.

When a programming language is specified, there is a choice between formal and informal specification:

- An *informal specification* is one written in English or some other natural language. Such a specification can be readily understood by any user of the programming language, if it is well-written. Experience shows, however, that it is very hard to make an informal specification sufficiently precise for all the needs of implementors and programmers; misinterpretations are common. Even for the language designer, an informal specification is unsatisfactory because it can too easily be inconsistent or incomplete.

- A *formal specification* is one written in a precise notation. Such a specification is more likely to be unambiguous, consistent, and complete, and less likely to be misinterpreted. However, a formal specification will be intelligible only to people who understand the notation in which the specification is written.

In practice, most programming language specifications are hybrids. Syntax is usually specified formally, using BNF or one of its variants, because this notation is easy and widely understood. But contextual constraints and semantics are usually specified informally, because their formal specification is more difficult, and the available notations are not yet widely understood. A typical language specification, with formal syntax but otherwise informal, may be found in Appendix B.

1.3.1   Syntax

Syntax is concerned with the form of programs. We can specify the syntax of a programming language formally by means of a ***context-free grammar***. This consists of the following elements:

- A finite set of *terminal symbols* (or just *terminals*). These are atomic symbols, the ones we actually use when writing a program in the language. Typical examples of terminals are ':', 'if', and '+'.
- A finite set of *nonterminal symbols* (or just *nonterminals*). A nonterminal symbol represents a particular class of phrases in the language. Typical examples of nonterminals are Program, Command, Expression, and Declaration.
- A *start symbol*, which is one of the nonterminals. The start symbol represents the principal class of phrases in the language. Typically this is Program.
- A finite set of *production rules*. These define how phrases are composed from terminals and subphrases.

Grammars are usually written in the notation ***BNF*** (Backus–Naur Form). In BNF, a production rule is written in the form $N ::= \alpha$, where N is a nonterminal symbol, and where α is a string of terminal and nonterminal symbols. Several production rules with a common nonterminal on their left-hand sides, $N ::= \alpha$, $N ::= \beta$, ..., may be grouped as $N ::= \alpha \mid \beta \mid ....$ The BNF symbol '::=' is pronounced 'may consist of', and '|' is pronounced 'or alternatively'.

Example 1.3
Mini-Δ is a subset of Δ, the language to be introduced in Section 1.4. Mini-Δ is not intended to be a realistic programming language, but will serve as a running example here and elsewhere. Here we present the context-free grammar of Mini-Δ.

The terminal symbols of Mini-Δ are:

```
begin   const   do      else    end     if
in      let     then    var     while
;       :       :=      ~       (       )
+       -       *       /       <       >       =       \
```

The nonterminal symbols are:

```
Program  (start symbol)
Command          single-Command
Expression       primary-Expression
Operator
```

V-name
Declaration   single-Declaration
Type-denoter
Identifier   Integer-Literal

The production rules are:

Program	::=	single-Command	(1.1)
Command	::=	single-Command	(1.2a)
	|	Command ; single-Command	(1.2b)
single-Command	::=	V-name := Expression	(1.3a)
	|	Identifier (Expression)	(1.3b)
	|	**if** Expression **then** single-Command	(1.3c)
		else single-Command	
	|	**while** Expression **do** single-Command	(1.3d)
	|	**let** Declaration **in** single-Command	(1.3e)
	|	**begin** Command **end**	(1.3f)
Expression	::=	primary-Expression	(1.4a)
	|	Expression Operator primary-Expression	(1.4b)
primary-Expression	::=	Integer-Literal	(1.5a)
	|	V-name	(1.5b)
	|	Operator primary-Expression	(1.5c)
	|	(Expression)	(1.5d)
Operator	::=	+ | − | * | / | < | > | = | \	(1.6a–h)
V-name	::=	Identifier	(1.7)
Declaration	::=	single-Declaration	(1.8a)
	|	Declaration ; single-Declaration	(1.8b)
single-Declaration	::=	**const** Identifier ~ Expression	(1.9a)
	|	**var** Identifier : Type-denoter	(1.9b)
Type-denoter	::=	Identifier	(1.10)
Identifier	::=	Letter | Identifier Letter | Identifier Digit	(1.11a–c)
Integer-Literal	::=	Digit | Integer-Literal Digit	(1.12a–b)
Letter	::=	**a** | **b** | **c** | ... | **x** | **y** | **z**	(1.13a–z)
Digit	::=	**0** | **1** | **2** | ... | **9**	(1.14a–j)

Production rule (1.3a) says that a single-command may consist of a value-or-variable-name, followed by the terminal symbol ':=', followed by an expression. (A value-or-variable-name, represented by the nonterminal symbol V-name, is the name of a declared constant or variable.)

Production rule (1.3f) says that a single-command may consist of the terminal symbol 'begin', followed by a command, followed by the terminal symbol 'end'.

Production rules (1.2a–b) say that a command may consist of a single-command alone, or alternatively a command followed by the terminal symbol '*;*' followed by a single-command. In other words, a command consists of a sequence of one or more single-commands separated by semicolons.   □

Each context-free grammar generates a language, which is a set of strings of terminal symbols. We define this language in terms of syntax trees and phrases. Consider a particular context-free grammar G.

A *syntax tree* of G is an ordered labeled tree such that: (a) the terminal nodes are labeled by terminal symbols; (b) the nonterminal nodes are labeled by nonterminal symbols; and (c) each nonterminal node labeled by N has children labeled by X_1, ..., X_n (in order from left to right) such that $N ::= X_1 ... X_n$ is a production rule. More specifically, an *N-tree* of G is a syntax tree whose root node is labeled by N.

A *phrase* of G is a string of terminal symbols labeling the terminal nodes (taken from left to right) of a syntax tree. More specifically, an *N-phrase* of G is a string of terminal symbols labeling the terminal nodes of an *N*-tree.

A *sentence* of G is an *S*-phrase, where S is the start symbol. The *language* generated by G is the set of all sentences of G.

Example 1.4

Figures 1.1 through 1.3 show some Mini-Δ syntax trees. Some of the nonterminal symbols have been abbreviated. Also, the syntax trees of identifiers and literals have been elided, as they are of little interest.

From the syntax tree of Figure 1.1 we can see that the following is an expression (formally, an **Expression**-phrase):

```
d + 10 * n
```

From the syntax tree of Figure 1.2 we can see that the following is a single-command (formally, a **single-Command**-phrase):

```
while b do begin n := 0; b := false end
```

From the syntax tree of Figure 1.3 we can see that the following is a program (formally, a sentence or **Program**-phrase):

```
let var y: Integer in y := y + 1
```

    □

There are two aspects to a grammar like that of Example 1.3:

- The grammar tells us, for each form of phrase, what its subphrases are. For example, a Mini-Δ assignment command (1.3a) has two subphrases: a value-or-variable-name and an expression. A Mini-Δ if-command (1.3c) has three subphrases: an expression and two (sub)commands. The way in which a program is composed from phrases and subphrases is called its *phrase structure*.

- The grammar also tells us in what order the subphrases must be written, and with what terminal symbols they must be delimited. For example, a Mini-Δ assignment command (1.3a) consisting of a value-or-variable-name V and an expression E must be written in the form '$V := E$'. A Mini-Δ if-command (1.3c) consisting of an expression E and subcommands C_1 and C_2 must be written in the form '$if\ E$ $then\ C_1\ else\ C_2$'. Moreover, the grammar tells us that C_1 and C_2 must be *single*-commands (in order to avoid ambiguity).

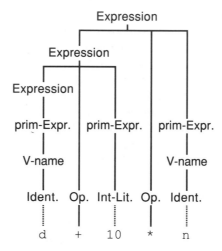

Figure 1.1 Syntax tree of a Mini-Δ expression.

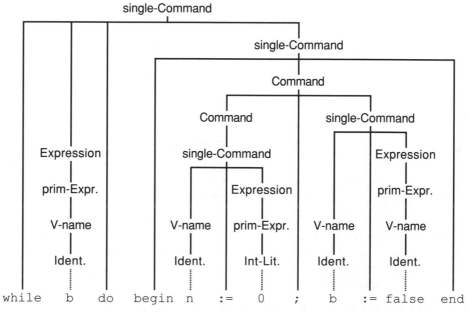

Figure 1.2 Syntax tree of a Mini-Δ single-command.

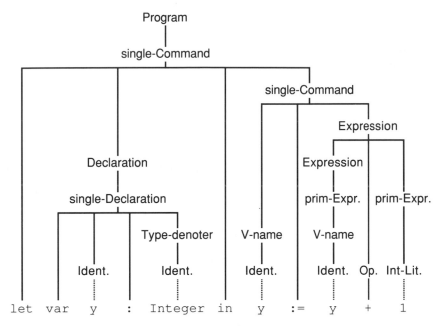

Figure 1.3 Syntax tree of a Mini-Δ program.

Because of its concentration on concrete syntactic details, a grammar such as this specifies what we call the ***concrete syntax*** of the language. The concrete syntax is important to the programmer, of course, who needs to know exactly how to write syntactically well-formed programs.

But concrete syntax has no influence on the *semantics* of the programs. For example, whether the assignment command is written in the form '$V := E$' or '$V \leftarrow E$' or '$E \rightarrow V$' or 'set $V = E$' or 'assign E to V' does not affect how the command will be executed. These are all different in terms of concrete syntax, but all the same in terms of phrase structure.

When specifying semantics, it is convenient to concentrate on phrase structure alone. This is the point of ***abstract syntax***. A grammar used to specify abstract syntax generates only a set of *abstract syntax trees* (*ASTs*). Each nonterminal node of an AST is labeled by a production rule, and it has just one subtree for each subphrase. The grammar does not generate sentences, for terminal symbols have no real role in abstract syntax.

Example 1.5
Here we present a grammar specifying the abstract syntax of Mini-Δ. This will specify only the phrase structure of Mini-Δ. Distinctions between commands and single-commands, between declarations and single-declarations, and between expressions and primary-expressions, will be swept away.

The nonterminal symbols are:

Program   (start symbol)
Command
Expression
Operator
Declaration
Type-denoter

The production rules are:

Program	::=	Command	(1.15)
Command	::=	V-name := Expression	(1.16a)
	|	Identifier (Expression)	(1.16b)
	|	Command ; Command	(1.16c)
	|	**if** Expression **then** Command	(1.16d)
		else Command	
	|	**while** Expression **do** Command	(1.16e)
	|	**let** Declaration **in** Command	(1.16f)
Expression	::=	Integer-Literal	(1.17a)
	|	V-name	(1.17b)
	|	Operator Expression	(1.17c)
	|	Expression Operator Expression	(1.17d)
Operator	::=	+ | − | * | / | < | > | = | \	(1.18a–h)
V-name	::=	Identifier	(1.19)
Declaration	::=	**const** Identifier ~ Expression	(1.20a)
	|	**var** Identifier : Type-denoter	(1.20b)
	|	Declaration ; Declaration	(1.20c)
Type-denoter	::=	Identifier	(1.21)

Figures 1.4 through 1.6 show some Mini-Δ ASTs, corresponding to the (concrete) syntax trees of Figures 1.1 through 1.3, respectively. The nonterminal nodes are labeled by production rules, which have been abbreviated in an obvious and systematic manner. For example, the labels 'V:=E', 'I(E)', 'C;C', 'ifEthenCelseC', 'whileEdoC', and 'letDinC' abbreviate production rules (1.16a–f), respectively.

Figure 1.5 represents the while-command:

```
while b do begin n := 0; b := false end
```

When we write down this command, the symbols 'begin' and 'end' are needed to bracket the subcommands 'n := 0' and 'b := false'. Thus they distinguish this command from the following:

```
while b do n := 0; b := false
```

whose meaning is quite different. (See Exercise 1.4.) There is no trace of these brackets in the abstract syntax, nor in the AST. They are not needed because the AST structure itself represents the bracketing of the subcommands.   □

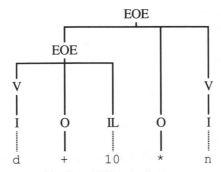

Figure 1.4 Abstract syntax tree of a Mini-Δ expression.

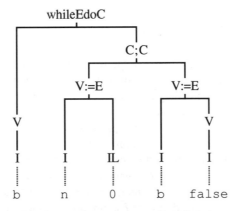

Figure 1.5 Abstract syntax tree of a Mini-Δ command.

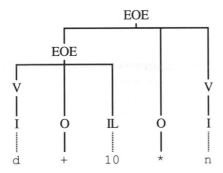

Figure 1.6 Abstract syntax tree of a Mini-Δ program (or command).

A program's AST represents its phrase structure explicitly. The AST is a convenient structure for specifying the program's contextual constraints and semantics. It is also a convenient representation for language processors such as compilers. For example, consider again the assignment command '$V := E$'. The meaning of this command can be specified in terms of the meanings of its subphrases V and E. The translation of this command into object code can be specified in terms of the translations of V and E into object code. The command is represented by an AST with root node labeled 'V:=E' and two subtrees representing V and E, so the compiler can easily access these subphrases.

In Chapter 3 we shall use ASTs extensively to discuss the internal phases of a compiler. In Chapter 4 we shall see how a compiler constructs an AST to represent the source program. In Chapters 5 and 7 we shall see how the AST is used to check that the program satisfies the contextual constraints, and to translate it into object code.

1.3.2   Contextual constraints

Contextual constraints are things like scope rules and type rules. They arise from the possibility that whether a phrase is well-formed or not may depend on its context.

Nearly every programming language allows identifiers to be declared, and thereafter used in ways consistent with their declaration. For instance, an identifier declared as a constant can be used as an operand in an expression; an identifier declared as a variable can be used either as an operand in an expression or on the left-hand side of an assignment; an identifier declared as a procedure can be used in a procedure call; and so on.

The occurrence of an identifier I at which it is declared is called a *binding occurrence*. Any other occurrence of I (at which it is used) is called an *applied occurrence*. At its binding occurrence, the identifier I is bound to some entity (such as a constant value, a variable, or a procedure). Each applied occurrence of I then denotes that entity. A programming language's rules about binding and applied occurrences of identifiers are called its **scope rules**.

The sorts of entity that can be bound to identifiers depend on the programming language; these entities are called *bindables*. For example, the bindables of Δ are values, variables, procedures, functions, and types.

If the programming language permits the same identifier I to be declared in several places, we need to be careful about which binding occurrence of I corresponds to a given applied occurrence of I. The language exhibits *static binding* if this can be determined by a language processor without actually running the program; the language exhibits *dynamic binding* if this can be determined only at run-time. In fact, nearly all major programming languages do exhibit static binding; only a few languages (such as Lisp and Smalltalk) exhibit dynamic binding.

Example 1.6
Mini-Δ is too simplistic a language for static binding to be an issue, so we shall use Δ itself for illustration. In the following Δ program outline, binding occurrences of identifiers are underlined, and applied occurrences are italicized:

```
let
    const m ~ 2;
    var n: Integer;
    func f (i: Integer) : Integer ~
        i * m
in
    begin
        ...;
①  n := f(n);
        ...
    end
```

Each applied occurrence of m denotes the constant value 2. Each applied occurrence of n denotes a particular variable. Each applied occurrence of f denotes a function that doubles its argument. Each applied occurrence of i denotes that function's argument. Each applied occurrence of Integer denotes the standard type *int*, whose values are integer numbers.

Δ exhibits static binding. Imagine a call to f in a block where m is redeclared:

```
let
    const m ~ 4
in
②   ... f(n) ...
```

Both the function calls at ① and ② would double their arguments, because the applied occurrence of m inside the function always denotes 2, regardless of what m denotes at the point of call.

In a language with dynamic binding, on the other hand, the applied occurrence of m would denote the value to which m was *most recently* bound. So the function call at ① would double its argument, whereas the function call at ② would *quadruple* its argument. □

Every programming language has a universe of discourse, the elements of which we call *values*. Usually these values are classified into *types*. Each operation in the language has an associated **type rule**, which tells us the types of value to which the operation is applicable, and the type of the operation's result (if any). Any attempt to apply an operation to a wrongly-typed value is called a *type error*.

A programming language is *statically typed* if a language processor can detect all type errors without actually running the program; the language is *dynamically typed* if type errors cannot be detected until run-time.

Example 1.7
Mini-Δ is statically typed. Consider the following Δ program outline:

```
let
    var n: Integer
in
    begin
```

```
      ...;
①    while n > 0 do
②       n := n - 1;
      ...
      end
```

The type rule of '>' is:

> If both operands are of type *int*, then the result is of type *bool*.

Thus the expression 'n > 0' at ① is indeed of type *bool*. Although we cannot tell in advance what particular values n will take, we know that such values will always be integers. Likewise, although we cannot tell in advance what particular values the expression 'n > 0' will take, we know that such values will always be truth values.

The type rule of '**while** *E* **do** *C*' is:

> If *E* is of type *bool*, then the while-command is well-typed.

Thus the while-command starting at ① is indeed well-typed.

The type rule of '−' is:

> If both operands are of type *int*, then the result is of type *int*.

Thus the expression 'n − 1' at ② is indeed of type *int*.

The type rule of '*V* : = *E*' is:

> If *V* and *E* are of equivalent type, then the assignment command is well-typed.

Thus the assignment command at ② is indeed well-typed.

In a dynamically-typed language, each variable, parameter, etc., may take values of any type. For example, a variable x might contain an integer or a truth value or a value of some other type. The same variable might even contain values of different types at different times. Thus we cannot tell in advance what *type* of value x will contain, never mind what individual value. It follows that we cannot tell in advance whether evaluating an expression such as 'x + 1' will satisfy the type rule of '+'. □

The fact that a programming language is statically typed implies the following:

- Every well-formed expression *E* has a unique type *T*, which can be inferred without actually evaluating *E*.

- Whenever *E* is evaluated, it will always yield a value of type *T*. (Evaluation of *E* might fail due to overflow or some other run-time error, but its evaluation will never fail due to a type error.)

In this book we shall generally assume that the source language exhibits static binding and is statically typed.

1.3.3   Semantics

Semantics is concerned with the meanings of programs. Many notations have been devised for specifying semantics, but so far none has achieved the widespread acceptance of BNF. However, the recently-developed notation of **action semantics** has many important advantages, not least of which is its unusual readability. We shall introduce action semantics here, very briefly, and mainly by example.

The basic idea of action semantics is to specify the semantics of each phrase of the programming language in terms of actions. An *action* is an entity that can be performed, perhaps using data propagated to it by other actions. When performed, an action might *complete* (producing data to be propagated to other actions) or *diverge* (go on forever) or *fail*.

Actions propagate data in various ways. An action can be given and can give *transients*, i.e., data intended to be used immediately (otherwise the data disappear). An action can receive and produce *bindings*, i.e., data bound to identifiers, which are propagated to actions over a defined scope. An action can inspect and/or change *storage*, where data are contained in cells, remaining undisturbed unless overwritten or deallocated.

An action may invoke *data operations* to retrieve or compute data. The simplest of these are the ordinary operations on truth values, integers, and so on. There are also operations that allow an action to access data from transients, bindings, and storage. Finally, there are operations on *abstractions*, an abstraction being a datum that embodies an action. (Abstractions are used to represent procedures and functions.) Some of the more common data operations are summarized in Table 1.1.

Table 1.1 Some data operations.

Data operation	Effect
false, true	Constant truth values.
not t	Yields the logical complement of truth value t.
0, 1, 2, ...	Constant integers.
sum (i, i')	Yields the sum of integers i and i'.
i is less than i'	Yields true if integer i is less than i', or false otherwise.
the given S	Yields the transient datum[†] (when given a single datum).
the given $S\#n$	Yields the nth transient datum[†] (when given a tuple of data).
the S bound to I	Yields the datum[†] bound to identifier I.
the S stored in c	Yields the datum[†] contained in cell c.
abstraction of A	Yields an abstraction that embodies action A.

[†] The datum must be of sort S, otherwise the enclosing action fails.

Table 1.2 Some primitive actions.

Primitive action	*Effect*
complete	Immediately completes, having no effect.
give d	Gives the transient datum d.
check d	Completes if datum d is true; fails otherwise.
bind I to d	Produces a binding of identifier I to datum d.
rebind	Reproduces all bindings received by the action.
store d in c	Changes cell c to contain datum d.
allocate a cell	Finds and reserves an unused cell, and gives that cell.
enact application of a to d	Performs the action embodied by abstraction a, giving datum d as a transient to that action.[†]

- The terms a, c, and d may invoke any data operations.
- [†] This action is actually a composition of two operations, 'enact _' and 'application of _ to _'.

Table 1.3 Some action combinators.

Composite action	*Effect*
A_1 or A_2	Chooses either A_1 or A_2 to be performed. If the chosen subaction fails, the other subaction is chosen instead.
A_1 and A_2	Causes A_1 and A_2 to be performed collaterally.[†¶]
A_1 and then A_2	Causes A_1 and A_2 to be performed sequentially.[†¶]
A_1 then A_2	Causes A_1 and A_2 to be performed sequentially. Transients given by A_1 are propagated to A_2.[¶]
A_1 hence A_2	Causes A_1 and A_2 to be performed sequentially. Bindings produced by A_1 are propagated to A_2.[†] (Thus A_2 is the scope of the bindings produced by A_1.)
A_1 before A_2	Causes A_1 and A_2 to be performed sequentially. Bindings produced by A_1 and A_2 are accumulated.[†]
A_1 moreover A_2	Causes A_1 and A_2 to be performed collaterally. Bindings produced by A_2 override those produced by A_1.[†]
unfolding A	Causes A to be performed iteratively. The dummy action 'unfold', whenever encountered inside A, causes 'unfolding A' to be performed again.

- A, A_1, and A_2 stand for any subactions.
- [†] This composite action propagates transients to its subactions, and combines any transients given by its subactions.
- [¶] This composite action propagates bindings to its subactions, and combines any bindings produced by its subactions.

Primitive actions correspond to single steps in a computation, such as binding an identifier to a datum, or storing a datum in a cell. Some of the more common primitive actions are summarized in Table 1.2.

Action combinators allow us to combine subactions into composite actions. Action combinators correspond to different patterns of control flow and data flow, such as sequencing, selection, and iteration. Some of the more common action combinators are summarized in Table 1.3.

The action notation allows us to express the semantics of programs in terms of simple well-known concepts. Moreover, the notation is English-like. In consequence, action-semantic specifications are remarkably easy to understand; they are even intelligible, at an informal level, to readers unfamiliar with action notation. (By contrast, other kinds of semantic specification are rather hard even for experts to understand, and quite unintelligible to readers unfamiliar with the notation used.)

We specify the action semantics of a programming language as follows:

- The *denotation* (meaning) of each source-language phrase is an action.

- For each class P of phrases in the abstract syntax, we introduce a *semantic function* f that maps each phrase in class P to its denotation:

$$f\ \_\ ::\ P \rightarrow \text{Action}$$

- We define the semantic function f by a number of *semantic equations*, with one semantic equation for each distinct form of phrase in class P. If one form of phrase in P has subphrases Q and R, then the corresponding semantic equation will look something like this:

$$f[\![... \ Q \ ... \ R \ ...]\!] = \\ ... \ f'Q \ ... \ f''R \ ...$$

where f' and f'' are the semantic functions appropriate for subphrases Q and R.

We illustrate this now by a fairly complete example.

Example 1.8
Here we outline the action semantics of Mini-Δ. First we introduce semantic functions for Mini-Δ programs, commands, expressions, etc.:

run $\_$	:: Program	$\rightarrow$ Action	(1.22)
execute $\_$	:: Command	$\rightarrow$ Action	(1.23)
evaluate $\_$	:: Expression	$\rightarrow$ Action	(1.24)
apply-unary $\_$	:: Operator	$\rightarrow$ Action	(1.25)
apply-binary $\_$	:: Operator	$\rightarrow$ Action	(1.26)
fetch $\_$	:: V-name	$\rightarrow$ Action	(1.27)
assign $\_$	:: V-name	$\rightarrow$ Action	(1.28)
elaborate $\_$	:: Declaration	$\rightarrow$ Action	(1.29)

Lines (1.22)–(1.29) state that the denotation of each program, command, expression, etc., will be an action. We can informally characterize these actions as follows:

- The action 'run P' runs the program P in the Mini-Δ standard environment.
- The action 'execute C' executes the command C, causing storage changes.
- The action 'evaluate E' gives the value obtained by evaluating the expression E.
- The action 'apply-unary O' applies the unary operator O to a given value, and gives the result of the operation.
- The action 'apply-binary O' applies the binary operator O to a pair of given values, and gives the result of the operation.
- The action 'fetch V' gives a value: either the value of the constant denoted by V, or the value currently contained in the variable denoted by V, as the case may be.
- The action 'assign V', when given a value, stores this value in the variable denoted by V.
- The action 'elaborate D' elaborates the declaration D, producing bindings.

We define these actions by means of semantic equations. There will be one semantic equation for each form of phrase in the Mini-Δ abstract syntax. More specifically, there will be one semantic equation for each form of command, one for each form of expression, and so on.

Let us start with the semantic equations for commands:

$$\text{execute } [\![V := E]\!] =$$ (1.30a)
  evaluate E then
  assign V

$$\text{execute } [\![I (E)]\!] =$$ (1.30b)
  evaluate E then
  enact application of (the abstraction bound to I) to the given value

$$\text{execute } [\![C_1 ; C_2]\!] =$$ (1.30c)
  execute C_1 and then
  execute C_2

$$\text{execute } [\![\textbf{if } E \textbf{ then } C_1 \textbf{ else } C_2]\!] =$$ (1.30d)
  | evaluate E
  then
  | | check (the given value is true) and then
  | | execute C_1
  | or
  | | check (the given value is false) and then
  | | execute C_2

$$\text{execute } [\![\textbf{while } E \textbf{ do } C]\!] =$$ (1.30e)
  unfolding
  | | evaluate E
  | then
  | | | check (the given value is true) and then
  | | | execute C and then
  | | | unfold

```
        or
        │ check (the given value is false)  and then
        │ complete
```

execute $[$**let** D **in** $C]$ =   (1.30f)
│ rebind moreover elaborate D
hence
│ execute C

Much of this should be self-explanatory. Indentation and vertical lines are used where necessary to bracket subactions. Emphatic brackets $[...]$ are used to enclose Mini-Δ phrases.

In (1.30a) the subaction 'evaluate E' is expected to give a value (either a truth value or an integer). This value is propagated (by the combinator 'then') to the sub-action 'assign V', whose effect is to store that value in the variable V.

In (1.30b) the subaction 'evaluate E' is likewise expected to give a value. This value is propagated to the subaction 'enact application of (the abstraction bound to I) to the given value', which uses both the given value and the received bindings. Mini-Δ procedures are represented by abstractions, so the operation 'the abstraction bound to I' yields the procedure to which identifier I is bound. (Since Mini-Δ has no procedure declarations, this binding must come from the standard environment.)

In (1.30d) the subaction 'evaluate E' is expected to give either true or false. If it gives true, the subaction 'check (the given value is true)' will just complete, allowing the subaction 'execute C_1' to be performed, but the subaction 'check (the given value is false)' will fail, preventing the subaction 'execute C_2' from being performed. If instead 'evaluate E' gives false, the converse will happen.

In (1.30e), the subaction 'evaluate E' is likewise expected to give either true or false. If it gives false, the subaction 'complete' will be performed, doing nothing. If instead it gives true, the subaction 'execute C and then unfold' will be performed. In this the effect of performing 'unfold' will be to perform the enclosing action 'unfolding ...' again. In other words, 'execute C' will be followed by a fresh iteration of the while-command.

In (1.30f) the net effect of 'rebind moreover elaborate D' is to reproduce the received bindings, overridden by the bindings produced by elaborating D. The resulting set of bindings is propagated (by the combinator 'hence') into the subaction 'execute C', which is therefore the scope of these bindings.

Here are the semantic equations for expressions:

evaluate $[IL]$ =   (1.31a)
    give valuation IL

evaluate $[V]$ =   (1.31b)
    fetch V

evaluate $[O\ E]$ =   (1.31c)
    evaluate E then
    apply-unary O

evaluate $\llbracket E_1 \; O \; E_2 \rrbracket$ = $\qquad\qquad\qquad\qquad$ (1.31d)
   | evaluate E_1 and
   | evaluate E_2
  then
   | apply-binary O

In (1.31a) 'valuation *IL*' is assumed to yield the integer value of the literal *IL*.

In (1.31d) the subaction 'evaluate E_1 and evaluate E_2' evaluates the two sub-expressions E_1 and E_2 collaterally (i.e., in no particular order). The resulting pair of values is propagated into the subaction 'apply-binary O', which gives the result of applying binary operator O to that pair of values.

Here are the semantic equations for some unary and binary operators:

apply-unary $\llbracket \setminus \rrbracket$ = $\qquad\qquad\qquad\qquad\qquad\qquad$ (1.32)
   give not (the given truth-value)

apply-binary $\llbracket + \rrbracket$ = $\qquad\qquad\qquad\qquad\qquad\qquad$ (1.33a)
   give sum (the given integer#1, the given integer#2)

apply-binary $\llbracket < \rrbracket$ = $\qquad\qquad\qquad\qquad\qquad\qquad$ (1.33b)
   give (the given integer#1 is less than the given integer#2)

Here are the semantic equations for value-or-variable-names:

fetch $\llbracket I \rrbracket$ = $\qquad\qquad\qquad\qquad\qquad\qquad\qquad$ (1.34)
   give the value bound to I or
   give the value stored in the cell bound to I

assign $\llbracket I \rrbracket$ = $\qquad\qquad\qquad\qquad\qquad\qquad\qquad$ (1.35)
   store the given value in the cell bound to I

In (1.35) the identifier I is assumed to be bound to a cell, which represents a variable. The action's effect is simply to store the given value in that cell.

In (1.34) I could be bound to either a value (a constant) or a cell (representing a variable). In the former case, the subaction 'give the value bound to I' will complete and the subaction 'give the value stored in the cell bound to I' will fail. In the latter case the converse will hold. In either case, the action gives a value.

Here are the semantic equations for declarations:

elaborate $\llbracket \textbf{const} \; I \sim E \rrbracket$ = $\qquad\qquad\qquad\qquad$ (1.36a)
   evaluate E then
   bind I to the given value

elaborate $\llbracket \textbf{var} \; I : T \rrbracket$ = $\qquad\qquad\qquad\qquad\qquad$ (1.36b)
   allocate a cell then
   bind I to the given cell

elaborate $\llbracket D_1 \; ; \; D_2 \rrbracket$ = $\qquad\qquad\qquad\qquad\qquad$ (1.36c)
   elaborate D_1 before
   elaborate D_2

The last semantic equation is that of a program:

run $[\![C]\!]$ =   (1.37)
        elaborate-standard-environ hence
        execute C

Here the auxiliary action 'establish-standard-environ' produces bindings for the Mini-Δ standard environment:

elaborate-standard-environ =   (1.38)
        bind "`false`" to false and
        bind "`true`" to true and
        bind "`putint`" to abstraction of ...

□

There is space here for only a thumbnail sketch of action semantics. The actions themselves have been specified very informally (and not even precisely). But one of the strengths of action semantics is that a semantic specification can be understood quite well at an informal level, as perhaps you appreciated while studying Example 1.8.

Although action semantics is founded on a rigorous mathematical theory of actions, it clearly has an operational flavor. Thus action semantics is well suited for one of the purposes of this textbook, which is to demonstrate how semantics underlies the compilation and interpretation of programs. In Chapter 7 we shall relate the action semantics of Mini-Δ to a code generator for Mini-Δ. In Chapter 8 we shall relate the action semantics of Mini-Δ to an interpreter for Mini-Δ.

1.4 Case study: the programming language Δ

In this book we shall use small examples – such as the toy language Mini-Δ – to illustrate various implementation methods without getting lost in details. Nevertheless, it is also important to illustrate how these methods can be applied to realistic programming languages.

A major language like Pascal is just *too* complicated for the purposes of an introductory textbook. Instead we shall use Δ (or *Triangle*), a small but realistic programming language, as a case study. Δ is a Pascal-like language, but generally simpler and more regular. Δ was also used as a case study in the companion textbook by Watt (1991). Here we give a brief overview of Δ. (By the way, the toy language Mini-Δ introduced earlier is a subset of Δ.)

Δ commands are similar to Pascal's, but for simplicity there is only one conditional command and one iterative command. Unlike Pascal, Δ has a block (let-) command with local declarations.

Example 1.9
The following illustrates the Δ if-command and let-command:

```
if x > y then
    let const xcopy ~ x
    in
        begin x := y; y := xcopy end
else
```

Note the empty else-part. (It is actually a skip command.)   □

Δ expressions are richer than Pascal's, but free of side effects. Conditional expressions, block (let-) expressions with local declarations, and aggregates (record and array expressions) are all provided. A function body is just an expression. For simplicity, only three primitive types (denoted by the identifiers Boolean, Char, and Integer), and two forms of composite type (records and arrays), are provided. Unlike Pascal, Δ is type-complete, i.e., no operations are arbitrarily restricted in the types of their operands. Thus values of any type may be passed as parameters, returned as function results, assigned, and compared using the binary operators '=' and '\='.

Example 1.10
The following illustrates a Δ let-expression and if-expression:

```
let
    const taxable ~ if income > allowance
                    then income - allowance
                    else 0
in
    taxable / 4
```

The following illustrates Δ record and array types and aggregates:

```
let
    type  Date ~ record
                     m: Integer,
                     d: Integer
                 end;
    const days ~ [31, 28, 31, 30, 31, 30,
                  31, 31, 30, 31, 30, 31];
    var   today: Date
in
    ...
    if today.d < days[today.m-1]
    then {m ~ today.m, d ~ today.d + 1}
    else if today.m \= 12
    then {m ~ today.m + 1, d ~ 1}
    else {m ~ 1, d ~ 1}
    ...
    if today = {m ~ 2, d ~ 29} then ... else ...
```

Here days is declared to be a constant of type 'array 12 of Integer', with elements 31, 28, 31, etc. The first if-expression yields a value of the record type `Date`, representing the day after `today`. The second if-expression illustrates record comparison.   □

Δ declarations are quite similar to Pascal's, but declarations of different kinds may be mixed freely. Constant, variable, and type declarations have been illustrated in Examples 1.9 and 1.10. Notice that a Δ constant declaration may have any expression, of any type, on its right-hand side. This expression must be evaluated at run-time, but thereafter the constant identifier's value is fixed. (The Δ constant declaration is more general than Pascal's, where the right-hand side is restricted to be a literal or another constant.)

Like Pascal, Δ has procedure and function declarations. A procedure body is just a command, which may be (but not necessarily) a block command. Likewise, a function body is just an expression, which may be (but not necessarily) a block expression. Functions are free of side effects.

Procedures and functions may have constant, variable, procedural, or functional parameters. These have uniform semantics: in each case the formal-parameter identifier is simply bound to the corresponding argument, which is a value, variable, procedure, or function, respectively. (Unlike Pascal value parameters, no copying is involved.)

Example 1.11
The following function and procedure implement operations on a type `Point`:

```
type Point ~ record
                x: Integer,
                y: Integer
             end;
func horizontalimage (pt: Point) : Point ~
     {x ~ pt.x, y ~ 0-pt.y};
proc movevertical (yshift: Integer, var pt: Point) ~
     pt.y := pt.y + yshift;
...
var p: Point; var q: Point;
...
movevertical(3, p);
q := horizontalimage(p)
```

□

Δ has the usual variety of operators, standard functions, and standard procedures. These behave exactly like ordinary declared functions and procedures; unlike Pascal, they have no special type rules or parameter mechanisms. In particular, Δ operators behave exactly like functions of one or two parameters.

Example 1.12
The Δ operator '`/\`' (logical conjunction) is, in effect, declared as follows:

```
func /\ (b1: Boolean, b2: Boolean) : Boolean ~
        if b1 then b2 else false
```

The expression 'a /\ b' is, in effect, a function call:

```
/\(a, b)
```

and the more complicated expression '(n > 0) /\ (sum/n > 40)' likewise:

```
/\(>(n, 0), >(/(sum, n), 40))
```

Note, by the way, that the above declaration of /\ does *not* imply short-circuit evaluation. The arguments passed to /\ are both *values*, computed at the time the function is called.   □

A complete informal specification of Δ may be found in Appendix B. Each section is devoted to a major construct, e.g., commands, expressions, or declarations. Within the section there are subsections describing the intended *usage* of the construct, its *syntax* (expressed in BNF), its *semantics* (and contextual constraints), and finally *examples*. Browse through Appendix B, attempting to fill the gaps in your understanding of Δ left by the brief overview here. Appendix B is intended to serve as a model of a carefully written informal specification of a programming language. (Nevertheless, a careful reader will almost certainly find loopholes!)

1.5   Further reading

This book assumes that you are familiar with the basic concepts of high-level programming languages, including those summarized in Section 1.1. A detailed study of these concepts, using terminology consistent with this book, may be found in the companion textbook by Watt (1990). Some other good textbooks cover similar material, including those by Ghezzi and Jazayeri (1987), Sethi (1988), and Tennent (1981).

A very brief review of syntax and semantics was given in Section 1.3. A much fuller treatment may be found in the companion textbook by Watt (1991). The advantages and disadvantages of formal and informal specification are discussed in detail, as are various methods for formally specifying syntax, contextual constraints, and semantics. There is an introduction to action semantics. Formal specifications of the syntax and semantics of Δ are given as case studies.

A comprehensive and definitive account of action semantics may be found in Mosses (1992). Action semantics is by no means restricted to specifying toy languages like the one used for illustration in this chapter. It can also specify languages with a variety of data types, procedures and functions, parameters, exceptions, concurrency, and so on. Mosses demonstrates this by specifying progressively larger subsets of Ada.

Exercises 1

1.1   In this chapter editors, compilers, and interpreters have been cited as kinds of language processor. Can you think of any other kinds of language processor?

1.2*   Recall Examples 1.1 and 1.2. Write a similar critical account of any other programming system with which you are familiar.

1.3**   Design an editor tailored to your favorite programming language.
       (*Hints:* Think of the editing operations you perform most frequently on your programs. You probably delete or replace complete symbols more often than individual characters, and you probably delete or replace complete phrases – expressions, commands, declarations – rather than individual lines. You probably spend a lot of time on chores such as good layout. Also think of the common syntactic errors that might reasonably be detected immediately.)

1.4   Draw the syntax tree and AST of the Mini-Δ command:

```
while b do n := 0; b := false
```

cited at the end of Example 1.5. Compare with Figures 1.2 and 1.5.

1.5   According to the context-free grammar of Mini-Δ in Example 1.3, which of the following are Mini-Δ expressions?

     (a)   `true`
     (b)   `sin(x)`
     (c)   `-n`
     (d)   `m >= n`
     (e)   `m - n * 2`

Draw the syntax tree and AST of each one that *is* an expression.
       Similarly, which of the following are Mini-Δ commands?

     (f)   `n := n + 1`
     (g)   `halt`
     (h)   `put(m, n)`
     (i)   `if n > m then m := n`
     (j)   `while n > 0 do n := n-1`

       Similarly, which of the following are Mini-Δ declarations?

     (k)   `const pi ~ 3.1416`
     (l)   `const y ~ x+1`
     (m)   `var b: Boolean`
     (n)   `var m, n: Integer`
     (o)   `var y: Integer; const dpy ~ 365`

1.6   According to the syntax and action semantics of Mini-Δ in Examples 1.3 and 1.8, what value is written by the following Mini-Δ program? (*Note:* The standard procedure `putint` writes the integer value given as an argument.)

```
let
    const m ~ 2;
    const n ~ m + 1
in
    putint (m + n * 2)
```

Do *not* rely on your knowledge of Pascal: it might mislead you!

1.7*   Write *informal* specifications of Mini-Δ's (a) syntax, and (b) semantics. Try to make your specifications clear and precise enough to be referred to by programmers.

CHAPTER TWO

Language Processors

In this book we shall study two particularly important kinds of language processor: translators (particularly compilers) and interpreters. In this chapter we start by reviewing the basic ideas of translation and interpretation, which will already be familiar to most readers. Then we build on these basic ideas to explore the more sophisticated ways in which language processors can be used. A language processor is itself a program, and thus can be processed (translated or interpreted) in just the same way as an ordinary program. The ultimate development of this idea is bootstrapping, whereby a language processor is used to process itself!

In this chapter we view translators and interpreters as 'black boxes'; we concentrate on what they do rather than how they do it. In subsequent chapters we shall look inside them to see how they work.

2.1 Translators and compilers

A *translator* is a program that accepts any text expressed in one language (the translator's *source language*), and generates a semantically-equivalent text expressed in another language (its *target language*).

Example 2.1
Here are some diverse examples of translators:

(a) A Chinese-into-English translator.
This is a program that translates Chinese texts into English. The source and target languages of this translator are both natural languages.

Natural-language translation is an advanced topic, related to artificial intelligence, and well beyond the scope of this textbook. We shall restrict our attention to translators whose source and target languages are programming languages.

(b) A 68000 assembler.
This is a program that translates 68000 assembly-language programs into 68000

machine code. The source language is 68000 assembly language, and the target language is 68000 machine code.

(c) A Pascal-into-68000 compiler.
This is a program that translates Pascal programs into 68000 machine code. The source language is Pascal, and the target language is 68000 machine code.

(d) An Ada-into-C translator.
This is a program that translates Ada programs into C. The source language is Ada, and the target language is C.

$\square$

An *assembler* translates from an assembly language into the corresponding machine code. An example is the 68000 assembler of Example 2.1(b). Typically, an assembler generates one machine-code instruction per source instruction.

A *compiler* translates from a high-level language into a low-level language. An example is the Pascal-into-68000 compiler of Example 2.1(c). Typically, a compiler generates several machine-code instructions per source command.

Assemblers and compilers are the most important kinds of programming language translator, but not the only kinds. We sometimes come across *high-level translators* whose source and target languages are both high-level languages, such as the Ada-into-C translator of Example 2.1(d). A *disassembler* translates a machine code into the corresponding assembly language. A *decompiler* translates a low-level language into a high-level language. (See Exercise 2.1.)

In all these cases, the translated texts are themselves programs. The source language text is called the *source program*, and the target language text is called the *object program*.

Before performing any translation, a compiler checks that the source text really is a well-formed program of the source language. (Otherwise it generates error reports.) These checks take into account the *syntax* and *contextual constraints* of the source language. Assuming that the source program is indeed well-formed, the compiler goes on to generate an object program that is semantically equivalent to the source program, i.e., that will have exactly the desired effect when run. Generation of the object program takes into account the *semantics* of the source and target languages.

Translators, and other language processors, are programs that manipulate programs. Several languages are involved: not only the source language and the target language, but also the language in which the translator is itself expressed! The latter is called the *implementation language*.

To help avoid confusion, we shall use *tombstone diagrams* to represent ordinary programs and language processors, and to express manipulations of programs by language processors. We shall use one form of tombstone to represent an ordinary program, and distinctive forms of tombstone to represent translators and interpreters.

An ordinary program is represented by a round-topped tombstone, as shown in Figure 2.1. The head of the tombstone names the program P. The base of the tombstone names the implementation language L, i.e., the language in which the program is expressed.

Figure 2.1 Tombstone representing a program *P* expressed in language *L*.

Example 2.2
The following diagrams show how we represent:

(a) A program named `sort` expressed in Pascal.
(b) A program named `sort` expressed in 68000 machine code. (By convention, we abbreviate '68000 machine code' to '68000'.)
(c) A program named `graph` expressed in Basic.

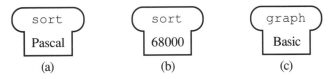

Programs run on machines. A machine that executes machine code *M* is represented by a pentagon inside which *M* is named, as shown in Figure 2.2.

Figure 2.2 Representation of a machine *M*.

Example 2.3
The following diagrams show how we represent:

(a) A 68000 machine.
(b) A MIPS machine.
(c) A SPARC machine.

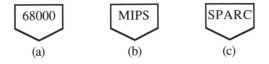

A program can run on a machine only if it is expressed in the appropriate machine code. Consider running a program P (expressed in machine code M) on machine M. We represent this by putting the P tombstone on top of the M pentagon, as shown in Figure 2.3.

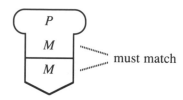

Figure 2.3 Running program P on machine M.

Example 2.4
The following diagrams show how we represent:

(a) Running program `sort` (expressed in 68000 machine code) on a 68000 machine.
(b) Running program `sort` (expressed in MIPS machine code) on a MIPS machine.
(c) Attempting to run program `sort` (expressed in MIPS machine code) on a 68000 machine. Of course, this will not work; the diagram clearly shows that the machine code in which the program is expressed does not match the machine on which we are attempting to run the program.
(d) Attempting to run program `sort` (expressed in Pascal) on a 68000 machine. This will not work either; a program expressed in a high-level language cannot run immediately on any machine. (It must first be translated into machine code.)

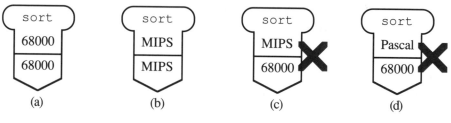

We have now introduced the elementary forms of tombstone. There are also distinctive forms of tombstone to represent different kinds of language processor. A translator is represented by a T-shaped tombstone, as shown in Figure 2.4. The head of the tombstone names the translator's source language S and target language T, separated by an arrow. The base of the tombstone names the translator's implementation language L.

(*Note:* Although we use tombstones of different shapes to represent ordinary programs, translators, and interpreters, the base of a tombstone always names the implementation language. Compare Figures 2.1, 2.4, and 2.6.)

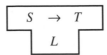

Figure 2.4 Tombstone representing an *S*-into-*T* translator expressed in language *L*.

Example 2.5
The following diagrams show how we represent:

(a) A Pascal-into-68000 compiler, expressed in C.
(b) A Pascal-into-68000 compiler, expressed in 68000 machine code.
(c) An Ada-into-C translator, expressed in Pascal.
(d) A 68000 assembler, which translates from 68000 assembly language into 68000 machine code, and is itself expressed in 68000 machine code.

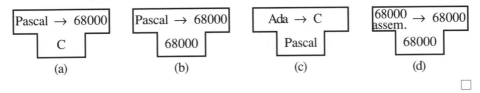

An *S*-into-*T* translator is itself a program, and can run on machine *M* only if it is expressed in machine code *M*. When the translator runs, it translates a source program *P*, expressed in the source language *S*, to an equivalent object program *P*, expressed in the target language *T*. This is shown in Figure 2.5. (The object program is shaded, to emphasize that it is newly generated, unlike the translator and source program, which must be given to start with.)

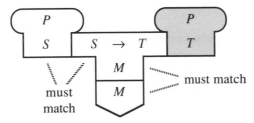

Figure 2.5 Translating a source program *P* expressed in language *S* to an object program expressed in language *T*, using an *S*-into-*T* translator running on machine *M*.

Example 2.6

The following diagram represents compilation of a Pascal program on a 68000 machine. Using the Pascal-into-68000 compiler, we translate the source program `sort` to an equivalent object program, expressed in 68000 machine code. Since the compiler is itself expressed in 68000 machine code, the compiler will run on a 68000 machine.

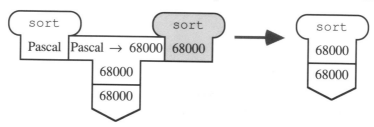

The second stage of the diagram shows the object program being run, also on a 68000 machine.   □

A *cross-compiler* is a compiler that runs on one machine (the *host machine*) but generates code for a dissimilar machine (the *target machine*). The object program must be generated on the host machine but transferred to the target machine to be run. Such a transfer is often called *downloading*. A cross-compiler is a useful tool if the target machine has too little memory to accommodate the compiler, or if the target machine is ill-equipped with program development aids. (Compilers tend to be large programs, needing a good programming environment to develop, and needing ample memory to run.)

Example 2.7

The following diagram represents cross-compilation of a Pascal program to enable it to run on a (hypothetical) XYZ microprocessor. Using a Pascal-into-XYZ cross-compiler, we translate the source program `sort` to an equivalent object program, expressed in XYZ machine code. Since the compiler is itself expressed in 68000 machine code, the compiler runs on a 68000 machine.

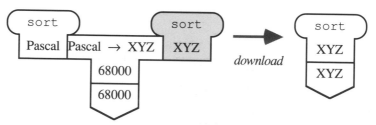

The second stage of the diagram shows the object program being run on an XYZ machine, having been downloaded from the 68000.   □

The behavior of a translator can be summarized by a few simple rules, which are clearly evident in Figure 2.5:

- A translator (like any other program) can run on a machine *M* only if it is expressed in machine code *M*.
- The source program must be expressed in the translator's source language *S*.
- The object program is, by construction, expressed in the translator's target language *T*.
- The object program is, by construction, semantically equivalent to the source program. (We emphasize this by giving the source and object programs the same name.)

Example 2.8
The following tombstone diagrams illustrate what we *cannot* do with a translator:

(a) A C compiler cannot translate a Pascal source program.
(b) A translator expressed in 68000 machine code cannot run on a MIPS machine.

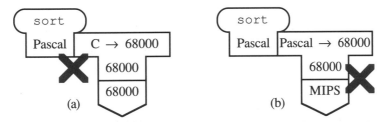

Similarly, it should be clear that a translator expressed in C or Pascal cannot run on any machine. (It must first be translated into machine code.) □

A *two-stage translator* is a composition of two translators. If we have an *S*-into-*T* translator and a *T*-into-*U* translator, we can compose them to make a two-stage *S*-into-*U* translator. The source language *S* is translated to the target language *U* not directly, but via an intermediate language *T*.

We can easily generalize this idea to multiple stages. An *n-stage translator* is a composition of *n* translators, and involves *n*–1 intermediate languages.

Example 2.9
Given an Ada-into-C translator and a C-into-68000 compiler, we can compose them to make a two-stage Ada-into-68000 compiler, as shown below. The Ada source program is translated into C, which is then compiled into 68000 machine code.

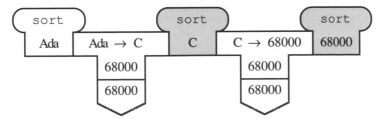

The two-stage compiler is functionally equivalent to an Ada-into-68000 compiler. □

A translator is itself a program, expressed in some language. As such, it can be translated into another language.

Example 2.10

Suppose we have a Pascal-into-68000 compiler expressed in C. We cannot run this compiler at all, because it is not expressed in machine code. But we can treat it as an ordinary source program to be translated by a C-into-68000 compiler:

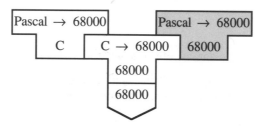

The object program is a Pascal-into-68000 compiler expressed in 68000 machine code (shaded). We can now use this to compile Pascal programs, as illustrated in Example 2.6. ☐

More generally, all language processors are themselves programs, and as such can be manipulated by other language processors. For example, language processors can be translated (as in Example 2.10) or interpreted. We shall see the importance of this later in the chapter.

2.2   Interpreters

A compiler allows us to prepare a program to be run on a machine, by first translating the program into machine code. The program will then run at full machine speed. This method of working is not without disadvantages, however: the entire program must be translated before it can even start to run and produce results. In an interactive environment, *interpretation* is often a more attractive method of working. Thus we come to a new kind of language processor, an interpreter, that also allows us to run programs.

An ***interpreter*** is a program that accepts any program (the *source program*) expressed in a particular language (the *source language*), and runs that source program immediately.

An interpreter works by fetching, analyzing, and executing the source program instructions, *one at a time*. The source program starts to run and produce results as soon as the first instruction has been analyzed. The interpreter does *not* pause to analyze the entire source program.

Interpretation is sensible when most of the following circumstances exist:

- The programmer is working in interactive mode, and wishes to see the results of each instruction before entering the next instruction.
- The program is to be used once and then discarded (i.e., it is a 'throw-away' program), and therefore running speed is not very important.
- Each instruction is expected to be executed only once (or at least not very frequently).
- The instructions have simple formats, and thus can be analyzed easily and efficiently.

Interpretation is very slow. Interpretation of a source program, in a high-level language, can be up to 100 times slower than running an equivalent machine-code program. Therefore interpretation is not sensible when:

- The program is to be run in production mode, and therefore speed is important.
- The instructions are expected to be executed frequently.
- The instructions have complicated formats, and are therefore time-consuming to analyze. (This is the case in most high-level languages.)

Example 2.11
Here are some well-known examples of interpreters:

(a) A Basic interpreter.
   Basic has expressions and assignment commands like other high-level languages. But its control structures are low-level: a program is just a sequence of commands linked by conditional and unconditional jumps. A Basic interpreter fetches, analyzes, and executes one command at a time.

(b) A Lisp interpreter.
   Lisp is a very unusual language in that it assumes a common data structure (trees) for both code and data. Indeed, a Lisp program can manufacture new code at run-time! The Lisp program structure lends itself to interpretation. (See also Exercise 2.11.)

(c) The Unix command language interpreter (*shell*).
   A Unix user instructs the operating system by entering textual commands. The *shell* program reads each command, analyzes it to extract a command-name together with some arguments, and executes the command by means of a system call. The user can see the results of a command before entering the next one. The commands constitute a command language, and the *shell* is an interpreter for that command language.

(d) An SQL interpreter.
   SQL is a database query language. The user extracts information from the database by entering an SQL query, which is analyzed and executed immediately. This is done by an SQL interpreter within the database management system.

□

An interpreter is represented by a rectangular tombstone, as shown in Figure 2.6. The head of the tombstone names the interpreter's source language. The base of the tombstone (as usual) names the implementation language.

$$\boxed{\begin{array}{c} S \\ \hline L \end{array}}$$

Figure 2.6 Tombstone representing an *S* interpreter expressed in language *L*.

Example 2.12
The following diagrams show how we represent:

(a) A Basic interpreter, expressed in 68000 machine code.
(b) An SQL interpreter, expressed in 68000 machine code.
(c) The Unix shell (command language interpreter), expressed in C.
(d) The Unix shell, expressed in 68000 machine code.

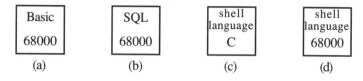

| (a) | (b) | (c) | (d) |

An *S* interpreter is itself a program, and can run on machine *M* only if it is expressed in machine code *M*. When the interpreter runs, it runs a source program *P*, which must be expressed in source language *S*. We say that *P* runs *on top of* the *S* interpreter. This is shown in Figure 2.7.

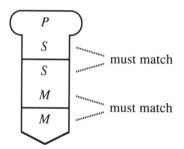

Figure 2.7 Interpreting a program *P* expressed in language *S*, using an *S* interpreter running on machine *M*.

Example 2.13
The following diagrams show how we represent:

(a) Running program `graph` (expressed in Basic) on top of a Basic interpreter, which itself runs on a 68000 machine.
(b) Running program `chess` (expressed in Lisp) on top of a Lisp interpreter, which itself runs on a 68000 machine.

(c) Attempting to run program `chess` (expressed in Lisp) on top of a Basic interpreter. Of course, this will not work; the diagram clearly shows that the language in which the program is expressed does not match the interpreter's source language.

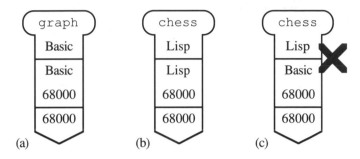

(a)   (b)   (c)

2.3 Real and abstract machines

The interpreters mentioned in Example 2.12 were all for (relatively) high-level languages. But interpreters for low-level languages are also useful.

Example 2.14
Suppose that a computer engineer has designed the architecture and instruction set of a radical new machine, Ultima. Now, actually constructing Ultima as a piece of hardware will be an expensive and time-consuming job. Modifying the hardware to implement design changes will likewise be costly. It would be wise to defer hardware construction until the engineer has somehow tested the design. But how can a paper design be tested?

There is a remarkably simple method that is both cheap and fast: we write an interpreter for Ultima machine code. We might well write the interpreter in C:

We can now translate the interpreter into some machine code, say M, using the C compiler:

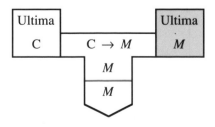

This gives us an Ultima interpreter expressed in *M* machine code (shaded above). Now we can run Ultima machine-code programs on top of the interpreter, which itself runs on *M*, as shown below left:

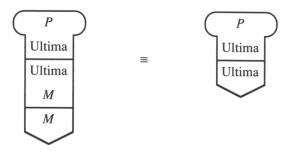

In all respects except speed, the effect is the same as running the programs on Ultima itself, as shown above right.

This kind of interpreter is often called an *emulator*. It cannot be used to measure the emulated machine's absolute speed, because interpretation slows everything down. But emulation can still be used to obtain useful quantitative information: counting memory cycles, estimating the degree of parallelism, and so on. It can also be used to obtain qualitative information about how well the architecture and instruction set meet the needs of programmers.   □

Running a program on top of an interpreter is functionally equivalent to running the same program directly on a machine, as illustrated in Example 2.14. The user sees the same behavior in terms of the program's inputs and outputs. The two processes are even similar in detail: an interpreter works in a fetch–analyze–execute cycle, and a machine works in a fetch–decode–execute cycle. The only difference is that an interpreter is a software artifact, whereas a machine is a hardware artifact (and therefore much faster).

Thus a machine may be viewed as an interpreter implemented in hardware. Conversely, an interpreter may be viewed as a machine implemented by software. We sometimes call an interpreter an ***abstract machine***, as opposed to its hardware counterpart which is a ***real machine***. An abstract machine is functionally equivalent to a real machine if they both implement the same language *L*. This is summarized in Figure 2.8.

A related observation is that there is no fundamental difference between machine codes and other low-level languages. By a machine code we just mean a language for which a hardware interpreter exists (at least on paper).

Figure 2.8 Abstract machines are functionally equivalent to real machines.

2.4 Interpretive compilers

A compiler may take quite a long time to translate a source program into machine code, but then the object program will run at full machine speed. An interpreter allows the program to start running immediately, but it will run very slowly (up to 100 times more slowly than the machine-code program).

An *interpretive compiler* is a combination of compiler and interpreter, giving some of the advantages of each. The key idea is to translate the source program into an *intermediate language*, designed to the following requirements:

* It is intermediate in level between the source language and ordinary machine code.
* Its instructions have simple formats, and therefore can be analyzed easily and quickly.
* Translation from the source language into the intermediate language is easy and fast.

Thus an interpretive compiler combines fast compilation with tolerable running speed.

Example 2.15
A Pascal/P-code interpretive compiler consists of a Pascal-into-P-code translator and a P-code interpreter, both of which run on some machine *M*:

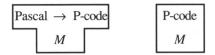

A Pascal program *P* is first translated into P-code, and then the P-code object program is interpreted:

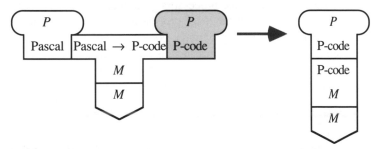

P-code is an intermediate language oriented to Pascal. It provides powerful instructions that correspond directly to Pascal operations such as array assignment, array indexing, and procedure call. Thus translation from Pascal into P-code is easy and fast (at least twice as fast as compilation from Pascal into machine code). Although powerful, P-code instructions have simple formats like machine-code instructions, with operation fields and operand fields, and so are easy to analyze. Thus P-code interpretation is relatively fast: 'only' about ten times slower than machine code. □

Interpretive compilers are exceedingly useful language processors. In the early stages of program development, the programmer might well spend more time compiling than running the program, since he or she is repeatedly discovering and correcting simple syntactic and logical errors. At that stage fast compilation is more important than fast running, so an interpretive compiler is ideal. (Later, and especially when the program is put into production use, the program will be run many times but rarely recompiled. At that stage fast running will assume paramount importance, so a compiler that generates efficient machine code will be required.)

2.5   Portable compilers

A program is *portable* to the extent that it can be (compiled and) run on any machine, without change. We can measure portability roughly by the proportion of code that remains unchanged when the program is moved to a dissimilar machine. Portability is an economic issue: a portable program is more valuable than an unportable one, because its development cost can be spread over more copies.

The language in which the program is expressed has a major impact on its portability. At one extreme, a program expressed in assembly language cannot be moved to a dissimilar machine unless it is completely rewritten, so its portability is 0%. A program expressed in a high-level language is much more portable. Ideally, it only needs to be recompiled when moved to a dissimilar machine, in which case its portability is 100%. However, this ideal is often quite elusive. For example, a program's behavior might be altered (perhaps subtly) by moving it to a machine with a different character set or different arithmetic. Written with care, however, programs expressed in high-level languages should achieve 95–99% portability.

Similar points apply to language processors, which are themselves programs. Indeed, it is particularly important for language processors to be portable because they are especially valuable and widely-used programs. For this reason language processors are commonly written in high-level languages such as Pascal and C.

Unfortunately, it is particularly hard to make compilers portable. A compiler's function is to generate machine code for a particular machine, a function that by its very nature is machine-dependent. If we have a Pascal-into-68000 compiler expressed in a high-level language, we should be able to move this compiler quite easily to run on a dissimilar machine, but it will still generate 68000 machine code! To change the compiler to generate different machine code would require about half the compiler to be rewritten, implying that the compiler is only about 50% portable.

It might seem that highly portable compilers are unattainable. However, the situation is not quite so gloomy: a compiler that generates intermediate language is potentially much more portable than a compiler that generates machine code.

Example 2.16
The Zürich Pascal compiler kit consists of a Pascal-into-P-code translator, expressed both in Pascal and in P-code, and a P-code interpreter, expressed in Pascal:

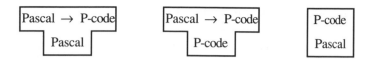

How can we make this work? It seems that we cannot compile Pascal programs until we have an implementation of P-code, and we cannot use the P-code interpreter until we can compile Pascal programs! Fortunately, a small amount of work can get us out of this chicken-and-egg situation.

Suppose that we want to get the system running on machine M, and suppose that we already have a compiler for (say) C on this machine. Then we rewrite the interpreter in C:

and then compile it:

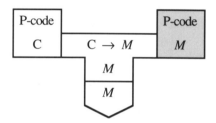

Now we have an interpretive compiler, similar to the one described in Example 2.15. There is one difference: the compiler itself, being expressed in P-code, has to run on top of the P-code interpreter:

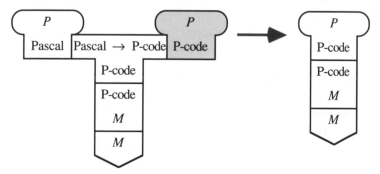

The P-code interpreter is much smaller and simpler than the compiler, so rewriting the interpreter is an easy job (a few days' work for an experienced programmer). Consequently, the Zürich compiler kit as a whole is about 95% portable. If no C compiler is available, it is even feasible to rewrite the interpreter in assembly language.

The Zürich Pascal compiler kit was designed and constructed at ETH Zürich in the early 1970s, at the instigation of Pascal's designer Niklaus Wirth. It was an extraordinarily successful invention, being largely responsible for the explosive growth of Pascal in the 1970s, because it proved so easy to move the compiler kit to a variety of machines, including the cheap microprocessors that were proliferating at the time.

Notice that the compiler expressed in Pascal is not actually needed to bootstrap the portable compiler. It was, however, originally used to generate the compiler expressed in P-code. Besides, it might prove to be useful in later development of the compiler after the initial move to machine M. (See Exercises 2.8 and 2.9.)   □

The Pascal compiler in Example 2.16 must be interpreted, so compilation of a Pascal source program will be slow. However, the compiler can be improved by bootstrapping, as we shall see in Section 2.6.1.

2.6   Bootstrapping

A language processor, such as a translator or interpreter, is a program that processes programs expressed in a particular language (the source language). Suppose, now, that a language processor is expressed in its own source language. Such a language processor can be used to process itself! This process is called *bootstrapping*. The idea seems at first to be paradoxical, but it can be made to work. Indeed, it turns out to be extremely useful. In this section we study several kinds of bootstrapping.

2.6.1   Bootstrapping a portable compiler

In Sections 2.4 and 2.5 we looked at interpretive and portable compilers. These work by translating from the high-level source language into an intermediate language, and then interpreting the latter.

A portable compiler can be bootstrapped to make a true compiler – one that generates machine code – by writing an intermediate-language-into-machine-code translator.

Example 2.17
Suppose that we have made the Zürich Pascal compiler kit into an interpretive compiler running on machine M, as described in Example 2.16. We can use this to build an efficient Pascal-into-M compiler, as follows.

First, we write a P-code-into-M translator, in Pascal:

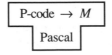

(This is a substantial job, but only about half as much work as writing a complete Pascal-into-M compiler.) Next, we compile this translator using the existing interpretive compiler:

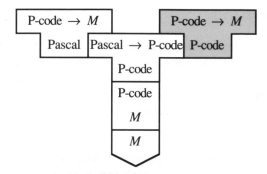

This gives a P-code-into-*M* translator expressed in P-code itself.

Next, we use this translator to translate *itself* :

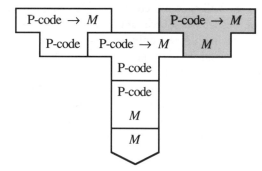

This, the actual bootstrap, gives a P-code-into-*M* translator expressed in machine code.

Finally, we translate the Pascal-into-P-code translator into machine code:

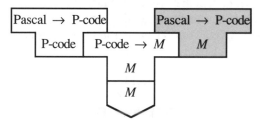

Now we have implemented a two-stage Pascal-into-*M* compiler:

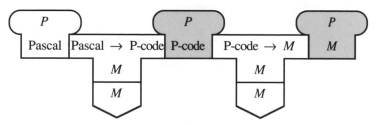

Moreover, the compiler is expressed in machine code, so compilation of a Pascal source program is much faster than in Example 2.16.   □

2.6.2   Full bootstrap

We have seen that a program, if it is to be portable, should be written in a suitable high-level language, *L*. That implies a commitment to the language *L* throughout the program's lifetime. If we wish to make a new version of the program (e.g., to remove known bugs, or to make it more efficient), we must edit the *L* source program and re-compile it. In other words, the program is maintainable only as long as an *L* compiler is available.

Exactly the same point applies to a language processor expressed in *L*. In Example 2.10, we saw how a Pascal compiler, expressed in C, could be translated into machine code by a C compiler (and thus enabled to run). However, this Pascal compiler can be maintained only as long as a C compiler is available. If we wish to make a new version of the Pascal compiler (e.g., to remove known bugs, or to generate better-quality machine code), we will need a C compiler to recompile the Pascal compiler.

In general, a compiler whose source language is *S*, expressed in a different high-level language *L*, can be maintained only as long as a compiler for *L* is available. This problem can be avoided by writing the *S* compiler in *S* itself! Whenever we make a new version of the *S* compiler, we use the old version to compile the new version. The only difficulty is how to get started: how can we compile the *first* version of the *S* compiler? The key idea is to start with a subset of *S* – a subset just large enough to be suitable for writing the compiler. The method is called *full boot-strap* – since a whole compiler is to be written from scratch.

Example 2.18

Suppose that we wish to build an Ada compiler for machine *M*. Now Ada is a very large language, so it makes sense to build the compiler incrementally. We start by selecting a small subset of Ada that will be adequate for compiler writing. (The Pascal-like subset of Ada would be suitable.) Call this subset Ada-S.

We write version 1 of our Ada-S compiler in C (or any suitable language for which a compiler is currently available):

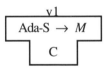

We compile version 1 using the C compiler:

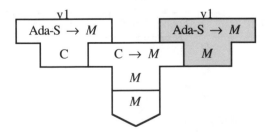

This gives an Ada-S compiler for machine *M*. We can test it by using it to compile and run Ada-S test programs.

But we prefer not to rely permanently on version 1 of the Ada-S compiler, because it is expressed in C, and therefore is maintainable only as long as a C compiler is available. Instead, we make version 2 of the Ada-S compiler, expressed in Ada-S itself:

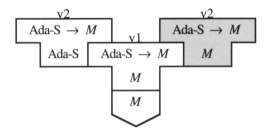

This rewriting of the compiler is not a hard job, because all the algorithms and data structures have already been developed and tested in version 1. (In fact, we could have wisely anticipated the rewriting, by refraining from using C features with no direct counterparts in Ada-S.)

Now we use version 1 to compile version 2:

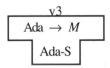

As usual, we can test version 2 of the Ada-S compiler by using it to compile and run Ada-S test programs. We have now broken our dependency on C, because the version 2 Ada-S compiler is expressed in Ada-S itself.

Finally, we extend the Ada-S compiler to a (full) Ada compiler, giving version 3:

and compile it using version 2:

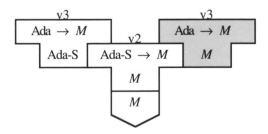

This gives us an Ada compiler expressed in Ada itself (actually in a subset of Ada, but no matter). This compiler can be used to maintain itself by using version 3 to compile version 4, and so on.   □

2.6.3   Half bootstrap

Suppose that we have a compiler that runs on a machine *HM*, and generates *HM*'s machine code; now we wish to move the compiler to run on a dissimilar machine *TM*. In this transaction *HM* is called the *host machine*, and *TM* is called the *target machine*.

If the compiler is expressed in a high-level language for which we have a compiler on *TM*, just getting the compiler to run on *TM* is straightforward, but we would still have a compiler that generates *HM*'s machine code. It would, in fact, be a cross-compiler.

To make our compiler generate *TM*'s machine code, we have no choice but to rewrite part of the compiler. As we shall see in Chapter 3, one of the major parts of a compiler is the *code generator*, which does the actual translation into the target language. Typically the code generator is about half of the compiler. If our compiler has been constructed in a modular fashion, it is not too difficult to strip out the old code generator, which generated *HM*'s machine code; then we can substitute the new code generator, which will generate *TM*'s machine code.

If the compiler is expressed in its own source language, this process is called a **half bootstrap** – since roughly half the compiler must be modified. It does not depend on any compiler or assembler being already available on the target machine – indeed, it depends *only* on the host machine compiler!

Example 2.19
Suppose that we have a Pascal compiler that generates machine code for machine *HM*. The compiler is expressed in Pascal itself, and in *HM*'s machine code:

We wish to bootstrap this compiler to machine *TM*. To be precise, we want a compiler that runs on *TM* and generates *TM*'s machine code.

First, we modify the compiler's code generator to generate *TM*'s machine code:

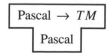

We compile the modified compiler, using the original compiler, to obtain a cross-compiler:

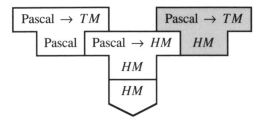

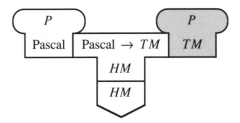

How do we test the cross-compiler? We can run it on *HM* to compile Pascal test programs into *TM*'s machine code:

We also want to run these test programs. (Visual inspection of the object code is possible, but practicable only for small test programs.) It might be possible to transfer the object programs to *TM* to be run. However, it might be easier to use an emulator.

We write an interpreter for *TM*'s machine code, to run on *HM*:

TM
HM

(In practice we would write the interpreter in Pascal or C, and then compile it on *HM*.) Now we can run the cross-compiler's object programs on *HM*:

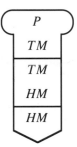

Once we are satisfied that the cross-compiler is correct, we can use it to compile *itself* into *TM*'s machine code (the actual bootstrap):

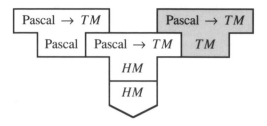

Finally, we transfer the Pascal-into-*TM* compiler (expressed in both Pascal and *TM*'s machine code) to the target machine *TM*, and subsequently maintain it there.   □

2.6.4   Bootstrapping to improve efficiency

The efficiency of an ordinary program can be measured with respect to either time or space: how fast does it run, and how much storage space does it require?

When we discuss the efficiency of a compiler, the situation is more complicated. We can measure the efficiency of the compiler program itself, and we can measure the efficiency of the object programs it generates. Here we are not concerned with the tactics of generating efficient object programs. But we can show that bootstrapping is a useful *strategy* for taking a simple compiler and upgrading it to generate more efficient object programs. The basic idea is to use the existing version of the compiler to compile the new version, and to do this repeatedly to make better and better versions.

Example 2.20
Suppose that we have a Pascal compiler, version 1, that generates slow machine code. Version 1 is expressed in slow machine code, as well as in Pascal:

In the diagrams we will use ✗ to indicate slow code and ✔ to indicate fast code. (Note that *M*✗ and *M*✔ are the same language, the machine code *M*; the ✗ and ✔ are merely indications of code *quality*.)

When we compile Pascal programs, both the version 1 compiler and its object programs will be slow. (Why?) Our objective is to make a fast compiler that generates fast object programs.

First, we modify version 1 to make a version 2 compiler that generates faster machine code:

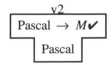

We can use version 1 to compile version 2:

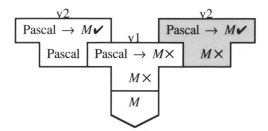

This gives us a better compiler, which we can use to compile Pascal programs:

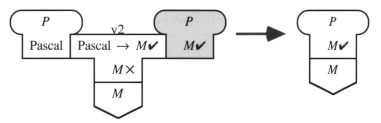

Compilation will still be slow (since the compiler is expressed in slow machine code), but the object program will be fast (since the generated machine code is fast).

The final stage of bootstrapping is to use version 2 to compile itself:

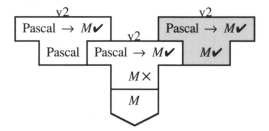

This gives us a fast compiler that generates fast object programs:

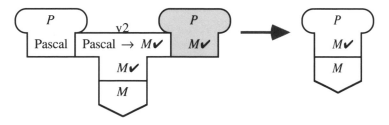

In practice, the bootstrapping steps illustrated in Example 2.20 would be used many times, as the compiler is gradually improved to generate better and better object code.

2.7   Case study: the Δ language processor

The Δ language processor will be used as a case study throughout this book. It is an integrated language processor, consisting of an editor, compiler, interpreter, and disassembler. Abridged listings of the interpreter and compiler may be found in Appendices D and E, respectively. We will study how they work in the following chapters. Here we examine the Δ language processor's overall structure. (See Figure 2.9.)

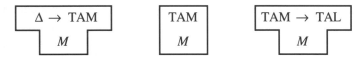

Figure 2.9 The compiler, interpreter, and disassembler components of the Δ language processor.

The compiler translates Δ source programs into TAM code. *TAM* (Triangle Abstract Machine) is an abstract machine, implemented by an interpreter. TAM has been designed to facilitate the implementation of Δ – although it would be equally suitable for implementing Algol, Pascal, and similar languages. Like P-code (Example 2.15), TAM's primitive operations are more similar to the operations of a high-level language than to the very primitive operations of a typical real machine. As a consequence, the translation from Δ into TAM code is straightforward and fast.

The Δ-into-TAM compiler and the TAM interpreter together constitute an interpretive compiler, much like the one described in Example 2.15. (See Exercise 2.2.)

The Δ language processor is integrated. The programmer may open a Δ source program, edit it, and compile it. Then the programmer may run and/or disassemble the TAM object program. All these operations are selected from menus.

2.8   Further reading

A number of authors have used tombstone diagrams to represent language processors and their interactions. The formalism was fully developed, complete with mathematical underpinnings, by Earley and Sturgis (1970). Their paper also presents an algorithm that systematically determines all the tombstones that can be generated from a given initial set of tombstones.

The Zürich Pascal compiler kit was developed at ETH Zürich. Its design and implementation are discussed in Nori *et al.* (1981). This article also outlines the various ways in which the compiler kit can be exploited to move and bootstrap Pascal compilers. Finally, it contains a detailed description of P-code.

A case study of compiler development by full bootstrap may be found in Wirth (1971). A case study of compiler development by half bootstrap may be found in Welsh and Quinn (1972). Finally, a case study of compiler improvement by bootstrapping may be found in Ammann (1981). Interestingly, all these three case studies are inter-linked: Wirth's Pascal compiler was the starting point for the other two developments.

Bootstrapping has a longer history, the basic idea being described by several authors in the 1950s. (At that time compiler development itself was still in its infancy!) The first well-known application of the idea seems to have been a program called `eval`, which was a Lisp interpreter expressed in Lisp itself (McCarthy *et al.* 1965).

Exercises 2

2.1*   Consider each of the following (hypothetical) translators. Do you think the translator might be useful in practice? Explain your answer. Also, what difficulties could be anticipated in making it generate a good-quality object program?
(a) A Fortran-into-Ada translator.
(b) An Ada-into-Fortran translator.
(c) An assembly-language-into-Pascal decompiler.

2.2   From the description of the Δ language processor in Section 2.7, use tombstone diagrams to show:
(a) compilation of a Δ source program *P*;
(b) running of the object program;
(c) disassembly of the object program.
Why do you think the disassembler has been provided?

2.3   Assume that you have the following: a machine *M*; a C compiler that runs on machine *M* and generates machine code *M*; a Pascal-into-C translator expressed in C. Use tombstone diagrams to represent these language processors. Also show how you would use these language processors to:
(a) compile and run a program *P* expressed in C;
(b) compile the Pascal-into-C translator into machine code;
(c) compile and run a program *Q* expressed in Pascal.

2.4   Assume that you have the following: a machine *M*; a C compiler that runs on machine *M* and generates machine code *M*; a TAM interpreter expressed in C; an Algol-into-TAM compiler expressed in C. Use tombstone diagrams to represent these language processors. Also show how you would use these language processors to:
(a) compile the TAM interpreter into machine code;
(b) compile the Algol-into-TAM compiler into machine code;
(c) compile and run a program *P* expressed in Algol.

2.5   The Gnu compiler kit uses a machine-independent register transfer language, RTL, as an intermediate language. The kit includes translators from several high-level languages (such as C, C++, Pascal) into RTL, and translators from RTL into several machine codes (such as VAX, 68000, SPARC). It also includes an RTL 'optimizer', i.e., a program that translates RTL into more efficient RTL. All these translators are expressed in C.
(a) Show how you would install these translators on a SPARC machine, given a C compiler for the SPARC.
   Now show how you would use these translators to:
(b) compile a program *P*, expressed in Pascal, into SPARC machine code;
(c) compile the same program, but using the RTL optimizer to generate more efficient object code;
(d) cross-compile a program *Q*, expressed in C++, into VAX machine code.

2.6   The Δ language processor (see Section 2.7) was written entirely in Pascal. Use tombstone diagrams to show how the compiler, interpreter, and disassembler would be made to run on machine *M*. Assume that a Pascal-into-*M* compiler is available.

2.7*   Suppose that you have designed a language XP, which is Pascal extended with packages. (A package is just a named group of declarations, some of which are designated as exported by the package; the remaining declarations are visible only inside the package. So packages are intended to support a programming discipline, rather than adding new functionality to the language.)
   A two-stage Pascal-into-*M* compiler is available, consisting of a Pascal-into-P-code translator and a P-code-into-*M* translator. The two-stage compiler is available both in Pascal and in machine code *M*, and a machine *M* is also available.
   Suggest *two* different strategies for implementing XP. What are the advantages and disadvantages of each strategy?

2.8   Consider the Zürich Pascal compiler kit (Example 2.16). This kit was developed originally by writing the Pascal-into-P-code compiler, and the P-code interpreter, in Pascal itself.
(a) Given that an earlier Pascal compiler (generating machine code) was already available on the local CDC 6000 machine, show how the compiler kit was generated.
(b) Imagine that only a C compiler had been available to start with. Show how the Pascal compiler kit could still have been generated, by bootstrapping.

2.9   Consider again the Zürich Pascal compiler kit (Example 2.16). Included in the compiler kit is a Pascal-into-P-code compiler expressed in Pascal itself, but this is not actually needed to move the portable compiler to machine *M*. Neither is it needed to develop a two-stage Pascal-into-*M* compiler by bootstrapping (Example 2.17). Show how we could use the compiler expressed in Pascal to develop a *one-stage* Pascal-into-*M* compiler.

2.10* Suppose that an ambitious new programming language, Utopia, has been designed to meet the needs of all programmers everywhere. Rather than a single language, it is actually a series of nested sublanguages Utopia-1, Utopia-2, and Utopia-3. The smallest sublanguage Utopia-1 has roughly the functionality of Pascal; Utopia-2 is intermediate in functionality; and the full language Utopia-3 supports a variety of advanced features such as concurrency.

The motivations for defining the sublanguages were as follows. Some implementors might prefer to develop compilers for the sublanguages only; whereas more ambitious implementors will aim to develop compilers for the full language. Programmers who do not need the functionality of the full language can use a compiler for a sublanguage (and such a compiler will be smaller and faster than a compiler for the full language); but they can easily graduate to the full language if the need arises, without having to rewrite any of their existing programs.

You are required to develop a complete set of compilers for Utopia-1, Utopia-2, and Utopia-3. What strategy would you adopt? You may assume that a C compiler is available. (*Note:* There are several possible strategies. Weigh their advantages and disadvantages carefully.)

2.11* Consider a programming language that allows code to be manufactured at runtime (such as Lisp, Example 2.11(b)).

(a) What would be unusual about the *specification* of this language?

(b) Why would this language normally be implemented by means of an *interpreter*?

(c) Suppose, nevertheless, that a *compiler* is to be designed for this language. What would be unusual about this compiler?

CHAPTER THREE

Compilation

In this chapter we study the internal structure of compilers. A compiler's basic function is to translate a high-level source program to a low-level object program, but before doing so it must check that the source program is well-formed. So compilation is decomposed into three *phases*: syntactic analysis, contextual analysis, and code generation. We study these phases and their relationships. We also examine some possible compiler structures, each structure being characterized by the number of passes over the source program or its internal representation, and discuss the issues underlying the choice of compiler structure.

In this chapter we restrict ourselves to a shallow exploration of compiler structure. We shall take a detailed look at syntactic analysis, contextual analysis, and code generation in Chapters 4, 5, and 7, respectively.

3.1   Phases

Inside any compiler, the source program is subjected to several transformations before an object program is finally generated. These transformations are called *phases*. The three principal phases of compilation are as follows:

- *Syntactic analysis:* the source program is parsed to check whether it conforms to the source language's syntax, and to determine its phrase structure.

- *Contextual analysis:* the parsed program is analyzed to check whether it conforms to the source language's contextual constraints.

- *Code generation:* the checked program is translated to an object program, in accordance with the semantics of the source and target languages.

The three phases of compilation correspond directly to the three parts of the source language's specification: its syntax, contextual constraints, and semantics.

Between the phases we need to represent the source program in such a way as to reflect the analysis already done on it. A suitable choice of representation is an abstract syntax tree (AST). The AST explicitly represents the source program's phrase structure. Its subtrees will correspond to the phrases (commands, expressions, declarations, etc.) of the source program. Its leaf nodes will correspond to the identifiers, literals, and operators of the source program. (Other symbols in the source program can be discarded after syntactic analysis.)

We can conveniently summarize the phases of a compiler by means of a data flow diagram[1]. Figure 3.1 shows the data flow diagram of a typical compiler. It shows the successive transformations effected by the three phases. It also shows that syntactic and contextual analysis may generate error reports, which will be transmitted to the programmer.

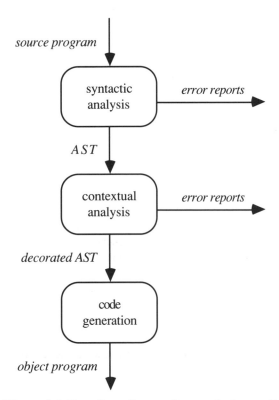

Figure 3.1 Data flow diagram for a typical compiler.

Let us now examine the three principal phases in more detail. We shall follow a tiny Δ program through all the phases of compilation. The source program is shown in Figure 3.2, and the results of successive transformations in Figures 3.3, 3.4, and 3.7.

In order to be concrete, we shall explain these transformations as implemented in

[1] A data flow diagram summarizes data flows and transformations in a system. An arrow represents a data flow, and is labeled by a description of the data. A rounded box represents a transformation, and is labeled accordingly.

the Δ compiler that is our case study (Appendix E). It should be understood, however, that another Δ compiler could implement the transformations in a different way. The main purpose of this section is to explain *what* transformations are performed, not *how* they are implemented. In Section 3.2.2 we shall emphasize this point by sketching an alternative Δ compiler with a very different internal structure, which nevertheless performs essentially the same processing on the source program.

```
! This program is useless
! except for illustration.
let
    var n: Integer;
    var c: Char
in
    begin
    c := '&';
    n := n+1
    end
```

Figure 3.2 A Δ source program.

3.1.1   Syntactic analysis

The purpose of syntactic analysis is to determine the source program's phrase structure. This process is called *parsing*. It is an essential part of compilation because the subsequent phases (contextual analysis and code generation) depend on knowing how the program is composed from commands, expressions, declarations, and so on.

The source program is parsed to check whether it conforms to the source language's syntax, and to construct a suitable representation of its phrase structure. Here we assume that the chosen representation is an AST.

Example 3.1
Syntactic analysis of the Δ source program of Figure 3.2 yields the AST of Figure 3.3. As we shall be studying the compilation of this program in detail, let us examine some parts of the AST.

① The program as a whole is a block (let-) command. It consists of a declaration ('var n: Integer; var c: Char' in the source program) and a subcommand ('c := '&'; n := n+1'). This is represented by an AST whose root node is labeled 'letDinC', and whose subtrees represent the declaration and subcommand.

② This is a variable declaration. It consists of an identifier (n) and a type-denoter (Integer).

③ This also is a variable declaration. It consists of an identifier (c) and a type-denoter (Char).

④ This is a sequential command. It consists of two subcommands ('c := '&'' and 'n := n+1').

⑤ This is an assignment command. It consists of a value-or-variable-name on the left-hand side (n) and an expression on the right-hand side (n+1).

⑥ This value-or-variable-name is just an identifier (n).

⑦ This is an expression that applies an operator ('+') to two subexpressions.

⑧ This expression is a value-or-variable-name (n).

⑨ This expression is an integer-literal (1).

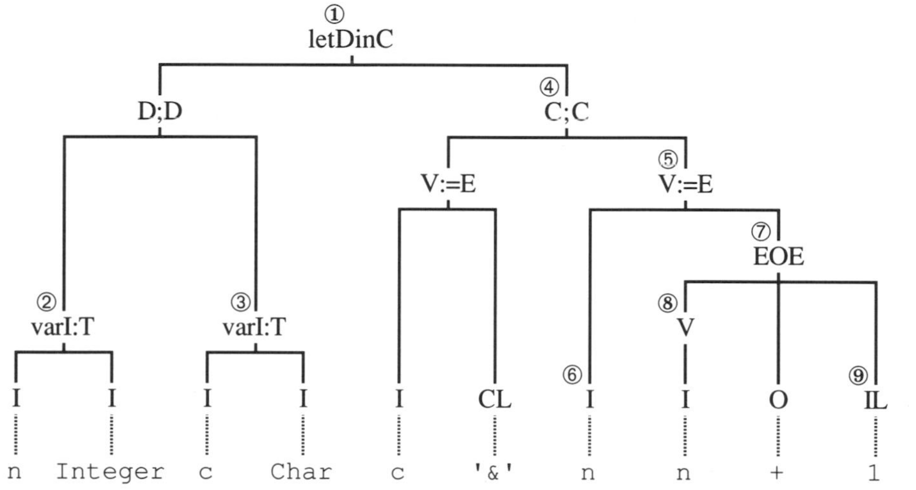

Figure 3.3 AST after syntactic analysis of Figure 3.2.

In general, the AST has terminal nodes that correspond to identifiers, literals, and operators in the source program, and subtrees that represent the phrases of the source program. Blank space and comments are not represented in the AST, because they contribute nothing to the source program's phrase structure. Punctuation and brackets also have no counterparts in the AST, because they serve only to separate and enclose phrases of the source program; once the source program has been parsed, they are no longer needed. For example, the 'begin' and 'end' brackets in Figure 3.2 serve only to enclose the sequential command 'c := '&'; n := n+1', thus ensuring that the sequential command as a whole is taken as the body of the let-command (rather than just the first assignment command). The AST's very structure represents this bracketing perfectly well.

If the source program contains syntactic errors, it has no proper phrase structure. In that case, syntactic analysis generates error reports instead of constructing an AST.

3.1.2   Contextual analysis

In contextual analysis the parsed program is further analyzed, to determine whether it conforms to the source language's contextual constraints:

- The source language's *scope rules* allow us, at compile-time, to associate each applied occurrence of an identifier (e.g., in an expression or command) with the corresponding declaration of that identifier, and to detect any undeclared identifiers. (Here we are assuming that the source language exhibits static binding.)

- The source language's *type rules* allow us, at compile-time, to infer the type of each expression and to detect any type errors. (Here we are assuming that the source language is statically typed.)

If the parsed program is represented by its AST, then contextual analysis will yield a *decorated AST*. This is an AST enriched with information gathered during contextual analysis:

- As a result of applying the scope rules, each applied occurrence of an identifier is linked to the corresponding declaration. We show this diagrammatically by a dotted arrow (◄┄┄┄┄).

- As a result of applying the type rules, each expression is decorated by its type *T*. We show this diagrammatically by marking the expression's root node ': *T*'.

Example 3.2
Δ exhibits static binding and is statically typed. Contextual analysis of the AST of Figure 3.3 yields the decorated AST of Figure 3.4.
    The contextual analyzer checks the declarations as follows:

② It notes that identifier n is declared as a variable of type *int*.
③ It notes that identifier c is declared as a variable of type *char*.

The contextual analyzer checks the second assignment command as follows:

⑥ At this applied occurrence of identifier n, it finds the corresponding declaration at ②. It links this node to ②. From the declaration it infers that n is a variable of type *int*.
⑧ Here, similarly, it infers that the expression n is of type *int*.
⑨ This expression, being an integer-literal, is manifestly of type *int*.
⑦ Since the operator '+' is of type *int* × *int* → *int*, it checks that the left and right subexpressions are indeed of type *int*, and infers that the whole expression is of type *int*.
⑤ It checks that the left-hand side of the assignment command is a variable, and that the right-hand side is an expression of equivalent type. Here both ⑥ and ⑦ are of type *int*, so the assignment command is indeed well-typed.

In this way the contextual analyzer verifies that the source program satisfies all the contextual constraints of Δ.   □

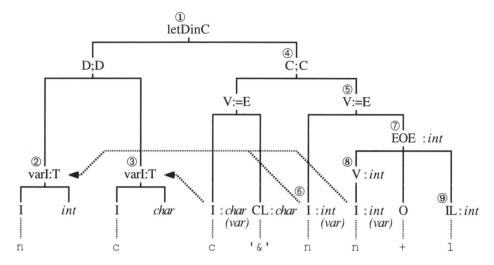

Figure 3.4 Decorated AST after contextual analysis of Figure 3.3.

If the source program does not satisfy the source language's contextual constraints, contextual analysis generates error reports.

Example 3.3

Figures 3.5 and 3.6 illustrate how contextual analysis will detect violations of scope rules and type rules. This particular Δ program contains three contextual errors:

① The expression of this while-command is not of type *bool*.
② Identifier m is used but not declared.
③ In this application of operator '>', which is of type *int* × *int* → *bool*, one subexpression has the wrong type.

□

```
let
    var n: Integer
in  ! ill-formed program
    while n/2 do
        m := 'n' > 1
```

Figure 3.5 An ill-formed Δ source program.

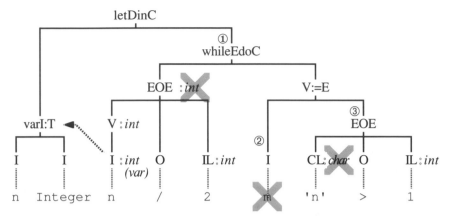

Figure 3.6 Discovering errors during contextual analysis of the Δ program of Figure 3.5.

3.1.3 Code generation

After syntactic and contextual analysis, the source program has been thoroughly checked and is known to be well-formed. Code generation is the final translation of the checked program to an object program, in accordance with the source and target languages' semantics.

A pervasive issue in code generation is the treatment of identifiers that are declared and/or used in the source program. In semantic terms, a declaration *binds* an identifier to some sort of entity. For example:

- A constant declaration such as 'const n ~ 7' binds the identifier n to the value 7. The code generator must then replace each applied occurrence of n by the value 7.
- A variable declaration such as 'var c: Char' binds the identifier c to a particular address (storage cell), which is decided by the code generator itself. The code generator must then replace each applied occurrence of c by the address to which it is bound.

A rather different issue for the compiler designer is the exact nature of the target language: should the compiler generate machine code or the assembly language of the target machine? Actually, the choice has only minor influence on the structure of the compiler, and we shall not pursue the issue in this book. When presenting examples of object code, however, we always write instructions mnemonically (as in Figure 3.7), since this is considerably more readable than the equivalent binary machine code!

Example 3.4
Code generation from the decorated AST of Figure 3.4 yields the TAM object program of Figure 3.7.

The code generator processes the declarations as follows:

② It allocates an address for the variable n, say 0[SB]. It stores that address at node ②, for later retrieval. (Here '0[SB]' means address 0 relative to the base register SB – but you will be able to follow this example without knowing TAM's addressing mechanism.)

③ It allocates an address for the variable c, say 1[SB]. It stores that address at node ③, for later retrieval.

The code generator processes the second assignment command as follows:

⑧ By following the link to the declaration of n, it retrieves this variable's address, namely 0[SB]. Then it generates the instruction 'LOAD 0[SB]'. (When executed, this instruction will fetch the current value of that variable.)

⑨ It generates the instruction 'LOADL 1'. (When executed, this instruction will fetch the literal value 1.)

⑦ It generates the instruction 'CALL add'. (When executed, this instruction will add the two previously-fetched values.)

⑤ By following the link to the declaration of n, it retrieves this variable's address, namely 0[SB]. Then it generates the instruction 'STORE 0[SB]'. (When executed, this instruction will store the previously-computed value in that variable.)

In this way the code generator translates the whole program into object code. □

```
PUSH   2
LOADL  38
STORE  1[SB]
LOAD   0[SB]
LOADL  1
CALL   add
STORE  0[SB]
POP    2
HALT
```

Figure 3.7 Object program after code generation from Figure 3.4.

3.2 Passes

In the previous section we examined the principal phases of compilation, and the flow of data between them. In this section we go on to examine and compare alternative compiler structures.

In designing a compiler, we wish to decompose it into modules, in such a way that each module is responsible for a particular phase. In practice there are several ways of doing so. The design of the compiler affects its modularity, its time and space requirements, and the number of passes over the program being compiled.

A *pass* is a complete traversal of the source program, or of an internal representation of the source program (such as an AST). A *one-pass* compiler makes a single traversal of the source program; a *multipass* compiler makes several traversals.

In practice, the structure of a compiler is inextricably linked to the number of passes it makes. In this section we contrast multipass and one-pass compilation, and summarize the advantages and disadvantages of each.

3.2.1   Multipass compilation

One possible compiler structure is shown by the structure diagram[2] of Figure 3.8.

The compiler consists of a top-level driver module together with three lower-level modules, the syntactic analyzer, the contextual analyzer, and the code generator. First, the compiler driver calls the syntactic analyzer, which reads the source program, parses it, and constructs a complete AST. Next, the compiler driver calls the contextual analyzer, which traverses the AST, checks it, and decorates it. Finally, the compiler driver calls the code generator, which traverses the decorated AST and generates an object program.

In general, a compiler with this structure makes at least three passes over the program being compiled. The syntactic analyzer invariably takes one pass, and the contextual analyzer and code generator take at least one pass each.

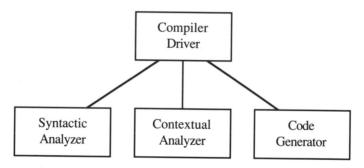

Figure 3.8 Structure diagram of a typical multipass compiler.

3.2.2   One-pass compilation

An alternative compiler structure is for the syntactic analyzer to control the other phases of compilation, as shown in Figure 3.9. A compiler with this structure makes a single pass over the source program.

Contextual analysis and code generation are performed 'on the fly' during syntactic

---

[2] A structure diagram summarizes the modules and module dependencies in a system. A rectangle represents a module. The higher-level modules are those near the top of the structure diagram. A connecting line represents a dependency of a higher-level module on a lower-level module. This dependency consists of the higher-level module calling procedures or functions in the lower-level module.

analysis. As soon as a phrase (e.g., expression, command, or declaration) has been parsed, the syntactic analyzer calls the contextual analyzer to perform any necessary checks. It also calls the code generator to generate any object code. Then the syntactic analyzer continues parsing the source program.

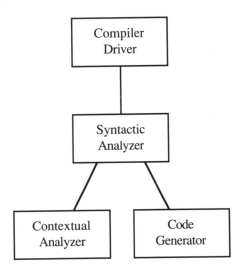

Figure 3.9 Structure diagram of a typical one-pass compiler.

Example 3.5

A one-pass Δ compiler would work as follows. Consider the following Δ source program:

```
! This program is useless
! except for illustration.
let
      var n: Integer①;
      var c: Char②
in
      begin
      c③  :=  '&'④⑤;
      n⑥  :=  n+1⑦⑧
      end
```

This is identical to the source program of Figure 3.2, but some of the key points in the program have been numbered for easy reference. There the following actions are taken:

① After parsing the variable declaration 'var n: Integer', the syntactic analyzer calls the contextual analyzer to note that identifier n is declared to be a variable of type *int*. It then calls the code generator to allocate an address for this variable, say 0[SB].

② After parsing the variable declaration 'var c: Char', the syntactic analyzer calls the contextual analyzer to note that identifier c is declared to be a variable of type *char*. It then calls the code generator to allocate an address for this variable, say 1[SB].

③ After parsing the value-or-variable-name c, the syntactic analyzer infers (by calling the contextual analyzer) that it is a variable of type *char*. It then calls the code generator to retrieve its address, 1[SB].

④ After parsing the expression '&', the syntactic analyzer infers that it is of type *char*. It then calls the code generator to generate the instruction 'LOADL 38'.

⑤ After parsing the assignment command 'c := '&'', the syntactic analyzer calls the contextual analyzer to check type compatibility. It then calls the code generator to generate the instruction 'STORE 1[SB]'.

⑥ After parsing the value-or-variable-name n, the syntactic analyzer infers (by calling the contextual analyzer) that it is a variable of type *int*. It then calls the code generator to retrieve the variable's address, 0[SB].

⑦ While parsing the expression n+1, the syntactic analyzer infers (by calling the contextual analyzer) that the subexpression n is of type *int*, that the operator '+' is of type *int* × *int* → *int*, that the subexpression 1 is of type *int*, and hence that the whole expression is of type *int*. It calls the code generator to generate the instructions 'LOAD 0[SB]', 'LOADL 1', and 'CALL *add*'.

⑧ After parsing the assignment command 'n := n+1', the syntactic analyzer calls the contextual analyzer to check type compatibility. It then calls the code generator to generate the instruction 'STORE 0[SB]'.

□

3.2.3   Compiler design issues

The choice between one-pass and multipass compilation is one of the first and most important design decisions for the compiler writer. It is not an easy decision, for both structures have important advantages and disadvantages. We summarize the main issues here.

• *Speed* is an issue where a one-pass compiler wins. Construction and subsequent traversals of the AST (or other internal program representation) is a modest time overhead in any multipass compiler. If the AST is stored on disk, however, the input–output overhead is likely to be large, even dominating compilation time.

• *Space* might also seem to favor a one-pass compiler. A multipass compiler must find memory to store the AST. But the situation is not really so clear-cut. In a multipass compiler, only one of the principal modules (syntactic analyzer, contextual analyzer, and code generator) is active at a time, so they can be overlaid in memory. In a one-pass compiler, all these modules are active throughout compile-time, so they must be coresident in memory. As a result, the code of a one-pass compiler occupies more memory than the code of a multipass compiler.

   Of course, a very large source program will give rise to a very large AST, perhaps occupying more memory than the compiler itself. Fortunately, modern programming languages allow very large programs to be decomposed into many compilation units, which are compiled separately; and individual compilation units tend to be moderately-sized. (See also Exercises 3.5 and 3.6.)

- *Modularity* favors the multipass compiler. In a one-pass compiler, the syntactic analyzer not only parses the source program but also coordinates the contextual analyzer and code generator. That is to say, it calls these modules, and maintains the data passed to and from them. In a multipass compiler, each module (including the syntactic analyzer) is responsible for a single function.

- *Flexibility* is an issue that favors the multipass compiler. Once the syntactic analyzer has constructed the AST, the contextual analyzer and code generator can traverse the AST in any convenient order. In particular, the code generator can translate phrases out of order, and sometimes this allows it to generate more efficient object code. A one-pass compiler is restricted to check and translate the phrases in exactly the order in which they appear in the source program.

- Semantics-preserving *transformations* of the source program or object program are performed by some compilers in order to make the object code as efficient as possible. (These are the so-called 'optimizing' compilers.) Such transformations generally require analysis of the whole program prior to code generation, so they force a multipass structure on the compiler.

- *Source language properties* might restrict the choice of compiler structure. A source program can be compiled in one pass only if every phrase (e.g., command or expression) can be compilcd using only information obtained from the preceding part of the source program. This requirement usually boils down to whether identifiers must be declared before use. If they must (as in Pascal, Ada, and Δ), then one-pass compilation is possible in principle. If identifiers need not be declared before use (as in Algol and ML), then multipass compilation is required.

Example 3.6
Pascal has a fairly strict rule that identifiers must be declared before use. Thus an applied occurrence of an identifier can be compiled in the sure knowledge that the identifier's declaration has already been processed (or is missing altogether).

Consider the following Pascal block:

```
var n: Integer;

procedure inc;
   begin
   n := n+1
   end;

begin
n := 0; inc
end
```

When the one-pass compiler encounters the command 'n := n+1', it has already processed the declaration of n. It can therefore retrieve the type and address of the variable, and subject the command to contextual analysis and code generation.

Suppose, instead, that the declaration of n *follows* the procedure. When the one-pass compiler encounters the command 'n := n+1', it has not yet encountered the declaration of n. So it cannot subject the command to contextual analysis and code generation. Fortunately, the compiler is not obliged to do so: it can safely generate an error report that the declaration of n is either misplaced or missing altogether.

Most Pascal compilers are, in fact, one-pass.   □

Example 3.7
The situation is different in Algol, in which declarations need not be in any particular order. The following Algol block is perfectly well-formed:

```
begin
    procedure inc;
        begin
        n := n+1
        end;

    integer n;

    n:= 0; inc
end
```

The command 'n := n+1' cannot be subjected to contextual analysis and code generation until the variable declaration 'integer n' has been processed. An Algol compiler must therefore process declarations in one pass, and commands and expressions in a later pass.   □

3.3   Case study: the Δ compiler

In Section 2.7 we introduced our case study, the Δ language processor. This consists of an editor, compiler, interpreter, and disassembler. In this section we look more closely at the Δ compiler, explaining its design.

The Δ compiler has the usual three phases of syntactic analysis, contextual analysis, and code generation, as shown in the data flow diagram of Figure 3.1. It has three passes, having the outline structure shown in Figure 3.8. The syntactic analyzer, contextual analyzer, and code generator modules take one pass each, communicating via an AST that represents the source program. This was illustrated in Examples 3.1, 3.2, and 3.4.

Omitting minor details, the compiler driver looks like this:

```
var theAST: AST;
...

parseProgram(theAST);    { calls the syntactic analyzer to parse the
                               source program and construct theAST}
```

```
checkProgram(theAST);    {calls the contextual analyzer to check and
                          decorate theAST}

encodeRun(theAST)        {calls the code generator to translate
                          theAST to an object program }
```

A one-pass Δ compiler would have been perfectly feasible, so the choice of a three-pass structure needs to be justified. The Δ compiler is intended primarily for educational purposes, so simplicity and clarity are paramount. Efficiency is a secondary consideration; in any case, efficiency arguments for a one-pass compiler are inconclusive, as we saw in Section 3.2.3. So the Δ compiler was designed to be as modular as possible, allowing the different phases to be studied independently of one another.

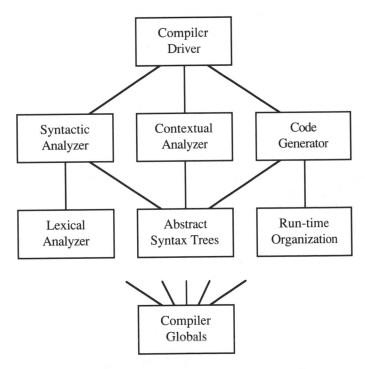

Figure 3.10 Structure diagram of the Δ compiler.

A detailed structure diagram of the Δ compiler is given in Figure 3.10, showing the lower-level modules. Here are brief explanations of the modules:

- The *compiler globals* module exports a number of generally useful constants and types. It also exports procedures for reporting compile-time errors. This module is used by all the other modules.

- The *abstract syntax trees* module exports types defining the AST data structure, and a number of simple functions and procedures for constructing and modifying ASTs.

(Other modules are allowed to inspect the AST structure directly, but are not supposed to modify it except through the procedures provided.)

- The *lexical analyzer* scans the source program, recognizing tokens (symbols relevant to parsing), but discarding blank space and comments.

- The *syntactic analyzer* parses the source program, and constructs the corresponding AST. It calls the lexical analyzer whenever it wishes to fetch the next token from the source program. It generates an error report if it detects a syntactic error.

- The *contextual analyzer* traverses the AST, links applied occurrences of identifiers to the corresponding declarations, infers the types of all expressions, and performs all necessary type checks. It decorates the AST with these types. It generates an error report if it detects a contextual error.

- The *run-time organization* module exports constants, types, and variables defining the target machine TAM. This information is used by the code generator.

- The *code generator* traverses the decorated AST, allocates addresses to variables, and generates TAM object code.

- The *compiler driver* module simply drives the other modules.

Each module is listed in detail in Appendix E (except for the run-time organization module, which is listed in Appendix D). At this stage you should read only the interface part of each module. This declares just the constants, types, variables, procedures, and functions exported by the module. Comments have been added to specify what each procedure and function does. In later chapters we shall continue this case study by looking inside the individual modules.

3.4 Further reading

The textbook by Aho *et al.* (1985) offers a comprehensive treatment of all aspects of compilation. Chapter 1 discusses compiler structures in general; Chapter 2 presents a complete example of one-pass compilation; Chapter 11 discusses compiler design issues; and Chapter 12 looks at several case studies of real compilers.

The present book concentrates on multipass compilation, in the interests of clarity and modularity. Other authors, such as Hoare (1973), have stressed the advantages of one-pass compilation. Welsh and McKeag (1980) devote a large part of their textbook to one-pass compilation. As a case study they develop a complete compiler for a subset of Pascal. Welsh and Hay (1986) is a complete one-pass Pascal compiler, together with an interpreter and post-mortem dump generator. This book is a fine example of literate programming.

The idea of using abstract syntax as a basis for compilation seems to be due to McCarthy (1963). Despite the attractions of this idea, it has received scant attention in the standard compiler textbooks.

Exercises 3

3.1   In Examples 3.2 and 3.4, the first assignment command 'c := ' & ' ' was ignored. Describe how this command would have been subjected to contextual analysis and code generation.

3.2   The Mini-Δ source program below left would be compiled to the object program below right:

```
let
    const m ~ 7;
    var x: Integer        PUSH  1
in
    x := m * x            LOADL 7
                          LOAD  0[SB]
                          CALL  mult
                          STORE 0[SB]
                          POP   1
                          HALT
```

Describe the compilation in the same manner as Examples 3.1, 3.2, and 3.4. (You may ignore the generation of the PUSH, POP, and HALT instructions.)

3.3   The Mini-Δ source program below contains several contextual errors:

```
let
    var a: Logical;
    var b: Boolean;
    var i: Integer
in
    if i then b := i = 0 else b := yes
```

In the same manner as Example 3.3, show how contextual analysis will detect these errors.

3.4*   Choose a compiler with which you are familiar. Find out and describe its phases and its pass structure. Draw a data flow diagram (like Figure 3.1) and a structure diagram (like Figure 3.8 or Figure 3.9).

3.5   Consider a source language, like Fortran or C, in which the source program consists of one or more distinct subprograms – a main program plus some procedures and functions. Design a compiler structure that uses ASTs, but (assuming that individual subprograms are moderately-sized) requires only a moderate amount of memory for ASTs.

3.6*   The Δ compiler would be unable to translate a very large source program, because of the memory required to store its AST. Consider the following proposal to restructure the compiler to improve its handling of very large source programs.

One procedure body is to be (completely) compiled at a time. Whenever the compiler has parsed a procedure declaration and constructed its AST, it breaks off to perform contextual analysis and code generation on the procedure body's AST, and then prunes the AST leaving a stub in place of the procedure body. Then the compiler resumes parsing the source program.

Would such a restructuring of the compiler be feasible? If *no*, explain why not. If *yes*, work through the following small source program, showing the steps that would be taken by the compiler, along the same lines as Example 3.5:

```
let
    var n: Integer;
    proc inc () ~
        n := n + 1
in
    begin n := 0; inc() end
```

CHAPTER FOUR

Syntactic Analysis

In Chapter 3 we saw how compilation can be decomposed into three principal phases, one of which is syntactic analysis. In this chapter we study syntactic analysis, and further decompose it into scanning, parsing, and abstract syntax tree construction. Section 4.2 explains this decomposition.

The main function of syntactic analysis is to parse the source program in order to discover its phrase structure. Thus the main topic of this chapter is parsing, and in particular the simple but effective method known as recursive-descent parsing. Section 4.1 introduces this topic, and Section 4.3 elaborates on it.

In a multipass compiler, the source program's phrase structure must be represented explicitly in some way. This choice of representation is a major design decision. One convenient and widely-used representation is the abstract syntax tree. Section 4.4 shows how to make the parser construct an abstract syntax tree.

In parsing it is convenient to view the source program as a stream of tokens: symbols such as identifiers, literals, operators, keywords, and punctuation. Since the source program text actually consists of individual characters, and a token may consist of several characters, scanning is needed to group the characters into tokens, and to discard other text such as blank space and comments. Scanning is the topic of Section 4.5.

4.1 Parsing algorithms

In Section 1.3.1 we briefly reviewed context-free grammars, and showed how a grammar generates a set of *sentences*. Each sentence is a string of terminal symbols. An (unambiguous) sentence has a unique *phrase structure*, embodied in its syntax tree.

Example 4.1
In this section, we shall use the following grammar as a running example. It is the grammar of a tiny fragment of English, which we shall call *micro-English*:

$$\text{Sentence} ::= \text{Subject Verb Object .} \qquad (4.1)$$

Subject	::=	**I** | **a** Noun | **the** Noun	(4.2a–c)
Object	::=	**me** | **a** Noun | **the** Noun	(4.3a–c)
Noun	::=	**cat** | **mat** | **rat**	(4.4a–c)
Verb	::=	**like** | **is** | **see** | **sees**	(4.5a–d)

The terminal symbols (shown in bold) are words and the punctuation mark ' . '. The nonterminal symbols are Sentence (the start symbol), Subject, Object, Noun, and Verb.

The following are among the sentences generated by the micro-English grammar:

```
the cat sees a rat .
I like the mat .
the cat likes me .
```

□

In this chapter we are not concerned with generating sentences, but with analyzing them. We are given as input a string of terminal symbols. Our task is to determine whether the input string is a sentence of the grammar, and if so to discover its phrase structure. The following definitions summarize this.

With respect to a particular context-free grammar G:

• **Recognition** of an input string is deciding whether or not the input string is a sentence of G.

• **Parsing** of an input string is recognition of the input string plus determination of its phrase structure. This can be done by reconstructing its syntax tree, or otherwise.

We require that G be *unambiguous*, i.e., that no sentence of G has more than one syntax tree. The possibility of an input string having two (or more) syntax trees is a complication we prefer to avoid.

Parsing is a task at which we humans are highly proficient. As we read a document, or listen to a speaker, we are continuously parsing the sentences to determine their phrase structure (and consequently their meaning). Parsing is subconscious most of the time, but occasionally it surfaces in our consciousness: when we notice a grammatical error, or realize that a sentence is ambiguous. Young children can be taught to parse simple sentences on paper.

In this chapter we are interested in parsing *algorithms*, which we can use in syntactic analysis. Many parsing algorithms have been developed, but they are all founded on one of two alternative strategies, *bottom-up parsing* and *top-down parsing*. These strategies are characterized by the order in which the input string's syntax tree is reconstructed. (A parser need not construct a syntax tree explicitly, in fact, but it is convenient to explain these parsing strategies in terms of syntax tree construction.) In the following subsections we compare bottom-up parsing and top-down parsing, then we introduce a particular top-down parsing algorithm known as *recursive descent*.

4.1.1 The bottom-up parsing strategy

Bottom-up parsing of an input string works as follows. The parser examines the terminals of the input string, in order from left to right, and reconstructs the syntax tree from the *bottom* (terminal nodes) *up* (towards the root node).

Example 4.2
Recall the grammar of micro-English, given in Example 4.1. Consider the following input string, consisting of six terminal symbols:

> `the cat sees a rat .`

Bottom-up parsing of this input string proceeds as follows:

(1) The first input terminal is '`the`'. The parser cannot do anything with this terminal yet, so it moves on to the next input terminal, '`cat`'. Here it can apply the production rule 'Noun ::= `cat`' (4.4a), forming a Noun-tree with the terminal '`cat`' as subtree:

(In these diagrams, input terminals not yet examined are shaded for emphasis.)

(2) Now the parser can apply the production rule 'Subject ::= `the` Noun' (4.2c), combining the input terminal '`the`' and the adjacent Noun-tree into a Subject-tree:

(3) Now the parser moves on to the next input terminal, '`sees`'. Here it can apply the production rule 'Verb ::= `sees`' (4.5d), forming a Verb-tree:

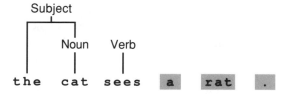

(4) The next input terminal is '`a`'. The parser cannot do anything with this terminal yet, so it moves on to the following input terminal, '`rat`'. Here it can apply the production rule 'Noun ::= `rat`' (4.4c), forming a Noun-tree:

(5) Now the parser can apply the production rule 'Object ::= **a** Noun' (4.3b), combining the input terminal '**a**' and the adjacent Noun-tree into an Object-tree:

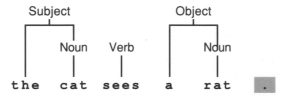

(6) The next (and last) input terminal is '**.**'. With this the parser can apply the production rule 'Sentence ::= Subject Verb Object **.**' (4.1), combining the adjacent Subject-tree, Verb-tree, Object-tree, and input terminal '**.**' into a Sentence-tree:

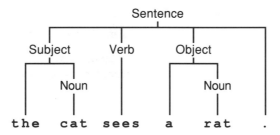

The parser has reduced the entire input string to a Sentence-tree. In other words, it has successfully parsed a sentence.   □

Consider a particular context-free grammar G. Each production rule is of the form $N ::= X_1...X_n$, where N is a nonterminal symbol of G, and each X_i is a terminal or nonterminal symbol of G.

In general, a bottom-up parser for G works as follows. When it encounters a sequence of terminals and trees that match the right-hand side of a production rule $N ::= X_1...X_n$, it may combine these terminals and trees into a single N-tree. The latter tree is then available for further matching. Parsing succeeds when and if the whole of the input string has been reduced to a single S-tree, where S is the start symbol of G.

How does the parser choose what to do at each step? This is an important issue, since a wrong choice can lead the parser into a blind alley. At step (5) in Example 4.2, the parser might have chosen to apply 'Subject ::= **a** Noun' (instead of the correct 'Object ::= **a** Noun'):

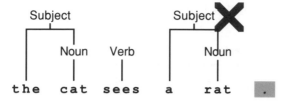

In this case, the trees would *not* match the right-hand side of the production rule 'Sentence ::= Subject Verb Object . ', nor indeed any other production rule, so the parser would be unable to make further progress. Having parsed a subject and verb, the parser has reached a state in which it should not parse another subject. In general, a bottom-up parser must, when choosing what to do next, take into account whatever information is available: the next input terminal, and the state it has reached as a result of previous parsing steps.

4.1.2 The top-down parsing strategy

Top-down parsing of an input string works as follows. The parser examines the terminals of the input string, in order from left to right, and reconstructs its syntax tree from the *top* (root node) *down* (towards the terminal nodes).

Example 4.3
Recall the grammar of micro-English, given in Example 4.1. Consider once more the input string:

    the cat sees a rat .

Top-down parsing starts by making a root node labeled Sentence. Then it proceeds as follows:

(1) The parser must decide which production rule to apply at the Sentence-node. In fact there is only one production rule with Sentence on the left-hand side, so it has no choice but to apply 'Sentence ::= Subject Verb Object . ' (4.1):

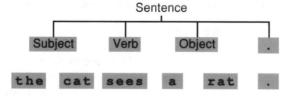

This step has made four stubs, i.e., nodes not yet connected to the input string. (In these diagrams the stubs, as well as the input terminals not yet examined, are shaded for emphasis.)

(2) Now the parser considers the leftmost stub, the node labeled Subject. It must decide which production rule to apply to it. There are three to choose from, but it should be clear that the appropriate one is 'Subject ::= **the** Noun' (4.2c). This

step connects up the first input terminal '**the**', and makes a new stub labeled Noun:

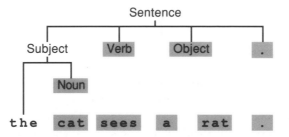

(3) The leftmost stub is now the node labeled Noun, and the parser must decide which production rule to apply to it. If it chooses 'Noun ::= **cat**' (4.4a), it can connect the next input terminal '**cat**' to the tree:

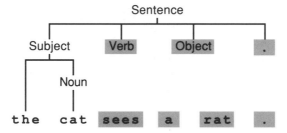

(4) The leftmost stub is now the node labeled Verb. If the parser chooses to apply the production rule 'Verb ::= **sees**' (4.5d), it can connect the input terminal '**sees**' to the tree:

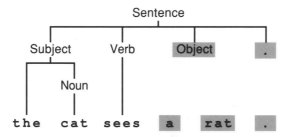

(5) The leftmost stub is now the node labeled Object. There are three production rules to choose from, but it should be clear that the appropriate production rule is 'Object ::= **a** Noun' (4.3b). This step connects up the next input terminal '**a**', and makes a new stub labeled Noun:

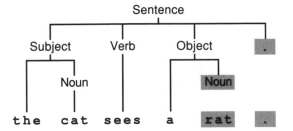

(6) The leftmost stub is now the (second) node labeled Noun. If the parser chooses to apply production rule 'Noun ::= **rat**' (4.4c), it can connect the input terminal '**rat**' to the tree. This step leaves the parser with a stub labeled '.' that matches the next (and last) input terminal:

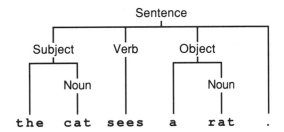

Thus the parser has successfully parsed the input string. □

Consider a particular context-free grammar G. In general, a top-down parser for G starts with just a stub for the root node, labeled by S (the start symbol of G). At each step, the parser takes the leftmost stub. If the stub is labeled by terminal symbol t, the parser connects it to the next input terminal, which must be t. (If not, the parser has detected a syntactic error.) If the stub is labeled by nonterminal symbol N, the parser chooses one of the production rules $N ::= X_1...X_n$, and grows branches from the node labeled by N to new stubs labeled X_1, ..., X_n (in order from left to right). Parsing succeeds when and if the whole input string is connected up to the syntax tree.

How does the parser choose which production rule to apply at each step? In the micro-English parser the choices are easy. For example, the parser can always choose which of the production rules 'Subject ::= ...' to apply simply by examining the next input terminal: if the terminal is '**I**', it chooses 'Subject ::= **I**'; or if the terminal is '**the**', it chooses 'Subject ::= **the** Noun'; or if the terminal is '**a**', it chooses 'Subject ::= **a** Noun'. (However, not all grammars are suited to this parsing strategy.)

4.1.3 The recursive-descent parsing algorithm

The parsing strategies outlined in the previous subsection are the basis of a variety of parsing algorithms. We observed that a parser often has to choose which production rule to apply next. A particular way of making such choices gives rise to a particular parsing algorithm.

Several parsing algorithms are commonly used in compilers. Here we describe just one, which is both effective and easy to understand.

Recursive descent is a top-down parsing algorithm. A recursive-descent parser for a grammar *G* consists mainly of a group of procedures `parseN`, one for each nonterminal symbol *N* of *G*. The task of each procedure `parseN` is to parse a single *N*-phrase. These procedures cooperate to parse complete sentences.

Example 4.4

Let us develop a recursive-descent parser for micro-English, whose grammar was given in Example 4.1.

This grammar has nonterminal symbols Noun, Verb, Subject, Object, and Sentence. So the parsing procedures will be:

`parseNoun`	– parses a noun, i.e., '**cat**', '**mat**', or '**rat**'.
`parseVerb`	– parses a verb, e.g., '**like**' or '**likes**'.
`parseSubject`	– parses a subject, e.g., '**I**' or '**a rat**'.
`parseObject`	– parses an object, e.g., '**me**' or '**a rat**'.
`parseSentence`	– parses a complete sentence.

These procedures should cooperate to parse the input string '**the cat sees a rat .**' as shown in Figure 4.1. The procedure `parseSentence` parses the whole input string, but delegates most of the work to procedures `parseSubject`, `parseVerb`, and `parseObject`, before itself accepting the last terminal '**.**'. The procedure `parseSubject` itself accepts the terminal '**the**', before delegating the rest of its work to procedure `parseNoun`. The latter simply accepts '**cat**'. And so on.

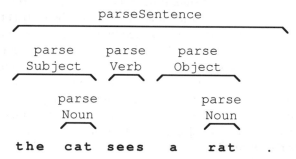

Figure 4.1 Recursive-descent parsing of a micro-English sentence.

Comparison of Figure 4.1 with the same sentence's syntax tree (at the end of Example 4.3) shows that the procedures have, in effect, discovered the sentence's phrase structure. Thus they really do constitute a parser.

Now let us see how to implement the parser. We need a variable, the *current terminal*, that will range over the terminals of the input string. (For example, given the input string of Figure 4.1, the current terminal will first contain '**the**', then '**cat**', then '**sees**', etc., and finally '**.**'.) In Pascal, the current terminal is declared as follows:

```
var currentTerminal: TerminalSymbol
```

The current terminal is accessed by the following auxiliary procedure:

```
procedure accept (expected: TerminalSymbol);
    begin
    if currentTerminal = expected then
        fetch the next input terminal into currentTerminal
    else
        report a syntactic error¹
    end
```

The parser will call '`accept (t)`' when it expects the current terminal to be *t*, and wishes to check that before fetching the next input terminal.

The parsing procedures themselves are implemented as follows. The comments on the right show how the parsing procedures are related to the grammar.

First, procedure `parseSentence`:

```
procedure parseSentence;              { Sentence ::=  }
    begin
    parseSubject;                     {        Subject }
    parseVerb;                        {        Verb    }
    parseObject;                      {        Object  }
    accept ('.')                      {        .       }
    end{parseSentence}
```

This is easy to understand. According to (4.1), a sentence consists of a subject, verb, object, and period, in that order. Therefore `parseSentence` should encounter the subject, verb, object, and period, in that same order. It calls procedures `parseSubject`, `parseVerb`, and `parseObject`, one after another, to parse the subject, verb, and object, respectively. Finally it calls `accept` to check that the (now) current terminal is indeed a period.

Now, procedure `parseSubject`:

```
procedure parseSubject;               { Subject ::=  }
    begin
    if currentTerminal = 'I' then
        accept ('I')                  {        I       }
    else                              {        |       }
    if currentTerminal = 'a' then
        begin
        accept ('a');                 {        a       }
        parseNoun                     {        Noun    }
        end
```

----

¹ This type style indicates a command or expression not yet refined into Pascal. We will use this convention to suppress unimportant details.

```
        else                              {    |        }
        if currentTerminal = 'the' then
           begin
           accept('the');                 {       the  }
           parseNoun                      {       Noun }
           end
        else
           report a syntactic error
        end{parseSubject}
```

This is a little more complicated. According to production rules (4.2a–c), a subject must have one of three forms: '**I**', '**a** Noun', or '**the** Noun'. Procedure `parseSubject` must decide which form it is, and the only way to decide is to inspect the current terminal. On entry to `parseSubject`, the current terminal should contain the first terminal of the subject. If the current terminal is '**I**', then clearly the subject is of the form '**I**'; if it is '**a**', then presumably the subject is of the form '**a** Noun'; if it is '**the**', then presumably the subject is of the form '**the** Noun'; otherwise the subject is ill-formed.

Now procedure `parseNoun`:

```
        procedure parseNoun;              { Noun ::=       }
           begin
           if currentTerminal = 'cat' then
              accept('cat')               {       cat  }
           else                           {    |        }
           if currentTerminal = 'mat' then
              accept('mat')               {       mat  }
           else                           {    |        }
           if currentTerminal = 'rat' then
              accept('rat')               {       rat  }
           else
              report a syntactic error
           end{parseNoun}
```

Procedure `parseObject` is analogous to `parseSubject`, and `parseVerb` to `parseNoun`, so we have omitted the details here. (See Exercise 4.2.)

The parser is initiated as follows:

fetch the first input terminal into `currentTerminal;`
`parseSentence;`
check that no terminal follows the sentence

This parser does not actually construct a syntax tree. But it does (implicitly) determine the input string's phrase structure. For example, `parseNoun` whenever called finds the beginning and end of a phrase of class Noun, and `parseSubject` whenever called finds the beginning and end of a phrase of class Subject. (See Figure 4.1.)   □

In general, the procedures of a recursive-descent parser cooperate as follows:

- The variable `currentTerminal` will successively contain each input terminal. All parsing procedures have access to this variable.

- On entry to procedure `parseN`, `currentTerminal` is supposed to contain the first terminal of an *N*-phrase. On exit from `parseN`, `currentTerminal` is supposed to contain the input terminal immediately following that *N*-phrase.

- On entry to procedure `accept` with argument *t*, `currentTerminal` is supposed to contain the terminal *t*. On exit from `accept`, `currentTerminal` is supposed to contain the input terminal immediately following *t*.

If the production rules are mutually recursive, then the parsing procedures will also be mutually recursive. It is for this reason (and the fact that the parsing strategy is top-down) that the method is called *recursive descent*.

In Section 4.3 we shall see how to apply recursive-descent parsing in syntactic analysis, and how we can systematically develop a recursive-descent parser from the source language's context-free grammar.

4.2 Subphases of syntactic analysis

Syntactic analysis in a compiler consists of the following subphases:

- *Scanning:* The source program is transformed to a stream of *tokens*: symbols such as identifiers, literals, operators, keywords, and punctuation. Blank space and comments are discarded. (They are present in the source program for the benefit of the human reader, but otherwise they are insignificant.) Scanning is also called *lexical analysis*.

- *Parsing:* The source program (now represented by a stream of tokens) is parsed to determine its phrase structure. The parser treats each token as a terminal symbol.

- *Representation of the phrase structure:* A data structure representing the source program's phrase structure is constructed. This representation is typically an abstract syntax tree (AST).

The first two subphases are present in every compiler. The third subphase is absent in a one-pass compiler, which has no need to construct an explicit representation of the source program's phrase structure.

Example 4.5
We shall use Mini-Δ to illustrate syntactic analysis in a compiler. A context-free grammar of Mini-Δ was given in Example 1.3.

Syntactic analysis of a small Mini-Δ source program is shown in Figures 4.2 through 4.5.

Scanning transforms the source program to a stream of tokens, as shown in Figure 4.3. Blanks (spaces, ends-of-lines, etc.) and comments (introduced by ' ! ') have been discarded. Each identifier, literal, and operator is treated as a single token.

Parsing determines the phrase structure of the stream of tokens. Figure 4.4 shows the effect of recursive-descent parsing.

Finally, the parser can be made to construct an AST explicitly representing the source program's phrase structure, as shown in Figure 4.5. ☐

```
let var y: Integer
in  !new year
    y := y+1
```

Figure 4.2 A Mini-Δ source program.

let	*var*	*ident.*	*colon*	*identifier*	*in*	*ident.*	*bec.*	*ident.*	*op.*	*intlit.*	*eot*
let	var	y	:	Integer	in	y	:=	y	+	1	

Figure 4.3 The program of Figure 4.2 represented by a stream of tokens.

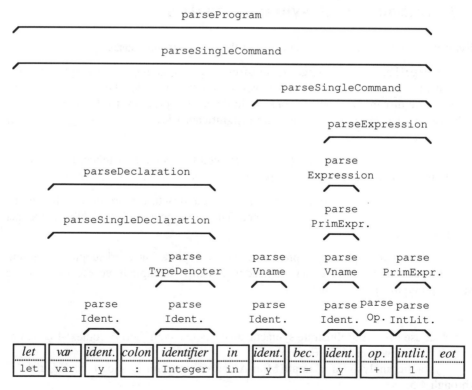

Figure 4.4 The program of Figure 4.2 after recursive-descent parsing.

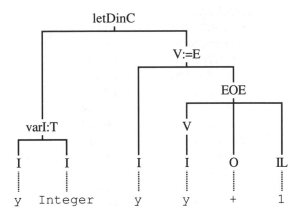

Figure 4.5 The program of Figure 4.2 represented by an AST.

4.2.1 Tokens

The interface between the scanner and the parser is a stream of tokens. A **token** is an atomic symbol of the source program. A token may consist of several characters, but these characters have little or no individual significance. For example, the letters of the keyword 'let' clearly have no individual significance; they serve only to distinguish this keyword from similarly-spelled identifiers like 'lot' and 'led'. The letters of an identifier also have no individual significance, except to distinguish between different identifiers.

As well as tokens, the source program may contain blank space and comments. These are not themselves tokens because they are completely insignificant. Part of the scanner's function is to discard blank space and comments.

Tokens may be classified, as shown in Figure 4.3. For example, the tokens 'y' and 'Integer' have been classified as identifiers, '1' as an integer-literal, and '+' as an operator. The criterion for classifying tokens is simply this: all tokens in the same class can be freely interchanged without affecting the program's phrase structure. Thus the identifier 'y' could be replaced by 'x' or 'banana', and the integer-literal '1' by '7' or '100', without affecting the program's phrase structure. On the other hand, the token 'let' could not be replaced by 'lot' or 'led' or anything else; it belongs in a class by itself.

Each token is completely described by its *class* and *spelling*. Thus a token can be represented simply by a record with these two fields.

Example 4.6
Mini-Δ tokens could be represented as follows:

```
type TokenClass =
        (semicolonToken,    {;}
         colonToken,        {:}
```

```
            becomesToken,    {:=}
            isToken,         {~}
            lParenToken,     {(}
            rParenToken,     {)}
            beginToken,      {begin}
            constToken,      {const}
            doToken,         {do}
            elseToken,       {else}
            endToken,        {end}
            ifToken,         {if}
            inToken,         {in}
            letToken,        {let}
            thenToken,       {then}
            varToken,        {var}
            whileToken,      {while}
            identifierToken, {e.g., y, putint, Integer}
            intLiteralToken, {e.g., 0, 7, 45, 1992}
            operatorToken,   {+, -, *, /, <, >, =, \}
            eotToken         {end of source text}
        );

    TokenString =
        packed array [1..10] of Char;

    Token =
        record
            class:    TokenClass;
            spelling: TokenString
        end;

procedure scan (var tok: Token);
    ...    {Fetch the next token from the source program,
             skipping any preceding blank space or comments.}
```

Note the token class `eotToken`, representing the physical end of the source text. In both scanning and parsing of the source program, the presence of this token will prove convenient.

The above definition of type `TokenString` assumes that no token needs to be longer than 10 characters, and that longer identifiers may be truncated to 10 characters. If the source language does not permit such an assumption, it will be necessary to use varying-length strings instead.   □

The definitions of types `TokenClass` and `TokenString` in Example 4.6 depend on the source language, but the definition of `Token` itself is quite general.

Only the class of each token will be examined by the parser, since different tokens in the same class do not affect the source program's phrase structure. The spellings of some tokens (identifiers, literals, operators) will be examined by the contextual analyzer and/or code generator, so their spellings must be retained and eventually incorporated into the AST. The spellings of other tokens (such as 'let') will never be examined after scanning. Nevertheless, it is convenient to have a uniform representation for all tokens.

4.2.2 Abstract syntax trees

A recursive-descent parser determines the source program's phrase structure *implicitly*, in the sense that it finds the beginning and end of each phrase. In a one-pass compiler, this is quite sufficient for the syntactic analyzer to know when to call the contextual analyzer and code generator. In a multipass compiler, however, the syntactic analyzer must construct an *explicit* representation of the source program's phrase structure. Here we shall assume that the representation is to be an AST.

The following example illustrates how we can define ASTs in Pascal, together with some useful auxiliary functions.

Example 4.7
Figure 4.5 shows an example of a Mini-Δ AST. Below we summarize all possible forms of Mini-Δ AST, showing how each form relates to one of the production rules of the Mini-Δ abstract syntax (Example 1.5):

- Command-ASTs (*C*):

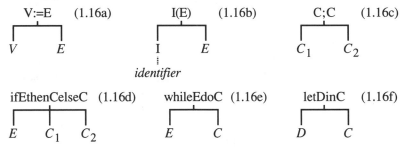

- Expression-ASTs (*E*):

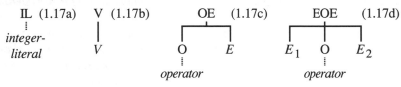

- V-name-ASTs (*V*):

- Declaration-ASTs (*D*):

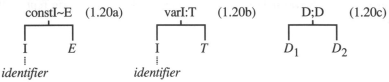

- Type-denoter-ASTs (*T*):

$$I \qquad (1.21)$$

identifier

The AST of a complete program is just a **Command-AST**.

   Each AST node has a tag that determines what (if any) subtrees that node has. For example:

- A node with tag 'ifEthenCelseC' is the root of a **Command-AST** with three subtrees, an **Expression-AST** and two **Command-ASTs**, respectively.
- A node with tag 'constI~E' is the root of a **Declaration-AST** with two subtrees, an **Identifier-AST** and an **Expression-AST**, respectively.
- A node with tag 'I' is the root of an **Identifier-AST**, which is just a terminal node.

   We need to define a type AST that captures the structure of Mini-Δ ASTs. There are several ways of doing so. The following Pascal type definitions are perhaps the simplest:

```
type ASTTag =
         (VbecomesE,        {V:=E, i.e., assignment command}
          IlpErp,           {I(E), i.e., procedure call}
          CsemicolonC,      {C;C, i.e., sequential command}
          ifEthenCelseC,    {if-command}
          whileEdoC,        {while-command}
          letDinC,          {let-command}
          V,                {value-or-variable-name}
          OE,               {application of unary operator}
          EOE,              {application of binary operator}
          constIisE,        {constI~E, i.e., constant declaration}
          varIcolonT,       {varI:T, i.e., variable declaration}
          DsemicolonD,      {D;D, i.e., sequential declaration}
          I,                {identifier}
          IL,               {integer-literal}
          O                 {operator}
         );

      AST = ^ ASTNode;
```

```
ASTNode =
    record
        case tag: ASTTag of
            {Nonterminal nodes ...}
            VbecomesE, IlpErp, CsemicolonC,
            ifEthenCelseC, whileEdoC, letDinC,
            V, OE, EOE,
            constIisE, varIcolonT, DsemicolonD:
                ( arity: 0..3;
                    child: array [1..3] of AST );
            {Terminal nodes ...}
            I, IL, O:
                ( spelling: TokenString )
    end
```

The tag field distinguishes nonterminal nodes from terminal nodes. A nonterminal node has up to three subtrees, which are themselves ASTs. A terminal node corresponds to a token (identifier, integer-literal, or operator) in the Mini-Δ source program. The only data at a terminal node is the spelling of that token.

We will need some AST constructor functions:

```
function leafAST (tag: ASTTag;
                    spelling: TokenString) : AST;
    ...; {Construct a terminal node with the given tag and token spelling.}

function nullaryAST (tag: ASTTag) : AST;
    ...; {Construct a nonterminal node with the given tag and no subtrees.}

function unaryAST  (tag: ASTTag;
                    child1: AST) : AST;
    ...; {Construct a nonterminal node with the given tag and one subtree.}

function binaryAST (tag: ASTTag;
                    child1, child2: AST) : AST;
    ...; {Construct a nonterminal node with the given tag and two
        subtrees.}

function ternaryAST (tag: ASTTag;
                    child1, child2, child3: AST)
                    : AST;
    ... {Construct a nonterminal node with the given tag and three
        subtrees.}
```

We might also need some auxiliary procedures for traversing ASTs, such as:

```
procedures displayAST (theAST: AST);
    ... {Display the given AST on the screen.}
```

The above definition of type AST is not the only possibility. See Exercise 4.7 for some alternative suggestions.   □

To make the syntactic analyzer construct the AST, we augment the parser with calls to the above constructor functions, as we shall see in Section 4.4.

4.3   Parsing

We have already introduced the method of recursive-descent parsing, in Section 4.1.3, and illustrated it with a parser for a natural language fragment. It only remains to show how this method is applied in a parser for a programming language. We shall do this by means of a running example. But first we briefly review a useful variant of BNF.

4.3.1   Regular expressions and EBNF

A ***regular expression*** (*RE*) is a convenient notation for expressing a set of strings. The main features of the RE notation are:

- '|' separates alternatives;
- '*' indicates that the previous item may be repeated zero or more times;
- '(' and ')' are grouping parentheses.

The notation is summarized in Table 4.1, and illustrated by Example 4.8 below.

Table 4.1 Regular expressions.

	Regular expression	This regular expression generates ...
(empty)	ε	just the empty string.
(singleton)	s	just the string consisting of s alone.
(concatenation)	$E\,F$ (or $E \cdot F$)	the concatenation of any string generated by E and any string generated by F.
(alternative)	$E \mid F$	any string generated by E or by F.
(iteration)	$E*$	the concatenation of zero or more of the strings generated by E.
(grouping)	(E)	any string generated by E.

Note: E and F are arbitrary regular expressions; s is any symbol.

Example 4.8
Here are some REs. Each generates a set of strings of letters, as shown:

ε	– generates {ε} (ε is the empty string)
M r | M s	– generates {**Mr, Ms**}
M (r | s)	– generates {**Mr, Ms**}
p s* t	– generates {**pt, pst, psst, pssst**, ...}
b a (n a)*	– generates {**ba, bana, banana, bananana**, ...}

□

An RE generates a set of strings, in other words a language. However, REs are capable of generating only very simple languages, called *regular languages*. REs are not capable of generating languages that exhibit *self-embedding*.

Consider a high-level language. Sublanguages such as identifiers and literals are typically regular. But expressions, commands, etc., typically exhibit self-embedding. For example:

- The expression 'a*(b+c)/d' contains an embedded subexpression, 'b+c'.
- The command 'if x > y then m := x else m := y' contains an embedded subcommand, 'm := x'.

Self-embedding in a high-level language is what allows us to write arbitrarily complex expressions, commands, etc. To generate languages with self-embedding, we must write recursive production rules in BNF.

EBNF (extended BNF) is a combination of BNF and the notation of REs. An EBNF production rule is of the form $N ::= E$, where N is a nonterminal symbol and E is an *extended RE*. Unlike BNF, the right-hand side E may use not only '|' but also '*' and '(' and ')'. Unlike an ordinary RE, E may contain nonterminal symbols as well as terminal symbols. Thus we can write recursive production rules, and an EBNF grammar is capable of generating a language with self-embedding.

Example 4.9
Consider the following EBNF grammar:

Expression	::=	primary-Expression (Operator primary-Expression)*
primary-Expression	::=	Identifier
	|	(Expression)
Identifier	::=	**a** | **b** | **c** | **d** | **e**
Operator	::=	**+** | **-** | ***** | **/**

This grammar generates expressions such as:

    e   a+b   a-b-c   a+(b*c)   a*(b+c)/d   a-(b-(c-(d-e)))

Because the production rules defining Expression and primary-Expression are mutually recursive, the grammar can generate self-embedded expressions.   □

EBNF combines the advantages of both BNF and REs. It is equivalent to BNF in expressive power. Its use of RE notation makes it more convenient than BNF for specifying some aspects of syntax. As we shall now see, EBNF is also a very useful notation to guide the systematic development of recursive-descent parsers.

4.3.2 Systematic development of a recursive-descent parser

A recursive-descent parser can be *systematically* developed from a (suitable) context-free grammar, in the following steps:

(1) If necessary, convert the grammar to EBNF, with a single production rule for each nonterminal symbol.

(2) Transcribe each EBNF production rule $N ::= E$ to a parsing procedure parse$N$, whose body is determined by E.

(3) The parser consists of:
   - a global variable currentToken;
   - auxiliary procedures accept and acceptIt (to be explained later), both of which call the scanner;
   - the parsing procedures developed in step (2);
   - a driver that calls parse$S$ (where S is the start symbol of the grammar), having called the scanner to store the first input token in currentToken.

Example 4.10
Consider the small language Mini-Δ whose BNF grammar was given in Example 1.3. We systematically develop a Mini-Δ parser as follows.
   Step (1) is to convert the grammar to EBNF. Recall production rules (1.2a–b):

```
Command  ::=   single-Command
         |  Command ; single-Command
```

These involve left recursion. This is a BNF device for specifying a sequence of phrases, in this case a sequence of single-commands separated by semicolons. We can specify this more directly using the '*' notation of EBNF:

```
Command ::= single-Command (; single-Command)*
```

Now recall production rule (1.7):

```
V-name ::= Identifier
```

We can simplify the grammar (for parsing purposes) by substituting Identifier for V-name wherever it appears on the right-hand side of a production rule, such as (1.3):

```
single-Command  ::=   Identifier := Expression
                |  Identifier ( Expression )
                |  if Expression then single-Command
                      else single-Command
                |  ...
```

The first two alternatives above can now be factorized using grouping parentheses[2]:

single-Command ::= Identifier (:= Expression | (Expression))
             | **if** Expression **then** single-Command
                  else single-Command
             | ...

These transformations are justified because they will make the grammar more convenient for parsing purposes. After making similar transformations to other parts of the grammar, we obtain the following complete EBNF grammar of Mini-Δ:

Program	::=	single-Command	(4.6)
Command	::=	single-Command (; single-Command)*	(4.7)
single-Command	::=	Identifier (:= Expression	(Expression))	(4.8)
			if Expression **then** single-Command	
			else single-Command	
			while Expression **do** single-Command	
			let Declaration **in** single-Command	
			begin Command **end**	
Expression	::=	primary-Expression	(4.9)
			(Operator primary-Expression)*	
primary-Expression	::=	Integer-Literal	
			Identifier	
			Operator primary-Expression	
			(Expression)	
Declaration	::=	single-Declaration (; single-Declaration)*	(4.10)
single-Declaration	::=	**const** Identifier ~ Expression	(4.11)
			var Identifier : Type-denoter	
Type-denoter	::=	Identifier	(4.12)

We have excluded production rules (1.11) through (1.15), which specify the syntax of identifiers, literals, and operators in terms of individual characters. This part of the syntax is called the language's *lexicon* (or *microsyntax*). The lexicon is of no concern to the parser, which will view each identifier, literal, and operator as a single token. (However, the lexicon will be taken into account in scanning, to be discussed in Section 4.5.)

Step (2) is to convert each EBNF production rule to a parsing procedure. Here is procedure parseSingleDeclaration:

```
procedure parseSingleDeclaration;     { single-Decl. ::=  }
   begin
```

---

[2] Distinguish carefully between '(' and ')', which are EBNF symbols, and the emboldened '**(**' and '**)**', which are terminal symbols of the source language. Similarly distinguish between the other EBNF symbols and any terminal symbols that happen to resemble them.

```
if currentToken.class
       = constToken then
     begin
     acceptIt;                        {    const     }
     parseIdentifier;                 {    Identifier }
     accept(isToken);                 {    ~          }
     parseExpression                  {    Expression }
     end
else                                  {    |          }
if currentToken.class
       = varToken then
     begin
     acceptIt;                        {    var        }
     parseIdentifier;                 {    Identifier }
     accept(colonToken);              {    :          }
     parseTypeDenoter                 {    Type-denoter }
     end
else
     report a syntactic error
end{parseSingleDeclaration}
```

Note the use of the auxiliary procedure `acceptIt`, which unconditionally fetches the next token from the source program. The following is also correct:

```
if currentToken.class = constToken then
     begin
     accept(constToken);
     parseIdentifier;
     accept(isToken);
     parseExpression
     end
     ...
```

Here '`accept(constToken)`' would check that the current token is of class `constToken`. In this context, however, such a check is redundant.

Now procedure `parseCommand`:

```
procedure parseCommand;               { Command ::=    }
     begin
     parseSingleCommand;              {    single-Com.  }
     while currentToken.class
            = semicolonToken do
        begin                         {    (           }
        acceptIt;                     {    ;           }
        parseSingleCommand            {    single-Com. }
        end                           {    ) *         }
     end{parseCommand}
```

This procedure illustrates something new. The EBNF notation '(; single-Command)*' signifies a sequence of zero or more occurrences of '; single-Command'. To parse this we use a while-loop, which is iterated zero or more times. The condition for continuing the iteration is simply that the current token is a semicolon.

Procedure `parseDeclaration` is similar to `parseCommand`. The remaining procedures are as follows:

```
procedure parseSingleCommand;            { single-Com. ::=  }
  begin
  if currentToken.class
        = identifierToken then
      begin
      parseIdentifier;                   {    Identifier    }
                                         {    (            }

      if currentToken.class
            = becomesToken then
          begin
          acceptIt;                      {    :=           }
          parseExpression               {    Expression    }
          end
      else                               {    |            }
      if currentToken.class
            = lParenToken then
          begin
          acceptIt;                      {    (            }
          parseExpression;               {    Expression    }
          accept(rParenToken)            {    )            }
          end
      else
          report a syntactic error        {    )            }
      end
  else                                   {    |            }
  if currentToken.class
        = ifToken then
      begin
      acceptIt;                          {    if           }
      parseExpression;                   {    Expression    }
      accept(thenToken);                 {    then         }
      parseSingleCommand;                {    single-Com.   }
      accept(elseToken);                 {    else         }
      parseSingleCommand                 {    single-Com.   }
      end
  else                                   {    |            }
  if currentToken.class
        = whileToken then
      begin
```

```
      acceptIt;                        {    while      }
      parseExpression;                 {    Expression }
      accept(doToken);                 {    do         }
      parseSingleCommand               {    single-Com. }
      end
    else                               {    |          }
    if currentToken.class
        = letToken then
      begin
      acceptIt;                        {    let        }
      parseDeclaration;                {    Declaration }
      accept(inToken);                 {    in         }
      parseSingleCommand               {    single-Com. }
      end
    else                               {    |          }
    if currentToken.class
        = beginToken then
      begin
      acceptIt;                        {    begin      }
      parseCommand;                    {    Command    }
      accept(endToken)                 {    end        }
      end
    else
      report a syntactic error
    end{parseSingleCommand}

procedure parseExpression;             { Expression ::=  }
    begin
    parsePrimaryExpression;            {    primary-Expr. }
    while currentToken.class
        = operatorToken do
      begin                            {    (          }
      parseOperator;                   {    Operator   }
      parsePrimaryExpression           {    primary-Expr. }
      end                              {    ) *        }
    end{parseExpression};

procedure parsePrimaryExpression;      { primary-Expr. ::= }
    begin
    if currentToken.class
        = intLiteralToken then
      parseIntegerLiteral              {    Integer-Literal }
    else                               {    |          }
    if currentToken.class
        = identifierToken then
      parseIdentifier                  {    Identifier }
    else                               {    |          }
```

```
if currentToken.class
       = operatorToken then
    begin
    parseOperator;                         {     Operator      }
    parsePrimaryExpression                 {     primary-Expr. }
    end
else                                       {   |              }
if currentToken.class
       = lParenToken then
    begin
    acceptIt;                              {     (            }
    parseExpression;                       {     Expression   }
    accept(rParenToken)                    {     )            }
    end
else
    report a syntactic error
end{parsePrimaryExpression};

procedure parseTypeDenoter;                { Type-denoter ::= }
    begin
    parseIdentifier                        {     Identifier   }
    end{parseTypeDenoter}
```

The nonterminal symbol Identifier corresponds to a single token, so the procedure `parseIdentifier` is similar to `accept`:

```
procedure parseIdentifier;
    begin
    if currentToken.class = identifierToken then
       scan(currentToken)
    else
       report a syntactic error
    end{parseIdentifier}
```

The procedures `parseIntegerLiteral` and `parseOperator` are analogous.

Step (3) is to assemble the complete parser:

```
procedure parseProgram;

    var currentToken: Token;

    procedure accept (expected: TokenClass);
       begin
       if currentToken.class = expected then
          scan(currentToken)
       else
          report a syntactic error
       end{accept};
```

```
procedure acceptIt;
   begin
   scan(currentToken)
   end{acceptIt};

...;       {parsing procedures, as above}

begin{parseProgram}
scan(currentToken);
parseSingleCommand;
if currentToken.class <> eotToken then
   report a syntactic error
end{parseProgram}
```

Note the following points:

- The parser examines only the class of the current token, ignoring its spelling.

- The parsing procedures are mutually recursive (because the production rules were mutually recursive). For example, `parseCommand` calls `parseSingleCommand`, which may call `parseCommand` recursively. (See Exercise 4.9.)

⊔

Having worked through a complete example, let us now study in general terms how we systematically develop a recursive-descent parser from a suitable grammar. The two main steps are: (1) to convert the grammar from BNF to EBNF, and (2) to convert the EBNF production rules to parsing procedures. It will be convenient to examine these steps in reverse order.

4.3.3 Conversion of EBNF production rules to parsing procedures

The conversion method depends on the following concept. The **starter set** of an (extended) regular expression E, written $starters[\![E]\!]$, is the set of terminal symbols that can start a string generated by E. For example:

$$starters[\![\mathbf{h\ i\ s\ |\ h\ e\ r\ |\ i\ t\ s}]\!] = \{\mathbf{h, i}\}$$
$$starters[\![(\mathbf{r\ e})^*\ \mathbf{s\ e\ t}]\!] \qquad = \{\mathbf{r, s}\}$$

since '$(\mathbf{r\ e})^*\ \mathbf{s\ e\ t}$' generates the set of strings {$\mathbf{set}$, $\mathbf{reset}$, $\mathbf{rereset}$, ...}.

The following is a precise and complete definition of *starters*. (E and F stand for arbitrary extended REs.)

$$starters[\![\varepsilon]\!] \qquad = \{\ \}$$

$$starters[\![t]\!] \qquad = \{t\} \qquad\qquad \text{where } t \text{ is a terminal symbol}$$

$$starters[\![N]\!] \qquad = starters[\![E]\!] \qquad \text{where } N \text{ is a nonterminal symbol}$$
$$\text{defined by production rule } N ::= E$$

$$starters[\![E\ F]\!] \quad = starters[\![E]\!] \cup starters[\![F]\!] \qquad \text{if } E \text{ generates } \varepsilon$$
$$starters[\![E]\!] \qquad\qquad\qquad\qquad \text{otherwise}$$

$$starters[\![E \mid F]\!] \quad = starters[\![E]\!] \cup starters[\![F]\!]$$

$$starters[\![E*]\!] \qquad = starters[\![E]\!]$$

Now we are ready to present the conversion method in detail. Consider an EBNF production rule $N ::= E$. We convert this production rule to a parsing procedure named parse$N$. This procedure's body is derived from the extended RE E:

```
procedure parseN;
   begin
   parse E
   end
```

Here '*parse E*' is supposed to parse an E-phrase, i.e., a terminal string generated by the extended RE E. (And of course the task of procedure parse$N$ is to parse an N-phrase.)

Next, we perform stepwise refinement on '*parse E*', decomposing it according to the structure of E. (In the following, E and F stand for arbitrary extended REs.)

- We refine '*parse ε*' to a skip command.

- We refine '*parse t*' (where t is a terminal symbol) simply to:

  ```
  accept (t)
  ```

  In a situation where the current terminal is already known to be t, the following is also correct, but more efficient:

  ```
  acceptIt
  ```

- We refine '*parse N*' (where N is a nonterminal symbol) to a call on the corresponding parsing procedure:

  ```
  parseN
  ```

- We refine '*parse E F*' to:

  ```
  begin
  parse E;
  parse F
  end
  ```

  The reasoning behind this is simple. The input must consist of an E-phrase followed by an F-phrase. Since the parser works from left to right, it must parse the E-phrase and then parse the F-phrase.

  This refinement rule is easily extended to '*parse $E_1 \ldots E_n$*'.

- We refine '*parse E | F*' to:

  ```
  if currentToken.class in starters[E] then
     parse E
  ```

```
else
if currentToken.class in starters[F] then
    parse F
else
    report a syntactic error
```

The reasoning behind this is also straightforward. The input must consist of *either* an *E*-phrase *or* an *F*-phrase. The parser must parse one of these, and it must decide immediately which it will be. It should choose '*parse E*' only if the current token is one that can start an *E*-phrase (since otherwise '*parse E*' would certainly fail). And likewise it should choose '*parse F*' only if the current token is one that can start an *F*-phrase (since otherwise '*parse F*' would certainly fail). We can express these conditions abstractly in terms of the starter sets of *E* and *F*, and concretely in terms of Pascal sets.

The parser will work correctly only if $starters[E]$ and $starters[F]$ are disjoint. Suppose that some token t is in both $starters[E]$ and $starters[F]$. When the current token is t, the parser will always choose '*parse E*', even when it ought to choose '*parse F*'. (See Example 4.13.)

This refinement rule is easily extended to '*parse E_1 | ... | E_n*'.

• We refine '*parse E**' to:

```
while currentToken.class in starters[E] do
    parse E
```

The reasoning behind this is as follows. The input must consist of zero or more consecutive *E*-phrases. The parser must repeatedly parse *E*-phrases, and it does this by means of a while-loop. Before each iteration, it must decide whether to terminate or to continue parsing *E*-phrases. It should continue only if the current token is one that can start an *E*-phrase (since otherwise '*parse E*' would certainly fail).

The parser will work correctly only if $starters[E]$ is disjoint from the set of tokens that can follow *E** in this particular context. Suppose that some token t is in $starters[E]$ and can also follow *E**. When the current token is t, the parser will continue parsing *E*-phrases even when it should terminate. (See Example 4.14.)

The following examples illustrate the stepwise refinement of parsing procedures.

Example 4.11

Let us follow the stepwise refinement of the procedure `parseCommand` of Example 4.10, starting from production rule (4.7):

Command ::= single-Command (; single-Command)*

We start with the following outline of the procedure:

```
procedure parseCommand;
    begin
    parse single-Command (; single-Command)*
    end
```

Now we refine '*parse* single-Command (; single-Command)*' to:

```
parseSingleCommand;
```
parse (; single-Command)*

Now we refine '*parse* (; single-Command)*' to:

while currentToken.class = semicolonToken **do**
    parse (; single-Command)

since *starters*⟦; single-Command⟧ = { ; }. This being a singleton set, we can use an equality test '=' rather than the slower set membership test '**in**'.

Finally we refine '*parse* (; single-Command)' to:

```
begin
acceptIt;
parseSingleCommand
end
```

In this situation we know already that the current token is a semicolon, so 'acceptIt' is a correct alternative to 'accept(semicolonToken)'. □

Example 4.12

Let us also follow the stepwise refinement of the procedure parseSingle-Declaration of Example 4.10, starting from production rule (4.11):

single-Declaration ::= **const** Identifier ~ Expression
                   | **var** Identifier : Type-denoter

We start with the following outline of the procedure:

procedure parseSingleDeclaration;
    begin
    parse **const** Identifier ~ Expression | **var** Identifier : Type-denoter
    end

Now we refine '*parse* **const** ... | **var** ...' to:

if currentToken.class = constToken **then**
    parse **const** Identifier ~ Expression
else
if currentToken.class = varToken **then**
    parse **var** Identifier : Type-denoter
else
    report a syntactic error

since *starters*⟦**const** ...⟧ = {**const**} and *starters*⟦**var** ...⟧ = {**var**}. Fortunately, these starter sets are disjoint.

Finally, we refine '*parse* **const** Identifier ~ Expression' to:

```
begin
acceptIt;
```

```
parseIdentifier;
accept(isToken);
parseExpression
end
```

and '*parse* **var** Identifier : Type-denoter' similarly, as shown in Example 4.10.   □

In defining how to refine '*parse E | F*' and '*parse E**', we stated certain conditions that must be satisfied. A grammar that satisfies all these conditions is called an *LL(1)* grammar. The method of recursive-descent parsing is suitable *only* for LL(1) grammars.

By no means are all programming language grammars LL(1). In practice, however, nearly every programming language grammar can easily be transformed to make it LL(1), without changing the language it generates. Why this should be so is a matter for conjecture, but often a language designer will consciously design the new language's syntax to be suitable for recursive-descent parsing. Pascal was a case in point.

The following examples illustrate grammars that are not LL(1). However, simple transformations of these grammars are sufficient to make them LL(1).

Example 4.13
Recall production rules (1.3a–f) in the grammar of Mini-Δ:

single-Command ::=   V-name := Expression
          | Identifier **(** Expression **)**
          | **if** Expression **then** single-Command
               else single-Command
          | ...

The relevant starter sets are:

starters⟦V-name := Expression⟧   = *starters*⟦V-name⟧
                     = {Identifier}

starters⟦Identifier **(** Expression **)** ⟧   = {Identifier}

starters⟦**if** Expression **then** ...⟧   = {**if**}

The first two are *not* disjoint, so the grammar is not LL(1).

Suppose, nevertheless, that we tried to develop a parsing procedure directly from the above production rules. The parsing procedure would turn out to be:

```
procedure parseSingleCommand;
   begin
   if currentToken.class = identifierToken then
      begin
      parseVname;
      accept(becomesToken);
      parseExpression
      end
   else
```

```
if currentToken.class = identifierToken then
  begin
  parseIdentifier;
  accept(lParenToken);
  parseExpression;
  accept(rParenToken)
  end
else
if currentToken.class = ifToken then
  ...
else
  ...
end{parseSingleCommand}
```

This parser is clearly incorrect. Whenever it encounters a command starting with an identifier – even a procedure call such as 'putint(n)' – the parser will try to parse it as an assignment command.

Fortunately the problematic production rule can easily be transformed, by substitution and factorization, to solve this particular problem. This was done in Example 4.10. ☐

Example 4.14
Consider the following production rules taken from a grammar of Algol:

> Block   ::= **begin** Declaration (; Declaration)* ; Command **end**
>
> Declaration ::= **integer** Identifier (, Identifier)* | ...

Here *starters*⟦; Declaration⟧ = { ; }, and the set of terminals that can follow '(; Declaration)*' in this situation is { ; }. These sets are not disjoint, so the grammar is not LL(1).

If we tried to develop a parsing procedure directly from this production rule, we would get:

```
procedure parseBlock;
  begin
  accept(beginToken);
  parseDeclaration;
  while currentToken.class = semicolonToken do
    begin
    acceptIt;
    parseDeclaration
    end;
  accept(semicolonToken);
  parseCommand
  end{parseBlock}
```

This is clearly incorrect. Iteration will continue as long as the current token is a semicolon. But this might be the semicolon that separates the declarations from the command, e.g., the second semicolon in:

```
begin integer i; integer j; i := j+1 end
```

Then `parseBlock` would attempt to parse the command 'i := j+1' as a declaration. Fortunately, we can transform the production rule defining Block:

Block ::= **begin** Declaration ; (Declaration ;)* Command **end**

This does not affect the generated language, but leads to the following correct parsing procedure:

```
procedure parseBlock;
  begin
  accept(beginToken);
  parseDeclaration;
  accept(semicolonToken);
  while currentToken.class
      in [integerToken, ...] do
    begin
    parseDeclaration;
    accept(semicolonToken)
    end;
  parseCommand
  end{parseBlock}
```

This eliminates the problem, assuming that *starters*⟦Declaration ; ⟧ is disjoint from *starters*⟦Command⟧.   □

The above examples are quite typical. Although the LL(1) condition is quite restrictive, in practice most programming language grammars can be transformed to make them LL(1) and thus suitable for recursive-descent parsing.

4.3.4   Conversion of a BNF grammar to EBNF

Since EBNF is an extension of BNF, a BNF grammar is in a sense already EBNF. However, we want to exploit the EBNF extensions, in particular grouping of alternatives '(...|...|...)' and iteration '*'. These extensions help us to ensure that the grammar is LL(1), if possible.

Here we summarize and illustrate some common transformations that we can exploit in EBNF.

Elimination of left recursion
Suppose that we have a production rule of the form:

$N ::= E \mid N F$

where N is a nonterminal symbol, and E and F are arbitrary extended REs. This production rule is *left-recursive*. We replace it by the equivalent EBNF:

$$N ::= E (F)*$$

Left recursion must always be eliminated if the grammar is to be LL(1). The following example illustrates the transformation, and also shows why it is essential.

Example 4.15
Recall production rules (1.2a–b) in the grammar of Mini-Δ:

```
Command ::=  single-Command
         |  Command ; single-Command
```

In Example 4.10 we eliminated this left recursion

What would happen if we omitted this transformation? The parsing procedure would then look like this:

```
procedure parseCommand;
  begin
  if currentToken.class
        in [identifierToken, ifToken,
            whileToken, letToken, beginToken] then
     parseSingleCommand
  else
  if currentToken.class
        in [identifierToken, ifToken,
            whileToken, letToken, beginToken] then
     begin
     parseCommand;
     accept(semicolonToken);
     parseSingleCommand
     end
  else
     report a syntactic error
  end{parseCommand}
```

where the sets used here are *starters*[single-Command] and *starters*[Command ; single-Command], respectively. It should be clear that the else-part of this procedure will never be chosen (even when parsing a command containing a semicolon).

See also Exercise 4.12, which draws attention to another way in which a recursive-descent parser can misbehave in the presence of left recursion. □

In general, a grammar that uses left recursion cannot be LL(1). Thus any attempt to convert left-recursive production rules directly into parsing procedures would result in an incorrect parser. It is easy to see why. Given the left-recursive production rule:

$$N ::= E \mid N F$$

we find:

$$starters[N\,F] = starters[N] = starters[E] \cup starters[N\,F]$$

so $starters\llbracket E \rrbracket$ and $starters\llbracket N\,F \rrbracket$ cannot be disjoint. (In fact, $starters\llbracket E \rrbracket = starters\llbracket N\,F \rrbracket$.)

Incidentally, it is possible for a more complicated production rule to be left-recursive:

$$N \;::=\; E_1 \mid \ldots \mid E_m \mid N\,F_1 \mid \ldots \mid N\,F_n$$

But factorization gives us:

$$N \;::=\; (E_1 \mid \ldots \mid E_m) \mid N\,(F_1 \mid \ldots \mid F_n)$$

and now we can apply our elimination rule:

$$N \;::=\; (E_1 \mid \ldots \mid E_m)\,(F_1 \mid \ldots \mid F_n)^*$$

Substitution of nonterminal symbols

Consider the production rule $N ::= E$. We may substitute E for any occurrence of N on the right-hand side of another production rule.

If we substitute E for *every* occurrence of N, then we may eliminate the production rule $N ::= E$ altogether. (This is possible, however, only if $N ::= E$ is nonrecursive.)

Whether we actually choose to make such transformations is a matter of convenience. If N occurs in only a few places, and if E is uncomplicated, then elimination of $N ::= E$ might well simplify the grammar as a whole.

Example 4.16
Consider the following production rules, taken from a grammar of Pascal:

```
single-Command ::=  for Control-Variable := Expression To-or-downto
                        Expression do single-Command
                |  ...

Control-Variable ::=  Identifier

To-or-downto    ::=  to
                |  downto
```

It makes sense to eliminate Control-Variable and To-or-downto by substitution:

```
single-Command ::=  for Identifier := Expression (to | downto)
                        Expression do single-Command
                |  ...
```

The nonterminal To-or-downto was present in the first place only because grouping of alternatives '(...|...)' is not possible in BNF. The nonterminal Control-Variable was present only to act as a 'semantic clue' – to emphasize the role this particular identifier plays in the for-command – and not for any grammatical reason. Eliminating such nonterminals simplifies the grammar.   □

Factorization

Suppose that we have alternatives of the form:

      E F G | EF' G

where *E*, *F*, *F'*, and *G* are arbitrary extended REs. We should replace these alternatives by the equivalent extended RE:

      E (F | F') G

This transformation is in fact essential if *E* is nonempty.

Example 4.17
In Example 4.10, the production rule 'V-name ::= Identifier' was eliminated. The occurrences of V-name on the right-hand sides of (1.3a) and (1.5b) were simply replaced by Identifier, giving:

    single-Command ::=   Identifier : = Expression
                | Identifier **(** Expression **)**
                | **if** Expression **then** single-Command
                        else single-Command
                | ...

    The substitution opened up a possibility for factorization:

    single-Command ::=   Identifier (: = Expression | **(** Expression **)**)
                | **if** Expression **then** single-Command
                        else single-Command
                | ...

This is an improvement, since the following are not disjoint:

      starters⟦Identifier : = Expression⟧   = {Identifier}
      starters⟦Identifier **(** Expression **)**⟧ = {Identifier}

but the following *are* disjoint:

      starters⟦ : = Expression⟧   = { :=}
      starters⟦ **(** Expression **)** ⟧   = { **(**}

□

4.4 Constructing the abstract syntax tree

It is straightforward to make a recursive-descent parser construct an AST to represent the source program's phrase structure. We enhance the parser as follows:

• We make each procedure parse*N*, as well as parsing a phrase of class *N*, return that phrase's AST as its result. If the implementation language is Pascal, the AST should be a variable parameter of parse*N*.

• We make the body of parse*N* construct the phrase's AST by combining the ASTs of any subphrases (or by creating a terminal node).

Thus, for production rule $N ::= E$:

```
procedure parseN (var itsAST: AST);
    begin
    parse E, at the same time constructing itsAST
    end
```

Example 4.18

Here we enhance the Mini-Δ parser of Example 4.10, to construct an AST representing the source program. We use the auxiliary functions of Example 4.7 to perform the actual tree construction.

Here is the enhanced procedure `parseSingleDeclaration` (with the enhancements italicized for emphasis):

```
procedure parseSingleDeclaration
                                    (var declAST: AST);
    var iAST, eAST, tAST: AST;
    begin
    if currentToken.class = constToken then
        begin
        acceptIt;
        parseIdentifier(iAST);
        accept(isToken);
        parseExpression(eAST);
        declAST := binaryAST(constIisE, iAST, eAST)
        end
    else
    if currentToken.class = varToken then
        begin
        acceptIt;
        parseIdentifier(iAST);
        accept(colonToken);
        parseTypeDenoter(tAST);
        declAST := binaryAST(varIcolonT, iAST, tAST)
        end
    else
        report a syntactic error
    end{parseSingleDeclaration}
```

This procedure is fairly typical. It has been enhanced by a variable parameter, `decl-AST`, in which will be stored (a pointer to) the AST of the single-declaration parsed by this procedure. The local variables `iAST`, `eAST`, and `tAST` will temporarily contain (pointers to) the ASTs of the subphrases.

Here is the enhanced procedure `parseCommand`:

```
procedure parseCommand (var comAST: AST);
    var c1AST, c2AST: AST;
    begin
```

```
parseSingleCommand(c1AST);
while currentToken.class = semicolonToken do
    begin
    acceptIt;
    parseSingleCommand(c2AST);
    c1AST := binaryAST(CsemicolonC, c1AST, c2AST)
    end;
comAST := c1AST
end{parseCommand}
```

This procedure contains a loop, arising from the iteration '*' in production rule (4.7) – which in turn was introduced by eliminating the left recursion in (1.2a–b). We must be careful to construct an AST with the correct structure. The local variable `c1AST` is used to accumulate this AST.

Suppose that the command being parsed is of the form '$C_1; C_2; C_3$'. Then after the procedure parses C_1, `c1AST` will contain the AST for C_1; after it parses C_2, it will update `c1AST` to the AST for '$C_1; C_2$'; and after it parses C_3, it will update `c1AST` to the AST for '$C_1; C_2; C_3$'.

Here is an outline of the enhanced procedure `parseSingleCommand`:

```
procedure parseSingleCommand (var comAST: AST);
    var c1AST, c2AST, dAST, eAST, iAST: AST;
    begin
    if currentToken.class = identifierToken then
        begin
        parseIdentifier(iAST);
        if currentToken.class = becomesToken then
            begin
            acceptIt;
            parseExpression(eAST);
            comAST := binaryAST(VbecomesE, iAST, eAST)
            end
        else
        if currentToken.class = lParenToken then
            begin
            acceptIt;
            parseExpression(eAST);
            accept(rParenToken);
            comAST := binaryAST(IlpErp, iAST, eAST)
            end
        else
            report a syntactic error
        end
    else
    if currentToken.class = ifToken then
        ...
    else
```

```
if currentToken.class = whileToken then
    ...
else
if currentToken.class = letToken then
    ...
else
if currentToken.class = beginToken then
    begin
    acceptIt;
    parseCommand(comAST);
    accept(endToken)
    end
else
    report a syntactic error
end{parseSingleCommand}
```

If the single-command turns out to be of the form '**begin** *C* **end**', there is no need to construct a new AST, since the '**begin**' and '**end**' are just command brackets. So in this case the procedure immediately stores *C*'s AST in comAST.

We enhance the remaining procedures similarly:

```
procedure parseExpression (var exprAST: AST);
    ...;

procedure parsePrimaryExpression
            (var exprAST: AST);
    ...;

procedure parseDeclaration (var declAST: AST);
    ...;

procedure parseTypeDenoter (var typeAST: AST);
    ...;

procedure parseIdentifier (var idAST: AST);
    begin
    if currentToken.class = identifierToken then
        begin
        idAST := leafAST(I, currentToken.spelling);
        scan(currentToken)
        end
    else
        report a syntactic error
    end{parseIdentifier}
```

The procedures parseIntegerLiteral and parseOperator are analogous to parseIdentifier. (See Exercise 4.14.)

The complete parser is:

```
procedure parseProgram (var progAST: AST);

    var currentToken: Token;

    ...;      {auxiliary procedures}

    ...;      {parsing procedures, as above}

    begin
    scan(currentToken);
    parseSingleCommand(progAST);
    if currentToken.class <> eotToken then
        report a syntactic error
    end{parseProgram}
```

□

4.5 Scanning

The purpose of scanning is to recognize tokens in the source program. Scanning is in some respects analogous to parsing, but works at a finer level of detail. In parsing, the terminal symbols are tokens, which are to be grouped into larger phrases such as expressions and commands. In scanning, the terminal symbols are individual characters, which are to be grouped into tokens.

As well as tokens, the source program contains *separators*: blank space, comments, and the like. They serve to separate tokens, and to assist human readers. But only tokens contribute to the program's phrase structure.

We can systematically develop a scanner in much the same way as a parser. We start with a *lexical grammar* specifying the source language's lexicon. This grammar's terminal symbols are individual characters, and its nonterminal symbols include Token and Separator. The lexical grammar must be non-self-embedding.

We develop the scanner as follows:

(1) If necessary, convert the lexical grammar to EBNF.

(2) Transcribe each EBNF production rule $N ::= E$ to a scanning procedure scanN, whose body is determined by E.

(3) The scanner consists of:
   - a global variable currentChar;
   - auxiliary procedures start, takeIt, leaveIt, finish, and screen;
   - the scanning procedures developed in step (2), enhanced to record the token's class and spelling;
   - a procedure scan that scans 'Separator* Token', and returns the latter token.

The scanning procedures will be somewhat analogous to the parsing procedures we have seen already. On entry to scanN, currentChar is supposed to contain the first character of a character sequence of class N; on exit, currentChar is supposed to contain the character immediately following that character sequence.

Likewise, the auxiliary procedures `takeIt` and `leaveIt` are somewhat analogous to the parser's auxiliary procedure `acceptIt`. Each of these procedures will fetch the next character from the source program into `currentChar`. (The difference is that `takeIt` will treat the previous character as part of a token, and therefore save it, whereas `leaveIt` will treat the previous character as part of a separator, and therefore discard it.)

The procedure `scan` is supposed to fetch the next token from the source program, each time it is called. But this token might turn out to be preceded by some separators. That is the reason for scanning 'Separator* Token'. In this we are assuming that the source language has a conventional lexicon: separators may be used freely between tokens. (Most modern languages do follow this convention.)

Example 4.19

The lexical grammar of Mini-Δ is partly given by production rules (1.11) through (1.15). We add production rules for tokens and separators:

Token	::=	Word | Integer-Literal | Operator | ; | : | : = | ~ | (|) | eot	(4.13)
Word	::=	Letter | Word Letter | Word Digit	(4.14)
Integer-Literal	::=	Digit | Integer-Literal Digit	(4.15)
Operator	::=	+ | - | * | / | < | > | = | \	(4.16)
Separator	::=	Comment | Blank	(4.17)
Comment	::=	! Graphic* eol	(4.18)

In these production rules:

- eot stands for an end-of-text 'character'.
- eol stands for an end-of-line 'character'.

(Visible characters can be expressed as themselves in EBNF, but these invisible characters cannot.) Also:

- Blank stands for a space or end-of-line.
- Digit stands for one of the digits '0', '1', ..., or '9'.
- Graphic stands for a space or visible character.
- Letter stands for one of the lowercase letters 'a', 'b', ..., or 'z'.

Each of these nonterminals represents a group of single characters. Specifying them formally would present no difficulty, of course.

Note an important point: identifiers and keywords are all represented by the nonterminal Word. It turns out that any attempt to distinguish between identifiers and keywords in the lexical grammar gets us into difficulties. (See Exercise 4.17 for the reason.) We shall return to this point later.

Let us now develop a scanner for Mini-Δ. A type definition for `Token` was given in Example 4.6.

Step (1) is to convert the lexical grammar to EBNF. We eliminate left recursion in (4.14) and (4.15), giving:

Word	::=	Letter (Letter | Digit)*	(4.19)
Integer-Literal	::=	Digit Digit*	(4.20)

We can simplify parts of the lexical grammar by substitution and factorization:

Token	::=	Word | Integer-Literal | Operator |	
		; | : (= | ε) | ~ | (|) | eot	(4.21)
Separator	::=	! Graphic* eol | Blank	(4.22)

Step (2) is to convert the production rules to scanning procedures. The procedures are given below. (The code in italics anticipates enhancements to be made in the third step; ignore this code for the moment.)

```
procedure scanToken;                        { Token ::=        }
   begin
   start;
   if currentChar in ['a'..'z'] then
      scanWord                              {      Word        }
   else                                     {      |          }
   if currentChar in ['0'..'9'] then
      scanIntegerLiteral                    {      Integer-Literal }
   else                                     {      |          }
   if currentChar
        in ['+', '-', '*', '/',
            '<', '>', '=', '\'] then
      scanOperator                          {      Operator    }
   else                                     {      |          }
   if currentChar = ';' then
      begin
      takeIt; finish(semicolonToken)  {    ;          }
      end
   else                                     {      |          }
   if currentChar = ':' then
      begin
      takeIt;                               {      :          }
      if currentChar = '=' then  {      (          }
         begin
         takeIt; finish(becomesToken){      =          }
         end
      else                                  {      |          }
         finish(colonToken)                 {      ε          }
      end                                   {      )          }
   else                                     {      |          }
   if currentChar = '~' then
```

```
            begin
              takeIt; finish(isToken)          {    ~            }
            end
          else                                 {    |            }
          if currentChar = '(' then
            begin
              takeIt; finish(lParenToken)       {    (            }
            end
          else                                 {    |            }
          if currentChar = ')' then
            begin
              takeIt; finish(rParenToken)       {    )            }
            end
          else                                 {    |            }
          if currentChar = eot then
              finish(eotToken)                  {    eot          }
          else
              report a lexical error
          end{scanToken};

      procedure scanWord;                      { Word ::=        }
        begin
          takeIt;                              {     Letter      }
          while currentChar
              in ['a'..'z', '0'..'9'] do
            takeIt;                            {     (Letter | Digit)* }
          screen
        end{scanWord};

      procedure scanIntegerLiteral;            { Integer-Literal ::= }
          ...;                                 {     ...         }

      procedure scanOperator;                  { Operator ::=    }
          ...;                                 {     ...         }

      procedure scanSeparator;                 { Separator ::=   }
        begin
          if currentChar = '!' then
            begin
              leaveIt;                         {    !            }
              while currentChar <> eol do
                leaveIt;                       {     Graphic*    }
              leaveIt                          {     eol         }
            end
          else                                 {    |            }
            leaveIt                            {     Blank       }
        end{scanSeparator}
```

Step (3) is to assemble the complete scanner, and make it determine the token's class and spelling. The necessary enhancements to the scanning procedures are italicized above. The auxiliary procedure `takeIt` appends the current character to the token's spelling, as well as fetching the next source character; the auxiliary procedure `leaveIt` does only the latter. The auxiliary procedure `start` initializes the token's spelling, and `finish` sets the token's class as directed.

We decided not to distinguish between identifiers and keywords in the lexical grammar. Nevertheless, the scanner *must* properly classify these tokens. This is done by `scanWord` calling an auxiliary procedure `screen`, which checks whether the token's spelling matches any of the keywords. If so, it classifies the token accordingly. If not, it classifies the token as an identifier.

Here is an outline of the complete scanner, including the auxiliary procedures:

```
var currentChar: Char;
                {must be initialized to the first source character}

procedure scan (var tok: Token);

    procedure start;
        ...; {Make tok.spelling empty.}

    procedure takeIt;
        ...; {Append currentChar to tok.spelling, and then
              fetch the next source character into currentChar.}

    procedure leaveIt;
        ...; {Fetch the next source character into currentChar.}

    procedure finish (class: TokenClass);
        ...; {Set tok.class to the given class.}

    procedure screen;
        ...; {Set tok.class according to tok.spelling. If
              tok.spelling contains a keyword, set tok.class to
              ifToken or thenToken or whatever. Otherwise set
              tok.class to identifierToken.}

    ...;     {scanning procedures, as above}

begin{scan}
while currentChar in ['!', ' ', eol] do
    scanSeparator;
scanToken
end{scan}
```

Some details have been omitted from this scanner. (See Exercise 4.16.) ☐

A lexical grammar is required to generate a regular language, so its scanner is always nonrecursive. (By contrast, the context-free grammar of a high-level language is invariably self-embedding, so the parser is always recursive.)

4.6 Case study: syntactic analysis in the Δ compiler

The Δ syntactic analyzer is listed in Sections E.2 through E.4. It consists of a module `SyntacticAnalyzer`, together with two lower-level modules `Abstract-SyntaxTrees` and `LexicalAnalyzer` on which it depends.

4.6.1   Scanning

The module `LexicalAnalyzer` (listed in Section E.3) performs scanning much as described in this chapter. The record type `Token` has fields `class` and `spelling` as shown in Example 4.6. It also has an additional field, `position`, which is used to note the token's position in the source program. The `spelling` and `position` fields are useful for generating error reports.

The lexical grammar of Δ may be found in Section B.8. Before developing the scanner, the lexical grammar was modified in two respects:

- The production rule for Token was modified to add eot as a distinct token.
- Keywords were grouped with identifiers. (See Exercise 4.17 for an explanation.)

In the Δ scanner, procedure `scan` has the task of scanning:

> Separator* Token

This extended RE was transformed, eliminating most nonterminals by substitution. The result was an extended RE containing only individual characters, nonterminals that represent individual characters (i.e., Letter, Digit, Blank, and Graphic), and the nonterminal Separator:

> Separator* (eot | Digit Digit* | ' Graphic ' |
> Letter (Letter | Digit)* | Op-character Op-character* |
> . | : (ε | =) | ; | , | ~ | (|) | [|] | { | }
>)

This extended RE was then used to develop procedure `scan`, much as described in Section 4.5.

The effect of the above transformation was to eliminate procedures such as `scanToken`, `scanIntegerLiteral`, etc. (The same effect could have been achieved in Example 4.19 by inline substitution of calls to these procedures.) Such a transformation is always possible, because a lexical grammar by definition generates a regular language, and therefore all nonterminals can be eliminated by repeated substitution. The transformation was motivated simply by efficiency: measurements have shown that scanning can consume a surprisingly large proportion of compilation time, if not carefully implemented.

4.6.2   Abstract syntax trees

The module `AbstractSyntaxTrees` (listed in Section E.2) defines the type `AST` together with a number of auxiliary functions and procedures. Users of the module are expected to use these functions and procedures for constructing and modifying ASTs. The module does not actually hide the AST representation, and no special procedures are provided for inspecting and traversing ASTs.

In the Δ compiler, an AST node contains more fields than shown in Example 4.7. One additional field, `position`, records the position of the corresponding phrase in the source program. This is derived from the `position` fields of constituent tokens, and is useful for generating error reports. There are other fields, `typ`, `decl`, and `obj`, that will later be used by the contextual analyzer and code generator to decorate the AST.

4.6.3   Parsing

The module `SyntacticAnalyzer` (listed in Section E.4) is a recursive-descent parser as described in this chapter. It calls upon module `LexicalAnalyzer` to scan the source program (one token at a time), and upon module `AbstractSyntax-Trees` to construct the AST representing the source program.

The grammar of Δ may be found in Appendix B, in the subsections entitled 'Syntax'. The parser was developed systematically from this grammar, much as described in Section 4.3.

The grammar transformations were mostly straightforward, but one transformation required particular care. The Δ grammar includes the following production rules:

single-Command	::=	V-name **:=** Expression	(4.23a)
	|	Identifier **(** Actual-Parameter-Sequence **)**	(4.23b)
	|	…	
primary-Expression	::=	V-name	(4.24a)
	|	Identifier **(** Actual-Parameter-Sequence **)**	(4.24b)
	|	…	
V-name	::=	Identifier	(4.25a)
	|	V-name **.** Identifier	(4.25b)
	|	V-name **[** Expression **]**	(4.25c)

The right-hand sides of both (4.23a) and (4.23b) have identifiers in their starter sets, and so fail to satisfy the LL(1) condition. For the same reason, (4.24a) and (4.24b) fail to satisfy the LL(1) condition.

After factorization and elimination of left recursion in (4.25a–c), we obtain:

V-name	::=	Identifier (**.** Identifier | **[** Expression **]**)*	(4.26)

Substitution for V-name in (4.23a) and (4.25a), followed by factorization, would now yield:

```
single-Command     ::=  Identifier ( (. Identifier | [ Expression ] )*
                                    : = Expression
                                    | ( Actual-Parameter-Sequence )
                                    )

                   | ...

primary-Expression ::=  Identifier ( (. Identifier | [ Expression ] )*
                                    | ( Actual-Parameter-Sequence )
                                    )

                   | ...
```

These production rules do satisfy the LL(1) condition, but they are messy. A nontrivial extended RE has been substituted for V-name in two places. If we proceed to develop a parser from these production rules, a nontrivial section of parsing code will appear in two different places.

Instead, we can further transform (4.26) by introducing an auxiliary nonterminal symbol:

$$V\text{-name} \quad ::= \quad \text{Identifier rest-of-V-name} \tag{4.27}$$

$$\text{rest-of-V-name} \quad ::= \quad (. \text{ Identifier} \mid [\text{ Expression }])* \tag{4.28}$$

and *now* substitute for V-name:

```
single-Command     ::=  Identifier ( rest-of-V-name : = Expression    (4.29)
                                    | ( Actual-Parameter-Sequence )
                                    )

                   | ...

primary-Expression ::=  Identifier ( rest-of-V-name                   (4.30)
                                    | ( Actual-Parameter-Sequence )
                                    )

                   | ...
```

These production rules satisfy the LL(1) condition, since:

$$
\begin{aligned}
\textit{starters}[\![\text{rest-of-V-name} : = \text{Expression}]\!] \quad &= \textit{starters}[\![\text{rest-of-V-name}]\!] \\
&\quad \cup \{ : = \} \\
&= \{ ., [, : = \}
\end{aligned}
$$

$$\textit{starters}[\![(\text{ Actual-Parameter-Sequence })]\!] = \{ (\}$$

Thus they are suitable for developing into parsing procedures.

4.6.4   Error handling

If the syntactic analyzer discovers that the source program is not, in fact, a sentence of the Δ grammar, it reports a syntactic error. It takes care to compose error reports that are helpful to the programmer. Let us see how this is done.

As already noted, positional information is recorded in tokens and in AST nodes.

This information allows error reports generated by the syntactic analyzer (and other modules) to be related to the source program.

Some syntactic errors are detected by procedure `accept`. Since its argument is the expected token *t*, this procedure can easily compose a suitable report. For example, the ill-formed command 'if m > n max := m else max := n' will trigger a report like 'error: "then" expected here' (together with positional information).

Other syntactic errors are detected in the kind of situation illustrated by:

```
procedure parseSingleDeclaration;
   begin
   if currentToken.class = constToken then
      begin
      acceptIt;
      ...
      end
   else
   if currentToken.class = varToken then
      begin
      acceptIt;
      ...
      end
   else
      report a syntactic error
   end{parseSingleDeclaration}
```

Here too it is easy to compose a suitable report. For example, the ill-formed declaration 'd ~ 7' will trigger a report like 'error: "d" cannot start a declaration'.

The way in which parsing procedures are written can influence the quality of error handling. Suppose that `parseSingleDeclaration` were written this way:

```
procedure parseSingleDeclaration;
   begin
   if currentToken.class = constToken then
      begin
      acceptIt;
      ...
      end
   else
      begin
      accept(varToken);
      ...
      end
   end{parseSingleDeclaration}
```

This procedure would correctly parse well-formed single-declarations, but its error reporting would be poor. For example, the ill-formed single-declaration 'd ~ 7' would trigger a misleading report like 'error: "var" expected here'. (The actual error is a missing 'const'.)

The Δ syntactic analyzer simply terminates after detecting and reporting a syntactic error. In the context of the integrated Δ language processor this is reasonable behavior, since the Δ programmer can immediately edit the erroneous part of the source program and recompile. (But in a compiler that functions as a self-contained software tool, the syntactic analyzer ought to recover and continue parsing, in an attempt to discover and report any further syntactic errors in the source program. This issue will be discussed further in Section 9.2.1.)

4.7   Further reading

A more detailed account of context-free grammars and regular expressions may be found in Chapter 2 of the companion textbook by Watt (1991).

The study of grammars, scanning, and parsing was one of the first major topics in computer science, and a large body of theory and practice has been accumulated over the years. A variety of parsing methods have been developed, both top-down (the recursive descent and backtracking methods) and bottom-up (Earley's algorithm, various precedence methods, and the LR method). The major triumph of this research has been the discovery of methods of generating scanners and parsers *automatically* from lexical grammars and (suitable) context-free grammars, respectively.

Comprehensive accounts of the theory of scanning and parsing may be found in Aho and Ullman (1972) and Backhouse (1979). Backhouse in particular pays a lot of attention to syntactic error recovery, i.e., the ability of a syntactic analyzer to continue after detecting and reporting a syntactic error.

For practical application in compilers, recursive descent and LR parsing are now generally held to be the best methods. Both methods are described in Chapter 4 of Aho *et al.* (1985), emphasizing practical application rather than theory. Chapter 3 of the same textbook covers scanning, including the finite-state method (a good alternative to the method described in Section 4.5 above).

In Section 4.3 we saw how to construct a parser from the source language's context-free grammar, and in Section 4.5 how to construct a scanner from its lexical grammar. It is striking how straightforward the construction methods are – almost mechanical. This is also true for other methods such as finite-state scanning and LR parsing. A variety of tools have been developed that generate scanners and parsers automatically. Among the best-known are the Unix tools Lex and Yacc. Lex accepts the lexical grammar of a source language *S*, and from it generates a finite-state scanner for *S*. Analogously, Yacc accepts the context-free grammar of *S*, and from it generates an LR parser for *S*. Both Lex and Yacc are described in Aho *et al.* (1985), explaining how they work, and showing how to use them in practical applications.

Exercises 4

Exercises for Section 4.1

4.1   (a) Perform a bottom-up parse of the micro-English sentence '**I like the mat**', along the lines of Example 4.2.
(b) Perform a top-down parse of the same sentence, along the lines of Example 4.3.
(c) Show how the micro-English recursive-descent parser (Example 4.4) would parse the same sentence, using a diagram like Figure 4.1.

4.2   Complete the procedures `parseObject` and `parseVerb` of the micro-English parser (Example 4.4).

4.3   The micro-English parser (Example 4.4) contains many duplicated checks. Point these out, and show how to eliminate them by using `acceptIt` rather than `accept`.

4.4*   (a) The micro-English grammar (Example 4.1) generates some sentences, such as '**I sees the cat**', that are ungrammatical in English itself. Modify the grammar to ensure that the subject *agrees* with the verb. '**I**' should agree with '**like**' and '**see**', and other subjects should agree with '**likes**' and '**sees**'.
(b) Modify the micro-English recursive-descent parser (Example 4.4) accordingly.

Exercises for Section 4.2

4.5   Perform syntactic analysis of the Mini-Δ program:

        `begin while true do putint(1); putint(0) end`

along the lines of Figures 4.3 through 4.5.

4.6   Using the definition of type `AST` in Example 4.7, *outline* an implementation of the following traversal procedure:

        procedure `displayAST (theAST: AST);`
            ... {*Display the structure and contents of* `theAST`.}

Make your procedure depend as little as possible on the source language.

4.7*   The definition of type `AST` in Example 4.7 allows us to construct trees that are not Mini-Δ ASTs. It makes no distinction among Command-ASTs, Expression-ASTs, Declaration-ASTs, and so on. Nor does it use the tag of a nonterminal node to fix its arity. For example, a node with tag 'whileEdoC' should have exactly two subtrees, an Expression-AST and a Command-AST, respectively; but the type definition in Example 4.7 allows such a node to have any number of subtrees (up to three), and allows these subtrees to be *any* ASTs.

(a) Modify the definition of AST to fix the arity of each node according to its tag.

(b) Split the definition of AST into definitions of CommandAST, ExpressionAST, DeclarationAST, and so on.

In (a) and (b), show how the AST constructor functions must be modified. Also, show how the traversal procedure displayAST (Exercise 4.6) would have to be modified in (a) and (b).

4.8* This exercise is similar to 4.7, but instead of Pascal you are to choose an implementation language (such as ML or Miranda) that allows you to write recursive type definitions.

(a) Define a recursive type AST to represent Mini-Δ ASTs (Example 4.7).

(b) Split the definition of AST into definitions of CommandAST, ExpressionAST, DeclarationAST, and so on.

You should not need to write constructor functions, but outline a traversal function displayAST in both (a) and (b).

Exercises for Section 4.3

4.9 The Mini-Δ parser of Example 4.10, expressed in Pascal, cannot be compiled in its present form. Why not? Show how to circumvent this problem.

4.10* The following EBNF grammar generates a subset of the Unix shell command language:

```
Command ::=  Name Argument* eol
        |  Variable = Argument eol
        |  if Name Argument* then eol
              Command*
              else eol
              Command*
              fi eol
        |  for Variable in Argument* eol
              do eol
              Command*
              od eol

Argument ::=  Name | Literal | Variable
```

The start symbol is single-Command. eol is a token, corresponding to an end-of-line. Treat names (i.e., filenames), literals, and variables as single tokens.

Construct a recursive-descent parser for this language.

4.11* Consider the rules for converting an EBNF production rule to a parsing procedure (Section 4.3.3).

(a) Suggest an alternative refinement rule for '*parse E | F*', using a case-command rather than an if-command.

(b) Suggest a new refinement rule for the special case '*parse E | ε*'.

(c) Suggest a new refinement rule for the special case '*parse E E**'.

In each case, state any condition that must be satisfied for the refinement rule to be correct.

4.12   The order of alternatives in BNF or EBNF makes no difference to the generated language. In other words, '*E | F*' is equivalent to '*F | E*'. So the following pair of production rules:

> Command ::=   Command ; single-Command
> | single-Command

is equivalent to (1.2a–b).

Attempt to develop a parsing procedure directly from the above. Like the parsing procedure of Example 4.15, your parsing procedure will be incorrect, but it will misbehave in a different way. How?

4.13*   Suppose that an if-command with no else-part is added to Mini-Δ:

> single-Command ::=   ...
> | **if** Expression **then** single-Command
> **else** single-Command
> | **if** Expression **then** single-Command
> | ...

This gives rise to the well-known 'dangling else' ambiguity, illustrated by the if-command:

$$\text{if } E_1 \text{ then if } E_2 \text{ then } C_1 \text{ else } C_2 \tag{4.31}$$

where C_1 and C_2 are (say) assignment commands. The if-command (4.31) has two possible phrase structures, depending on whether '*else C_2*' is associated with '*if E_1 then ...*' or with '*if E_2 then ...*'. Demonstrate the ambiguity by showing two different syntax trees for (4.31).

Modify the parsing procedure `parseSingleCommand` (Example 4.10) to include the new form of if-command. How will your parsing procedure behave when required to parse (4.31)?

The 'dangling else' ambiguity is also found in Pascal. It is *specified* that the ambiguity is to be resolved by pairing each 'else' with the nearest unmatched 'if'. How does your parser's behavior relate to this specification?

Exercises for Section 4.4

4.14   Complete the enhanced Mini-Δ parser of Example 4.18. Take particular care to construct correct ASTs for expressions. For example, the AST for the expression '`a - b + c`' must be left-branching as in (a) below. (The right-branching tree (b) is the AST for '`a - (b + c)`'.)

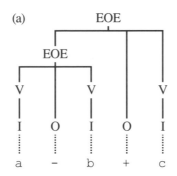 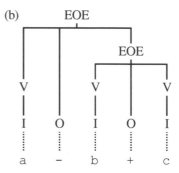

4.15   The grammar of expressions in Mini-Δ treats all binary operators alike: they all have the same priority, and they all associate to the left. Thus 'a − b * c' is treated as equivalent to '(a − b) * c'.

The following grammar of expressions gives '*' and '/' higher priority than '+' and '−':

> Expression ::= secondary-Expression
> | Expression add-Operator secondary-Expression
>
> secondary-Expression
> ::= primary-Expression
> | secondary-Expression mult-Operator
> primary-Expression
>
> primary-Expression ::= Numeral
> | Variable
> | (Expression)
>
> add-Operator ::= + | −
>
> mult-Operator ::= * | /

In this grammar, 'a − b * c' is treated as equivalent to 'a − (b * c)', but 'a − b + c' is treated as equivalent to '(a − b) + c'.
(a) Construct a recursive-descent parser from this grammar of expressions.
(b) Extend your parser to construct an AST. (Note that the concrete syntactic changes do not affect the abstract syntax.)

Exercises for Section 4.5

4.16   Fill in the missing details in the Mini-Δ scanner of Example 4.19.

4.17*   Suppose that the Mini-Δ lexical grammar of Example 4.19 were modified as follows, in an attempt to distinguish between identifiers and keywords (such as 'if', 'then', 'else', etc.):

```
Token    ::=  Identifier | Integer-Literal | Operator |
              if | then | else | ... |
              ; | : | := | ~ | ( | ) | eot

Identifier ::=  Letter (Letter | Digit)*
```

Point out a serious problem with this lexical grammar. (Remember that the terminal symbols are individual characters.) Can you see any way to remedy this problem?

4.18   (a) Modify the Mini-Δ lexical grammar to allow identifiers to contain single embedded underscores, e.g., `set_up` (but not `set__up`, nor `set_`, nor `_up`). Modify the scanner accordingly.
(b) Modify the Mini-Δ lexical grammar to allow real-literals, with a decimal point surrounded by digits, e.g., `3.1416` (but not `4.`, nor `.125`). Modify the scanner accordingly.

General exercises

4.19*   Consider a hypothetical programming language, NewSpeak, with an English-like syntax (expressed in EBNF) as follows:

```
Program         ::=  Command .

Command         ::=  single-Command single-Command *

single-Command ::=  do nothing
                |  store Expression in Variable
                |  if Condition : single-Command
                        otherwise : single-Command
                |  do Expression times : single-Command

Expression      ::=  Numeral
                |  Variable
                |  sum of Expression and Expression
                |  product of Expression and Expression

Condition       ::=  Expression is Expression
                |  Expression is less than Expression

Numeral         ::=  Digit Digit *

Variable        ::=  Letter Letter *
```

Consecutive keywords and variables must be separated by blank space; otherwise blank space may be inserted freely between symbols.

Design and implement a syntactic analyzer for Newspeak:
(a) Decide which NewSpeak symbols should be tokens, and how they should be classified. Define the type `Token`. Then implement a NewSpeak scanner.
(b) Name and specify the parsing procedures in a recursive-descent parser for NewSpeak. Then implement the NewSpeak parser. You may assume that the

variable `currentToken`, and the procedures `accept` and `acceptIt`, are already available.

4.20** Design and implement a complete syntactic analyzer for your favorite programming language.

CHAPTER FIVE

Contextual Analysis

Given a parsed program, the purpose of contextual analysis is to check that the program conforms to the source language's contextual constraints. For a typical programming language (statically typed and with static bindings), contextual constraints consist of:

- *Scope rules:* These are rules governing declarations and applied occurrences of identifiers.

- *Type rules:* These are rules that allow us to infer the types of expressions, and to decide whether each expression has a valid type.

It follows that contextual analysis consists of two subphases:

- *Identification:* applying the source language's scope rules to relate each applied occurrence of an identifier to its declaration (if any).

- *Type checking:* applying the source language's type rules to infer the type of each expression, and compare that type with the expected type.

In Section 5.1 we study identification, and in Section 5.2 type checking. In Section 5.3 we develop a particular contextual analysis algorithm, combining identification and type checking in a single pass, and show how the results of contextual analysis may be recorded. Throughout, we assume that the source language exhibits static bindings and is statically typed.

5.1 Identification

The first task of the contextual analyzer is to relate each applied occurrence of an identifier in the source program to the corresponding declaration. If there is no corresponding declaration, the source program is ill-formed, and the contextual analyzer must generate an error report. This task is called *identification*. Once an applied occurrence of an identifier has been identified, the contextual analyzer will check that the identifier is used in a way consistent with its declaration. But that is type checking, which will be considered in Section 5.2.

Identification can have a disproportionate effect on the efficiency of the whole compiler. The longer the source program, the more applied occurrences of identifiers it is likely to contain, and hence the more identifications will have to be performed. But also, the longer the source program, the more declarations it is likely to contain, and consequently the more time each identification is likely to take – especially if identification is carelessly implemented. Some compilers (and assemblers) are indeed very slow, for this reason.

If the source program is represented by an AST, a naive identification algorithm would be to search the AST: starting from a leaf node representing an applied occurrence of an identifier, find the subtree representing the corresponding declaration of that identifier. But such an algorithm would be very cumbersome. (See Exercise 5.2.)

A better method is to employ an *identification table* that associates identifiers with their attributes. The basic operations on the identification table are as follows:

- Make the identification table empty.
- Add an entry associating a given identifier with a given attribute.
- Retrieve the attribute (if any) associated with a given identifier.

An identifier's *attribute* consists of information relevant to contextual analysis, and is obtained from the identifier's declaration. An attribute could be information distilled from a declaration, or just a pointer to the declaration itself. For the moment we need not be more specific, since the attributes do not influence the structure of the identification table. We shall return to attributes in Section 5.1.4.

Each declaration in a program has a definite *scope*, that is the portion of the program over which the declaration takes effect. A *block* is any program phrase that delimits the scope of declarations within it. For example, Δ has a block command, of the form '`let` D `in` C', in which the scope of each declaration in D extends over the subcommand C. A Δ procedure declaration, of the form '`proc` I $(FPS) \sim C$', is also a block, in which the scope of each formal parameter in FPS is the procedure body C.

The organization of the identification table depends on the source language's *block structure*, that is the textual relationship of blocks in programs. There are three possibilities:

- Monolithic block structure (exemplified by Basic and Cobol).
- Flat block structure (exemplified by Fortran).
- Nested block structure (exemplified by Algol, Pascal, and similar languages).

These block structures are covered in the following subsections.

5.1.1 Monolithic block structure

A programming language exhibits *monolithic block structure* if the only block is the entire program. All declarations are global in scope.

A language with monolithic block structure has very simple scope rules, typically:

(1a) No identifier may be declared more than once.

(1b) For every applied occurrence of an identifier *I*, there must be a corresponding declaration of *I*. (In other words, no identifier may be used unless declared.)

In the case of monolithic block structure, the identification table should contain
entries for all declarations in the source program. There will be at most one entry for
each identifier. Each entry in the table consists of an identifier *id* and the attribute *attr*
associated with it.

Example 5.1
Consider a hypothetical programming language in which a program takes the form:

```
program
    D
    C
end
```

D is a sequence of declarations (the only ones in the program). *C* is a command sequence, the executable part of the program. In this example it is not important what kinds
of declaration and command are provided. What is important is that the only block is
the whole program.

Figure 5.1 shows a program outline, together with a picture of the identification
table after all declarations have been processed. The table contains one entry for each
declared identifier. The declarations are numbered for cross-referencing, and in the table
each identifier's attribute is shown as a cross-reference to the identifier's declaration. □

```
        program
 ①      integer b = 10
 ②      integer n
 ③      char c
        ...
        n = n * b           ┌──────────┐
                            │ id   attr │
        ...                 ├──────────┤
        write c             │  b    ① │
                            │  n    ② │
        ...                 │  c    ③ │
        end                 └──────────┘
```

Figure 5.1 Identification table: monolithic block structure.

The basic operations on the identification table are as follows:

type Attribute = ...;   {*information obtained from a declaration*}

procedure startIdentification;
    ...;   {*Make the identification table empty.*}

```
procedure enter (id: TokenString;
                     attr: Attribute);
   ...;      {Add an entry associating identifier id with attribute attr.}

procedure retrieve (id: TokenString;
                     var found: Boolean;
                     var attr: Attribute);
   ...       {Make attr the attribute associated with identifier id. If
              there is no entry for id, set found to false.}
```

The contextual analyzer will use these operations as follows:

- To initialize the table, startIdentification will be called.
- At a declaration of identifier *I*, enter will be called to add an entry for *I*.
- At an applied occurrence of identifier *I*, retrieve will be called to find the entry for *I*. If there is no such entry, an error report will be generated.

The identification table should be organized for efficient retrieval. A good implementation would be an ordered binary tree or a hash table. These are standard data structures, so we need not go into the implementation details here. (See Exercise 5.1.)

5.1.2   Flat block structure

A programming language exhibits *flat block structure* if a program can be partitioned into several disjoint blocks. There are two scope levels:

- Some declarations are *local* in scope. That is to say, applied occurrences of the declared identifiers are restricted to a particular block.
- Other declarations are *global* in scope. That is to say, applied occurrences of the declared identifiers are allowed anywhere in the program. In effect, the program as a whole is a block, enclosing all the other blocks.

The scope rules for a language with flat block structure might be:

(2a) No globally declared identifier may be redeclared anywhere in the program.

(2b) No locally declared identifier may be redeclared in the same block. (But the same identifier may be declared locally in several different blocks.)

(2c) For every applied occurrence of an identifier *I* in a block *B*, there must be a corresponding declaration of *I*. This must be either a global declaration of *I* or a declaration of *I* local to *B*.

In the case of flat block structure, the identification table should contain entries for both global and local declarations. The contents of the table will vary during contextual analysis. During analysis of block *B*, the table should contain entries both for global declarations and for declarations local to *B*. Once analysis of *B* is completed, the entries for local declarations should be discarded. It follows that the entries for local and global declarations must be distinguished in some way.

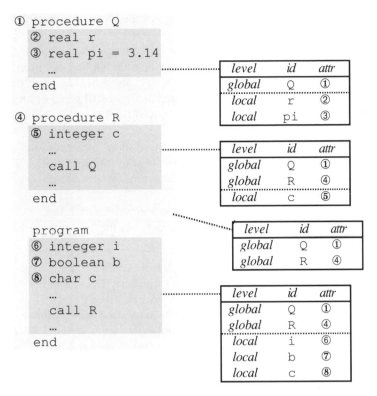

Figure 5.2 Identification table: flat block structure.

Example 5.2

Consider a hypothetical programming language in which a main program takes the form:

```
program
    D
    C
end
```

The main program's body is a block, and the declarations *D* are local to it. The main program may be preceded by any number of procedure declarations, which take the form:

```
procedure I
    D
    C
end
```

The procedure body is a block, and the declarations *D* are local to it. The procedure declaration itself is global in scope.

Figure 5.2 shows a program outline, with the blocks shaded to distinguish between global and local scopes. It also shows a picture of the identification table as it stands during contextual analysis of each block.

During analysis of procedure Q, the table contains a *global* entry for Q itself, and *local* entries for r and pi. The body of Q may contain applied occurrences of these identifiers only. If the contextual analyzer encounters any other identifier, that identifier will not be found in the table, and the contextual analyzer will generate an error report. After analysis of Q, all the *local* entries are removed from the table. Similar points can be made about the other two blocks.

Note that the program contains two local declarations of identifier c. This causes no confusion, because the two declarations are local to different blocks. Their entries never appear in the identification table at the same time.   □

We still need the identification table operations `startIdentification`, `enter`, and `retrieve` specified in Section 5.1, but the last of these has a slightly more complicated specification:

> **procedure** retrieve (id: TokenString;
>   **var** found: Boolean;
>   **var** attr: Attribute);
>
> …   {*Make* attr *the attribute associated with identifier* id. *If there are both global and local entries for* id, *take the attribute from the local entry. If there is no entry for* id, *set* found *to* false.}

In addition, we need the following new operations:

> **procedure** openScope;
>
> …;   {*Add a local scope level to the identification table, with no entries yet belonging to it.*}
>
> **procedure** closeScope;
>
> …   {*Remove the local scope level from the identification table, and all entries belonging to it.*}

The contextual analyzer will use the operations as follows:

- To initialize the table, `startIdentification` will be called.
- At the start of a block, `openScope` will be called.
- At the end of a block, `closeScope` will be called.
- At a declaration of identifier *I*, `enter` will be called to add an entry for *I*. If `openScope` has been called but not canceled by `closeScope`, the new entry will be marked as *local*; otherwise it will be marked as *global*.
- At an applied occurrence of an identifier *I*, `retrieve` will be called to find the entry for *I*. If there is no such entry, an error report will be generated.

It is still easy to implement the identification table. The only minor complication is to distinguish the global and local declaration entries, so that the latter can be efficiently discarded when contextual analysis of a block is completed. (See Exercise 5.3.)

5.1.3   Nested block structure

A programming language exhibits *nested block structure* if blocks may be nested one within another. Thus there may be many scope levels:

- Declarations in the outermost block are global in scope. We say that the outermost block is at *scope level 1*.
- Declarations inside an inner block are local to that block. Every inner block is completely enclosed by another block. If enclosed by the outermost block, we say that the inner block is at *scope level 2*; if enclosed by a level-2 block, we say that the inner block is at *scope level 3*; and so on.

The scope rules for a language with nested block structure are typically as follows:

(3a) No identifier may be declared more than once in the same block. (But the same identifier may be declared in different blocks, even if they are nested.)

(3b) For every applied occurrence of an identifier *I* in a block *B*, there must be a corresponding declaration of *I*. This declaration must be in *B* itself, or (failing that) in the block *B'* that immediately encloses *B*, or (failing that) in the block *B''* that immediately encloses *B'*, etc. (In other words, the corresponding declaration is in the smallest enclosing block that contains any declaration of *I*.)

In the case of nested block structure, the identification table should contain entries for declarations at all scope levels. Again, the contents of the table will vary during contextual analysis. During analysis of block *B*, the table should contain entries for declarations in *B*, entries for declarations in the block *B'* that encloses *B*, entries for declarations in the block *B''* that encloses *B'*, etc. Once analysis of *B* is completed, the entries for the declarations in *B* should be discarded. To make this possible, each entry should contain a scope level number.

Example 5.3
The language Mini-Δ introduced in Example 1.3 has block commands of the form '**let** *D* **in** *C*'. These may be nested. Mini-Δ's scope rules are (3a) and (3b).

Figure 5.3 shows a program outline, with the blocks shaded to indicate their scope levels. It also shows a picture of the identification table as it stands during contextual analysis of each block.

During analysis of the outermost block, the table contains only entries for identifiers a (declaration ①) and b (declaration ②). These entries are marked as level 1.

During analysis of the innermost block, the table contains entries for all the declarations in this block (marked as level 3), the enclosing block (level 2), and the outermost block (level 1). Notice that there are two entries for b (declarations ② and ③), but this is legitimate since they are in different blocks, and so their scope levels are different. If the innermost block contains an applied occurrence of b, the table must be searched in such a way as to retrieve attribute ③ – in accordance with scope rule (3b).

□

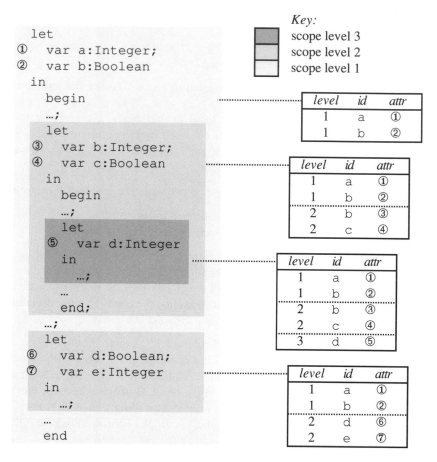

Figure 5.3 Identification table: nested block structure.

We still need the identification table operations `startIdentification`, `enter`, `retrieve`, `openScope`, and `closeScope`, but some of these have modified specifications:

```
procedure retrieve (id: TokenString;
                        var found: Boolean;
                        var attr: Attribute);
    ...;    {Make attr the attribute associated with identifier id. If
            there are several entries for id, take the attribute from the
            entry at the highest scope level. If there is no entry for id,
            set found to false.}

procedure openScope;
    ...;    {Add a new highest scope level to the identification table.}
```

procedure closeScope;
...   {*Remove the highest scope level from the identification table, and all entries belonging to it.*}

These are generalizations of the operations specified in Section 5.1.2.

The contextual analyzer will use the operations as follows:

- To initialize the table, startIdentification will be called.
- At the start of a block, openScope will be called.
- At the end of a block, closeScope will be called.
- At a declaration of identifier *I*, enter will be called to add an entry for *I*. (This entry will contain a scope level number determined by the number of calls on openScope not yet canceled by calls on closeScope.)
- At an applied occurrence of identifier *I*, retrieve will be called to find the correct entry for *I*. If there is more than one entry for *I*, the one with the highest scope level number must be retrieved. If there is no entry for *I*, an error report will be generated.

Nested block structure makes implementation of the identification table a rather challenging problem. There is no longer at most one entry for each identifier; instead there is at most one entry for each (scope level, identifier) combination. The table must be searched in such a way that the highest-level entry is retrieved when there are several entries for the same identifier. And, as usual, retrieval efficiency is important. Some possible implementations are outlined in Section 5.4 and in Exercises 5.4 and 5.5.

5.1.4   Attributes

So far we have been deliberately unspecific about the nature of the attributes associated with identifiers in the identification table. These attributes are stored in the table, and later retrieved, but they have no influence on the *structure* of the table.

Let us now look at these attributes in more detail. At an applied occurrence of an identifier *I*, the attribute associated with *I* is retrieved for use in type checking. If *I* occurs as an operand in an expression, the type checker will need to ensure that *I* has been declared as a constant or variable, and will need to know its type. If *I* occurs as the left-hand side of an assignment command, the type checker will need to ensure that *I* has been declared as a variable (not a constant), and will need to know its type (for comparison with the type of the expression on the right-hand side). If *I* occurs in a procedure call, the type checker will need to ensure that *I* has indeed been declared as a procedure, and will need to know the types of its formal parameters (for comparison with the types of the actual parameters). These examples illustrate the kind of information that must be included in attributes.

One possibility is for the contextual analyzer to extract type information from declarations, and store that information in the identification table. Later that information can be retrieved whenever required.

Example 5.4

Consider a Mini-Δ contextual analyzer that extracts type information from a declaration, and uses that information to construct an attribute.

For Mini-Δ, the relevant information is just whether the declaration is of a constant or variable, and whether its type is *bool* or *int*. (Other information, such as the actual value of a constant, is irrelevant in contextual analysis of Mini-Δ.)

Thus the type `Attribute` could be defined as follows:

```
type Type      = (bool, int);
     AttrKind  = (const, var);
     Attribute = record
                    kind: AttrKind;
                    valueType: Type
                 end
```

Consider the Mini-Δ program outlined in Example 5.3. When the contextual analyzer processes declaration ①, it calls `enter` with identifier `'a'` and an attribute whose fields are `var` and `int`. Whenever it processes an applied occurrence of a, it calls `retrieve` with identifier `'a'`, and thus retrieves that attribute. Using the latter, it determines that a denotes an integer variable. The other declarations are treated similarly.   □

Example 5.5

Now imagine a one-pass compiler for Δ itself. Here the information to be extracted from a declaration is rather complicated, for several reasons. First, there are several kinds of declaration – constant, variable, procedure, function, and type – with different information provided in each case. Secondly, a procedure or function declaration includes a list of formal parameters, and each formal parameter may be a constant, variable, procedural, or functional parameter. Third, the language provides not only primitive types, but also whole families of record and array types.

The type `Attribute` could be defined as follows:

```
type Type      = ^ TypeRecord;
     FieldList  = ...;   {list of (identifier, type) pairs}
     TypeKind   = (bool, char, int, rec, arr);
     TypeRecord =
          record
             case kind: TypeKind of
                bool, char, int:
                    ( );
                rec:
                    ( fields: FieldList );
                arr:
                    ( elementCount: Natural;
                      elementType:  Type    )
          end;
     Attribute  = ^ AttrRecord;
```

```
FormalList = ...;    { list of (identifier, attribute) pairs }
AttrKind   = (const, var, proc, func, ...);
AttrRecord =
       record
          case kind: AttrKind of
             const, var:
                  ( valueType:   Type );
             proc:
                  ( procFormals: FormalList );
             func:
                  ( funcFormals: FormalList;
                    resultType:  Type          );
             ...
       end
```

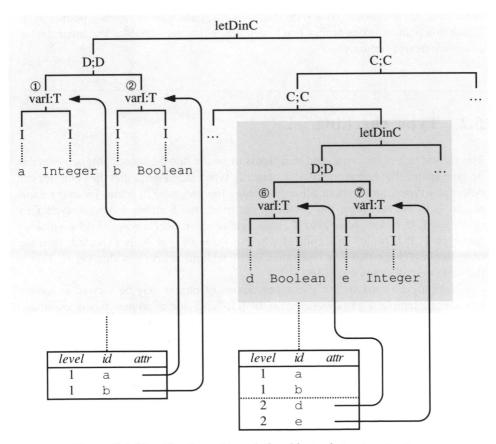

Figure 5.4 Identification table: relationship to abstract syntax tree.

For a realistic source language, the information to be stored in the identification table is quite complex, as Example 5.5 illustrates. A lot of tedious programming is required to declare and construct the attributes.

Fortunately, this can be avoided if the source program is represented by an AST. The point is that the AST itself contains the information we need to store and retrieve. The information associated with an identifier *I* can be accessed via a pointer to the subtree that represents the declaration of *I*. In other words, we can define the type `Attribute` simply as follows:

```
type Attribute = AST
```

Example 5.6

Consider once more the Mini-Δ program outlined in Example 5.3. Figure 5.4 shows part of the AST representing this program, including one of the inner blocks, with the subtree representing each block shaded to indicate its scope level. Figure 5.4 also shows a picture of the identification table as it stands during contextual analysis of each block.

When the contextual analyzer visits the declaration at subtree ①, it calls `enter` with identifier `'a'` and a pointer to subtree ①. Whenever it visits an applied occurrence of a, it calls `retrieve` with identifier `'a'`, and thus retrieves a pointer to ①. Using this pointer, it determines that a denotes an integer variable. The other declarations are treated similarly.   □

5.2 Type checking

The second task of the contextual analyzer is to ensure that the source program contains no type errors. The key property of a statically typed language is that the compiler can detect any type errors without actually running the program. In detail, for every expression *E* in the language, the compiler can infer that *E either* has some type *T or* is ill-typed. If *E* does have type *T*, then evaluating *E* will always yield a value of that type *T*. If *E* occurs in a context where a value of type *T'* is expected, then the compiler can check that *T* is equivalent to *T'*, without actually evaluating *E*. This is the task we call *type checking*.

Not only expressions but also other classes of phrase may be viewed as having types. For example, a variable-name on the left-hand side of an assignment command has a type. Even an operator has a type. We write a unary operator's type in the form $T_1 \rightarrow T_2$, meaning that the operator must be applied to an operand of type T_1, and will yield a result of type T_2. We write a binary operator's type in the form $T_1 \times T_2 \rightarrow T_3$, meaning that the operator must be applied to a left operand of type T_1 and a right operand of type T_2, and will yield a result of type T_3. In our discussion of type rules and type checking, terms such as *expression*, *type*, and *value* should therefore be interpreted broadly.

For most statically-typed programming languages, type checking is straightforward. The type checker infers the type of each expression bottom-up (i.e., starting with literals and identifiers, and working up through larger and larger subexpressions):

- The type of a literal is immediately known.
- The type of an applied occurrence of an identifier I is obtained from the corresponding declaration of I.
- Consider an expression of the form '$\oplus E$', where $\oplus$ is a unary operator of type $T_1 \rightarrow T_2$. The type checker ensures that E's type is equivalent to T_1, and thus infers that the type of '$\oplus E$' is T_2. Otherwise there is a type error.
- Consider an expression of the form '$E_1 \otimes E_2$', where $\otimes$ is a binary operator of type $T_1 \times T_2 \rightarrow T_3$. The type checker ensures that E_1's type is equivalent to T_1, and that E_2's type is equivalent to T_2, and thus infers that the type of '$E_1 \oplus E_2$' is T_3. Otherwise there is a type error.

In general, the type of a nontrivial expression is inferred from the types of its subexpressions, using the appropriate type rule.

In some phrases the type checker must test whether an inferred type is equivalent to an expected type, or test whether two inferred types are equivalent to each other. In a typical language, the type of the expression in an if- or while-command must be equivalent to the type *bool*; and the type of an actual parameter must be equivalent to the type of the corresponding formal parameter. So the type checker must be able to compare two given types T and T', to test whether T is equivalent to T'.

Example 5.7
Mini-Δ has only two types (denoted by `Boolean` and `Integer`), so they can be represented easily as follows:

    type Type = (bool, int)

Testing type equivalence is thus trivial.

An applied occurrence of a constant or variable identifier I would be handled in the manner illustrated below:

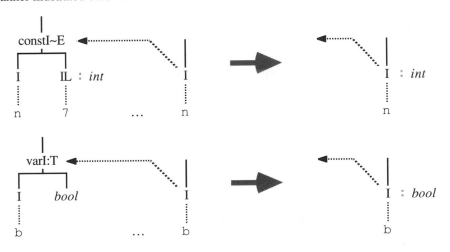

Assuming that a link has already been established to the declaration of *I*, it is a simple matter to infer the type of the applied occurrence of *I*. If the declaration is of the form '**var** *I*: *T*', then the type of *I* is *T*. If the declaration is of the form '**const** *I* ~ *E*', and if *E*'s type has been inferred to be *T*, then the type of *I* is *T*. (We show the inferred type *T* by annotating the expression's AST node with '∶ *T*'.)

An application of a binary operator such as '<' would be handled as follows:

The binary operator '<' is of type *int* × *int* → *bool*. Suppose that E_1's type has been inferred to be T_1, and that E_2's type has been inferred to be T_2. Having checked that T_1 is equivalent to *int*, and that T_2 is also equivalent to *int*, the type checker infers that the type of '$E_1 < E_2$' is *bool*. Other operators would be handled similarly.

□

Of course, Mini-Δ type checking is exceptionally simple: the representation of types is trivial, and testing for type equivalence is also trivial. If the source language has composite types, on the other hand, type checking is more complicated. For example, Δ array and record types have component types, which are unrestricted. Thus we need to represent types by trees. Furthermore, there are two possible definitions of type equivalence.

Some programming languages (such as Δ) adopt *structural equivalence*, whereby two types are equivalent if and only if their structures are the same. If types are represented by trees, structural equivalence can be tested easily by comparing the structures of these trees.

Other programming languages (such as Pascal) adopt so-called *name equivalence*. Every occurrence of a type constructor (e.g., `array` or `record`) creates a new and distinct type. In this case type equivalence can be tested simply by comparing the *pointers* to the trees representing the types: two trees created at different times (and therefore pointed to by different pointers) represent types that are not equivalent, even if they happen to be structurally similar.

In Section 5.4 we shall return to look at a more realistic example of type checking, in the context of the Δ compiler.

5.3   A contextual analysis algorithm

Contextual analysis consists of identification and type checking. Each applied occurrence of an identifier must be identified before type checking can proceed. Identification could, in principle, be completed before type checking is started, but there is little advantage in such an order. Usually identification and type checking are interleaved in a single pass over the source program (or its representation). If the source program is represented by an AST, contextual analysis can be done in a single depth-first traversal.

The results of contextual analysis can be recorded by **decorating** the AST, as explained in Section 3.1.2. The following decorations prove to be useful:

- The results of *identification* can be recorded by making an explicit link from each applied occurrence of an identifier *I* to the corresponding declaration of *I*. This has the advantage of making the decorated AST a self-contained representation of the source program; the identification table may be discarded once identification is complete. In the compiler, we represent this link by a pointer field in each (terminal) AST node. In diagrams, we show this link as a dotted arrow (◄··············).

- The results of *type checking* can be recorded by storing each expression *E*'s inferred type *T* at the root node of *E*. In the compiler, we represent this by a type field in each AST node. In diagrams, we show this inferred type by an annotation ': *T*' to the right of the AST node.

Example 5.8
A type AST suitable for representing Mini-Δ undecorated ASTs was defined in Example 4.7. Here we extend the definition of AST to make it suitable for Mini-Δ decorated ASTs:

```
type ASTTag = ...;

     AST = ^ ASTNode;

     ASTNode =
         record
             typ: Type;
             case tag: ASTTag of
                 {Nonterminal nodes ...}
                 VbecomesE, ..., DsemicolonD:
                     ( arity: 0..3;
                         child: array [1..3] of AST );
                 {Terminal nodes ...}
                 I, IL, O:
                     ( spelling: TokenString;
                         decl: AST )
         end
```

The additional fields are italicized for emphasis. The field typ can be used to decorate each expression node with its type. The field decl can be used to link each identifier node to the corresponding declaration.   □

The work to be done by the contextual analyzer depends on the class of phrase to be checked. Checking of a command *C* determines simply whether *C* is well-formed or not. Checking of an expression *E* determines whether *E* is well-formed or not, and also infers the type of *E*. Checking of a declaration *D* determines whether *D* is well-formed or not, and also makes new entries in the identification table. And so on.

Therefore we shall implement the contextual analyzer by a set of *checking procedures*, which cooperate to traverse the AST representing the source program. For each phrase class named *P* in the source language's abstract syntax, there will be a corresponding checking procedure, `checkP`. This procedure's parameter will be an AST representing a phrase of class *P*. The procedure will generate an error report if it determines that the phrase is ill-formed.

Example 5.9

Mini-Δ has the following classes of phrase: programs, commands, expressions, operators, value-or-variable-names, declarations, and type-denoters. A Mini-Δ contextual analyzer will therefore consist of the following checking procedures:

> **procedure** checkProgram (program: AST);
> ...;   {*Check whether* program *is well-formed.*}
>
> **procedure** checkCommand (command: AST);
> ...;   {*Check whether* command *is well-formed.*}
>
> **procedure** checkExpression (expression: AST;
>   **var** exprType: Type);
> ...;   {*Check whether* expression *is well-formed. If so, infer its type, and decorate its root node with this type.*}
>
> **procedure** checkUnaryOperator
>   (operator: AST;
>   **var** operandType, resultType: Type);
> ...;   {*Check whether* operator *is a unary operator. If so, return the types of its operand and result.*}
>
> **procedure** checkBinaryOperator
>   (operator: AST;
>   **var** lType, rType, resultType: Type);
> ...;   {*Check whether* operator *is a binary operator. If so, return the types of its left operand, right operand, and result.*}
>
> **procedure** checkVname (vname: AST;
>   **var** vnameType: Type;
>   **var** variable: Boolean);
> ...;   {*Check whether* vname *is well-formed. If so, infer its type, and whether it is a variable, and decorate its root node with this type.*}
>
> **procedure** checkDeclaration (declaration: AST);
> ...;   {*Check whether* declaration *is well-formed.*}
>
> **procedure** checkTypeDenoter (typedenoter: AST);
> ...   {*Check whether* typedenoter *is well-formed. If so, decorate its root node with the type it denotes.*}

Recall the representation of Mini-Δ types, from Example 5.7:

```
type Type = (bool, int)
```

The following outlines illustrate how the checking procedures would be written:

```
procedure checkCommand (command: AST);
    var eType, vType: Type;
        variable: Boolean;
    begin
    with command^ do
        case tag of

            VbecomesE:
                begin
                checkVname(child[1], vType, variable);
                checkExpression(child[2], eType);
                if not variable then
                    report an error – the left-hand side is not a variable;
                if eType <> vType then
                    report an error – the left-hand side and right-hand side
                                  are not of equivalent type
                end;

            IlpErp:
                ...;

            CsemicolonC:
                begin
                checkCommand(child[1]);
                checkCommand(child[2])
                end;

            ifEthenCelseC:
                ...;

            whileEdoC:
                begin
                checkExpression(child[1], eType);
                if eType <> bool then
                    report an error – the expression is not of type bool;
                checkCommand(child[2])
                end;

            letDinC:
                begin
                openScope;
                checkDeclaration(child[1]);
                checkCommand(child[2]);
                closeScope
```

```
                              end

                          end{case}
                      end{checkCommand}
```

Procedure `checkCommand` is fairly self-explanatory. There is one case for each form of command. In the case of an assignment command ($V := E$), it checks that V is indeed a variable, whose type is equivalent to the type of E. In the case of a while-command (**while** E **do** C), it checks that the type of E is *bool*. In the case of a let-command (**let** D **in** C), it first opens a new scope level, then calls `check-Declaration` to check the local declaration D (and to make new entries in the identification table for the declared identifier(s)), then calls `checkCommand` recursively to check the subcommand C, and finally closes the new scope level (and thus removes the new entries from the table).

```
        procedure checkExpression (expression: AST;
                                        var exprType: Type);
            var e1Type, e2Type, lType, rType: Type;
                variable: Boolean;
            begin
            with expression^ do
              case tag of

                IL:
                    exprType := int;

                V:
                    checkVname(child[1],
                        exprType, variable);

                OE:
                    ...;

                EOE:
                    begin
                    checkExpression(child[1], e1Type);
                    checkExpression(child[3], e2Type);
                    checkBinaryOperator(child[2],
                        lType, rType, exprType);
                    if e1Type <> lType then
                        report an error – the left subexpression's type is not
                                the operator's left operand type;
                    if e2Type <> rType then
                        report an error – the right subexpression's type is not
                                the operator's right operand type
                    end

              end{case};
            expression^.typ := exprType    {decorate with its type}
            end{checkExpression}
```

Procedure `checkExpression` is also largely self-explanatory.

Procedure `checkBinaryOperator` will ensure that the given operator is indeed a binary operator, and return information about its type. Procedure `checkUnary-Operator` is similar.

```
procedure checkVname (vname: AST;
                          var vnameType: Type;
                          var variable: Boolean);
    var idDecl: AST;
        declared: Boolean;
    begin
    with vname^ do
      case tag of

          I:
            begin
            retrieve(spelling, declared, idDecl);
            if not declared then
                begin
                report an error – this identifier is not declared;
                vnameType := error-type;
                variable := false
                end
            else
                begin
                case idDecl^.tag of
                  constIisE:
                      begin
                      vnameType :=
                              idDecl^.child[2]^.typ;
                      variable := false
                      end;
                  varIcolonT:
                      begin
                      vnameType :=
                              idDecl^.child[2]^.typ;
                      variable := true
                      end
                  end{case};
                decl := idDecl
                {... link this identifier occurrence to its declaration}
                end
            end

      end{case};
    vname^.typ := vnameType     {decorate vname with its type}
    end{checkVname}
```

As well as determining the value-or-variable-name's type, and whether it is a variable or not, procedure `checkVname` links the applied occurrence of identifier *I* to the corresponding declaration of *I*.

```
procedure checkDeclaration (declaration: AST);
    var eType: Type;
    begin
    with declaration^ do
        case tag of

            constIisE:
                begin
                checkExpression(child[2], eType);
                enter(child[1]^.spelling, declaration)
                end;

            varIcolonT:
                begin
                checkTypeDenoter(child[2]);
                enter(child[1]^.spelling, declaration)
                end;

            DsemicolonD:
                begin
                checkDeclaration(child[1]);
                checkDeclaration(child[2])
                end

        end{case}
    end{checkDeclaration}
```

Procedure `checkDeclaration` makes an entry in the identification table for each constant or variable declaration. This entry consists of the declared identifier and a pointer to the declaration's root node.

Procedure `checkTypeDenoter` (not shown) checks whether the given typedenoter is the identifier 'Boolean' or 'Integer', and decorates `typedenoter` with *bool* or *int* accordingly.

```
procedure checkProgram (program: AST);
    begin
    startIdentification;
    enter('false', ...);
    enter('true', ...);
    ...;
    enter('putint', ...);
    checkCommand(program)
    end{checkProgram}
```

Procedure `checkProgram` illustrates how the source language's standard environment can be handled. It initializes the identification table with entries for all standard constants, types, procedures, and so on. These entries will then be retrieved in the usual way at applied occurrences of the standard identifiers. The technique will be explained more fully in Section 5.4.1.   □

5.4 Case study: contextual analysis in the Δ compiler

Δ has static bindings and is statically typed. The Δ contextual analyzer works in much the same way as described in Section 5.3, interleaving identification and type checking in a single traversal of the AST. The contextual analyzer is listed in Section E.5.

5.4.1 Identification

Δ exhibits nested block structure, so identification is performed with the aid of a multilevel identification table as described in Section 5.1.3. The attribute stored in each table entry is a pointer to a declaration in the AST. At each applied occurrence of an identifier *I*, the table is used to find the corresponding declaration of *I*, and the applied occurrence is linked to this declaration. Once contextual analysis of the source program is completed, the identification table is no longer required and is discarded.

The current implementation of the identification table is simplistic. It is a stack in which each entry contains a scope level, an identifier, and a declaration pointer. Procedure `enter` pushes a new entry on to the stack. Procedure `retrieve` searches the stack from the top down, i.e., it uses linear search. Procedure `openScope` simply increments the current scope level. Procedure `closeScope` pops entries belonging to the current scope level, which it then decrements.

Two rather better implementations of the identification table are suggested by Exercises 5.4 and 5.5.

5.4.2 Type checking

Δ has not only primitive types (denoted by `Boolean`, `Char`, and `Integer`) but also array types and record types. An array type is characterized by the number and type of the elements. A record type is characterized by the identifiers, types, and order of its fields. These types are conveniently represented by small ASTs, as shown in Figure 5.5. Thus:

```
type Type = AST
```

In Δ type equivalence is structural. Of the types shown in Figure 5.5, only ⑤ and ⑥ are equivalent to each other. To test whether two types are equivalent, the type checker just compares their ASTs structurally. This test is performed by the following recursive function:

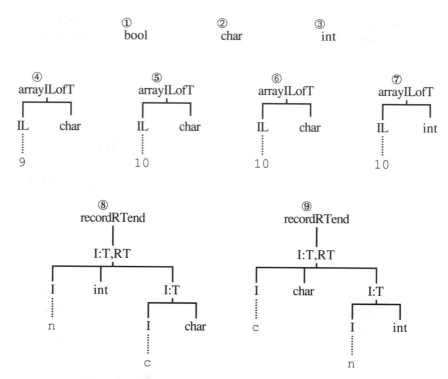

Figure 5.5 Representation of Δ types by small ASTs.

```
function equivalent (type1, type2: Type) : Boolean;
   ...        {Returns true if and only if the given types are structurally
              equivalent.}
```

Type *identifiers* in the AST would complicate the type equivalence test. To remove this complication, procedure checkTypeDenoter must be modified:

```
procedure checkTypeDenoter (var typedenoter: AST);
   ...        {Check whether typedenoter is well-formed. Also
              eliminate all type identifiers in typedenoter, replacing
              each type identifier by the type it denotes.}
```

Figure 5.6 shows the ASTs representing the following Δ declarations:

```
type Word ~ array 8 of Char;
var  w1: Word;
var  w2: array 8 of Char
```

Initially the type subtrees ① and ② in the two variable declarations are different. But after procedure checkTypeDenoter has checked these subtrees, and eliminated the type identifiers 'Char' and 'Word', the resulting subtrees ③ and ④ are structurally similar. The elimination of type identifiers makes it clear that the types of variables w1 and w2 are equivalent.

A consequence of this transformation is to make each type tree into a directed acyclic graph. This does not give rise to any serious complications. (But recursive types – as found in Pascal, Ada, and ML – do give rise to a complication. See Exercise 5.9.)

The Δ type checker infers and checks the types of expressions and value-or-variable-names in much the same way as in Example 5.7. The most important difference is that types are tested for structural equivalence by the above function equivalent. (Instead, testing types by '=' would implement name equivalence.)

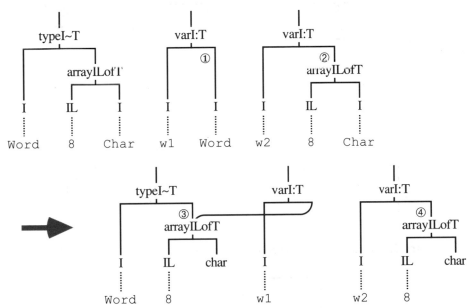

Figure 5.6 Elimination of type identifiers in Δ ASTs.

5.4.3 Standard environment

Like all programming languages, Δ has a standard environment (described in Section B.9). This is represented by a collection of small ASTs, representing the 'declarations' of the standard identifiers. Some of these 'declarations' are shown in Figure 5.7. There are 'type declarations' for standard types, such as Boolean ①; 'constant declarations' for standard constants, such as false ② and true ③; 'function declarations' for standard functions, such as eof ④; and 'procedure declarations' for standard procedures, such as put ⑤ and get ⑥.

Before analyzing a source program, the contextual analyzer initializes the identification table with entries for the standard identifiers, at scope level 0, as shown in Figure 5.8. The attribute stored in each of these entries is a pointer to the appropriate 'declaration'. Thus standard identifiers are treated in exactly the same way as identifiers declared in the source program.

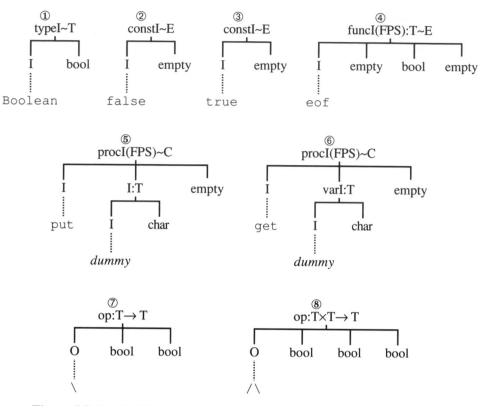

Figure 5.7 Small ASTs representing the Δ standard environment (abridged).

level	id	attr
0	Boolean	①
0	false	②
0	true	③
0	eof	④
0	put	⑤
0	get	⑥
0	\	⑦
0	/\	⑧
...	...	...

Figure 5.8 Identification table for the Δ standard environment (abridged).

The Δ standard environment also includes a collection of unary and binary operators. It is convenient to treat operators in much the same way as identifiers, as shown in Figures 5.7 and 5.8. (Indeed, some programming languages, such as ML and Ada, actually allow operators to be declared like functions in the source program. This emphasizes the analogy between operators and function identifiers.)

The representation of the Δ standard environment therefore includes small ASTs representing 'operator declarations', such as one for the unary operator '\' ⑦, and one for the binary operator '/\' ⑧. (See Figure 5.7.) An 'operator declaration' merely declares the types of the operator's operand(s) and result. Entries are also made for operators in the identification table. (See Figure 5.8.) At an application of operator O, the table is used to retrieve the 'operator declaration' of O, and thus to find the operand and result types for type checking.

5.5 Further reading

For a more detailed discussion of declarations, scope, and block structure, see Chapter 4 of the companion textbook by Watt (1990). Section 2.5 of the same textbook discusses simple type systems (of the kind found in Δ, Pascal, and indeed most programming languages). Chapter 7 goes on to explore more advanced type systems. *Coercions* (found in most languages) are implicit conversions from one type to another. *Overloading* (found in Ada) allows a group of functions with different bodies and different types to have a common identifier, even in the same scope. In a function call with this common identifier, a technique called *overload resolution* is needed to identify which of the group of functions is being called. *Parametric polymorphism* (found in ML) allows a single function to operate uniformly on arguments of a family of types (e.g., the list types). Moreover, the types of functions, parameters, etc., need not be declared explicitly. *Polymorphic type inference* is a technique that allows all types to be inferred in the context of a polymorphic type system.

For a comprehensive account of type checking, see Chapter 6 of Aho *et al.* (1986). As well as elementary techniques, the authors discuss techniques required by the more advanced type systems: type checking of coercions, overload resolution, and polymorphic type inference. For some reason, they defer discussion of identification to Chapter 7 (run-time organization).

A paper on polymorphic type inference by Milner (1978) was the genesis of the type system that was adopted by ML, and borrowed by later functional languages. Although it is difficult reading, Milner's paper is now regarded as a classic.

For a good short account of contextual analysis in a one-pass compiler for a Pascal subset, see Chapter 2 of Welsh and McKeag (1980). The authors clearly explain ways of representing the identification table, attributes, and types. They also present a simple error recovery technique that enables the contextual analyzer to generate sensible error reports when an identifier is declared twice in the same scope, or not declared at all.

The technique of linking applied occurrences of identifiers to the corresponding declarations in the AST, although simple and effective, is not described in the standard compiler textbooks. The idea seems to be due to Frank DeRemer – see DeRemer and Jüllig (1981).

The reader should be aware of a lack of standard terminology in this area. Identification tables are often called 'symbol tables' or 'declaration tables'. Contextual analysis itself is often misnamed 'semantic analysis'.

Exercises 5

5.1   Consider a source language with monolithic block structure, and consider the following ways of implementing the identification table:
(a) an ordered list;
(b) an ordered binary tree;
(c) a hash table structure of your choice.
In each case, declare the identification table, and implement the operations `startIdentification`, `enter`, and `retrieve`.

In terms of efficiency, how do these implementations compare with one another?

5.2*   Outline an identification algorithm that does not use an identification table, but instead searches the AST. For simplicity, assume monolithic block structure.

In terms of efficiency, how does this algorithm compare with one based on an identification table?

5.3   Consider a source language with flat block structure. Devise an efficient way of implementing the identification table. Implement the operations `startIdentification`, `enter`, `retrieve`, `openScope`, and `closeScope`.

5.4*   For a source language with nested block structure, we can implement the identification table by a stack of ordered binary trees. Each binary tree contains entries for declarations at one scope level. Consider the innermost block of Figure 5.3, for example. At the stack top there would be a binary tree containing the level-3 entry for declaration ⑤; below that there would be a binary tree containing the level-2 entries for declarations ③ and ④; and below that there would be a binary tree containing the level-1 entries for declarations ① and ②.

Declare the identification table, and implement the operations `startIdentification`, `enter`, `retrieve`, `openScope`, and `closeScope`.

In terms of efficiency, how does this implementation compare with that used in the Δ compiler (Section 5.4.1)?

5.5*   For a source language with nested block structure, we can alternatively implement the identification table by a sparse matrix, with columns indexed by scope levels and rows indexed by identifiers. Each column links the entries at a particular scope level. Each row links the entries for a particular identifier, in order from innermost scope to outermost scope. In the innermost block of Figure 5.3, for example, the table would look like Figure 5.9.

Declare the identification table, and implement the operations `startIdentification`, `enter`, `retrieve`, `openScope`, and `closeScope`.

In terms of efficiency, how does this implementation compare with that used in the Δ compiler (Section 5.4.1), and with the stack of binary trees (Exercise 5.4)?

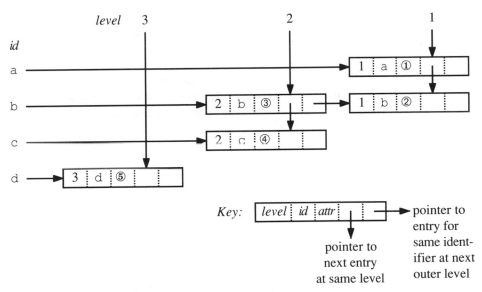

Figure 5.9 Representation of the identification table by a sparse matrix.

5.6   (a) Consider the types defined by the following Δ declarations:

```
type  Age      = Integer;
type  Letter   = Char;
type  Alphanum = Char;
type  Name     = array 20 of Letter;
type  Address  = array 20 of Char;
type  City     = array 10 of Letter;
type  ZipCode  = array 10 of Alphanum
```

Draw the (undecorated) ASTs representing these declarations. Then eliminate the type identifiers (as in Figure 5.6). Which of the types are structurally equivalent to one another?

(b) Repeat with the corresponding type definitions in Pascal. (*Note:* Pascal adopts name equivalence, rather than structural equivalence, of types.)

5.7   Suppose that name equivalence were to be adopted in Δ. Modify the function `equivalent` in the Δ contextual analyzer (Section E.5) accordingly.

5.8*   Consider the following Δ record types:

```
type  T1 = record i: Integer; c: Char end;
type  T2 = record j: Integer; d: Char end;
type  T3 = record c: Char; i: Integer end
```

None of these types are equivalent, since a Δ record type is characterized by the identifiers, types, and order of its fields. See the function `equivalent` in the Δ contextual analyzer (Section E.5).

(a) Suppose, instead, that a record type were to be characterized only by the types and order of its fields (and not by their identifiers). Thus types T1 and T2 would be equivalent. Modify the function `equivalent` accordingly.

(b) Suppose, now, that a record type were to be characterized only by the identifiers and types of its fields (and not by their order). Thus types T1 and T3 would be equivalent. Modify the function `equivalent` accordingly.

5.9   In Pascal, type definitions may be mutually recursive, e.g.:

```
type  IntList  = ^ IntNode;
      IntNode  = record
                        head: Integer;
                        tail: IntList
                 end
```

Draw (undecorated) ASTs representing these type definitions. Then eliminate the type identifiers (as in Figure 5.6). What do you observe about the transformed ASTs? How does this complicate type checking?

5.10   Suppose that Mini-Δ were to be extended with single-parameter function declarations:

```
single-Declaration   ::=  ...
                      |  func Identifier
                            ( Identifier : Type-denoter )
                            : Type-denoter ~
                            Expression
```

and function calls:

```
primary-Expression ::=  ...
                      |  Identifier ( Expression )
```

Describe how function calls would be type-checked.

CHAPTER SIX

Run-time Organization

A programming language supports high-level concepts such as types and values, expressions, variables, procedures, functions, and parameters. The target machine (whether a real machine or an abstract machine) supports low-level concepts such as bits, bytes, words, registers, stacks, addresses, and routines. The gap between the higher and lower levels is often called the *semantic gap*. Bridging this gap is the task of the compiler, and in particular the code generator.

Before writing a code generator, however, we must decide how to marshall the resources of the target machine (instructions, storage, and system software) in order to implement the source language. This is called *run-time organization*, and is the subject of this chapter.

The following are key issues in run-time organization:

- *Data representation:* How should we represent the values of each source-language type in the target machine?

- *Expression evaluation:* How should we organize the evaluation of expressions, taking care of intermediate results?

- *Storage allocation:* How should we organize storage for variables, taking into account the different lifetimes of global, local, and heap variables?

- *Routines:* How should we implement source-language procedures and functions, together with parameter passing?

We shall study all these topics in this chapter.

A thorough knowledge of run-time organization is essential for implementors of language processors, but a basic knowledge is useful to any serious programmer. In order to make rational design decisions, the application programmer should have a feel for the efficiency of various high-level language constructs. An example is the choice of data structures: as we shall see, records and static arrays can be represented very efficiently, but the representations of dynamic arrays and recursive types carry overheads (indirect addressing, garbage collection) that might be unacceptable in some applications. This chapter covers all of these topics, for the sake of completeness, although not all of them are essential to understand the Δ language processor.

6.1   Data representation

Programming languages provide high-level data types such as truth values, integers, characters, records, and arrays, together with operations over these types. Target machines provide only machine 'types' such as bits, bytes, words, and multiple words, together with low-level arithmetic and logical operations. To bridge the semantic gap between the source language and the target machine, the implementor must decide how to *represent* the source language's types and operations in terms of the target machine's types and operations.

In the following subsections we shall survey representations of various types. As we study these representations, we should bear in mind the following fundamental principles of data representation:

• *Nonconfusion:* different values of a given type should have different representations.

• *Uniqueness:* each value should always have the same representation.

The *nonconfusion* requirement should be self-evident. If two different values are confused, i.e., have the same representation, then comparison of these values will incorrectly treat the values as equal.

Nevertheless, confusion does arise in practice. A well-known example is the approximate representation of real numbers: real numbers that are slightly different mathematically might have the same approximate representation. This confusion is inevitable, however, given the design of our digital computers. So language designers must formulate the semantics of real-number operations with care; and programmers on their part must learn to live with the problem, by avoiding naive comparisons of real numbers.

On the other hand, confusion can and must be avoided in the representations of discrete types, such as truth values, characters, and integers.

If the source language is statically typed, the nonconfusion requirement refers only to values of the same type; values of distinct types need not have distinct representations. Thus the word $00...00_2$ could serve simultaneously to represent the truth value *false*, the integer 0, and so on. Compile-time type checks will ensure that values of different types cannot be used interchangeably at run-time, and therefore cannot be confused. Thus we can be sure that if $00...00_2$ turns up as an operand of an OR operation, it is representing *false*, whereas if it turns up as an operand of an ADD operation, it is representing the integer 0.

The *uniqueness* requirement is likewise fairly self-evident. Comparison of values would be complicated by the possibility of any value having more than one representation. Correct comparison is possible, however, so uniqueness is desirable rather than essential.

An example of nonuniqueness is the ones-complement representation of integers, in which zero is represented both by $00...00_2$ and by $11...11_2$. (These are +0 and –0!) A simple bit-string comparison would incorrectly treat these values as unequal, so a more specialized integer comparison must be used. The alternative twos-complement representation does give us unique representations of integers.

As well as these fundamental principles, we should bear in mind the following pragmatic issues in data representation:

- *Constant-size representation:* the representations of all values of a given type should occupy the same amount of space.

- *Direct or indirect representation:* should the values of a given type be represented directly, or indirectly through pointers?

Constant-size representation makes it possible for a compiler to plan the allocation of storage. Knowing the type of a variable, but not its actual value, the compiler will know exactly how much storage space the variable will occupy.

The *direct representation* of a value x is just the binary representation of x itself, which consists of one or more bits, bytes, or words. This is illustrated in Figure 6.1(a).

The *indirect representation* of x is a *handle*, which points to a storage area (usually in the heap) that contains the binary representation of x. This is illustrated in Figure 6.1(b).

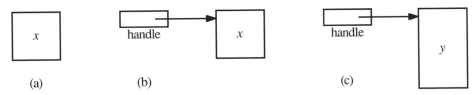

(a) (b) (c)

Figure 6.1 (a) Direct representation of a value x. (b) Indirect representation of the value x. (c) Indirect representation of a value y, of the same type but requiring more space.

To understand the distinction, it may be helpful to visualize what happens when the value x is passed around (e.g., passed as an argument). With the direct representation, it is the binary representation of x that is passed around. With the indirect representation, it is only the handle to x that is passed around. The direct representation is so called because x can be accessed by direct addressing; the indirect representation is so called because x must be accessed by indirect addressing.

The choice of direct or indirect representation is a key design decision in run-time organization. Direct representation is usually preferred in compilers for languages like Pascal, because values can be accessed more efficiently by direct addressing, and because the overheads of heap storage management are avoided. Indirect representation is usually preferred in compilers for functional languages like ML, because it simplifies the implementation of polymorphic functions.

Indirect representation is essential for types whose values vary greatly in size. For example, a list or dynamic array may have any number of elements, and clearly the total amount of space depends on the number of elements. For types such as this, indirect representation is the only way to satisfy the constant-size requirement. This is illustrated in Figure 6.1(b) and (c) where, although the values x and y occupy different amounts of space, the handles to x and y occupy the same amount of space.

We now survey representations of the more common types found in programming languages. We shall assume direct representation wherever possible, i.e., for primitive types, records, disjoint unions, and static arrays. But we shall see that indirect representation is necessary for dynamic arrays and recursive types.

We shall use the following notation:

- #*T* stands for the cardinality of type *T*, i.e., the number of distinct values of type *T*. For example, #⟦Boolean⟧ = 2.

- *size T* stands for the amount of space (in bits, bytes, or words) occupied by each value of type *T*. If indirect representation is used, only the handle is counted.

We use emphatic brackets to enclose a specific type-denoter, as in #⟦Boolean⟧ or *size*⟦Boolean⟧ or *size*⟦array 8 of Char⟧.

If a direct representation is chosen for values of type *T*, we can assert the following inequality:

$$size\ T \geq \log_2 (\#T), \quad \text{or equivalently} \quad 2^{(size\ T)} \geq \#T \tag{6.1}$$

where *size T* is expressed in bits. This follows from the nonconfusion requirement: in *n* bits we can represent at most 2^n distinct values if we are to avoid confusion.

6.1.1   Primitive types

The *primitive types* of a programming language are those whose values are primitive, i.e., cannot be decomposed into simpler values. Examples of primitive types are Boolean, Char, and Integer. Most programming languages provide these types, equipped with the elementary logical and arithmetic operations.

Machines typically support such types and operations directly, so the choice of representation is straightforward.

The values of the type Boolean are the truth values *false* and *true*. We can represent a truth value by one word, one byte, or even a single bit. (Since #⟦Boolean⟧ = 2, clearly *size*⟦Boolean⟧ ≥ 1 bit.)

Using a single bit, the conventional representations are 0 for *false* and 1 for *true*. Using a byte or word, the conventional representations are $00...00_2$ for *false*, and either $00...01_2$ or $11...11_2$ for *true*. The operations on truth values – negation, conjunction, and disjunction – can be implemented by the machine's logical NOT, AND, and OR operations. (See also Exercise 6.2.)

The value of the type Char are the elements of a character set. Sometimes the source language specifies a particular character set. For example, Ada specifies the ASCII character set, which consists of 2^7 distinct characters. Most programming languages are deliberately unspecific about the character set, however. This allows the compiler writer to choose the target machine's 'native' character set. Typically this consists of 2^7 or 2^8 distinct characters. In any case, the choice of character set determines the representation of individual characters. For example, ASCII defines the representation of character 'A' to be 0110001_2. We can represent a character by one byte or one word.

The values of the type `Integer` are integer numbers. Obviously we cannot represent an unbounded range of integers within a fixed amount of space. All major programming languages take account of this in their semantics: `Integer` denotes an implementation-defined[1] bounded range of integers. The binary representation of integers is determined by the target machine's arithmetic unit, and almost always occupies one word. The source language's integer operations can then, for the most part, be implemented by the corresponding machine operations.

In Pascal and Δ, `Integer` denotes the range $-maxint$, ..., -1, 0, $+1$, ..., $+maxint$, where the constant *maxint* is implementation-defined. In this case we have #Integer $= 2 \times maxint+1$, and therefore we can specialize (6.1) as follows:

$$2^{size[\texttt{Integer}]} \geq 2 \times maxint+1 \tag{6.2}$$

If the word size is w bits, then $size[\texttt{Integer}] = w$. To ensure that (6.2) is satisfied, the implementation should define $maxint = 2^{w-1} - 1$.

Example 6.1
TAM is the target machine of the Δ compiler. Storage is organized in 16-bit words. There are no smaller storage units, but multiple-word objects are addressable. The Δ primitive types are represented as follows:

Type	Representation	Size
`Boolean`	$00...00_2$ for *false*; $00...01_2$ for *true*	1 word
`Char`	ASCII representation	1 word
`Integer`	twos-complement representation	1 word

Thus $maxint = 2^{15} - 1 = 32767$. □

Example 6.2
The MC68020 is a ubiquitous processor. Storage is organized in 8-bit bytes, 16-bit words, and 32-bit double-words. Primitive types could be represented as follows:

Type	Representation	Size
`Boolean`	00000000_2 for *false*; 11111111_2 for *true*	1 byte
`Char`	ASCII representation	1 byte
`Integer`	twos-complement representation	1 word *or* 1 double-word

Thus $maxint = 2^{15} - 1 = 32767$, *or* $maxint = 2^{31} - 1 = 2147483647$. □

Some programming languages allow the programmer to define new primitive types. An example is the *enumeration type* of Pascal. The values of such a type are called *enumerands*. Enumerands can be represented by small integers.

---

[1] An attribute of a programming language L is *implementation-defined* if it is not defined by the specification of L, but must be defined by each individual L language processor.

Example 6.3
Consider the following Pascal type definition:

```
type Color = (red, orange, yellow, green, blue)
```

This creates a new enumeration type consisting of five enumerands, which we shall write as *red*, *orange*, *yellow*, *green*, and *blue*. It also binds the identifiers `red`, `orange`, etc., to these enumerands. (We must distinguish between the identifiers and the enumerands they denote, because the identifiers could be redeclared.)

The enumerands will be represented by $00...000_2$ for *red*, $00...001_2$ for *orange*, $00...010_2$ for *yellow*, $00...011_2$ for *green*, and $00...100_2$ for *blue*. Since $\#[\texttt{Color}]$ = 5, clearly $size[\texttt{Color}] \geq 3$ bits. In practice we would use one byte or one word. $\square$

To generalize, consider the enumeration type defined by:

$$\texttt{type } T = (I_0, \ I_1, \ ..., \ I_{n-1})$$

We can represent each I_i by (the binary equivalent of) i. Since $\#T = n$, $size \ T \geq \log_2 n$ bits.

The enumeration type is equipped with operations such as `succ` and `ord`. The representation chosen allows `succ` to be implemented by the target machine's `INC` operation (if available). The `ord` operation becomes an identity (`NOP`) operation!

6.1.2   Records

Now we proceed to examine the representation of *composite types*. These are types whose values are composed from simpler values.

A *record* consists of several *fields*, each of which has an identifier. A record type designates the identifiers and types of its fields, and all the records of a particular type have fields with the same identifiers and types. The fundamental operation on records is *field selection*, whereby we use one of the field identifiers to access the corresponding field.

There is an obvious and good direct representation for records: we simply juxtapose the fields, i.e., make them occupy consecutive positions in storage. This representation is compact, and makes it easy to implement field selection very efficiently.

Example 6.4
Consider the record types and variables introduced by the following Δ declarations:

```
type Date    = record
                  y: Integer,
                  m: Integer,
                  d: Integer
               end;

type Details = record
                  female: Boolean,
                  dob:    Date,
```

```
        status: Char
    end;

var today: Date;
var her:   Details
```

Assume for simplicity that each primitive value occupies one word. Then the variables today and her (after initialization) would look like this:

Each box in the diagram is a word. The variable today (or any other variable of type Date) occupies three consecutive words, one for each of its fields. The variable her (or any other variable of type Details) occupies five consecutive words, one for its field female, three for its field dob, and one for its field status.

As well as the total size of each record variable, we can predict the position of each field relative to the base of the record. If today is located at address 100 (i.e., it occupies the words at addresses 100 through 102), then today.y is located at address 100, today.m is located at address 101, and today.d is located at address 102. In other words, the fields y, m, and d have *offsets* of 0, 1, and 2, respectively, within any record of type Date. Likewise, the fields female, dob, and status have offsets of 0, 1, and 4, respectively, within any record of type Details.

Summarizing:

$size[\texttt{Date}]$ $= 3$ words

$address[\texttt{today.y}]$ $= address[\texttt{today}] + 0$
$address[\texttt{today.m}]$ $= address[\texttt{today}] + 1$
$address[\texttt{today.d}]$ $= address[\texttt{today}] + 2$

$size[\texttt{Details}]$ $= 5$ words

$address[\texttt{her.female}]$ $= address[\texttt{her}] + 0$
$address[\texttt{her.dob}]$ $= address[\texttt{her}] + 1$
$address[\texttt{her.dob.y}]$ $= address[\texttt{her.dob}] + 0$ $= address[\texttt{her}] + 1$
$address[\texttt{her.dob.m}]$ $= address[\texttt{her.dob}] + 1$ $= address[\texttt{her}] + 2$
$address[\texttt{her.dob.d}]$ $= address[\texttt{her.dob}] + 2$ $= address[\texttt{her}] + 3$
$address[\texttt{her.status}]$ $= address[\texttt{her}] + 4$

We use the notation *address v* to stand for the address of variable *v*. If the variable occupies several words, this means the address of the first word. We use emphatic brackets $[\ldots]$ to enclose a specific variable-name.

Let us now generalize from this example. Consider a record type *T* and variable *r*:

$$\texttt{type } T = \texttt{record } I_1: T_1, \;...,\; I_n: T_n \texttt{ end;} \qquad (6.3)$$
$$\texttt{var } r: T$$

We represent each record of type T by juxtaposing its n fields, as shown in Figure 6.2. It is clear that:

$$size \; T \;=\; size \; T_1 + ... + size \; T_n \qquad (6.4)$$

This satisfies the constant-size requirement. If $size \; T_1$, ..., and $size \; T_n$ are all constant, then $size \; T$ is also constant.

The implementation of field selection is simple and efficient. To access field I_i of the record r, we use the following address computation:

$$address[\![r.I_i]\!] \;=\; address \; r + (size \; T_1 + ... + size \; T_{i-1}) \qquad (6.5)$$

Since $size \; T_1$, ..., and $size \; T_{i-1}$ are all constant, the address of the field $r.I_i$ is just a constant offset from the base address of r itself. Thus, if the compiler knows the address of the record, it can determine the exact address of any field, and can generate code to access the field directly. In these circumstances, field selection is a zero-cost operation!

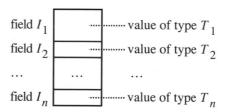

Figure 6.2 Representation of a record.

6.1.3 Disjoint unions

A *disjoint union* consists of a *tag* and a *variant part*, in which the *value* of the tag determines the *type* of the variant part. Mathematically we define a disjoint union type as follows:

$$T \;=\; T_1 + ... + T_n \qquad (6.6)$$

In each value of type T, the variant part is a value chosen from one of the types T_1, ..., or T_n; the tag indicates which one. The fundamental operations on disjoint unions are: (a) testing of the tag; and (b) projection of the variant part to give an ordinary value of type T_1 or ... or T_n. (The projection operation must be designed with care to avoid any loophole in the type rules of a statically-typed language.)

Disjoint unions crop up as *variant records* in Pascal and Ada, as *unions* in Algol-68, as *constructions* in ML, and as *algebraic types* in Miranda. In a variant record, the tag is just a field, and each possible variant is a distinct field (or tuple of fields); projection is then similar to field selection from an ordinary record. In the other languages mentioned, projection is done by pattern matching.

A suitable representation for a disjoint union is juxtaposition of the tag and variant part. But there is a complication: the variant part may have several possible types, and therefore several possible sizes. Therefore, we must be careful to satisfy the constant-size requirement. Fortunately, this is not difficult.

Example 6.5
Consider the following Pascal variant record type:

```
type Number =   record
                    case acc: Boolean of
                        true:   (i: Integer);
                        false: (r: Real)
                end;

    var num: Number
```

Every value of type `Number` has a tag field, named `acc`, and a variant part. The value of the tag determines the form of the variant part. If the tag is *true*, the variant part is an integer field named `i`. If the tag is *false*, the variant part is a real field named `r`.

Assume that a truth value or integer occupies one word, but a real number occupies two words. Then the variable `num` would look like this:

```
num.acc [ true ]     or    num.acc [ false ]
num.i   [  7  ]            num.r
        [      ]                   [ 3.1416 ]
```

Some values of type `Number` occupy two words; others occupy three words. This apparently contradicts the constant-size requirement, which we wish to avoid at all costs. We want the compiler to allocate a fixed amount of space to each variable of type `Number`, and let it change form within this space. To be safe we must allocate three words: one word for the tag field, and two words for the variant part. The fields `i` and `r` can be overlaid within the latter two words. When the tag is *true*, one word is unused (shaded in the diagram), but this is a small price to pay for satisfying the constant-size requirement. Thus:

$$size[\text{Number}] \qquad = 3 \text{ words}$$

$$address[\text{num.acc}] = address[\text{num}] + 0$$
$$address[\text{num.i}] \quad = address[\text{num}] + 1$$
$$address[\text{num.r}] \quad = address[\text{num}] + 1$$

Now consider the following variant record type, which illustrates an empty variant and a variant with more than one field:

```
type Shape  =   (point, circle, box);
     Figure =   record
                    case s: Shape of
                        point:  ( );
                        circle: (r: Integer);
```

```
                            box:      (b, w: Integer)
                end;

    var fig: Figure
```

Every value of type `Figure` has a tag field, named s, and a variant part. The value of the tag (*point*, *circle*, or *box*) determines the form of the variant part. If the tag is *point*, the variant part is empty. If the tag is *circle*, the variant part is an integer field named r. If the tag is *box*, the variant part is a pair of integer fields named b and w.

Assume that each primitive value occupies one word. Then the variable `fig` would look like this:

```
fig.s | point |   or   fig.s | circle |   or   fig.s |  box  |
      |       |        fig.r |   5    |        fig.h |   3   |
      |       |              |        |        fig.w |   4   |
```

(The enumerands *point*, *circle*, and *box* would be represented by small integers, as discussed in Section 6.1.1.)

It is easy to see that:

$$size[\text{Figure}] = 3 \text{ words}$$

$$address[\text{fig.s}] = address[\text{fig}] + 0$$
$$address[\text{fig.r}] = address[\text{fig}] + 1$$
$$address[\text{fig.h}] = address[\text{fig}] + 1$$
$$address[\text{fig.w}] = address[\text{fig}] + 2$$

□

Let us now generalize. Consider a Pascal variant record type T and variable u:

```
    type T =   record                                          (6.7)
                   case I_tag : T_tag of
                       v_1:  (I_1 : T_1) ;
                       ...;
                       v_n:  (I_n : T_n)
               end;
    var u: T
```

where each variant is labeled by one possible value of type T_{tag}. We represent each record of type T by juxtaposing its tag field and variant part. Within the variant part we overlay the different variants, which are of types $T_1, T_2, ...,$ and T_n. This representation is shown in Figure 6.3. It is clear that:

$$size\ T = size\ T_{tag} + max\ (size\ T_1, ..., size\ T_n)\qquad(6.8)$$

This satisfies the constant-size requirement. If $size\ T_{tag}$, $size\ T_1$, ..., and $size\ T_n$ are all constant, then $size\ T$ is also constant.

The operations on variant records are easily implemented. To access the tag and variant fields of the variant record u, we use the following address computations:

$$address[u.I_{tag}] \quad = address\ u + 0 \tag{6.9}$$

$$address[u.I_i] \quad = address\ u + size\ T_{tag} \tag{6.10}$$

– both being constant offsets from the base address of *u*.

This analysis can easily be generalized to variants with no fields or many fields, as in Example 6.5.

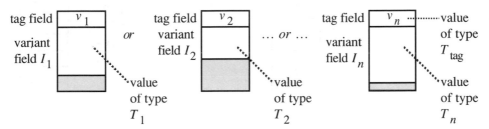

Figure 6.3 Representation of a disjoint union (variant record).

6.1.4   Static arrays

An *array* consists of several *elements*, which are all of the same type. The array has a bounded range of *indices* (which are usually integers), and for each index it has exactly one element. The fundamental operation on arrays is *indexing*, whereby we access an individual element by giving its index; in general, this index is evaluated at run-time.

A *static array* is an array whose index bounds are known at compile-time. A suitable direct representation for a static array is to juxtapose the array elements, in order of increasing indices. The indexing operation is implemented by a run-time address computation.

We start our analysis with the simplifying assumption that the lower index bound is zero. This is the case in the programming languages Δ and C. (Later we shall relax this assumption.)

Example 6.6
Consider the array types and variables introduced by the following Δ declarations:

```
type Name   = array 6 of Char;
type Coding = record
                c: Char, n: Integer
              end;

var me:   Name;
var them: array 2 of Name;
var code: array 3 of Coding
```

The variable me is just an array of six characters (indexed from 0 through 5). The variable them is an array of two elements, each of which is itself an array of six characters. The variable `code` is an array of three elements, each of which is a record with two fields.

Assume again that each primitive value occupies one word. Then the variables `me`, `them`, and `code` would be represented as follows:

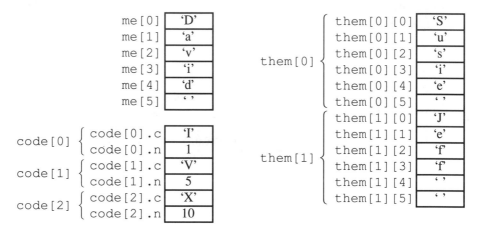

It is easy to see that:

$$size[\text{Name}] = 6 \times size[\text{Char}] = 6 \text{ words}$$
$$size[\text{array 2 of Name}] = 2 \times size[\text{Name}] = 12 \text{ words}$$
$$size[\text{array 3 of Coding}] = 3 \times size[\text{Coding}] = 6 \text{ words}$$

$$address[\text{me}[4]] = address[\text{me}] + 4$$
$$address[\text{me}[i]] = address[\text{me}] + i$$
$$address[\text{code}[2]] = address[\text{code}] + 4$$
$$address[\text{code}[i]] = address[\text{code}] + 2i$$
$$address[\text{code}[i].\text{n}] = address[\text{code}[i]] + 1$$
$$= address[\text{code}] + 2i + 1$$
$$address[\text{them}[i]] = address[\text{them}] + 6i$$
$$address[\text{them}[i][j]] = address[\text{them}[i]] + j$$
$$= address[\text{them}] + 6i + j$$

□

Let us now generalize from this example. Consider a Δ array type T and array variable a:

$$\text{type } T = \text{array } n \text{ of } T_{\text{elem}}; \tag{6.11}$$
$$\text{var } a: T$$

Each array of type T has n elements, indexed from 0 through $n-1$. We represent each array by juxtaposing its elements, as shown in Figure 6.4. It is clear that:

$$size\ T = n \times size\ T_{\text{elem}} \tag{6.12}$$

This satisfies the constant-size requirement. The number of elements n is constant, so if $size\ T_{\text{elem}}$ is constant, then $size\ T$ is also constant.

Since the elements of the array *a* are positioned in order of increasing index, and since the first element has index 0, the element with index *i* is addressed as follows:

$$address[\![a\,[i]]\!] = address\ a + (i \times size\ T_{elem}) \tag{6.13}$$

Here *size* T_{elem} is known at compile-time, but (in general) the value of *i* is known only at run-time. Thus array indexing implies a run-time address computation.

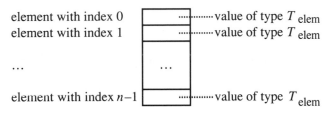

Figure 6.4 Representation of a zero-based static array.

Now let us consider static arrays where the programmer may choose both the lower and upper index bounds, as in Pascal. (See also Exercise 6.5.)

Example 6.7
Consider the array variables introduced by the following Pascal declarations:

```
var grade: array [-2..3] of Char;
    gnp:   array [1988..1992] of Integer
```

Assume that each primitive value occupies one word. Then the arrays would be represented as follows:

grade[-2]	'G'
grade[-1]	'F'
grade[0]	'N'
grade[1]	'C'
grade[2]	'B'
grade[3]	'A'

gnp[1988]	13500
gnp[1989]	14200
gnp[1990]	15000
gnp[1991]	15200
gnp[1992]	15100

It is easy to see that:

$$size[\![\texttt{array [-2..3] of Integer}]\!] = 6\ words$$

$$address[\![\texttt{grade[-1]}]\!] = address[\![\texttt{grade}]\!] + 1$$
$$address[\![\texttt{grade[2]}]\!] = address[\![\texttt{grade}]\!] + 4$$
$$address[\![\texttt{grade[i]}]\!] = address[\![\texttt{grade}]\!] - (-2) + i$$

$$size[\![\texttt{array [1988..1992] of Integer}]\!] = 5\ words$$

$$address[\![\texttt{gnp[1991]}]\!] = address[\![\texttt{gnp}]\!] + 3$$
$$address[\![\texttt{gnp[i]}]\!] = address[\![\texttt{gnp}]\!] - 1988 + i$$

To be concrete, suppose that *address*[grade] = 2000 (i.e., grade occupies the words at addresses 2000 through 2004). Then *address*[grade[*i*]] = 2000 − (−2) + *i* = 2002 + *i*. So we can compute the address of any element of this array with a single run-time addition (rather than a subtraction and an addition).

But what is the significance of this number 2002? It is just *address*[grade[0]]. We call this address the *origin* of the array grade.

Similarly, *address*[gnp[*i*]] = *address*[gnp[0]] + *i*, where the origin of the array gnp is *address*[gnp[0]] = *address*[gnp] − 1988. Of course, this particular array has no element with index 0, but that does not prevent us from using its origin (which is just a number!) to compute the addresses of its elements at run-time.   □

Let us now generalize. Consider a Pascal array type *T* and array variable *a*:

$$\text{type } T = \text{array } [l..u] \text{ of } T_{\text{elem}}; \tag{6.14}$$
$$\text{var } a: T$$

The constants *l* and *u* are the lower and upper index bounds, respectively, of the array type. Each array of type *T* has (*u* − *l* + 1) elements, indexed from *l* through *u*. As before, we represent each array by juxtaposing its elements, as shown in Figure 6.5. It is clear that:

$$size\ T = (u − l + 1) \times size\ T_{\text{elem}} \tag{6.15}$$

Again, this satisfies the constant-size requirement, since *l* and *u* are constant.

The element of array *a* with index *i* is addressed as follows:

$$address[a[i]] \quad = address\ a + (i − l) \times size\ T_{\text{elem}}$$
$$= address\ a − (l \times size\ T_{\text{elem}}) + (i \times size\ T_{\text{elem}})$$

From this we can determine *address*[a[0]], and use it to simplify the formula:

$$address[a[0]] \quad = address\ a − (l \times size\ T_{\text{elem}}) \tag{6.16}$$
$$\therefore\ address[a[i]] \quad = address[a[0]] + (i \times size\ T_{\text{elem}}) \tag{6.17}$$

Equation (6.17) has the same form as (6.13). The only difference is that *a*[0] no longer need be the first element of the array *a*. Indeed, *a*[0] might not even exist! But that does not matter, as we saw in Example 6.7, because *address*[a[0]] is just a number.

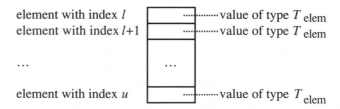

element with index *l* — value of type *T*elem
element with index *l*+1 — value of type *T*elem

... ...

element with index *u* — value of type *T*elem

Figure 6.5 Representation of a static array.

There is more to array indexing than an address computation. An *index check* is also needed, to ensure that the evaluated index lies within the array's index range. When an array of the type T of (6.14) is indexed by i, the index check must ensure that:

$$l \le i \le u \tag{6.18}$$

Since the index bounds l and u are known at compile-time, the compiler can easily generate such an index check.

6.1.5 Dynamic arrays

A *dynamic array* is an array whose index bounds are not known until run-time. Dynamic arrays are found in Algol and Ada. In such languages, different dynamic arrays of the same type may have different index bounds, and therefore different numbers of elements. How then can we make dynamic arrays satisfy the constant-size requirement?

We must adopt an indirect representation, in which the dynamic array's handle (also called an *array descriptor*) contains the array's index bounds as well as a pointer to the array's elements. Here we shall not concern ourselves with where the elements themselves are stored; all that matters is that they are stored separately from the array's handle. The handle therefore has a constant size.

Example 6.8
Consider the array type and variables introduced by the following Ada declarations:

```
type String is
      array (Integer range <>) of Character;
d: String (1 .. k);
s: String (m .. n - 1);
```

(Ada uses parentheses rather than square brackets for arrays.)

The values of type String are arrays of characters, indexed by integers. Different arrays of type String may have different index bounds; moreover, these index bounds may be evaluated at run-time. Operations such as concatenation and lexicographic comparison are applicable to any arrays of type String, even if they have different numbers of elements. But any attempt to assign one array of type String to another will fail at run-time unless they happen to have the same number of elements.

A suitable representation for arrays of type String is as follows. Each array's handle contains the array's origin, i.e., the address of the (possibly notional) element with index 0. The handle also contains the array's lower and upper index bounds. The array's elements are stored separately.

Suppose that the variables k, m, and n turn out to have values 7, 0, and 4, respectively. Then the array d will have index bounds 1 through 7, and the array s will have index bounds 0 through 3. The arrays will look like this:

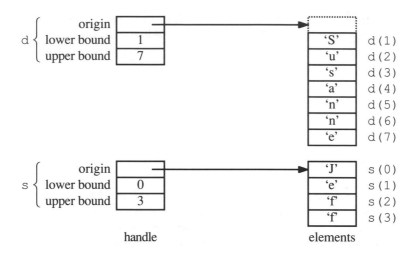

handle   elements

Each array's handle occupies 3 words exactly (assuming that integers and addresses occupy one word each). The elements of d occupy 7 words, but the elements of s occupy 4 words (assuming that characters occupy one word each). Since the elements are stored separately, we take $size[\text{String}]$ to be the size of the handle of an array of type String. Thus:

$$size[\text{String}] = 3 \text{ words}$$

Likewise, we shall take $address[\text{d}]$ to be the address of d's handle. The address of element d(0) is stored at offset 0 within the handle. Thus the address of an arbitrary element can be computed as follows:

$$\begin{aligned}
address[\text{d}(i)] &= address[\text{d}(0)] + i \\
&= content(address[\text{d}]) + i
\end{aligned}$$

where $content(x)$ stands for the content of the word at address x.   □

Let us now generalize. Consider an Ada array type T and array variable a:

$$\text{type } T \text{ is array (Integer range <>) of } T_{\text{elem}}; \qquad (6.19)$$
$$a: T \ (E_1 \ .. \ E_2);$$

We represent each array of type T by a handle, consisting of an address and two integers, as shown in Figure 6.6. Thus:

$$size \ T = address\text{-}size + 2 \times size[\text{Integer}] \qquad (6.20)$$

where *address-size* is the amount of space required to store an address – usually one word. Equation (6.20) clearly satisfies the constant-size requirement.

The declaration of array variable a is elaborated as follows. First the expressions E_1 and E_2 are evaluated to yield a's index bounds. Suppose that their values turn out to be l and u, respectively. Space is then allocated for $(u - l + 1)$ elements, juxtaposed in the usual way, but located separately from a's handle. The array's origin is computed as follows:

$$address[\![a(0)]\!] = address[\![a(l)]\!] - (l \times size\ T_{\text{elem}}) \tag{6.21}$$

The values $address[\![a(0)]\!]$, l, and u are stored in a's handle, as shown in Figure 6.6. As usual, $a(0)$ might not actually exist; but that does not matter, because $address[\![a(0)]\!]$ is just a number.

The element with index i will be addressed as follows:

$$\begin{aligned}
address[\![a(i)]\!] \quad &= address[\![a(0)]\!] + (i \times size\ T_{\text{elem}}) \\
&= content(address[\![a]\!]) + (i \times size\ T_{\text{elem}}) \tag{6.22}
\end{aligned}$$

The index bounds of a are stored at constant offsets within a's handle. Using these, the above address computation should be preceded by the following index check:

$$l \le i \le u \tag{6.23}$$
$$\begin{aligned}
\text{where}\ l\ &= content(address[\![a]\!] + address\text{-}size) \\
u\ &= content(address[\![a]\!] + address\text{-}size + size[\![\texttt{Integer}]\!])
\end{aligned}$$

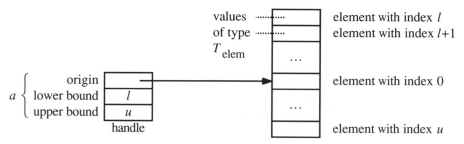

Figure 6.6 Representation of a dynamic array.

6.1.6 Recursive types

A *recursive type* is one defined in terms of itself. Values of a recursive type T have components that are themselves of type T. Typical examples are lists (the tail of a list being itself a list) and trees (the subtrees being themselves trees).

In Pascal recursive types are defined by means of pointers. A record cannot contain a record of the same type, but may contain a pointer to a record of the same type.

Example 6.9
In Pascal we define linked lists of integers by means of a pair of mutually recursive type definitions:

```
type  IntList = ^IntNode;
      IntNode = record
                     head: Integer;
                     tail: IntList
                end;

var ns: IntList
```

A nonempty list is represented by a pointer to a record, whose fields contain the list's head and tail. An empty list is represented by the special pointer value *nil*, which points to nothing.

A list consisting of the integers 2, 3, 5, and 7 would be represented as follows:

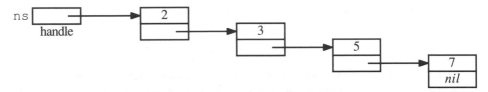

A value of type `IntList` is represented by a pointer, so typically:

$$size[\![\texttt{IntList}]\!] = 1 \text{ word}$$

Each node of the list will occupy two words (assuming that integers also occupy one word). There may be any number of nodes, of course, so the total amount of space occupied by the list is unbounded. However, the size of its handle is constant.   □

In general, the amount of storage occupied by a pointer will be:

$$size[\![\char`\^T]\!] = \textit{address-size} \tag{6.24}$$

The value *address-size* is implementation-defined. It is, however, the same for all pointer types in a given implementation.

The same indirect representation can be adopted for lists in other programming languages, whether the list type is built-in or programmer-defined. Even if the language supports recursive type definitions (without pointers), pointers must still be used to *represent* values of the recursive type. For example, in ML:

```
datatype intlist = nil | cons of (int * intlist);
val ns = cons(2, cons(3, cons(5, cons(7, nil))))
```

the representation illustrated in Example 6.9 would still be suitable. Thus:

$$size[\![\texttt{intlist}]\!] = \textit{address-size}$$

Similar principles apply to the representation of other recursive types such as trees.

6.2   Expression evaluation

Historically, one of the first distinguishing characteristics of high-level programming languages was that they allowed the programmer to write algebraic expressions, such as the following Δ expressions:

```
2 * (h + w)     (0 < i) /\ (i <= n)     a * b + (1 - (c * 2))
```

Such expressions are concise, and the notation is familiar from mathematics.

The implementation problem is the need to keep intermediate results somewhere, during evaluation of the more complicated expressions. For example, during evaluation of the expression 'a * b + (1 - (c * 2))', the subexpressions 'a * b', 'c * 2', and '1 - (c * 2)' will give rise to intermediate results.

The problem can be seen in a more general setting if we consider the semantics of such expressions (1.17d). To evaluate an expression of the form '$E_1 \, O \, E_2$', we must evaluate both the subexpressions E_1 and E_2, then apply the binary operator O to the two intermediate results. If we evaluate E_1 first, then its result must be kept somewhere safe during the evaluation of E_2.

Many machines provide a small pool of **registers** that can be used to store intermediate results. Such a machine typically provides registers named R0, R1, R2, and so on, and instructions like the following:

- LOAD Ri x   – fetch the value of x and place it in register i.
- ADD Ri x   – fetch the value of x and add it to the value in register i.
- SUB Ri x   – fetch the value of x and subtract it from the value in register i.
- MULT Ri x   – fetch the value of x and multiply it into the value in register i.

Depending on the details of the instruction set, x could be the address of a storage cell, a literal, another register, etc.

Example 6.10
To evaluate the expression 'a * b + (1 - (c * 2))' on our register machine, we could use the following sequence of instructions:

LOAD	R1	a	– now R1 contains the value of a
MULT	R1	b	– now R1 contains the value of a*b
LOAD	R2	#1	– now R2 contains the literal value 1
LOAD	R3	c	– now R3 contains the value of c
MULT	R3	#2	– now R3 contains the value of c*2
SUB	R2	R3	– now R2 contains the value of 1-(c*2)
ADD	R1	R2	– now R1 contains the value of a*b+(1-(c*2))

Of course, if *address*[a] = 100 (say), the first instruction would really be 'LOAD R1 100', and the other instructions likewise. In order to make our examples of object code readable, however, we will adopt the convention that a stands for *address*[a], b for *address*[b], and so on.   □

The object code for expression evaluation in registers is efficient but rather complicated. A compiler generating such code must assign a specific register to each intermediate result. It is important to do this well, but quite tricky. In particular, a problem arises when there are not enough registers for all the intermediate results! (See Exercise 6.10.)

A very different kind of machine is one that provides a **stack** for holding intermediate results. This allows us to evaluate expressions in a very natural way. Such a machine typically has instructions like the following:

- LOAD x   – fetch the value of x and push it on to the stack (x being an address).

- `LOADL` *n*   – push the value *n* on to the stack (*n* being a literal).
- `ADD`   – replace the top two values on the stack by their sum.
- `SUB`   – replace the top two values on the stack by their difference.
- `MULT`   – replace the top two values on the stack by their product.

Example 6.11
To evaluate the expression '`a * b + (1 - (c * 2))`' on our stack machine, we could use the sequence of instructions shown below left. Note the one-to-one correspondence with the same expression's *postfix* representation, shown below right.

```
LOAD    a              a
LOAD    b              b
MULT                   *
LOADL 1                1
LOAD    c              c
LOADL 2                2
MULT                   *
SUB                    -
ADD                    +
```

Figure 6.7 shows the effect of each instruction on the stack, assuming that the stack is initially empty.   ☐

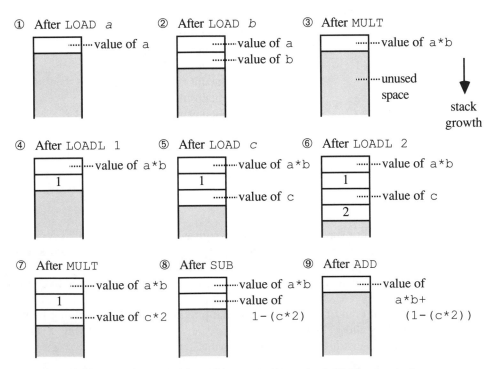

Figure 6.7 Evaluation of '`a * b + (1 - (c * 2))`' on a stack.

(*Note:* In Figure 6.7 and throughout this book, the stack is shown growing downwards, with the stack top nearest the bottom of the diagram. If this convention seems perverse, recall the convention for drawing trees in computer science textbooks! Shading indicates the unused space beyond the stack top.)

The stack machine requires more instructions to evaluate an expression than a register machine, but the individual instructions are simpler. There is one instruction for each operator, and one for each operand. In fact, as we noted in Example 6.11, the instruction sequence is in one-to-one correspondence with the expression's postfix representation. Because the problem of register assignment is removed, code generation for a stack machine is much simpler than code generation for a register machine.

The *net effect* of evaluating a (sub)expression on the stack is to leave its result at the stack top, on top of whatever was there already. For example, consider the evaluation of the subexpression 'c * 2' – steps ⑤ through ⑦ in Figure 6.7. The net effect is to push the value of 'c * 2' on to the stack top, and meanwhile the two values already on the stack remain undisturbed.

These desirable and simple properties of evaluation on the stack hold true however complicated the expression. An expression involving function calls, or operands of different types (and therefore different sizes), can be evaluated in just the same way.

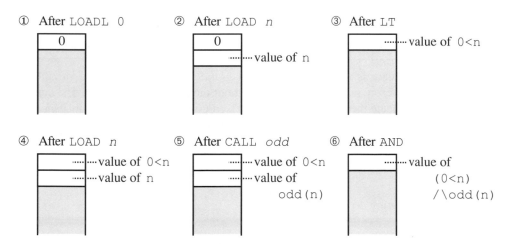

Figure 6.8 Evaluation of '(0 < n) /\ odd(n)' on a stack.

Example 6.12
To evaluate the expression '(0 < n) /\ odd (n)' on our stack machine, we could use the following sequence of instructions:

```
LOADL  0
LOAD   n
LT
LOAD   n
```

```
CALL    odd
AND
```

Figure 6.8 shows the effect of each instruction on the stack, assuming that the stack is initially empty. The instructions 'LT' and 'AND' are analogous to 'ADD', 'AND', etc., in that each replaces two values at the stack top by a single value, but some of the values involved are truth values rather than integers.

Note the analogy between 'CALL *odd*' and instructions like 'ADD', 'LT', etc. – each takes its argument(s) from the stack top, and replaces them by its result. □

6.3   Static storage allocation

We now study the allocation of storage to variables. In this section we consider only global variables. In Section 6.4 we shall consider local variables, and in Section 6.6 heap variables.

Each variable in the source program requires enough storage to contain any value that might be assigned to it. The compiler cannot know, in general, which particular values will be assigned to the variable. But if the source language is statically typed, the compiler will know the variable's type, *T*. Thus, as a consequence of constant-size representation, the compiler will know how much storage needs to be allocated to the variable, namely *size T*.

The simplest case is storage allocation for *global variables*. These are variables that exist (and therefore occupy storage) throughout the program's run-time. The compiler can simply locate these variables at some fixed positions in storage. In this way it can decide each global variable's exact address. (More precisely, the compiler decides each global variable's address relative to the base of the storage region in which global variables are located.) This is called ***static storage allocation***.

Example 6.13
Consider the following Δ program outline:

```
let
    type Date = record ... end;    ! as in Example 6.4
    var a: array 3 of Integer;
    var b: Boolean;
    var c: Char;
    var t: Date
in
    ...
```

Assuming that each primitive value occupies one word, the global variables a, b, c, and t would be laid out as shown in Figure 6.9. Thus:

$$address[\text{a}] \ = 0$$
$$address[\text{b}] \ = 3$$

$$address[\text{c}] = 4$$
$$address[\text{t}] = 5$$

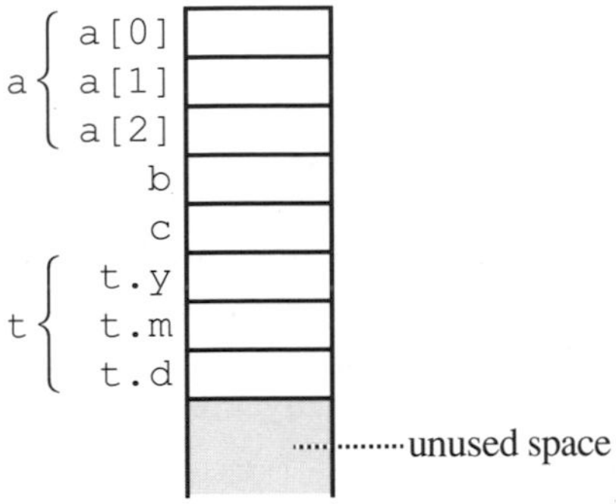

a [0]
a [1]
a [2]
b
c
t.y
t.m
t.d

······· unused space

Figure 6.9 Layout of global variables for the program of Example 6.13.

6.4 Stack storage allocation

Let us now take into account *local variables*. A local variable *v* is one that is declared inside a procedure (or function). The variable *v* exists (i.e., occupies storage) only during an activation of that procedure. This time interval is called a *lifetime* of *v*. If the same procedure is activated several times, then *v* will have several lifetimes. (Each activation really creates a distinct variable.)

Example 6.14
Consider the following outline of a Δ program, containing parameterless procedures Y and Z:

```
let
    var a: array 3 of Integer;
    var b: Boolean;
    var c: Char;

    proc Y () ~
        let
            var d: Integer;
            var e: record
                    c: Char,
                    n: Integer
                  end
        in
            ...;
```

```
proc Z () ~
    let
        var f: Integer
    in
        begin ...; Y(); ... end
in
    begin ...; Y(); ...; Z(); ... end
```

The variables a, b, and c are global. The variables d and e are local to procedure Y. The variable f is local to procedure Z.

The main program calls Y directly. Later it calls Z, which itself calls Y.

The lifetimes of the global and local variables are summarized in Figure 6.10. The lifetime of each local variable corresponds to an activation of the procedure within which it is declared. Since there are two activations of Y, its local variables have two lifetimes.   □

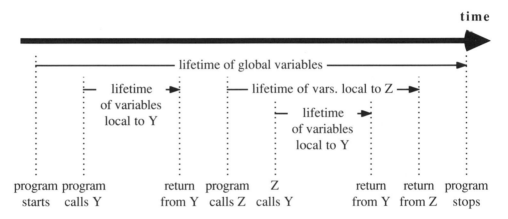

Figure 6.10 Lifetimes of global and local variables in Example 6.14.

There are two important observations that we can make about programs with global and local variables:

- The global variables are the only ones that exist throughout the program's run-time.
- The lifetimes of local variables are properly nested. That is to say, the later a local variable is created, the sooner it must be deleted. The reason why variables' lifetimes are nested is simply that the procedure activations themselves are nested.

The first observation suggests that we should use static allocation only for global variables. The second observation suggests that for local variables we should use a *stack*. On entry to a procedure, we expand the stack to make space at the stack top for that procedure's local variables. On return, we release that space by contracting the stack. This is ***stack storage allocation***.

6.4.1   Accessing local and global variables

For the moment, we assume that a procedure may access global variables and its own local variables only. (This is the case in languages such as Fortran and C.)

The stack allocation method, in detail, works as follows. The global variables are always at the base of the stack (and therefore in fixed locations). At each point during run-time, the stack also contains a number of *frames* – one frame for each currently active procedure. Each procedure's frame contains space for its own local variables. Whenever a procedure is called, a new frame is pushed on to the stack. Whenever a procedure returns, its frame is popped off the stack.

Example 6.15
Consider again the Δ program of Example 6.14. Successive snapshots of the stack are shown in Figure 6.11. (SB, ST, and LB are registers. The roles of these registers and of the dynamic links will be explained shortly.)

Initially, when the main program is running, only the global variables are occupying storage (snapshot ①). When the program calls procedure Y, a frame with space for Y's local variables is pushed on to the stack (snapshot ②). When Y returns, this frame is popped, leaving only the global variables (snapshot ③). Later, when the program calls procedure Z, a frame for Z is pushed on to the stack (snapshot ④). When Z in turn calls Y, a frame for Y is pushed on top of that one (snapshot ⑤). And so on.

Compare Figure 6.11 in detail with Figure 6.10. This shows that the period during which the frame for Z is on the stack coincides with the lifetime of Z's local variables, i.e., the activation of Z. Similarly, each period during which the frame for Y is on the stack coincides with a lifetime of Y's local variables, i.e., an activation of Y.   □

The stack of course varies in size. Furthermore, the position of a particular frame within the stack cannot always be predicted in advance. For example, during the two activations of procedure Y, the frames that provide space for Y's local variables are in two different positions. In order that variables can be addressed within the frames, the target machine will need to dedicate registers to point to the frames. These dedicated registers, named SB, ST, and LB, are shown in Figure 6.11.

Register *SB* (Stack Base) is fixed, pointing to the base of the stack. This is where the global variables are located. Therefore the global variables can be addressed relative to SB:

> LOAD   *d*[SB]   – fetch the value of the global variable at address *d*.
> STORE *d*[SB]   – store a value in the global variable at address *d*.

Register *LB* (Local Base) points to the base of the topmost frame in the stack. This frame always contains the local variables of the currently running procedure. Therefore these local variables can be addressed relative to LB:

> LOAD   *d*[LB]   – fetch the value of the local variable at address *d* relative
>   to the frame base.
> STORE *d*[LB]   – store a value in that local variable.

Register *ST* (Stack Top) points to the very top of the stack, i.e., the top of the topmost frame. If the currently running procedure evaluates an expression on the stack, the topmost frame expands and contracts, and ST keeps track of the frame boundary.

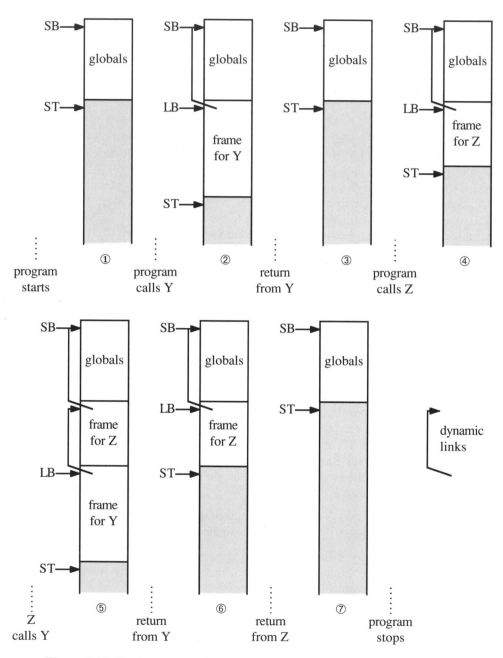

Figure 6.11 Stack snapshots in Example 6.14 (showing dynamic links).

What about the other frames, which lie below the topmost one? Each such frame contains the local variables of a procedure that is not currently running. That frame is temporarily fixed in size. In the absence of a register pointing to the frame, the variables it contains cannot (currently) be accessed. Therefore only the global variables and the currently running procedure's local variables can be accessed.

As well as space for local variables, a frame contains certain housekeeping information, known collectively as *link data*:

- The **return address** is the code address to which control will be returned at the end of the procedure activation. It is the address of the instruction following the call instruction that activated the procedure in the first place.

- The **dynamic link** is a pointer to the base of the underlying frame in the stack. It is the old content of LB, which will be restored at the end of the procedure activation.

The dynamic links are shown in Figure 6.11. Notice that they link together all the frames on the stack, in reverse order of creation.

A frame typically has the layout shown in Figure 6.12. The order of the link data items is arbitrary. The part shown as 'local data' contains space for local variables. It may be expanded to make space for anonymous data, such as the intermediate results of expression evaluation – but only when the frame is topmost in the stack. Since there are two words of link data, the local variables start at address displacement 2 within each frame.

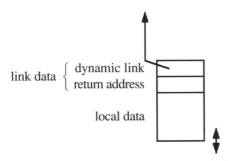

Figure 6.12 Layout of a frame (without static link).

Example 6.16
Consider again the Δ program of Example 6.14. The layout of the globals and of the two procedures' frames would be as shown in Figure 6.13.

Here are some examples of instructions to access global and local variables:

```
LOAD  0[SB]    – for any part of the program to fetch global variable a[0]
LOAD  4[SB]    – for any part of the program to fetch global variable c

LOAD  2[LB]    – for procedure Y to fetch its own local variable d
LOAD  4[LB]    – for procedure Y to fetch its own local variable e.n

LOAD  2[LB]    – for procedure Z to fetch its own local variable f
```

It might appear that the local variables d and f have the same address, 2[LB]. But remember that d can be accessed only by procedure Y, and while that procedure is running LB is pointing to the base of a frame containing Y's local variables. Similarly, f can be accessed only by procedure Z, and while that procedure is running LB is pointing to the base of a frame containing Z's local variables.   □

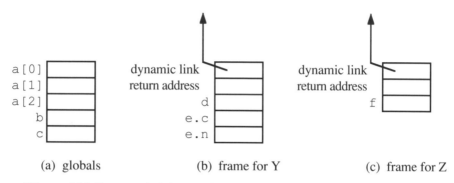

Figure 6.13 Layout of globals and frames for the program of Example 6.14.

The compiler cannot determine the *absolute* address of a local variable; but it can determine its address displacement *relative to the base of the frame* containing it. In order that the local variable can be accessed at run-time, we need only arrange that a particular register (such as LB) points to the base of the frame.

Stack allocation is economical of storage. If static allocation were used on the program of Example 6.14, every variable would occupy storage space throughout the program's run-time. With stack allocation, however, only some of the local variables occupy storage at any particular time. This is illustrated by Figure 6.11. (At snapshot ⑤, all the local variables are occupying storage at the same time; but this rarely happens in real programs with many procedures.)

Even more importantly, stack storage allocation works well in the presence of recursive procedures, whereas static allocation would not work at all. The effect of recursion will be discussed in Section 6.5.4.

6.4.2   Accessing nonlocal variables

So far we have assumed that a procedure can access global variables and its own local variables only. Now we drop this restriction. Procedures are allowed to be nested. Moreover, a procedure *P* may directly access any *nonlocal* variable, i.e., a variable that is not local to *P* but is local to an enclosing procedure.

As we have already observed, the compiler cannot determine the absolute address of any variable (other than a global), but only its address displacement within a frame. To access the variable at run-time, we must arrange for a particular register to point to the base of that frame. We use SB to point to the global variables, and LB to point to the frame containing variables local to the running procedure. Now we also need registers pointing to any frames that contain accessible nonlocal variables. We introduce registers L1, L2, etc., for this purpose.

```
let
   var g1: Integer;
   var g2: Boolean;

   proc P () ~
      let
         var p1: Boolean;
         var p2: Integer;

         proc Q () ~
            let
               var q: Integer;

               proc R () ~
                  let
                     var r: Boolean
                  in
                     begin ... end

            in
               begin ... end;

         proc S () ~
            let
               var s: Integer
            in
               begin ... end

      in
         begin ... end

   in
      begin ... end
```

Key:
- routine level 3
- routine level 2
- routine level 1
- routine level 0

Figure 6.14 A Δ program with global and local variables.

Example 6.17

Figure 6.14 shows an outline of a Δ program with nested procedures. The bodies of the procedures are shaded, with the most deeply nested procedure shaded darkest. In consequence of Δ's scope rules:

- Procedure P can access global variables, and its own local variables.
- Procedure Q can access global variables, its own local variables, and variables local to the enclosing procedure P.
- Procedure R can access global variables, its own local variables, and variables local to the enclosing procedures P and Q.
- Procedure S can access global variables, its own local variables, and variables local to the enclosing procedure P.

Figure 6.15 shows a possible sequence of stack snapshots as this program runs.

Consider snapshot ②, taken when procedure P has called procedure Q. At this time, register LB points to the frame that contains Q's local variables, and register L1 points to the underlying frame that contains P's local variables. This is necessary because Q can access P's local variables. Q might contain instructions like the following:

```
LOAD  d[SB]      – for procedure Q to fetch a global variable
LOAD  d[LB]      – for procedure Q to fetch a variable local to itself
LOAD  d[L1]      – for procedure Q to fetch a variable local to P
```

where in each case d is the appropriate address displacement.

Now consider snapshot ⑤, also taken when procedure P has called procedure Q, but this time indirectly through S. At this time also, LB points to the frame that contains Q's local variables, and L1 points to the underlying frame that contains P's local variables. So the above instructions will still work correctly. No register points to the frame that contains S's local variables. This is correct, because Q may not directly access these variables.

The following snapshot ⑥ illustrates a situation where R, the most deeply-nested procedure, has been activated by Q. Now register LB points to R's frame, register L1 points to the frame belonging to Q (the procedure immediately enclosing R), and register L2 points to the frame belonging to P (the procedure immediately enclosing Q). This allows R to access not only its own local variables, but also variables local to Q and P:

```
LOAD  d[SB]      – for procedure R to fetch a global variable
LOAD  d[LB]      – for procedure R to fetch a variable local to itself
LOAD  d[L1]      – for procedure R to fetch a variable local to Q
LOAD  d[L2]      – for procedure R to fetch a variable local to P
```

But no register points to the frame containing S's local variables, since R may not directly access these variables.   □

By arranging for registers L1, L2, etc., to point to the correct frames, we allow each procedure to access nonlocal variables. In order to arrange this, we need to add a third item to the link data in each frame. Consider a routine (procedure or function) R that is enclosed by routine R' in the source program. In a frame that contains variables local to routine R:

- The ***static link*** is a pointer to the base of an underlying frame that contains variables local to R'. The static link is set up when R is called. (This will be demonstrated in Section 6.5.1.)

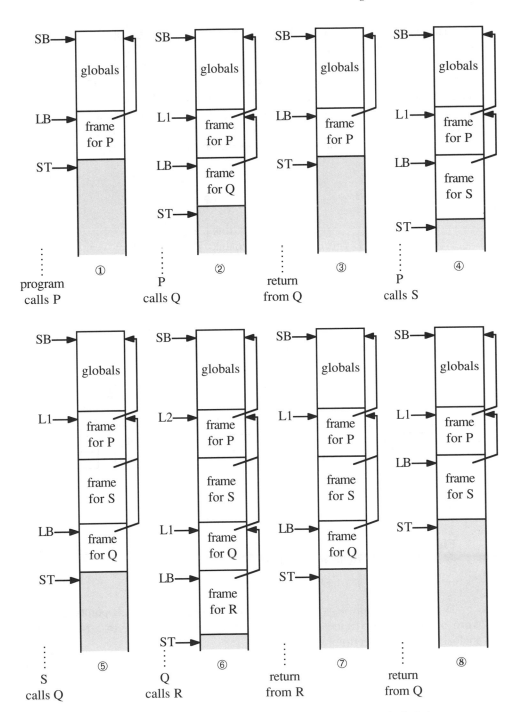

Figure 6.15 Stack snapshots in Example 6.17 (showing static links).

The static links were shown in Figure 6.15. Notice that the static link in a frame for Q always points to a frame for P, since it is P that immediately encloses Q in the source program. Similarly, the static link in a frame for R always points to a frame for Q, and the static link in a frame for S always points to a frame for P. (The static link in a frame for P always points to the globals, but that static link is actually redundant.)

The layout of a stack frame is now as shown in Figure 6.16. Since there are now three words of link data, the local variables now start at address displacement 3. Figure 6.17 shows the layout of frames for some of the procedures in Figure 6.14.

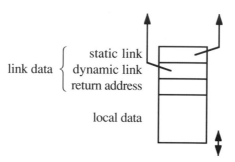

Figure 6.16 Layout of a frame (with static link).

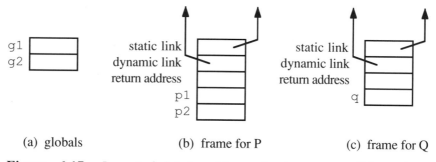

(a) globals   (b) frame for P   (c) frame for Q

Figure 6.17   Layout of globals and frames for the program of Figure 6.14 (with static links).

The static links allow us to set up the registers L1, L2, etc. LB points to the first word of the topmost frame, which is the static link and points to a frame for the enclosing routine. Therefore:

$$L1 = content(\text{LB}) \qquad\qquad (6.25)$$

where $content(r)$ stands for the content of the word to which register r points. In turn, L1 points to the next static link. Therefore:

$$L2 = content(\text{L1}) = content(content(\text{LB})) \qquad\qquad (6.26)$$
$$L3 = content(\text{L2}) = content(content(content(\text{LB}))) \qquad\qquad (6.27)$$

And so on. These equations are invariants: L1, L2, etc., automatically change whenever LB changes, i.e., on a routine call or return.

At any moment during run-time:

- Register SB points to the global variables.
- Register LB points to the topmost frame, which always belongs to the routine R that is currently running.
- Register L1 points to a frame belonging to the routine R' that encloses R in the source program.
- Register L2 points to a frame belonging to the routine R'' that encloses R' in the source program.

And so on.

The collection of registers LB, L1, L2, ..., and SB is often called the *display*. The display allows access to local, nonlocal, and global variables. The display changes whenever a routine is called or returns.

The critical property of the display is that the *compiler* can always determine which register to use to access any variable. A global variable is always addressed relative to SB. A local variable is always addressed relative to LB. A nonlocal variable is addressed relative to one of the registers L1, L2, ... Which one is determined only by the nesting levels of the routines in the source program. These levels are indicated by shading in Figure 6.14.

We assign routine levels as follows: the main program is at *routine level 0*; the body of each routine declared at level 0 is at *routine level 1*; the body of each routine declared at level 1 is at *routine level 2*; and so on.

Let v be a variable declared at routine level l, and let v's address displacement be d. Then the current value of v is fetched by various parts of the code as follows:

If $l = 0$ (i.e., v is a global variable):

LOAD d[SB]   – for any code to fetch v

If $l > 0$ (i.e., v is a local variable):

LOAD d[LB]   – for code at level l to fetch v

LOAD d[L1]   – for code at level $l+1$ to fetch v

LOAD d[L2]   – for code at level $l+2$ to fetch v

...

Storing to v is analogous.

6.5 Routines

A *routine* (or *subroutine*) is the machine-code equivalent of a procedure or function in a high-level language. Control is transferred to a routine by means of a *call* instruction (or instruction sequence). Control is transferred back to the caller by means of a *return* instruction in the routine.

When a routine is called, some **arguments** may be passed to it. An argument could be, for example, a value or address. There may be zero, one, or many arguments.

A routine may return a **result** – that is if it corresponds to a function in the high-level language. (This is not to be confused with any side effects that the routine may cause by updating the store. Here we are not concerned with the issue of side effects.)

We have already studied one aspect of routines, namely allocation of storage for local variables. In this section we study other important aspects:

- Protocols for passing arguments and returning results.
- The arguments themselves.
- The implementation of recursive routines.

6.5.1 Parameter passing protocols

When a routine is called, the arguments are computed by the caller, and used by the called routine. Thus we need a suitable *parameter passing protocol*, a convention to ensure that the caller deposits the arguments in a place where the called routine expects to find them. Conversely, the routine's result (if any) is computed by the routine, and used by the caller. Thus our protocol must also ensure that, on return, the called routine deposits its result in a place where the caller expects to find it.

There are numerous possible parameter passing protocols. Sometimes the implementor has to design a protocol from scratch. More often, the operating system dictates a standard protocol to which all compilers must conform. In every case, the choice of protocol is influenced by the target machine, such as whether the latter is a register machine or a stack machine.

Example 6.18
In a register machine, the parameter passing protocol might be:

- Pass the first argument in R1, the second argument in R2, etc.
- Return the result (if any) in R0.

Such a protocol works only if there are fewer arguments than registers, and if every argument and result is small enough to fit into a register. In practice, a more elaborate protocol is needed.   □

Example 6.19
In a stack machine, the parameter passing protocol might be:

- Pass the arguments at the stack top.
- Return the result (if any) at the stack top, in place of the arguments.

This protocol places no limits on the number of arguments, nor on the sizes of the arguments or result.   □

The stack-based parameter passing protocol of Example 6.19 is simple and general. For that reason it is adopted by the abstract machine TAM. Variants of this protocol are also adopted by machines equipped with both registers and stacks (such as the MC68000). Because of the popularity of this protocol, we shall study the TAM protocol in detail.

Some routines (functions) have results, whereas others (procedures) do not. For the sake of simplicity, we shall discuss the protocol in terms of the more general case, namely a routine with a result. A procedure is then just the special case of a routine with a 0-word 'result'. (Compare the use of a **void** function in C, or a `unit` function in ML, to achieve the effect of a procedure.)

Before calling a routine, the caller is responsible for evaluating the arguments and pushing them on to the stack top. (Since expression evaluation is done on the stack, as in Section 6.2, the stack top is where the arguments will be evaluated anyway.) After return, the caller can expect to find the result at the stack top, in the place formerly occupied by the arguments. This is shown in Figure 6.18. The net effect of calling the routine (ignoring any side effects) will be to replace the arguments by the result at the stack top.

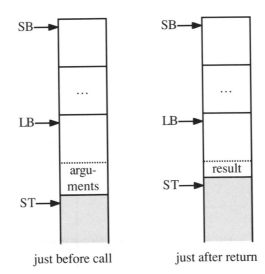

Figure 6.18 The TAM parameter passing protocol.

The called routine itself is responsible for evaluating its result and depositing it in the correct place. Let us examine a call to some routine R, from the point of view of the routine itself (see Figure 6.19):

(1) Immediately before the call, the arguments to be passed to R must be at the stack top.

(2) The call instruction pushes a new frame, on top of the arguments. Initially, the new frame contains only link data. Its return address is the address of the code

following the call instruction. Its dynamic link is the old content of LB. Its static link is supplied by the call instruction. Now LB is made to point to the base of the new frame, and control is transferred to the first instruction of *R*.

(3) The instructions within *R* may expand the new frame, to make space for local variables and to perform expression evaluation. These instructions can access the arguments relative to LB. Immediately before return, *R* evaluates its result and leaves it at the stack top.

(4) The return instruction pops the frame and the arguments, and deposits the result in the place formerly occupied by the arguments. LB is reset using the dynamic link, and control is transferred to the instruction at the return address.

TAM has a single call instruction that does all the work described in step (2). Some other machines have a less powerful call instruction, and we need a *sequence* of instructions to do the same work. TAM also has a single return instruction that does all the work described in step (4).

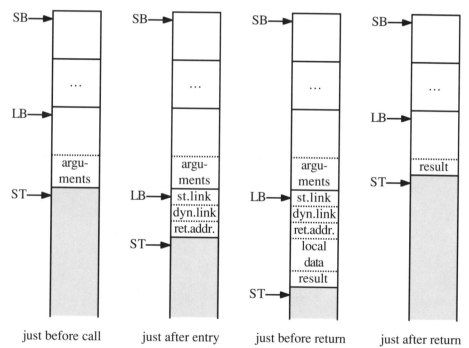

Figure 6.19 Routine call and return (in detail).

Example 6.20

Consider the following Δ program, containing a function F with two parameters, and a procedure W with one parameter:

```
let
    var g: Integer;
```

```
func F (m: Integer, n:Integer) : Integer ~
   m * n;

proc W (i: Integer) ~
   let
      const s ~ i*i
   in
      begin
      putint(F(i, s));
      putint(F(s, s))
      end

in
   begin
   getint(var g);
   W(g+1)
   end
```

This (artificial) program reads an integer, and writes the cube and fourth power of its successor.

Figure 6.20 shows a sequence of stack snapshots. The main program first reads an integer, say 3, into the global variable g (snapshot ①). Then it evaluates 'g+1', which yields 4, and leaves that value at the stack top as the argument to be passed to procedure W (snapshot ②).

On entry to procedure W, a new frame is pushed on to the stack top, and the argument becomes known to the procedure as i. The constant s is defined by evaluating 'i*i', which yields 16 (snapshot ③). Next, the procedure prepares to evaluate 'F(i, s)' by pushing the two arguments, 4 and 16, on to the stack top (snapshot ④).

On entry to function F, a new frame is pushed on to the stack, and the arguments become known to the function as m and n, respectively. F immediately evaluates 'm*n' to determine its result, 64, and leaves that value on the stack top (snapshot ⑤). On return from F, the topmost frame and the arguments are popped, and the result is deposited in place of the arguments (snapshot ⑥). This value is used immediately as an argument to putint, which writes it out.

Similarly, W evaluates 'F(s, s)', yielding 256, and passes the result as an argument to putint. Finally, on return from W, the topmost frame and the argument are popped; this time there is no result to replace the arguments (snapshot ⑦).

It is instructive to study the corresponding object code. It would look something like this (using symbolic names for routines, and omitting some minor details):

```
PUSH       1            – expand globals to make space for g
LOADA      0[SB]        – push the address of g
CALL       getint       – read an integer into g
LOAD       0[SB]        – push the value of g
CALL       succ         – add 1
CALL(SB)   W            – call W (using SB as static link)
POP        1            – contract globals
HALT
```

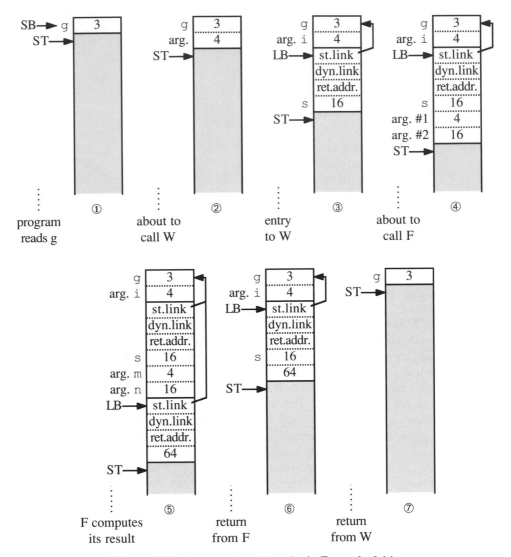

Figure 6.20 Arguments and results in Example 6.14.

```
W:
    LOAD      -1[LB]      – push the value of i
    LOAD      -1[LB]      – push the value of i
    CALL      mult        – multiply; the result will be the value of s
    LOAD      -1[LB]      – push the value of i
    LOAD      3[LB]       – push the value of s
    CALL(SB)  F           – call F (using SB as static link)
    CALL      putint      – write the value of F(i,s)
    LOAD      3[LB]       – push the value of s
```

```
         LOAD        3[LB]        – push the value of s
         CALL(SB)    F            – call F (using SB as static link)
         CALL        putint       – write the value of F(s,s)
         RETURN(0)   1            – return, replacing the 1-word argument
                                  –   by a 0-word 'result'
F:
         LOAD        -2[LB]       – push the value of m
         LOAD        -1[LB]       – push the value of n
         CALL        mult         – multiply
         RETURN(1)   2            – return, replacing the 2-word argument pair
                                  –   by a 1-word result
```

(*Note:* In TAM, operations like addition, subtraction, logical negation, etc., are performed by calling primitive routines – *add*, *sub*, *not*, etc. This avoids the need to provide many individual instructions – ADD, SUB, NOT, etc.)   □

6.5.2   Static links

One loose end in our description of the parameter passing protocol is how the static link is determined. Recall that the static link is needed only if the source language exhibits nested block structure. The scope rules of such a language guarantee that, at the time of call, the correct static link is in one or other of the display registers. The caller need only copy it into the newly-created frame.

Example 6.21
Consider the outline Δ program of Figure 6.14. Some stack snapshots were shown in Figure 6.15.

When P calls Q, the required static link is a pointer to a frame for P itself, since P encloses Q in the source program, and the caller can find that pointer in LB (snapshots ① and ②). Similarly, when P calls S, the required static link is a pointer to a frame for P itself, since P encloses S, and the caller can find that pointer in LB (snapshots ③ and ④).

When S calls Q, the required static link is a pointer to a frame for P, since P encloses Q, and the caller can find that pointer in L1 (snapshots ④ and ⑤).

If R were to call Q or S, the required static link would be a pointer to a frame for P, since P encloses Q and S, and the caller could find that pointer in L2 (snapshot ⑥).

Here is a summary of all the possible calls in this program:

```
         CALL(SB)    P     – for any call to P

         CALL(LB)    Q     – for P to call Q
         CALL(L1)    Q     – for Q to call Q (recursively)
         CALL(L2)    Q     – for R to call Q
         CALL(L1)    Q     – for S to call Q

         CALL(LB)    R     – for Q to call R
         CALL(L1)    R     – for R to call R (recursively)
```

```
CALL(LB)  S   – for P to call S
CALL(L1)  S   – for Q to call S
CALL(L2)  S   – for R to call S
CALL(L1)  S   – for S to call S (recursively)
```

(In the TAM call instruction, the field in parentheses nominates the register whose content is to be used as the static link.)   □

In general, the *compiler* can always determine which register to use as the static link in any call instruction. A call to a global routine (i.e., one declared at the outermost level of the source program) always uses SB. A call to a local routine (i.e., one declared inside the currently running routine) always uses LB. A call to any other routine uses one of the registers L1, L2, …. Which one is determined only by the nesting levels of the routines in the source program.

Let R be a routine declared at routine level l (thus the *body* of R is at level $l+1$). Then R is called as follows:

If $l = 0$ (i.e., R is a global routine):
```
CALL(SB)  R      – for any call to R
```

If $l > 0$ (i.e., R is enclosed by another routine):
```
CALL(LB)  R      – for code at level l to call R
CALL(L1)  R      – for code at level l+1 to call R
CALL(L2)  R      – for code at level l+2 to call R
…
```

(Compare this with the code used for addressing variables, at the end of Section 6.4.2.)

6.5.3 Arguments

We have already seen some examples of argument passing. We now examine two other aspects of arguments: how the called routine accesses its own arguments, and how arguments are represented under different parameter mechanisms.

According to the parameter passing protocol studied in the previous subsection, the arguments to be passed to a routine are deposited at the top of the *caller*'s frame (or at the top of the globals, if the caller is the main program). Since the latter frame is just under the *called* routine's frame, the called routine can find its arguments just under its own frame. In other words, the arguments have small negative addresses relative to the base of the called routine's frame. In all other respects, they can be accessed just like variables local to the called routine.

Example 6.22
In the Δ program of Example 6.17, the two routines accessed their arguments as follows:

```
LOAD  -1[LB]     – for procedure W to fetch its argument i

LOAD  -2[LB]     – for function F to fetch its argument m
```

```
LOAD  -1[LB]      – for function F to fetch its argument n
```

□

We can easily implement a variety of parameter mechanisms:

- *Constant parameter* (as in Δ and ML) or *value parameter* (as in Algol and Pascal):
  The argument is an ordinary value (such as a truth value, integer, or record). The caller computes the argument by evaluating an expression, and leaving the value on the stack.

- *Variable parameter* (as in Δ or Pascal):
  The argument is the address of a variable. The caller simply pushes this address on to the stack.

- *Procedural/functional parameter* (as in Δ or Pascal):
  The argument is a (static link, code address) pair representing a routine. This pair, known as a *closure*, contains just the information that will be needed to call the argument routine.

Constant parameters have already been illustrated, in Example 6.20. Value parameters differ in only one respect: the formal parameter is treated as a local *variable*, and thus may be updated. If procedure W had a *value* parameter i, the procedure body could contain assignments to i, implemented by 'STORE -1[LB]'. Note, however, that the word corresponding to i will be popped on return from P, so any such updating would have no effect outside the procedure. This conforms to the intended semantics of value parameters.

The following example illustrates a variable parameter.

Example 6.23
Consider the following outline Δ program, containing a procedure S with a variable parameter n as well as a constant parameter i:

```
let
    proc S (var n: Integer, i: Integer) ~
        n := n + i;

    var b: record
                y: Integer, m: Integer, d: Integer
            end

in
    begin
    b := {y ~ 1978, m ~ 5, d ~ 5};
    S(var b.m, 6);
    ...
    end
```

Figure 6.21 shows some snapshots of the stack as this program runs.

The procedure call 'S(var b.m, 6)' works by first pushing the *address* of the variable b.m, along with the value 6, and then calling S.

The procedure S itself works as follows. Its first argument is the address of some variable (not necessarily b.m, of course). S can access the variable by indirect addressing. It can fetch the variable's value by an indirect load instruction, and update it by an indirect store instruction.

We can see this by studying the TAM code corresponding to the above program:

```
      ...
      LOADL      1978
      LOADL      5
      LOADL      5
      STORE(3)   0[SB]        – store a record value in b
      LOADA      1[SB]        – push the address of b.m
      LOADL      6            – push the literal value 6
      CALL(SB)   S            – call S
      ...
S:
      LOAD       -2[LB]       – push the argument address n
      LOADI                   – push the value contained at that address
      LOAD       -1[LB]       – push the argument value i
      CALL       add          – add (giving the value of n+i)
      LOAD       -2[LB]       – push the argument address n
      STOREI                  – store the value of n+i at that address
      RETURN(0)  2            – return, replacing the 2 words of arguments
                              –   by a 0-word 'result'
```

Here the instruction LOADI (load indirect) pops an address off the stack, and then fetches a value from that address. STOREI (store indirect) pops an address and a value, and then stores that value at that address.   □

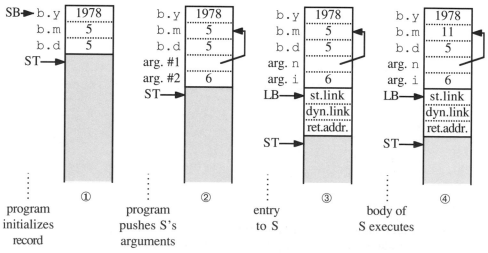

Figure 6.21 Variable and constant parameters in Example 6.23.

6.5.4 Recursion

We have already noted that stack allocation is more economical of storage than static allocation. As a bonus, stack allocation supports the implementation of *recursive* routines. In fact, there is nothing to add to the techniques introduced in Section 6.4; we need only illustrate how stack allocation works in the presence of recursive routines.

Example 6.24

Consider the following Δ program. It includes a recursive procedure, P, that writes a given nonnegative integer, i, to a given base in the range two through ten, b:

```
let
    proc P (i: Integer, b: Integer) ~
        let const d ~ chr(i//b + ord('0'))
        in
            if i < b then
                put (d)
            else
                begin P(i/b); put(d) end;

    var n: Integer;

in
    begin
    ...;  P(n, 8);  ...
    end
```

Figure 6.22 shows the lifetimes of the variables in this program (and also formal parameters such as i and b, and declared constants such as d, because they too occupy storage). Note that each recursive activation of P creates a new set of local variables, which coexist with the local variables of continuing activations. Figure 6.22 is essentially similar to Figure 6.10, in that all the variable's lifetimes are nested. This suggests that stack allocation will cope with recursion.

Figure 6.23 shows some stack snapshots as this program runs. Having stored a value in n, say 92, the main program pushes a pair of arguments, here 92 and 8, in preparation for calling P (snapshot ①). Inside P these arguments are known as i and b, respectively. In the constant definition, d is defined to be '4'. Now, since the value of 'i < b' is *false*, P pushes a pair of arguments, here 11 and 8, in preparation for calling itself recursively (snapshot ②). Inside P these arguments are known as i and b. At this point there are two activations of P, the original one and the recursive one, and each activation has its own arguments i and b. In the constant definition, using the *current* activation's i and b, d is defined to be '3'. Now, since the value of 'i < b' is again *false*, P pushes a pair of arguments, here 1 and 8, in preparation for calling itself recursively (snapshot ③). In this third activation of P, d is defined to be '1', but the value of 'i < b' turns out to be *true* (snapshot ④). So P merely writes '1', then returns to the second activation of itself (snapshot ⑤). This activation writes '3', and then returns to the original activation of P (snapshot ⑥). This activation writes '4', and then returns to the main program (snapshot ⑦). □

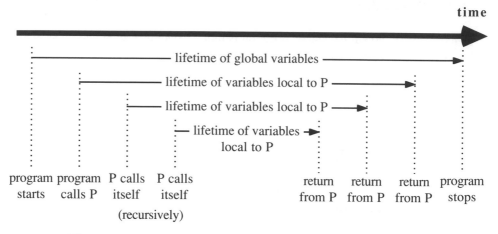

Figure 6.22 Lifetimes of variables local to a recursive procedure.

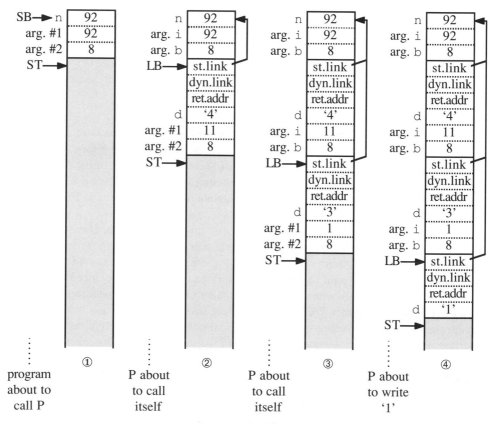

Figure 6.23 Stack snapshots for the recursive procedure in Example 6.24.

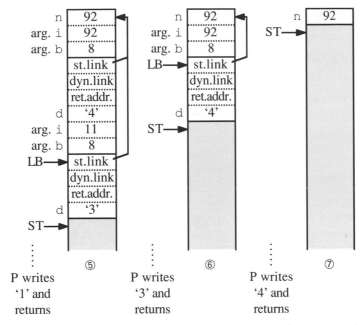

Figure 6.23 Stack snapshots for the recursive procedure in Example 6.24.
(continued)

6.6   Heap storage allocation

In Section 6.4 we saw how local variables are allocated storage. A lifetime of a local variable corresponds exactly to an activation of the procedure, function, or block within which the local variable was declared. Since their lifetimes are always nested, local variables can be allocated storage on a stack.

On the other hand, a ***heap variable*** is created by executing an *allocator* (such as `new` in Pascal). The allocator returns a pointer through which the heap variable can be accessed. Later the heap variable may be deallocated, either explicitly by executing a *deallocator* (such as `dispose` in Pascal), or automatically. The heap variable's lifetime extends from the time it is allocated until the time it is deallocated.

Thus heap variables behave quite differently from local variables. Consequently they demand a different method of storage allocation.

Example 6.25
Consider the following outline of a Pascal program, which manipulates linked lists:

```
type IntList = ...;      {linked list of integers}

procedure insertI (i: Integer; var l: IntList);
    ...;      {Insert a node containing i at the front of list l.}
```

```
procedure deleteI (i: Integer; var l: IntList);
    ...;    {Delete the (first) node containing i from list l.}

type Symbol  = array [1..2] of Char;
     SymList = ...;    {linked list of symbols}

procedure insertS (s: Symbol; var l: SymList);
    ...;    {Insert a node containing s at the front of list l.}

procedure deleteS (s: Symbol; var l: SymList);
    ...;    {Delete the (first) node containing s from list l.}

var ns: IntList;  ps: SymList;

ns := nil;        ps := nil;             ①
insertI(6, ns);   insertS('Cu', ps);
insertI(9, ns);   insertS('Ag', ps);
insertI(10, ns);  insertS('Au', ps);    ②
...;
deleteI(10, ns);  deleteS('Cu', ps);    ③
...;
insertI(12, ns);  insertS('Pt', ps);    ④
...
```

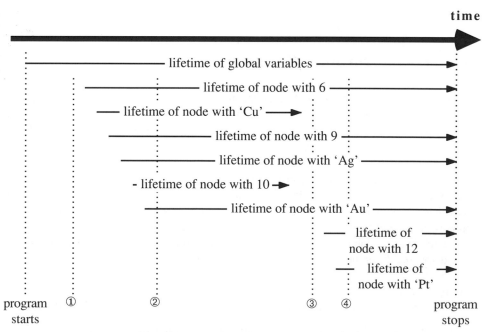

Figure 6.24 Lifetimes of heap variables in Example 6.25.

In this program, the heap variables are nodes of linked lists. Procedures `insertI` and `insertS` allocate nodes, and procedures `deleteI` and `deleteS` deallocate nodes.

Figure 6.24 shows the lifetimes of the heap variables. Observe that there is no particular pattern to their lifetimes: the program allocates and deallocates them whenever it chooses. The ones not deallocated by the program cease to exist when the program stops.   □

6.6.1   Heap management

Since heap variables can be allocated and deallocated at any time, their lifetimes bear no particular relationship to one another. So these variables are allocated on a ***heap***, a storage region managed differently from a stack.

The heap will expand and (occasionally) contract as the program runs. Let us assume that registers HB (Heap Base) and HT (Heap Top) point to the boundaries of the heap. (Note the analogy with SB and ST, which point to the boundaries of the stack.)

Since the stack and the heap both expand and contract, it is a good idea to place them at opposite ends of the available storage space. Contraction of the stack leaves more space for the heap to expand, and *vice versa*. It is only when the stack and heap crash into one another that the program must fail due to storage exhaustion.

Figure 6.25 shows several snapshots of the heap as the program of Example 6.25 runs. The heap is initially empty, but expands as nodes are allocated (snapshot ②). When nodes are deallocated, gaps appear (snapshot ③). Some of these gaps may be partly or wholly refilled as further nodes are allocated (snapshot ④).

Deallocation of a heap variable at the heap top causes the heap to contract. But deallocation elsewhere in the heap leaves a *gap*, i.e., a piece of unused storage surrounded by used storage. (This never happens in the stack, where deallocation always takes place at the stack top.) Gaps may appear in the heap at any time, and they have to be managed. Thus the object program must be supported by a run-time module called the *heap manager*.

The heap manager privately maintains a *free list*, which is a linked list of gaps within the heap. Each gap contains a size field, and a link to the next gap. The size fields are necessary because the gaps are of differing sizes. The heap manager needs a pointer to the first gap in the free list; we shall call this HF (Heap Free-list pointer). In Figure 6.25, the free list is initially empty (snapshot ②), but later accumulates some gaps (snapshots ③ and ④).

A simple heap manager works as follows. To *allocate* a heap variable of size s, the heap manager tries to find a gap of size at least s in the free list:

- If it finds a gap whose size is s exactly, it removes that gap from the free list.
- If it finds a gap whose size is greater than s, it replaces that gap in the free list by the residual gap.
- If there is no gap big enough, it expands the heap by the amount s.
- If there is no room to expand the heap, storage is exhausted and the program fails.

To *deallocate* a heap variable, the heap manager simply adds it to the free list.

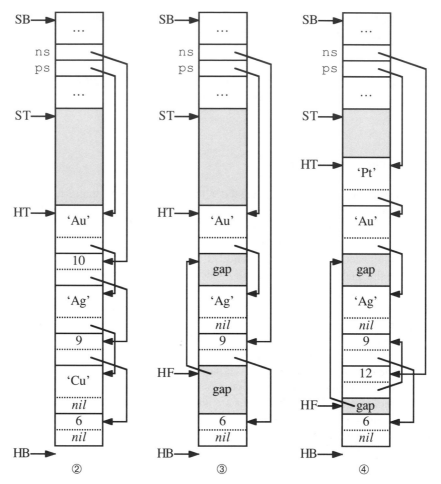

Figure 6.25 Snapshots of the heap in Example 6.25.

All this seems very straightforward, but in practice such a simple heap manager does not work very well. One major problem is *fragmentation*. As many allocations and deallocations take place, gaps tend to become smaller and more numerous. (This can already be seen in snapshot ④ of Figure 6.25.) When the heap manager tries to allocate a heap variable, there might be no *single* gap big enough, although the *total* amount of free space is sufficient.

There are several methods of reducing fragmentation:

- When allocating a heap variable, the heap manager could choose the *smallest* gap that is big enough (rather than choosing just any gap). This preserves large gaps for when they are really needed. This method implies a small time overhead on allocation, because the free list must be searched – unless the heap manager keeps the gaps sorted by size, which implies a small time overhead on deallocation.
- When deallocating a heap variable, the heap manager could *coalesce* the heap vari-

able with any adjacent gap(s). This method implies a small time overhead on deallocation, because the free list must be searched. (See Example 6.26 and Exercise 6.21.)

- The heap manager could occasionally *compact* the heap by shifting heap variables together. This method is quite complicated to manage: to shift a heap variable, the heap manager must find and redirect all pointers to that heap variable. The method implies a large time overhead whenever the heap is compacted, because the whole heap is affected. (See Example 6.27 and Exercise 6.22.)

Example 6.26

Figure 6.26 illustrates coalescence of gaps in the heap. Deallocating heap variable c allows the space it occupied to be coalesced with an adjacent gap. Deallocating heap variable b is even more effective, since the space it occupied can be coalesced with two adjacent gaps. (As an exercise, work out what the free list would look like without coalescence of gaps.) ◻

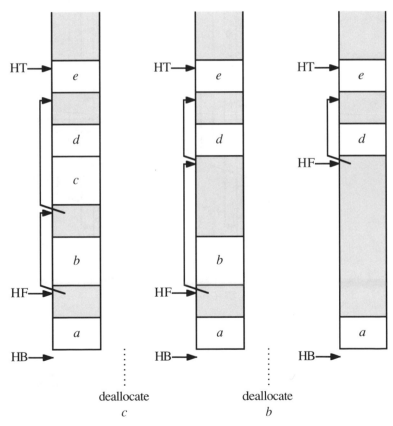

Figure 6.26 Coalescing deallocated variables with adjacent gaps in the heap.

Example 6.27

Figure 6.27 illustrates heap compaction. To understand this, start by convincing your-self that the states of the heap before and after compaction are equivalent.

Since a pointer is represented by the address of the heap variable it points to, mov-ing a heap variable to a different address implies that every pointer to it must be ad-justed. There are two pointers to heap variable c : one in the stack, a second in another heap variable, b. Indeed, b and c point to each other. All these pointers have to be adjusted consistently.   □

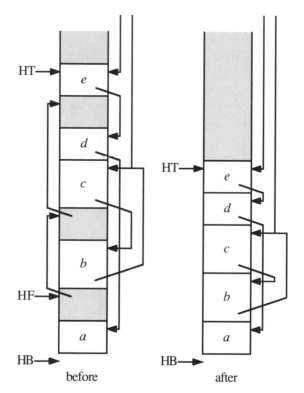

Figure 6.27 Compacting the heap.

This example illustrates the complications that can arise in heap compaction. There may be several pointers to the same heap variable. Pointers may be located both in the stack and in other heap variables. *All* such pointers must be found and adjusted.

To implement heap compaction, the heap manager must create a table containing the old address and new address of each heap variable. Then, for every pointer in the stack or heap, it must use the table to replace the old address by the new address. Final-ly it can actually copy the heap variables to their new addresses.

Compaction is usually combined with garbage collection, so we defer a more detailed explanation until Section 6.6.3.

6.6.2   Explicit deallocation

Programming languages differ in how they allow heap variables to be deallocated. In this subsection we study *explicit deallocation*. Pascal programs, for example, explicitly deallocate heap variables by calling the standard procedure dispose.

Example 6.28
The procedure deleteI of Example 6.25 might be implemented as follows:

```
procedure deleteI (i: Integer; var l: IntList);
   {Delete the (first) node containing i from list l.}
   var p, q: IntList;
   begin
   ...; {Make q point to the (first) node containing i in list l,
         and make p point to the preceding node (if any).}
   if q = l then
      l := q^.tail
   else
      p^.tail := q^.tail;
   dispose(q)
   end{deleteI}
```

□

Explicit deallocation is efficient, and allows the programmer fine control over heap storage allocation.

In Examples 6.25 and 6.28 explicit deallocation was used in a controlled manner. In practice, however, explicit deallocation is notoriously error-prone. Two problems arise frequently in practice: garbage accumulation and dangling pointers.

A heap variable is *inaccessible*, or *garbage*, if there exists no pointer to it. If such a heap variable has not been deallocated, the space it occupied is wasted.

Example 6.29
Figure 6.28 illustrates how garbage can appear. At first p and q point to different heap variables, *a* and *b*, respectively (snapshot ①). After the assignment 'p := q', both p and q point to *b* (snapshot ②). Now there exists no pointer to *a*, so the latter is garbage. Worse still, there is no way to retrieve this situation; without a pointer to *a*, it cannot be explicitly deallocated.

This situation could have been averted by greater care on the programmer's part: *a* should have been deallocated *before* the assignment 'p := q'.   □

Since pointers can be copied, several pointers to the same heap variable might exist at the same time. When one of these pointers is used to deallocate the heap variable, the other pointers are left pointing to a gap. They are called *dangling pointers*.

The program might accidentally use a dangling pointer to update a heap variable that no longer exists. The effect will be to corrupt the gap left by deallocation, or perhaps to corrupt a new heap variable subsequently allocated (by chance) in that gap.

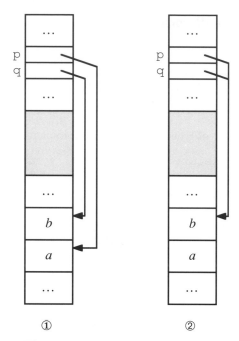

Figure 6.28 Garbage in the heap.

Example 6.30
The following program illustrates a possible effect of a dangling pointer:

```
var p, q: ^T1;
     r   : ^T2;
...
new(p);   p^ := value of type T1;
q := p;                              ①
...;
dispose(p);                          ②
...;
new(r);   r^ := value of type T2;    ③
...;
q^ := value of type T1               ④
```

Figure 6.29 shows the effect. At first, both p and q point to the same heap variable, which contains a value of type T1 (snapshot ①). Now the program uses dispose(p) to deallocate p^, which adds this heap variable to the free list, and which (in a typical implementation) changes p to *nil*. But of course dispose knows nothing about q. (How could it?) So q still contains the same address, which is a dangling pointer (snapshot ②). Any assignment to q^ now would corrupt the gap.

Later the program executes 'new(r)', and then stores a value of type T2 in the newly allocated heap variable (snapshot ③). This new heap variable might (purely by chance) be located at the same address as the old one, as shown in snapshot ③.

This is a situation in which a disaster is just waiting to happen. The program might attempt to inspect q^, expecting to find a value of type T1. Worse still, it might attempt to store a value of type T1 in q^, which would corrupt the value already there.   □

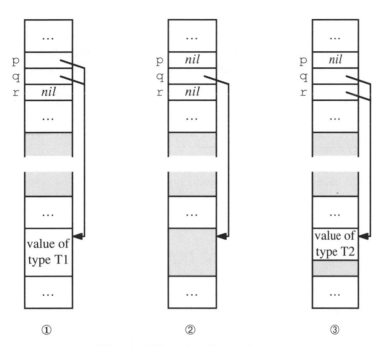

Figure 6.29 A dangling pointer.

The situation illustrated in Figure 6.29 is no less than a violation of Pascal's type rules, which are supposed to guarantee that every pointer of type ^{T} is either *nil* or points to a heap variable of type *T*. To restore the guarantee, extreme measures would be necessary. One measure would be never to allocate a heap variable in space released by deallocation. But this would prevent the heap from ever contracting. An alternative measure would be to make dispose find, and change to *nil*, *all* pointers to the deallocated heap variable. But this would imply a large time overhead, negating the main advantage of explicit deallocation.

6.6.3 Automatic deallocation and garbage collection

In a programming language that supports explicit deallocation, the appearance of garbage is usually a consequence of a programming error. In a language that does not support explicit deallocation, garbage must inevitably appear. A heap variable becomes inaccessible when the last pointer to it is overwritten (as in Example 6.29) or otherwise ceases to exist.

Fortunately, *automatic deallocation* of inaccessible heap variables is possible. The space they occupied can then be recycled by being added to the free list. The recycling process is called *garbage collection*, and is performed by a heap manager routine called the *garbage collector*.

Garbage collection is a feature of the run-time support for some imperative languages (such as Ada) and all functional languages (such as Lisp and ML). It is generally not provided for languages (such as Pascal and C) that have explicit deallocation.

Many garbage collection algorithms have been invented. *Mark–sweep garbage collection* is a simple and commonly used algorithm. The idea is to mark as accessible every heap variable that can be reached (directly or indirectly) by pointers from the stack. All other heap variables are inaccessible and may be deallocated.

Example 6.31
Figure 6.30 illustrates mark–sweep garbage collection. The initial state of the heap shows typical patterns. The stack contains pointers to some of the heap variables (*b* and *j*). These heap variables in turn contain pointers to other heap variables (*f* and *h*), and so on (*d*). But there are also some inaccessible heap variables to which no pointers exist (*c*, *e*, *g*, and *i*), and others to which the only pointers are themselves in inaccessible heap variables (*a*).

The garbage collector starts by marking *all* heap variables as inaccessible. In Figure 6.30, heap variables marked as inaccessible are indicated by small white circles, and those marked as accessible by small black circles.

Next, the garbage collector follows all chains of pointers from the stack, marking as accessible each heap variable it reaches. By following the first pointer from the stack it reaches *b*. It marks *b* as accessible. By following the second pointer from the stack it reaches *j*; by following the pointers in *j* it reaches *f* and *h*; and by following the pointer in *f* it reaches *d*. It marks all these heap variables as accessible. By following the third pointer from the stack it reaches *j*. But it has already marked *j* as accessible, so it need take no further action.

The garbage collector finishes by scanning the heap for heap variables still marked as inaccessible: *a*, *c*, *e*, *g*, and *i*. These really *are* inaccessible, so the garbage collector deallocates them.   □

Mark–sweep garbage collection may be seen to be a simple graph algorithm. The heap variables and the stack are the nodes of a directed graph, and the pointers are the edges. Our aim is to determine the largest subgraph in which all nodes can be reached from the stack node. The *mark–sweep garbage collection algorithm* can be expressed as follows (in pseudo-Pascal):

```
procedure collectGarbage;

    procedure markAccessible (var hv);
        {Mark heap variable hv as accessible, along with all other
          heap variables that can be reached from it.}
    begin
```

```
if hv is marked inaccessible then
    begin
    mark hv as accessible;
    for each pointer p in hv do
        markAccessible(p^)
    end
end{markAccessible};
```

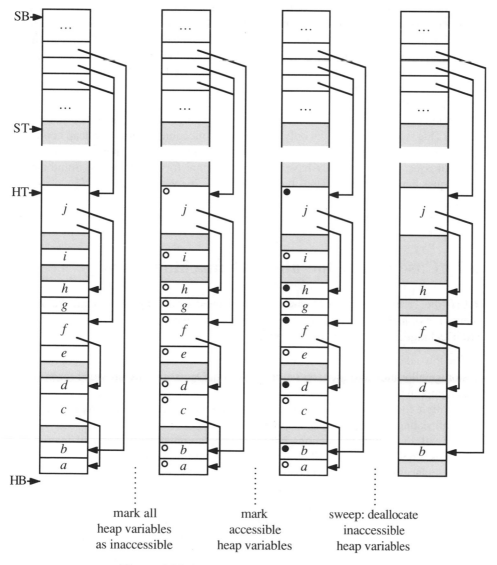

Figure 6.30 Mark–sweep garbage collection.

```
begin{collectGarbage}
for each heap variable hv do
    mark hv as inaccessible;
for each pointer p in the stack do
    markAccessible(p^);
for each heap variable hv do
    if hv is marked inaccessible then
        add hv to the free list
end{collectGarbage}
```

For this algorithm to work, it must be able to visit all heap variables, it must know the size of each, and it must be able to mark each as accessible or inaccessible. One way to meet these requirements is to extend each heap variable with hidden fields (which are used by the garbage collector but invisible to the programmer): a size field; a link field (used to connect all heap variables into a single linked list, to permit them all to be visited); and a 1-bit accessibility field (represented by a small black or white circle in Figure 6.30).

Another requirement is that pointers must be distinguishable from other data in the store. (This is a requirement not only for garbage collection, but also for heap compaction as described in Section 6.6.2.) This is an awkward problem: pointers are represented by addresses, which typically have exactly the same form as integers. Some clever techniques have been devised to solve this problem. See Wilson (1992).

6.7 Case study: the abstract machine TAM

TAM (the Triangle Abstract Machine) was designed specifically to support the implementation of high-level programming languages, and in particular the run-time organization techniques described in this chapter. Thus:

- The low-address end of the data store is reserved as a stack. This is used both for stack storage allocation and for expression evaluation. Operations are provided for pushing and popping values at the stack top.
- The high-address end of the data store is reserved as a heap. Operations are provided for allocating and deallocating heap variables.
- The call and return instructions handle frames automatically. The call instruction pushes a new frame, with all its link data. The return instruction pops a frame, and also replaces the routine's arguments by its result (if any).
- There are no general-purpose registers that could be used for storing data. All registers are dedicated to specific purposes: registers SB and ST delimit the stack; registers HB and HT delimit the heap; register LB points to the topmost frame on the stack; and so on. Updating of registers is always implicit: LB is updated by call and return instructions; ST is updated by load, store, and many other instructions; and so on.

In these respects TAM is quite similar to some other real and abstract stack machines (such as the P-code abstract machine, see Section 2.4). But a detailed look at TAM reveals a number of interesting design features, some of which are discussed below. A complete description of TAM may be found in Appendix C.

TAM is implemented by an interpreter. This interpreter is described in Section 8.4, and a complete listing may be found in Appendix D.

Addressing and registers

Most instructions have address operands. An address operand is always of the form '$d[r]$', where r names a register that points to the base of a store segment or frame, and d is a displacement:

$$\text{address denoted by } d[r] \quad = d + \text{register } r$$

This method of addressing is used uniformly for accessing global variables within the global segment, local and nonlocal variables within stack frames, and instructions within the code segment.

The registers SB, LB, L1, L2, etc., together form a display: SB allows access to global variables; LB allows access to local variables; and L1, L2, etc., allow access to nonlocal variables.

An interesting implementation decision is how exactly to maintain the registers L1, L2, etc. They are related to LB by the invariants:

$$L1 = content(LB)$$
$$L2 = content(content(LB))$$

and so on. Thus these registers change whenever LB changes, i.e., on a routine call or return. But it turns out that these registers are rarely needed in practice.[2] So, rather than updating L1, L2, and the others on every routine call or return, it is more efficient to compute L1 or L2 or whichever only when and if needed. In fact, the interpreter can compute the address of any variable as follows:

$$\text{address denoted by } d[\text{SB}] \quad = d + \text{SB}$$
$$\text{address denoted by } d[\text{LB}] \quad = d + \text{LB}$$
$$\text{address denoted by } d[\text{L1}] \quad = d + \text{L1} \quad = d + content(\text{LB})$$
$$\text{address denoted by } d[\text{L2}] \quad = d + \text{L2} \quad = d + content(content(\text{LB}))$$

and so on. Thus L1, L2, etc., are redundant! Although they can be named in the address operands of instructions, they need not exist as actual registers.

Primitive routines

The machine's primitive operations are provided by a set of *primitive routines*, such as `add`, `mult`, `lt`, and `not`. A primitive routine behaves like an ordinary routine, as far as the caller is concerned. That is to say, the caller must evaluate and push its arguments before calling the primitive routine, and on return the caller can expect to find the result at the stack top in place of the arguments. This design avoids the need for a large number of distinct instructions (such as `ADD`, `MULT`, `LT`, and `NOT`). It has the

---

[2] One study of a collection of Pascal programs suggested that, in practice, accesses to global variables (49%) and to local variables (49%) are far more common than accesses to nonlocal variables (2%).

further advantage of allowing a primitive to be treated exactly like an ordinary routine, e.g., we can pass it as an argument represented by a closure (see Section 6.5.2).

Each primitive routine has a dedicated address in the code store. Thus a call to a primitive routine can be trapped by the interpreter and treated appropriately.

Data representation

TAM storage is organized in words. However, the instruction set provides consistent support for composite values of any size from 1 word to 255 words. In the `LOAD`, `STORE`, and some other instructions there is an 8-bit size field, n, that indicates how many words are to be loaded, stored, or whatever. For example, the following instruction sequence:

```
LOAD(6)    4[LB]    – push 6 words from address 4 in the local frame
STORE(6) 21[SB]    – store them to address 21 in the global segment
```

copies a 6-word value (perhaps a record or array) from one place to another in the store. As well as copying multiword values, we can pass them as arguments to routines, return them as results, and so on.

In practice, most load and store instructions work on single-word values. By convention, therefore, we abbreviate '`LOAD(1)`' to '`LOAD`', '`STORE(1)`' to '`STORE`', etc., when writing instructions in mnemonic form.

6.8   Further reading

The essential background to the material presented in this chapter is a knowledge of basic programming language concepts. See the companion textbook by Watt (1990), and in particular Chapter 2 (primitive and composite types), Chapter 3 (variables and storage), and Chapter 5 (procedures, functions, and parameters).

The main topics of this chapter are covered in any good compiler textbook. See, for example, Chapter 7 of Aho *et al.* (1985).

Data representation has long been part of compiler writers' folklore. An early – but still unsurpassed – treatment of the topic may be found in a pair of illuminating papers by Hoare (1972, 1975). A more theoretical view of data representation issues – in the context of algebraic specification of data types – may be found in Chapter 6 of the companion textbook by Watt (1991).

Static storage allocation was used in implementations of the earliest programming languages (Fortran and Cobol). These languages deliberately rejected recursion in order to make static allocation feasible. When the Algol-like languages (Algol-60 and its successors) introduced recursion and nested block structure, stack storage allocation was developed to implement them, along with the use of display registers to access nonlocal variables. An early account of this method may be found in Dijkstra (1960).

Heap storage allocation and garbage collection were first developed when Lisp introduced recursive data structures. All functional languages rely heavily on garbage collection, as do those imperative languages (such as Ada) that eschew explicit deallocation. This topic is both fascinating and difficult, and remains an active research area. (See Wilson (1992) for a more detailed account.)

In functional programming languages, functions are first-class values, i.e., they can be passed as arguments, returned as function results, incorporated in data structures, and so on. In such a language local variables have lifetimes that are not strictly nested, so stack storage allocation as described in Section 6.4 is unsuitable. See Cardelli (1984) for an account of a run-time organization suitable for ML, a typical example of this kind of language. (The run-time organization described in this chapter is, however, perfectly suitable for languages – such as Δ, Pascal, and even Fortran – that allow functions and procedures to be passed as arguments.)

Exercises 6

Exercises for Section 6.1

6.1   Consider the following Pascal types:

```
type
    Player   =  (white, black);
    Piece    =  (pawn, knight, bishop,
                 rook, queen, king);
    Square   =  record
                    case empty: Boolean of
                        true:  ( );
                        false: (occupant: Piece;
                                  owner: Player)
                end;
    Board    =  array [1..8] of
                    array [1..8] of Square;
    State    =  record
                    pos:    Board;
                    next:   Player;
                    moves:  Integer
                end
```

(a) Show how these types would be represented, and state the size of each type. Assume that the target machine is TAM, in which every primitive value occupies one word.

(b) Repeat, but now assume that the target machine has byte addressing, with 1 word = 4 bytes = 32 bits.

6.2   In Pascal, the type `Boolean` behaves like an enumeration type:

```
type Boolean = (false, true)
```

and is therefore equipped with operations such as succ, pred, and ord as well as the logical operations. How does this influence the choice of representation for Pascal truth values?

6.3 Many real machines have a choice of integer representations (word or double-word), and a corresponding choice of machine operations (ADD or DADD, MULT or DMULT, etc.).

Assuming that the source language has a single type Integer, the compiler writer has to make a choice between the two representations. List the arguments in favor of each. How does your favorite compiler make this choice?

6.4 Consider the record type T of (6.3). Express $\#T$ in terms of $\#T_1$, ..., and $\#T_n$. Check that your $\#T$, together with *size* T (6.4), satisfies (6.1).

6.5 In Pascal, the programmer can choose not only the index *bounds* but also the index *type* of a static array.
(a) Show how the following arrays would be represented:

```
var freq:  array ['a'..'z'] of Integer;
    pixel: array [Color] of 0..15
```

where Color is defined as in Example 6.3.
(b) Generalize (6.15), (6.16), and (6.17) to cater for the general case:

$$\text{type } T = \text{array } [T_{\text{index}}] \text{ of } T_{\text{elem}}$$

where T_{index} may be any primitive discrete type, i.e., Boolean, Char, Integer, an enumeration type, or a subrange thereof.

6.6 In Δ (or Pascal), the effect of a multidimensional array may be obtained by an array of arrays: see array them in Example 6.6. Generalize (6.12) and (6.13) to cater for the two-dimensional case:

$$\text{type } T = \text{array } m \text{ of array } n \text{ of } T_{\text{elem}}$$

6.7 In Ada, the programmer can choose the index type of a dynamic array, as freely as in Pascal.
(a) Show how the array freq would be represented:

```
type Profile is
        array (Character range <>) of Integer;
first: Character := 'a';
last:  Character := 'z';
freq:  Profile (first .. last);
```

(b) Generalize (6.20), (6.21), and (6.22) to cater for the general case:

$$\text{type } T \text{ is array } (T_{\text{index}} \text{ range } <>) \text{ of } T_{\text{elem}};$$
$$a: T \ (E_1 \ .. \ E_2);$$

where T_{index} may be any primitive discrete type, i.e., `Boolean`, `Character`, `Integer`, or an enumeration type, and where E_1 and E_2 are expressions of type T_{index}.

6.8*   Suggest a representation for two-dimensional dynamic arrays, as in Ada:

```
type T is array (T₁ range <>,
                 T₂ range <>) of Telem;
a: T(E₁..E₂, E₃..E₄);
```

Exercises for Section 6.2

6.9   Consider the Δ expression '$(0 < n) /\backslash odd(n)$' whose evaluation on a stack machine was illustrated in Example 6.12. Illustrate the same expression's evaluation on a different stack machine with byte addressing: each stack element may be one or more bytes in size; a truth value occupies 1 byte, and an integer 4 bytes.

6.10   In most programming languages, the semantics of the expression '$E_1 \oplus E_2$' (where $\oplus$ is a binary operator) are such that the subexpressions E_1 and E_2 may be evaluated in any order.
(a) Consider the expression '$a * b + (1 - (c * 2))$' and the corresponding instruction sequence in Example 6.10. Find a shorter instruction sequence that evaluates this expression using only two registers.
(b) Now consider a machine with a single register (accumulator). How could this expression be evaluated on such a machine?

Exercises for Section 6.3

6.11   Consider a Pascal program with the type definitions of Exercise 6.1 and the following global variable declarations:

```
var computer, human: Player;
    initial: Board;
    current: State
```

Show how the global variables would be located in storage, assuming a target machine with 1 word = 4 bytes = 32 bits. Write down the address of each variable, assuming that the first variable is located at address 0.

6.12   Suppose that a Δ program has the following global variable declarations:

$$var \ v_1: T_1; \quad ...; \quad var \ v_n: T_n$$

Write down a formula for *address* v_i. Assume that *address* $v_1 = 0$.
Observe that each variable's address depends on the order of the variable declarations. But the semantics of Δ places no significance on the order of variable declarations. Discuss this paradox.

Exercises for Section 6.4

6.13　Consider the Δ program of Example 6.20. Suppose that the main program calls procedure Y, which in turn calls procedure Z. Draw a stack snapshot at each point during this sequence. Show frames and dynamic links as in Figure 6.11; also show individual global and local variables.

6.14　Consider the Δ program of Figure 6.14. Suppose that the main program calls procedure P, which in turn calls procedure Q, which in turn calls procedure R, which in turn calls procedure S.

(a) Draw a stack snapshot at each point during this sequence. Show frames and static links as in Figure 6.15; also show individual global, local, and nonlocal variables.

(b) According to Example 6.17, procedure R can fetch a variable local to Q by an instruction of the form 'LOAD d[L1]'. Write down the instruction that R would use to fetch q. Verify that this instruction will work correctly at the point when R is running during the above sequence.

(c) Which nonlocal variables may procedure S access? Verify that these nonlocal variables, and no others, are indeed accessible at the point when S is running during the above sequence. Write down instructions for S to fetch each of these nonlocal variables.

6.15* Algol is a programming language with nested block structure. (In this respect it is much like Δ, with procedures and block commands.) It has a few primitive types, namely Boolean, integer, and real. Its only composite type is the (dynamic) array. Arrays are indexed by integers, and their elements are always primitive – arrays of arrays are not supported. An example of an array declaration is:

```
real array v [1 : n]
```

where n must have been declared in an enclosing scope.

Design a run-time organization suitable for Algol. In particular, decide where the handle and elements of a dynamic array such as v should be located.

6.16** SB, LB, L1, L2, and so on are classified as display registers. SB always points to the globals; LB points to the topmost frame, which belongs to the currently running routine R; L1 points to a frame belonging to the routine R' immediately enclosing R; L2 points to a frame belonging to the routine R'' immediately enclosing R'; and so on.

An alternative form of display consists of registers D0, D1, D2, and so on. D0 always points to the globals; D1 points to a frame belonging to a routine whose body is at level 1; D2 points to a frame belonging to a routine whose body is at level 2; and so on. If the currently running routine R has its body at level n, Dn points to the topmost frame (which belongs to R), and D(n+1), D(n+2), and so on are undefined. This is illustrated in Figure 6.31, which corresponds to part of Figure 6.15.

How should D0, D1, D2, etc., be updated:
(a) when code at level *m* calls a routine *S* whose body is at level *n* ($1 \leq n \leq m+1$)?
(b) when *S* returns?
Discuss the advantages and disadvantages of this form of display.

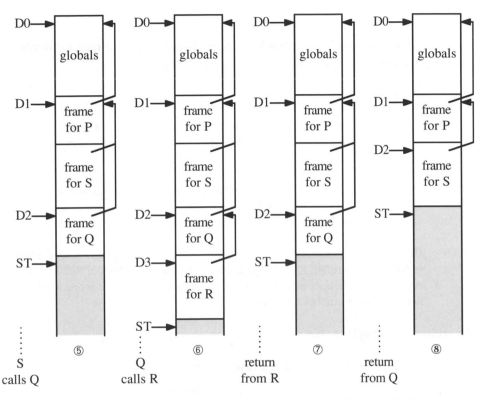

Figure 6.31 An alternative form of display (program of Figure 6.14).

Exercises for Section 6.5

6.17* Consider the following Δ program:

```
let
    func sqr (i: Integer) : Integer ~
        i * i;

    func even (i: Integer) : Boolean ~
        ((i // 2) = 0);

    func power (x: Integer, n: Integer)
            : Integer ~
```

```
                    if n = 0 then
                        1
                    else if even(n) then
                        sqr(power(x, n / 2))
                    else
                        sqr(power(x, n / 2)) * x
        in

            ...
```

Draw stack snapshots, showing arguments and results, at relevant points as this program evaluates:

(a) `power(2, 1)`

(b) `power(2, 6)`

6.18 Consider the parameter passing protocols of Examples 6.18 and 6.19. Compare the code that would be used to evaluate the following function calls:

(a) `f(a, b, c)`

(b) `f(g(a), h(b, c), d)`

In the case of the register machine, assume that instructions are of the form 'STORE R*i* *a*', 'LOAD R*i* *v*', 'ADD R*i* *v*', 'SUB R*i* *v*', and so on, where *a* is an address, and where *v* is an address, a literal, or a register.

6.19* Consider a target machine that has just eight general-purpose single-word registers, R0 through R7. Design a parameter passing protocol that uses these registers as much as possible, but also allows for multiple-word arguments and for a large number of arguments.

Exercises for Section 6.6

6.20 Consider the following outline Pascal program:

```
    type IntList = ...;      {linked list of integers}

    var p: Integer;
        ps, ns: IntList;

    function cons (n: Integer; n: IntList)
                    : IntList;
        ...;      {Return the list obtained by inserting n at the front
                    of ns.}

    procedure removeMultiples
                (n: Integer; var ns: IntList);
        ...;      {Remove n and all its multiples from ns.}

    begin
    ps := nil;
    ns := cons(3, cons(5, cons(7, cons(9,
            cons(11, cons(13, cons(15, cons(17,
```

```
             cons(19, cons(21, cons(23, cons(25,
             cons(27, cons(29, cons(31, cons(33,
             cons(35, cons(37, cons(39, cons(41,
             nil))))))))))))))))))))));
    repeat
       p := ns^.head;
       removeMultiples(p, ns);
       ps := cons(p, ps)
       until ns = nil
    end
```

Function `cons` allocates a new node, and procedure `removeMultiples` deallocates one or more nodes. Draw snapshots of the heap after the first six iterations of the loop. Do this for each of the following versions of the heap manager:

Version 1: On allocation, the heap manager just uses the first gap in the free list. On deallocation, the heap manager just adds the new gap to the front of the free list.

Version 2: On allocation, the heap manager uses the smallest gap that is big enough. On deallocation, the heap manager coalesces the new gap with any adjacent gap(s).

6.21* Design an algorithm that coalesces adjacent gaps in the heap whenever a heap variable is deallocated, as illustrated by Figure 6.26.

6.22* Design an algorithm that compacts the heap, as illustrated by Figure 6.27. When should heap compaction be done?

CHAPTER SEVEN

Code Generation

Syntactic and contextual analysis are concerned with analysis of the source program; thus they are dependent only on the source language. Code generation, on the other hand, is concerned with translation of the source program to object code, and so is dependent on both the source language and the target machine. It is possible to expound general principles of syntactic or contextual analysis, as in Chapters 4 and 5. But the influence of the target machine makes it much harder to expound general principles of code generation.

The main problem is that target machines are extremely varied. Some machines provide registers for storage of intermediate results; others provide a stack; still others provide both. Some machines provide instructions with zero, one, two, or three operands, or a mixture of these. Some machines provide a single addressing mode; others provide many. The structure of a code generator is dominated by such aspects of the target machine architecture. A code generation algorithm suitable for one target machine might be difficult or impossible to adapt to a dissimilar target machine.

The major subproblems of code generation are the following:

- *Code selection.* This is the problem of deciding which sequence of target machine instructions will be the object code of each phrase in the source program. For this purpose we write *code templates*, a code template being a general rule specifying the object code of all phrases of a particular form (e.g., assignment commands, or function calls). In practice, code selection is often complicated by special cases.

- *Storage allocation.* This is the problem of deciding the storage address of each variable in the source program. The code generator can decide the address of each global variable exactly (*static storage allocation*), but it can decide the address of each local variable only relatively (*stack storage allocation*).

- *Register allocation.* If the target machine has registers, they should be used to hold intermediate results during expression evaluation. The code generator, knowing that a particular register contains the current value of variable v, should take advantage of that to save a memory cycle when the value of v is needed. Many complications arise in practice: there might not be enough registers to evaluate a complex expression; or some registers might be reserved for particular purposes (such as indexing).

Code generation for a stack machine is significantly easier than code generation for a register machine. As we saw in Chapter 6, we need a stack anyway to implement (recursive) procedures and local variables. A stack is also convenient for expression evaluation. The problem of register allocation simply disappears. In this book, therefore, we consider only code generation for a stack machine, and concentrate on the subproblems of code selection and storage allocation. The abstract machine TAM is used as an illustrative target machine. (TAM was introduced in Chapter 6, and is fully explained in Appendix C.)

7.1   Code selection

The function of the code generator is to translate source programs to semantically equivalent object programs. When we design a code generator, therefore, we must be guided by the semantic specification of the source language – whether it be formal or informal. Now a semantic specification is generally structured in terms of the semantics of phrases such as expressions, commands, and declarations. In code generation we should follow the same structure: we should specify the translation of source programs to object programs inductively, by specifying the translation of individual phrases to object code.

Usually there are many correct translations of a given program or phrase. There may be several sequences of instructions that correctly perform a given source-language operation. So a basic task of the code generator is to decide which sequence of instructions is to be generated in each case. This is called *code selection*.

7.1.1   Code templates

How should we go about code selection? In general, we specify code selection inductively over the phrases of the source language, using *code functions* and *code templates*. If a phrase is primitive (i.e., contains no subphrases), then a code template can specify its object code directly. In general, however, a phrase contains one or more subphrases; then a code template should specify its object code by combining the object code of the subphrases, perhaps together with some additional instructions. The following example illustrates the method.

Example 7.1
Consider translation of some hypothetical source language to object code. We can specify the translation of commands to object code by introducing the following code function:

   execute : Command → Instruction*

This function will translate each command to a sequence of target-machine instructions. We must define this function over all the commands in the source language. This we do by means of code templates.

Consider a sequential command, typically of the form 'C_1; C_2'. Its semantics may be expressed informally as follows: to execute 'C_1; C_2', first execute C_1, and then execute C_2. We can easily specify the translation of 'C_1; C_2' to object code by means of the following code template:

execute $[C_1 ; C_2] =$
   execute C_1
   execute C_2

This code template may be read as follows: the code to execute 'C_1; C_2' consists of the code to execute C_1, followed by the code to execute C_2. For instance, here is a translation of the sequential command 'p := p + 7; f := f + 1':

$$
\textit{execute } \left[\begin{matrix} \texttt{p := p+7;} \\ \texttt{f := f+1} \end{matrix}\right] \left\{ \begin{matrix} \textit{execute } [\texttt{p := p+7}] \left\{ \begin{matrix} \texttt{LOAD} & p \\ \texttt{LOADL} & 7 \\ \texttt{CALL} & add \\ \texttt{STORE} & p \end{matrix} \right. \\ \textit{execute } [\texttt{f := f+1}] \left\{ \begin{matrix} \texttt{LOAD} & f \\ \texttt{CALL} & succ \\ \texttt{STORE} & f \end{matrix} \right. \end{matrix} \right.
$$

(The actual machine instructions will contain numerical addresses. Here we write p to stand for the address of variable p, f for the address of variable f, and add and $succ$ for the addresses of the respective primitive routines. We will use this convention freely, to make the examples readable.)

Most code templates contain specific instructions. For example, the code template for a simple assignment command might look like this:

execute $[I := E] =$
   evaluate E
   STORE a where a = address of variable I

This code template may be read as follows. The code to execute '$I := E$' consists of the code to evaluate E, followed by a STORE instruction whose operand field is the address of the variable I. For instance, see the translations of two assignment commands above.   □

Each code template specifies the object code to which a phrase is translated, in terms of the object code to which its subphrases are translated. A complete set of code functions and code templates specifies the translation of the entire source language to object code. More precisely:

- The **object code** of each source-language phrase is the sequence of instructions to which it will be translated. In other words, the object code is in Instruction*.
- For each phrase class P in the source language's abstract syntax, we introduce a **code function**, f, that translates each phrase in class P to object code:

   $f : P \rightarrow$ Instruction*

- We define the code function *f* by a number of **code templates**, with (at least) one code template for each distinct form of phrase in class **P**. If one form of phrase in **P** has subphrases *Q* and *R*, then the corresponding code template will look something like this:

$$f[\ldots Q \ldots R \ldots] =$$
$$\ldots$$
$$f' Q$$
$$\ldots$$
$$f'' R$$
$$\ldots$$

where *f'* and *f''* are the code functions appropriate for subphrases *Q* and *R*. (The order shown above is not fixed: *Q*'s object code may either precede or follow *R*'s object code.)

A **code specification** is a collection of code functions and code templates. It must cover the entire source language, i.e., it must specify the translation of every well-formed source program to object code. Let us now examine a complete code specification.

Example 7.2
Consider the language Mini-Δ, whose syntax was given in Example 1.3, and semantics in Example 1.8. We will present a code specification for the translation from Mini-Δ to TAM code.

The relevant phrase classes in this language are Program, Command, Expression, Operator, V-name, and Declaration. We first introduce code functions for these phrase classes:

run	: Program	→ Instruction*	(7.1)
execute	: Command	→ Instruction*	(7.2)
evaluate	: Expression	→ Instruction*	(7.3)
apply-unary	: Operator	→ Instruction*	(7.4)
apply-binary	: Operator	→ Instruction*	(7.5)
fetch	: V-name	→ Instruction*	(7.6)
assign	: V-name	→ Instruction*	(7.7)
elaborate	: Declaration	→ Instruction*	(7.8)

(There is also a phrase class Type-denoter, but we do not introduce a code function for type-denoters since they will not be translated to object code. There are *two* code functions for the phrase class V-name, which will be used in different contexts.)

The object code of each program, command, expression, operator, value-or-variable-name, or declaration is a sequence of TAM instructions that will behave as follows:

- '*run P*' is code that will run the program *P* and then halt, starting and finishing with an empty stack. (In other words, '*run P*' is a complete object program.)

- '*execute C*' is code that will execute the command *C*, possibly updating variables, but neither expanding nor contracting the stack.
- '*evaluate E*' is code that will evaluate the expression *E*, pushing its result on to the stack top, but having no other effect.
- '*apply-unary O*' is code that will pop a value from the stack top, and in its place push the result of applying unary operator *O* to that value.
- '*apply-binary O*' is code that will pop two values from the stack top, and in their place push the result of applying binary operator *O* to these values.
- '*fetch V*' is code that will push the value of the constant or variable *V* on to the stack top.
- '*assign V*' is code that will pop a value from the stack top, and store it in the variable *V*.
- '*elaborate D*' is code that will elaborate the declaration *D*, expanding the stack to make space for any constants and variables declared therein.

A Mini-Δ program is simply a command *C*. The program is run simply by executing *C* and then halting. The code template for a program is therefore as follows:

$$run \; [\![C]\!] = \tag{7.9}$$
$$\quad execute \; C$$
$$\quad \texttt{HALT}$$

The code templates for commands are as follows:

$$execute \; [\![V := E]\!] = \tag{7.10a}$$
$$\quad evaluate \; E$$
$$\quad assign \; V$$

This is easy to understand: '*evaluate E*' will have the net effect of pushing the value yielded by *E* on to the stack, and '*assign V*' will pop that value and store it in the variable *V*.

$$execute \; [\![I \; (\; E \;)]\!] = \tag{7.10b}$$
$$\quad evaluate \; E$$
$$\quad \texttt{CALL} \; d \texttt{[PB]} \qquad \text{where } d = \text{address of primitive routine } I$$
$$\qquad\qquad\qquad\qquad\qquad\qquad \text{relative to PB}$$

This is the code template for a procedure call. Since there are no procedure declarations in Mini-Δ, *I* must be the identifier of a predefined procedure such as `putint`. The above CALL instruction calls the corresponding primitive routine in TAM (which is addressed relative to the register PB).

$$execute \; [\![C_1 \; ; \; C_2]\!] = \tag{7.10c}$$
$$\quad execute \; C_1$$
$$\quad execute \; C_2$$

This was explained in Example 7.1.

$$execute \; [\![\textbf{if } E \textbf{ then } C_1 \textbf{ else } C_2]\!] = \tag{7.10d}$$
$$\quad evaluate \; E$$

```
        JUMPIF(0)  g
        execute C₁
        JUMP  h
g:      execute C₂
h:
```

Here the code '*evaluate E*' will have the net effect of pushing a truth value on to the stack. The JUMPIF instruction will pop and test this value. If it is 0 (representing *false*), the code '*execute C_2*' will be selected; otherwise the code '*execute C_1*' will be selected. (The labels g and h stand for the addresses of the following instructions.)

$$execute \; [\textbf{while } E \textbf{ do } C] = \qquad\qquad\qquad (7.10e)$$

```
        JUMP  h
g:      execute C
h:      evaluate E
        JUMPIF(1)  g
```

Here again, the code '*evaluate E*' will have the net effect of pushing a truth value on to the stack. The JUMPIF instruction will pop and test this value. If it is 1 (representing *true*), the code '*execute C*' will be iterated; otherwise iteration will cease. The initial JUMP instruction ensures that the code '*evaluate E*' will be executed before the code '*execute C*' in every iteration. This is in accordance with the semantics of the while-command. (See Exercise 7.1 for discussion of an alternative code template.)

$$execute \; [\textbf{let } D \textbf{ in } C] = \qquad\qquad\qquad (7.10f)$$

```
        elaborate D
        execute C
        POP(0)  s        if s > 0
                         where s = amount of storage allocated by D
```

This code template shows how storage allocation and deallocation comes in. The code '*elaborate D*' will expand the stack, as a consequence of allocating space for (constants and) variables declared in D. The code '*execute C*' will be able to access these variables. The POP instruction must contract the stack to its original size – in effect, deallocating these variables.

The code templates for expressions are as follows. (Recall that the object code in each case must have the net effect of pushing a value on to the stack.)

$$evaluate \; [IL] = \qquad\qquad\qquad (7.11a)$$

```
        LOADL  d        where d = valuation IL
```

The LOADL instruction will simply push the integer-literal's value on to the stack top.

$$evaluate \; [V] = \qquad\qquad\qquad (7.11b)$$

```
        fetch V
```

This is self-explanatory.

$$evaluate \; [O \; E] = \qquad\qquad\qquad (7.11c)$$

```
        evaluate E
        apply-unary O
```

$$evaluate \; [\![E_1 \; O \; E_2]\!] = \tag{7.11d}$$
$$evaluate \; E_1$$
$$evaluate \; E_2$$
$$apply\text{-}binary \; O$$

The above two code templates show how applications of unary and binary operators will be translated. Note how expression evaluation exploits the stack: the object code will first evaluate the operand(s), and then apply the operation corresponding to O. The latter is achieved by calling an appropriate primitive routine, e.g.:

$$apply\text{-}unary \; [\![\backslash]\!] = \tag{7.12}$$
```
CALL not
```

$$apply\text{-}binary \; [\![+]\!] = \tag{7.13a}$$
```
CALL add
```

$$apply\text{-}binary \; [\![<]\!] = \tag{7.13b}$$
```
CALL lt
```

In Mini-Δ, a value-or-variable-name is just an identifier that has been declared as a (global) constant or variable. Being a global, it will be addressed relative to register SB. Here we assume that its address has already been determined:

$$fetch \; [\![I]\!] = \tag{7.14}$$
```
LOAD d[SB]
```
where d = address of I relative to SB

$$assign \; [\![I]\!] = \tag{7.15}$$
```
STORE d[SB]
```
where d = address of I relative to SB

The code templates for declarations are as follows. In each case the object code must expand the stack to make space for the declared constants and variables.

$$elaborate \; [\![\textbf{const} \; I \sim E]\!] = \tag{7.16a}$$
$$evaluate \; E$$

The code '*evaluate E*' will determine the value of the constant, pushing it on to the stack. There the constant will remain, to be fetched whenever required. The address of the constant must be bound to I for future reference – this address will be needed whenever (7.14) is applied.

$$elaborate \; [\![\textbf{var} \; I : T]\!] = \tag{7.16b}$$
```
PUSH 1
```

This PUSH instruction will expand the stack by one word, enough space to accommodate the newly allocated variable. (The only types in Mini-Δ are truth values and integers, and these occupy one word each in TAM: *size T* = 1 word.) The newly allocated variable is not initialized. Its address must be bound to I for future reference – this address will be needed whenever (7.14) or (7.15) is applied.

$$elaborate \; [\![D_1 \; ; \; D_2]\!] = \tag{7.16c}$$
$$elaborate \; D_1$$
$$elaborate \; D_2$$

Note that in code templates (7.16a–c) it is a simple matter to predict the total amount of storage allocated by the declaration. This information is required in (7.10f). □

Example 7.3

The following translation illustrates code templates (7.10a) and (7.10e), among others:

$$
\textit{execute}\left[\!\!\left[\begin{array}{l}\texttt{while}\\ \quad\texttt{i > 0}\\ \texttt{do}\\ \quad\texttt{i := i-2}\end{array}\right]\!\!\right]\left\{\begin{array}{l}\textit{execute}\left[\!\!\left[\texttt{i := i-2}\right]\!\!\right]\left\{\begin{array}{llll}\texttt{30:} & \texttt{JUMP} & \texttt{35}\\ \texttt{31:} & \texttt{LOAD} & \textit{i}\\ \texttt{32:} & \texttt{LOADL} & \texttt{2}\\ \texttt{33:} & \texttt{CALL} & \textit{sub}\\ \texttt{34:} & \texttt{STORE} & \textit{i}\end{array}\right.\\[2ex]\textit{evaluate}\left[\!\!\left[\texttt{i > 0}\right]\!\!\right]\left\{\begin{array}{lll}\texttt{35:} & \texttt{LOAD} & \textit{i}\\ \texttt{36:} & \texttt{LOADL} & \texttt{0}\\ \texttt{37:} & \texttt{CALL} & \textit{gt}\end{array}\right.\\ \qquad\qquad\texttt{38:} \quad \texttt{JUMPIF(1)} \quad \texttt{31}\end{array}\right.
$$

Here we are assuming that the while-command's object code starts at address 30. The numbers to the left of the instructions are their addresses. (In this example we show the instruction addresses, but more usually we omit them.) □

Example 7.4

The following translation of a let-command illustrates code templates (7.10f) and (7.16b), among others:

$$
\textit{execute}\left[\!\!\left[\begin{array}{l}\texttt{let}\\ \quad\texttt{var i:}\\ \qquad\texttt{Integer}\\ \texttt{in}\\ \quad\texttt{i := i+2}\end{array}\right]\!\!\right]\left\{\begin{array}{l}\textit{elaborate}\left[\!\!\left[\begin{array}{l}\texttt{var i:}\\ \quad\texttt{Integer}\end{array}\right]\!\!\right]\{\ \ \texttt{PUSH} \quad \texttt{1}\\[2ex]\textit{execute}\left[\!\!\left[\texttt{i := i+2}\right]\!\!\right]\left\{\begin{array}{ll}\texttt{LOAD} & \textit{i}\\ \texttt{LOADL} & \texttt{2}\\ \texttt{CALL} & \textit{add}\\ \texttt{STORE} & \textit{i}\end{array}\right.\\ \qquad\qquad\texttt{POP(0)} \quad \texttt{1}\end{array}\right.
$$

The code generated from this let-command expands the stack by one word to allocate space for the local variable $\texttt{i}$, and later contracts the stack by one word to deallocate it. The address of this word, i say, is used to access the variable within the let-command. □

Example 7.5

Code templates (7.14), (7.15), and (7.16b) took advantage of the fact that every Mini-Δ value occupies one word exactly. This is because the language supports only truth values and integers, which occupy one word each in TAM.

On the other hand, Δ itself supports a variety of types including arrays and records. A value or variable of type T will occupy a number of words given by *size* T. (See Section 6.1.) We must generalize the code templates to take this into account:

$$\textit{fetch}\,[\![I]\!] = \tag{7.17}$$
$$\texttt{LOAD}\,(s)\ \ d\,[\texttt{SB}] \qquad \text{where } s = \textit{size}(\text{type of } I),$$
$$d = \text{address of } I \text{ relative to SB}$$

$$assign \; [\![I]\!] = \tag{7.18}$$
$$\text{STORE} \, (s) \quad d[\text{SB}] \qquad \text{where } s = size(\text{type of } I),$$
$$d = \text{address of } I \text{ relative to SB}$$

$$elaborate \; [\![\textbf{var} \, I : T]\!] = \tag{7.19}$$
$$\text{PUSH} \; s \qquad \qquad \text{where } s = size \; T$$

We shall use these more general code templates from now on. They are still valid for Mini-Δ (in which *size T* is always 1). $\qquad\qquad\qquad\qquad\qquad\square$

7.1.2   Special-case code templates

There are often several ways to translate a given source-language phrase to object code, some more efficient than others. For example, the TAM code to evaluate the expression 'n + 1' could be:

```
(a)   LOAD    n          or (b)  LOAD    n
      LOADL 1                    CALL    succ
      CALL    add
```

Object code (a) follows code template (7.11d). That code template is always applicable, being valid for any binary operator and any subexpressions. Object code (b) is correct only in the special case of the binary operator '+' being applied to the literal value 1. When applicable, this special case gives rise to more efficient object code. It could be specified as follows:

$$evaluate \; [\![E_1 + 1]\!] =$$
$$evaluate \; E_1$$
$$\text{CALL} \; succ$$

All practical code specifications include some special cases. A *special case* is a code template that is applicable only to phrases of a special form. These phrases might well be covered by a more general code template. A special-case code template is worth specifying if phrases of the special form occur frequently, and if they allow translation into particularly efficient object code. The following example illustrates this further.

Example 7.6
The right-hand side of a constant declaration is frequently a literal, as in:

```
let
    const n ~ 7
in
    ... n ... n ...
```

Code template (7.16a) specifies that the code '*elaborate* $[\![$const n ~ 7$]\!]$' will push the value 7 on to the stack and leave it there. Whenever n is used, code template (7.14) specifies that the value will be copied to the top of stack. The following translation illustrates these code templates:

$$
\textit{execute} \, \llbracket \texttt{let} \\
\qquad \texttt{const n ~ 7} \\
\qquad \texttt{in} \\
\qquad \texttt{putint} \\
\qquad\qquad \texttt{(i*n)} \rrbracket
\begin{cases}
\textit{elaborate} \, \llbracket \texttt{const} \\
\qquad\qquad \texttt{n ~ 7} \rrbracket \left\{
\begin{array}{ll}
\texttt{LOADL} & \texttt{7} \\
\end{array}
\right. \\
\\
\textit{execute} \, \llbracket \texttt{putint} \\
\qquad\qquad \texttt{(i*n)} \rrbracket
\left\{
\begin{array}{ll}
\texttt{LOAD} & \textit{i} \\
\texttt{LOAD} & \textit{n} \\
\texttt{CALL} & \textit{mult} \\
\texttt{CALL} & \textit{putint} \\
\texttt{POP(0)} & \texttt{1}
\end{array}
\right.
\end{cases}
$$

The value of the constant n is pushed on to the stack. The address where this value is located (say *n*) is used to access the constant, wherever required within the block, by means of the instruction 'LOAD *n*'. Finally, the value of n is popped.

A better translation is simply to use the literal value 7 wherever n is used. This special treatment is possible whenever an identifier is bound to a known value in a constant declaration. This is expressed by the following special-case code templates:

$$\textit{fetch} \, \llbracket I \rrbracket = \tag{7.20}$$
$$\qquad \texttt{LOADL} \;\; d \qquad\qquad \text{where } d = \text{value of } I, \text{ if that value is known}$$

$$\textit{elaborate} \, \llbracket \textbf{const} \; I \sim IL \rrbracket = \tag{7.21}$$
$$\qquad\qquad (\text{i.e., no code})$$

In (7.21) no code is required to elaborate the constant declaration. It is sufficient that the value of the integer-literal *IL* is bound to *I* for future reference. In (7.20) that value is incorporated into a LOADL instruction. Thus the object code is more efficient in both places. The following alternative translation illustrates the special cases:

$$
\textit{execute} \, \llbracket \texttt{let} \\
\qquad \texttt{const n ~ 7} \\
\qquad \texttt{in} \\
\qquad \texttt{putint} \\
\qquad\qquad \texttt{(i*n)} \rrbracket
\begin{cases}
\textit{elaborate} \, \llbracket \texttt{const} \\
\qquad\qquad \texttt{n ~ 7} \rrbracket \left\{ \right. \\
\\
\textit{execute} \, \llbracket \texttt{putint} \\
\qquad\qquad \texttt{(i*n)} \rrbracket
\left\{
\begin{array}{ll}
\texttt{LOAD} & \textit{i} \\
\texttt{LOADL} & \texttt{7} \\
\texttt{CALL} & \textit{mult} \\
\texttt{CALL} & \textit{putint}
\end{array}
\right.
\end{cases}
$$

In this object code, the applied occurrence of n has been translated to the literal value 7. The instruction to elaborate the constant declaration, and the final instruction to pop the constant value, have both been eliminated. □

7.2 A code generation algorithm

A code specification does more than specify a translation from the source language to object code. It also suggests an algorithm for performing this translation. This algorithm recursively traverses the decorated AST representing the source program, emitting target-machine instructions one by one. Both the order of traversal and the instructions to be emitted are determined straightforwardly by the code templates.

In this section we see how to develop a code generator from a code specification. We illustrate this with the code specification of Example 7.2.

7.2.1   Representation of the object program

Since its basic function is to generate an object program consisting of target-machine instructions, the code generator must obviously define representations of instructions and instruction sequences. This is easy, as the following example illustrates.

Example 7.7

A code generator that generates TAM object code must include representations of TAM instructions and fields of instructions.

The following constants represent the TAM register numbers (Table C.1):

```
const
        CBr =  0;    CTr =  1;    PBr =  2;    PTr =  3;
        SBr =  4;    STr =  5;    HBr =  6;    HTr =  7;
        LBr =  8;    L1r =  9;    L2r = 10;    L3r = 11;
        L4r = 12;    L5r = 13;    L6r = 14;    CPr = 15
```

The following constants represent the TAM operation codes (Table C.2):

```
const
        LOADop   =  0;    LOADAop  =  1;
        LOADIop  =  2;    LOADLop  =  3;
        STOREop  =  4;    STOREIop =  5;
        CALLop   =  6;    CALLIop  =  7;
        RETURNop =  8;
        PUSHop   = 10;    POPop    = 11;
        JUMPop   = 12;    JUMPIop  = 13;
        JUMPIFop = 14;    HALTop   = 15
```

The following types represent TAM instructions (Section C.2):

```
type OpCode          = 0..15;
     Length          = 0..255;
     RegisterNumber  = 0..15;
     Operand         = -32768..+32767;
     Instruction     = packed record
                           op: OpCode;
                           n: Length;
                           r: RegisterNumber;
                           d: Operand
                       end
```

Now the object program can be represented as follows:

```
type CodeAddress = 0..32767;
var  code: array [CodeAddress] of Instruction;
     nextInstrAddr: CodeAddress
```

Instructions will be stored in `code`, using `nextInstrAddr` as a counter. We will use the following auxiliary procedures to construct the object program:

```
procedure startCodeGeneration;
         {Initialize the object program.}
   begin
   nextInstrAddr := 0
   end;

procedure emit (op: OpCode; n: Length;
                r: RegisterNumber; d: Operand);
         {Append a single instruction to the object program.}
   begin
   store an instruction with fields op, n, r, and d
            in code[nextInstrAddr];
   nextInstrAddr := nextInstrAddr + 1
   end
```

The code generator must call `startCodeGeneration` to empty the object program, and thereafter append instructions in the correct order by successive calls to `emit`.   □

7.2.2 Systematic development of a code generator

A code specification determines the action of a code generator. The latter will consist of a set of *encoding procedures*, which cooperate to traverse the decorated AST representing the source program. For each code function *f* there will be a corresponding encoding procedure, `encodef`. Since *f* is defined by several code templates, `encodef` will have several corresponding cases.

Example 7.8
Let us develop a code generator that translates Mini-Δ to TAM object code, in accordance with the code specification of Example 7.2. The code generator will consist of the following encoding procedures, one for each code function:

```
procedure encodeRun (program: AST);
   ...      {Generate code as specified by 'run program'.}

procedure encodeExecute (command: AST);
   ...;     {Generate code as specified by 'execute command'.}

procedure encodeEvaluate (expression: AST);
   ...;     {Generate code as specified by 'evaluate expression'.}

procedure encodeApplyUnary (operator: AST);
   ...;     {Generate code as specified by 'apply-unary operator'.}

procedure encodeApplyBinary (operator: AST);
   ...;     {Generate code as specified by 'apply-binary operator'.}

procedure encodeFetch (vname: AST);
   ...;     {Generate code as specified by 'fetch vname'.}
```

```
procedure encodeAssign (vname: AST);
    ...;      {Generate code as specified by 'assign vname'.}

procedure encodeElaborate (declaration: AST);
    ...       {Generate code as specified by 'elaborate declaration'.}
```

Each encoding procedure's parameter is an AST representing a phrase of the appropriate class. We shall assume Example 4.7's definition of type AST.

This procedure generates code for a complete program, using code template (7.9):

```
procedure encodeRun (program: AST);
  begin
  startCodeGeneration;
                                    { run [[C]] =                 }
  encodeExecute(program);           { execute C       }
  emit(HALTop, null, null, null)    { HALT            }
  end{encodeRun}
```

(For ease of comparison, each code template is shown as a comment alongside the corresponding code generator steps.)

Now let us develop the procedure encodeExecute. This procedure's parameter is an AST representing a command, and its function is to translate that command to object code. By inspecting the tag of the AST's root node, the procedure can determine which form of command is to be translated. It generates code from the different forms of command according to the corresponding code templates (7.10a–f):

```
procedure encodeExecute (command: AST);
  begin
  with command^ do
    case tag of

        VbecomesE:                    { execute [[V := E]] =      }
          begin                       {                 }
          encodeEvaluate(child[2]);   { evaluate E      }
          encodeAssign(child[1])      { assign V        }
          end;

        IlpErp:                       { execute [[I ( E )]] =     }
          begin                       {                 }
          encodeEvaluate(child[2]);   { evaluate E      }
          emit(CALLop, SBr, PBr,      { CALL d[PB]  }
               address of primitive routine I  { where d = ...   }
               relative to PB)
          end;

        CsemicolonC:                  { execute [[C₁ ; C₂]] =     }
          begin                       {                 }
          encodeExecute(child[1]);    { execute C₁      }
          encodeExecute(child[2])     { execute C₂      }
          end;
```

```
ifEthenCelseC:              { execute ⟦if E              }
                            {          then C₁          }
                            {          else C₂⟧ =        }
    ...;                    { ...                        }

whileEdoC:                  { execute ⟦while E           }
                            {          do C⟧ =           }
    ...;                    { ...                        }

letDinC:                    { execute ⟦let D             }
    begin                   {          in C⟧ =           }
    encodeElaborate(child[1]); { elaborate D             }
    encodeExecute(child[2]);   { execute C               }
    if amount of storage    {                            }
        allocated by D > 0 then { if s > 0               }
            emit(POPop, 0, null,  { POP(0)  s            }
                amount of storage { where s = ...        }
                allocated by D)
    end

    end{case}
end{encodeExecute}
```

We shall deal with the if-command and while-command cases in Example 7.9. We shall fill in the missing details of the let-command case in Example 7.13.

Now let us develop the procedure `encodeEvaluate`. Its parameter is an AST representing an expression, and its function is to translate that expression to object code, according to code templates (7.11a–d):

```
procedure encodeEvaluate (expression: AST);
    begin
    with expression^ do
        case tag of

            IL:                     { evaluate ⟦IL⟧ =        }
                emit(LOADLop,       { LOADL  d               }
                    null, null,     {                        }
                    valuation(spelling)); { where d = ...    }

            V:                      { evaluate ⟦V⟧ =         }
                encodeFetch(child[1]); { fetch V             }

            OE:                     { evaluate ⟦O E⟧ =       }
                begin               {                        }
                encodeEvaluate(child[2]); { evaluate E       }
                encodeApplyUnary(child[1]) { apply-unary O   }
                end;

            EOE:                    { evaluate ⟦E₁ O E₂⟧ =   }
                begin               {                        }
```

```
        encodeEvaluate(child[1]);    { evaluate E₁    }
        encodeEvaluate(child[3]);    { evaluate E₂    }
        encodeApplyBinary(child[2]) { apply-binary O  }
     end

  end{case}
end{encodeEvaluate}
```

The following auxiliary function was used here:

```
function valuation (intLit: TokenString) : Integer;
   ...      {Return the value of the given integer-literal.)
```

The procedure `encodeApplyBinary` works as follows. Its parameter is an AST leaf node representing a binary operator. Its function is to generate code that applies that operation to its two operands, according to code templates (7.13):

```
procedure encodeApplyBinary (operator: AST);
   begin
   emit(CALLop, SBr, PBr,
            address relative to PB of primitive routine
            corresponding to operator)
   end{encodeApplyBinary}
```

The procedure `encodeApplyUnary` is similar.

The procedures `encodeElaborate`, `encodeFetch`, and `encodeAssign` will be considered in Example 7.13.   □

Compare the code generator developed in Example 7.8 with the code specification of Example 7.2. For the most part, it is easy to see how the code generator was developed:

- To each code function, $f: P \rightarrow$ Instruction*, there corresponds an encoding procedure, `encodef`. The parameter of `encodef` is an AST representing a phrase of class P. Within the body of `encodef` there is one case for each possible form of the phrase. Each case is developed from the corresponding code template.
- Wherever a code template invokes a code function f, the corresponding encoding procedure `encodef` is called. Its first argument is the subAST representing the particular subphrase.
- Wherever a code template contains a specific instruction, the auxiliary procedure `emit` is called to append that instruction to the object program.

The encoding procedures developed in this way cooperate to traverse the AST recursively, generating the object program one instruction at a time.

In a code template, the order of the object code most commonly follows the order of the subphrases. But sometimes the order is different, as in code templates (7.10a) and (7.10e). This causes no difficulty to our code generator, which simply traverses the AST in the order specified by the code templates. (Out-of-order code generation cannot easily be achieved by a one-pass compiler, on the other hand, since such a compiler generates object code 'on the fly' as it parses the source program.)

Now we have the outline of a code generator, but a number of particular problems require particular solutions. The following subsection deals with the problem of generating code for control structures. Thereafter Sections 7.3 and 7.4 deal with the problems of generating code for declared constants and variables, procedures and parameters.

7.2.3   Control structures

The code generator appends one instruction at a time to the object program. It can easily determine the address of each instruction, simply by counting the instructions as they are generated.

Source-language control structures, such as if-commands and while-commands, are implemented using conditional and conditional jump instructions. The address of the destination instruction (i.e., the instruction to which the jump is directed) is an operand of the jump instruction. A *backward* jump causes no problem, because the jump instruction is generated *after* the destination instruction – so the destination address is already known. But a *forward* jump is awkward, because the jump instruction must be generated *before* the destination instruction – and the destination address cannot generally be predicted at the time the jump instruction is generated.

Fortunately, there is a simple solution to the problem of forward jumps, a solution known as *backpatching*. When the code generator has to generate a forward jump, it generates an incomplete jump instruction, with a null destination address field, but it also notes the address of the jump instruction. Later, when the destination address becomes known, the code generator goes back and patches it into the jump instruction. (A similar solution to a similar problem is also used in one-pass assemblers.)

The following example illustrates the method. Recall that the code generator maintains a global variable, the *next instruction address*, that contains the address of the next instruction to be generated. The next instruction address is incremented whenever an instruction is appended to the object program. (See Example 7.7.)

Example 7.9
Recall code template (7.10e):

> *execute* $[$**while** E **do** $C]$ =
>   JUMP h
> $g:$ *execute C*
> $h:$ *evaluate E*
>   JUMPIF(1) g

Here g stands for the address of the first instruction of the object code '*execute C*', and h stands for the address of the first instruction of the object code '*evaluate E*'. Let us see how encodeExecute implements this code template.

The backward jump instruction 'JUMPIF(1) g' is easily generated as follows. Immediately before code is generated for '*execute C*', the next instruction address is saved in a variable, say loopAddr, local to encodeExecute. When the backward jump instruction is later generated, the address in loopAddr is used as its destination address.

When the forward jump instruction 'JUMP *h*' is to be generated, on the other hand, its destination address is not yet known. Instead, an incomplete JUMP instruction is generated, with a null address field. The address of this incomplete instruction is saved in another local variable, say jumpAddr. Later, just before code is generated for '*evaluate E*', the next instruction address is noted, and patched into the instruction at address jumpAddr.

For instance, in Example 7.3 we saw the translation of '**while** i > 0 **do** i := i - 2'. Here we show how encodeExecute generates this object code:

(1) It saves the next instruction address (say 30) in jumpAddr.

(2) It generates a JUMP instruction with a null address field:

        30:     JUMP   *null*

(3) It saves the next instruction address (namely 31) in loopAddr.

(4) It translates the subcommand 'i := i - 2' to object code:

        31:     LOAD   *i*
        32:     LOADL 2
        33:     CALL   *sub*
        34:     STORE *i*

(5) It takes the next instruction address (namely 35), and patches it into the address field of the instruction whose address was saved in jumpAddr (namely 30):

        30:     JUMP   <u>35</u>

(6) It translates the expression 'i > 0' to object code:

        35:     LOAD   *i*
        36:     LOADL 0
        37:     CALL   *gt*

(7) It generates a JUMPIF instruction whose address field contains the address that was saved in loopAddr (namely 31):

        38:     JUMPIF(1) 31

Below we apply this method to generate code for the while-command, and for the if-command similarly:

```
procedure encodeExecute (command: AST);
    var jumpAddr, jumpifAddr, loopAddr: CodeAddress;
    begin
    with command^ do
        case tag of

            ...

            whileEdoC:                      { execute [while E     }
                begin                       {          do C] =     }
                jumpAddr := nextInstrAddr; {                       }
```

```
        emit(JUMPop, null, CBr,      { JUMP h           }
             null);                  {                  }
        loopAddr := nextInstrAddr;   { g:               }
        encodeExecute(child[2]);     { execute C        }
        patch(jumpAddr,              {                  }
             nextInstrAddr);         { h:               }
        encodeEvaluate(child[1]);    { evaluate E       }
        emit(JUMPIFop, 1, CBr,       { JUMPIF(1) g      }
             loopAddr)
    end;

    ifEthenCelseC:                   { execute ⟦if E              }
                                     {             then C₁       }
        begin                        {             else C₂⟧ =     }
        encodeEvaluate(child[1]);    { evaluate E       }
        jumpifAddr := nextInstrAddr; {                  }
        emit(JUMPIFop, 0, CBr,       { JUMPIF(0) g      }
             null);                  {                  }
        encodeExecute(child[2]);     { execute C₁       }
        jumpAddr := nextInstrAddr;   {                  }
        emit(JUMPop, null, CBr,      { JUMP h           }
             null);                  {                  }
        patch(jumpifAddr,            {                  }
             nextInstrAddr);         { g:               }
        encodeExecute(child[3]);     { execute C₂       }
        patch(jumpAddr,              {                  }
             nextInstrAddr)          { h:               }
    end;

    ...

    end{case}
end{encodeExecute}
```

Here we have used the following auxiliary procedure for patching instructions:

```
procedure patch (addr: CodeAddress; d: Operand);
    ...      {Put d into the d field of the instruction at address addr.}
```

7.3   Constants and variables

The role of a *declaration* in a programming language is to bind an identifier to an entity such as a value, variable, or procedure. Within the scope of its declaration, the identifier may be used in expressions, commands, and so on. Each such applied occurrence of the identifier denotes the entity to which the identifier was bound.

In an object program, entities such as values, variables, and procedures will be represented by *run-time objects*. The identifiers themselves have no direct counterparts in machine code. Instead, each applied occurrence of an identifier will be translated to a run-time object.

How the code generator handles identifiers and declarations is the topic of this and the following sections. In this section we concentrate on declarations and applied occurrences of constants and variables, and the closely related topic of storage allocation. In Section 7.4 we go on to consider procedures, functions, and parameters.

7.3.1   Constant and variable declarations

A constant declaration binds an identifier to an ordinary value (such as a truth value, integer, or record). The representation of values of various types was discussed in Section 6.1.

A variable declaration allocates a variable and binds an identifier to it. A variable will be represented by one or more consecutive storage cells, based at a particular data address.

The code generator, when it visits a constant or variable declaration, must decide what run-time object will represent the declared entity. It should create an *object description*, containing details of the run-time object (value or address), and bind that object description to the identifier for future reference. The following example illustrates the idea, and also suggests a simple method by which the code generator can represent the binding of object descriptions to identifiers.

Example 7.10
Consider the following Mini-Δ command:

```
let
    const b ~ 10;
    var i: Integer
in
    i := i * b
```

Figure 7.1(a) shows the decorated AST representing this command. The subAST ① represents the declaration of b, and the applied occurrence of b at ⑤ has been linked to ①. The subAST ② represents the declaration of i, and the applied occurrences of i at ③ and ④ have been linked to ②.

The constant declaration binds the identifier b to the integer value 10. The variable declaration binds the identifier i to a newly allocated integer variable, whose address must be decided by the code generator. Let us suppose that this address is 4 (relative to SB).

In the subcommand 'i := i * b', the applied occurrence of b should be translated to the value 10 (more precisely, to the representation of 10), and each applied occurrence of i should be translated to the address 4. So the subcommand should be translated to the following object code:

```
LOAD   4[SB]          – fetch from the address denoted by i
LOADL 10              – fetch the value denoted by b
CALL   mult
STORE 4[SB]           – store to the address denoted by i
```

Now let us see how this treatment of identifiers can be achieved. The code generator first visits the declarations. It creates an object description for the known value 10, and attaches that object description to the declaration of b at ①. It creates an object description for the known address 4, and attaches that object description to the declaration of i at ②. Figure 7.1(b) shows the AST at this point.

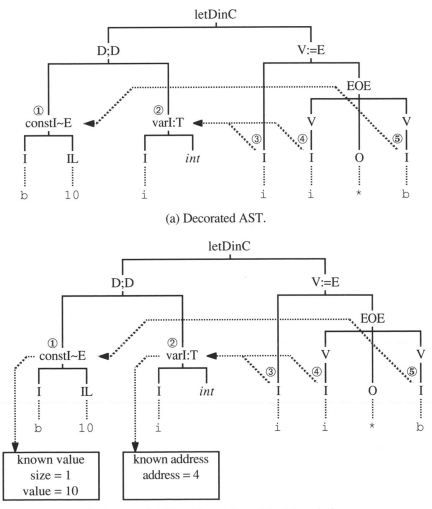

(a) Decorated AST.

(b) Decorated AST with attached object descriptions.

Figure 7.1 Object descriptions for a known value and a known address.

Thereafter, when the code generator encounters an applied occurrence of b, it follows the link to the declaration ①. From the object description attached to ① it determines that b denotes the known value 10. Likewise, when the code generator encounters an applied occurrence of i, it follows the link to the declaration ②. From the object description attached to ② it determines that i denotes the known address 4.   □

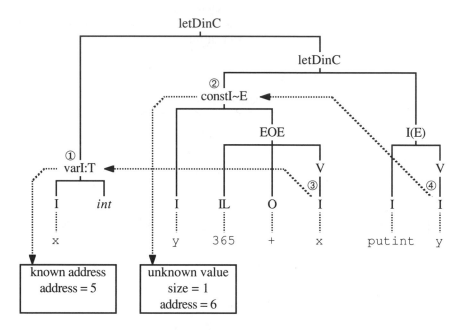

Figure 7.2 Object descriptions for a known address and an unknown value.

Example 7.11
Consider the following Mini-Δ command:

```
let var x: Integer
in
    let const y ~ 365 + x
    in
        putint (y)
```

Figure 7.2 shows the decorated AST representing this command. The applied occurrences of x and y at ③ and ④ have been linked to the corresponding declarations (① and ②, respectively).

The variable declaration binds the identifier x to a newly allocated integer variable. Let us suppose that its address is 5 (relative to SB).

The constant declaration binds the identifier y to an integer value that is *unknown* at compile-time. Thus the code generator cannot simply translate each applied occurrence of y to the value that it denotes. (This contrasts with the constant declaration of

Example 7.10, in which an identifier was bound to a value *known* at compile-time, thus allowing the code generator to incorporate that known value into a `LOADL` instruction.)

Fortunately, there is a simple solution to this problem. The code generator translates the constant declaration to object code that evaluates the unknown value and stores it *at a known address*. Suppose that the value of y is to be stored at address 6 (relative to SB). Then the applied occurrence of y in 'putint(y)' should be translated to an instruction to fetch the value contained at address 6:

```
LOAD  6[SB]         – fetch the value denoted by y
CALL  putint
```

The code generator first visits the declarations. It creates an object description for the known address 5, and attaches that object description to the declaration of x at ①. It creates an object description for an unknown value at address 6, and attaches that object description to the declaration of y at ②. These object descriptions are shown in Figure 7.2.

Thereafter, whenever the code generator encounters an applied occurrence of y, it follows the link to the declaration ②. From the object description attached to ② it determines that y denotes the unknown value contained at address 6.   □

In summary, the code generator handles declarations and applied occurrences of identifiers as follows:

- When it encounters a declaration of identifier *I*, the code generator creates an object description, and binds that object description to *I*. This object description contains details of the run-time object that represents the entity bound to *I*.
- When it encounters an applied occurrence of *I*, the code generator consults the object description bound to *I*, and translates *I* to the corresponding run-time object.

If the source program is represented by a decorated AST, there is a particularly simple way to bind an object description to an identifier *I*: simply attach the object description to the subAST that represents the declaration of *I*. Every applied occurrence of *I* has already been linked to the corresponding declaration of *I*. So, whenever the code generator encounters an applied occurrence of *I*, it follows the link to the declaration of *I*, and there finds the attached object description.

Identifiers may be bound to run-time objects such as *values* and *addresses*. Each object may be either *known* or *unknown* (at compile-time). All combinations are possible, and all actually occur in Δ:

- *Known value.* This describes a value bound in a constant declaration whose right-hand side is a literal.
- *Unknown value.* This describes a value bound in any other constant declaration, or an argument value bound to a constant parameter.
- *Known address.* This describes an address allocated and bound in a variable declaration.
- *Unknown address.* This describes an argument address bound to a variable parameter.

(Constant and variable parameters will be discussed in Section 7.4.3.)

We can systematically deal with both known and unknown objects by the techniques illustrated in Examples 7.10 and 7.11. In general:

- If an identifier *I* is bound to a *known* object, the code generator creates an object description containing that known object, and attaches that object description to the declaration of *I*. It translates each applied occurrence of *I* to that known object.
- If an identifier *I* is bound to an *unknown* object, the code generator generates code to evaluate the unknown object and store it at a known address, creates an object description containing that address, and attaches that object description to the declaration of *I*. At each applied occurrence of *I*, the code generator generates code to fetch the unknown object from that address.

An important task for the code generator is to allocate addresses for variables. We study this topic in the following subsections. (As we have just seen, the code generator must also allocate addresses for unknown values. For the sake of simplicity, we discuss the topic of storage allocation in terms of variables, but exactly the same principles apply to allocation of storage for unknown values.)

Throughout we shall take advantage of the constant-size requirement explained in Section 6.1. Given the type of a variable, the code generator knows exactly how much storage must be allocated for it.

7.3.2 Static storage allocation

Consider a source language with only global variables. As explained in Section 6.3, static storage allocation is appropriate for such a language. The code generator can determine the exact address of every variable in the source program.

Example 7.12
Consider the following Mini-Δ program:

```
let
    var a: Integer;
    var b: Boolean;
    var c: Integer;
    var d: Integer
in
    begin
    ...
    end
```

If the target machine is TAM, then variables of types `Boolean` and `Integer` will occupy one word each, and the variables in this program will have the addresses (relative to SB) shown in the middle column below. If instead the target machine is the MC68000, then variables of types `Boolean` and `Integer` will occupy one byte and one word, respectively, and the variables will have the addresses shown in the rightmost column below. (These are byte addresses; 1 word = 2 bytes.)

Variable	TAM address	MC68000 address
a	0	0
b	1	2
c	2	3
d	3	5

Now consider the following Mini-Δ program with nested blocks:

```
let var a: Integer
in
    begin
    ...;

    let var b: Boolean;
        var c: Integer
    in
        begin ... end;

    ...;

    let var d: Integer
    in
        begin ... end;

    ...
    end
```

If the target machine is TAM, then the variables in this program will have the addresses (relative to SB) shown in the middle column below. If instead the target machine is the MC68000, then the variables will have the addresses shown in the rightmost column below. Note that the variables b and c can safely occupy the same storage as the variable d, since they can never coexist.

Variable	TAM address	MC68000 address
a	0	0
b	1	2
c	2	3
d	1	2

□

The code generator must keep track of how much storage has been allocated at each point in the source program. We can arrange this by giving each encoding procedure a parameter indicating how much storage is already in use. Since elaborating a declaration may allocate *extra* storage, we give encodeElaborate an additional parameter through which it can pass back the amount of extra storage it has allocated. We also give encodeEvaluate an additional parameter through which it can pass back the size of the expression's result.

Example 7.13

In the Mini-Δ code generator, we enhance the encoding procedures as follows:

```
procedure encodeExecute
                (command: AST;
                 globalSize: Natural);
    ...;      {Generate code as specified by 'execute command'.
              globalSize is the amount of storage already in use.}

procedure encodeEvaluate
                (command: AST;
                 globalSize: Natural;
                 var valSize: Natural);
    ...;      {Generate code as specified by 'evaluate expression'.
              globalSize is the amount of storage already in use.
              Set valSize to the size of the result.}

procedure encodeElaborate
                (declaration: AST;
                 globalSize: Natural;
                 var extraSize: Natural);
    ...       {Generate code as specified by 'elaborate declaration'.
              globalSize is the amount of storage already in use.
              Set extraSize to the amount of extra storage allocated.}
```

We define object descriptions as follows:

```
type ObjectKind =
            (knownValue,    unknownValue,
             knownAddress, unknownAddress);
     ObjectDescription =
            record
               size: Natural;
               case kind: ObjectKind of
                  knownValue:
                        ( value: Word );
                  unknownValue,
                  knownAddress,
                  unknownAddress:
                        ( address: DataAddress )
            end;
     ObjectPointer = ^ObjectDescription
```

In addition, to each nonterminal node of the AST we add a field `obj` that can be made
to point to an object description:

```
type ASTNode =
            record
               ...;
```

```
case tag: ASTTag of
   {Nonterminal nodes ...}
   ...:
         ( ...;
           obj: ObjectPointer );
   {Terminal nodes ...}
   ...:
         ( ... )
end
```

The field obj will be initialized to **nil** when an AST node is created.

Recall the code templates for declarations (7.16a), (7.21), (7.19), and (7.16c):

elaborate ⟦**const** *I* ~ *E*⟧ =
   evaluate E

elaborate ⟦**const** *I* ~ *IL*⟧ =   (special case)
             (i.e., no code)

elaborate ⟦**var** *I* : *T*⟧ =
   PUSH *s*   where *s* = *size T*

elaborate ⟦*D*₁ ; *D*₂⟧ =
   *elaborate D*₁
   *elaborate D*₂

These are implemented by the following encoding procedure:

```
procedure encodeElaborate
                (declaration: AST;
                 globalSize: Natural;
                 var extraSize: Natural);
   var valSize, extraSize1, extraSize2: Natural;
begin
with declaration^ do
   case tag of
      constIisE:
         begin
         if child[2]^.tag     { elaborate [const      }
             = IL then        {               I ~ IL] = }
         begin                {      (i.e., no code) }
         new(obj);
         obj^.kind := knownValue;
         obj^.size := 1;
         obj^.value :=
               valuation(child[2]^.spelling);
         extraSize := 0
         end
```

```
                      else              { elaborate ⟦const      }
                         begin         {            I ~ E⟧ =    }
                         encodeEvaluate(            { evaluate E      }
                                 child[2],
                                 globalSize,
                                 valSize);
                         new(obj);
                         obj^.kind := unknownValue;
                         obj^.size := valSize;
                         obj^.address := globalSize;
                         extraSize := valSize
                         end
                      end;

              varIcolonT:                  { elaborate ⟦var      }
                 begin                     {            I : T⟧ =    }
                 extraSize :=                      {              }
                        typeSize(child[2]);   {              }
                 emit(PUSHop, null, null,   { PUSH s       }
                        extraSize);          { where s = ...    }
                 new(obj);
                 obj^.kind := knownAddress;
                 obj^.size := 1;
                 obj^.address := globalSize
                 end;

              DsemicolonD:                  { elaborate ⟦D₁ ; D₂⟧ =    }
                 begin                            {              }
                 encodeElaborate(child[1],   { elaborate D₁    }
                        globalSize,          {              }
                        extraSize1);         {              }
                 encodeElaborate(child[2],   { elaborate D₂    }
                        globalSize + extraSize1,
                        extraSize2);
                 extraSize :=
                        extraSize1 + extraSize2
                 end

              end{case}
          end{encodeElaborate}
```

Here the command 'new(obj)' – in other words, 'new(declaration^.obj)' – creates an object description and attaches it to the declaration node in the AST.

Recall the code template for a let-command (7.10f):

$$execute \ ⟦\textbf{let } D \textbf{ in } C⟧ =$$
$$elaborate \ D$$
$$execute \ C$$

```
POP (0)  s              if s > 0
                        where s = amount of storage allocated by D
```

The corresponding case in Example 7.8 omitted one important detail: how does it determine the amount of storage allocated by *D*? We can now see that this information is supplied by `encodeElaborate`:

```
procedure encodeExecute
                    (command: AST;
                     globalSize: Natural);
    var extraSize: Natural;
    begin
    with command^ do
      case tag of
          ...;

          letDinC:                        { execute [let D       }
             begin                        {          in C] =    }
             encodeElaborate(child[1],    { elaborate D          }
                 globalSize,              {                      }
                 extraSize);              {                      }
             encodeExecute(child[2],      { execute C            }
                 globalSize + extraSize);{                      }
             if extraSize > 0 then        { if s > 0             }
                emit(POPop, 0, null,      { POP (0)  s           }
                     extraSize)           { where s = ...        }
             end

      end{case}
    end{encodeExecute}
```

Recall the code templates for value-or-variable-names, (7.17), (7.20), and (7.18):

fetch $[I]$ =
    LOAD (s) d[SB]   where s = *size*(type of *I*),
                            d = address of *I* relative to SB

fetch $[I]$ $\doteq$ (special case)
    LOADL d where d = value of *I*, if that value is known

assign $[I]$ =
    STORE (s) d[SB]   where s = *size*(type of *I*),
                           d = address of *I* relative to SB

These are implemented by the following encoding procedures. (Recall that each applied occurrence of identifier *I* has been linked, by the contextual analyzer, to the corresponding declaration of *I*. The field `decl` represents this link. So `decl^.obj` points to the object description bound to *I*.)

```
procedure encodeFetch (vname: AST);
    begin
```

```
        with vname^ do
          case tag of

             I:
                 with decl^.obj^ do
                      {... object description bound to I}
                      case kind of
                         knownValue:     { fetch [[I]] =          }
                              emit(LOADLop,   { LOADL d          }
                                   null, null,
                                   value);
                         unknownValue,
                         knownAddress:   { fetch [[I]] =          }
                              emit(LOADop,    { LOAD (s) d[SB]   }
                                   typeSize(type of I),
                                   SBr, address)
                         end{case}

             end{case}
        end{encodeFetch};

      procedure encodeAssign (vname: AST);
         begin
         with vname^ do
           case tag of

              I:                          { assign [[I]] =          }
                  with decl^.obj^ do      {                        }
                  {... object description bound to I} {            }
                      emit(STOREop,       { STORE (s) d[SB]  }
                           typeSize(type of I),
                           SBr, address)

              end{case}
        end{encodeAssign}
```

In `encodeAssign` we can safely assume that `decl^.obj^.kind` is equal to `knownAddress`. (The contextual analyzer will already have checked that *I* is a *variable* identifier.)

Procedure `encodeRun` starts off code generation with no storage allocated:

```
      procedure encodeRun (program: AST);
         begin
         startCodeGeneration;
         encodeExecute(program, 0);
         emit(HALTop, null, null, null)
         end{encodeRun}
```

□

7.3.3 Stack storage allocation

Consider now a source language with procedures and local variables. As explained in Section 6.4, stack storage allocation is appropriate for such a language. The code generator cannot predict a local variable's absolute address. What it can do is to predict the variable's address displacement relative to the base of a frame – a frame belonging to the procedure within which the variable was declared. At run-time, a display register will point to the base of that frame, and the variable can be addressed relative to that register. Which register is determined entirely by the routine level of the variable's declaration, and the routine level of the code that is addressing the variable. These routine levels are known to the code generator. (See Section 6.4.2 for details.)

To make the code generator implement stack storage allocation, we must modify the form of addresses in object descriptions. The address of a variable will now be held as a pair (l, d), where l is the routine level of the variable's declaration, and d is the variable's address displacement relative to its frame base. As in Section 6.4.2, we assign a routine level of 0 to the main program, a routine level of 1 to the body of each procedure or function declared at level 0, a routine level of 2 to the body of each procedure or function declared at level 1, and so on.

Example 7.14
Recall the Δ program of Figure 6.14. The same program is outlined in Figure 7.3, with each procedure body shaded to indicate its routine level.

Object descriptions are shown attached to the variable declarations in the source program. (This is for clarity. In reality, of course, the object descriptions would be attached to the subASTs that represent these declarations, as in Figures 7.1 and 7.2.)

The address of the global variables g1 and g2 are shown as (0, 0) and (0, 1), meaning displacements of 0 and 1, respectively, relative to the base of the level-0 frame (i.e., the globals).

The addresses of the local variables p1 and p2 are shown as (1, 3) and (1, 4), meaning displacements of 3 and 4, respectively, relative to the base of a level-1 frame (i.e., a frame belonging to a procedure whose body is at level 1). The address of the local variable q is shown as (2, 3), meaning a displacement of 3 relative to the base of a level-2 frame. And so on.

Notice that the address displacements of local variables start at 3. The reason is that the first three words of a frame contain link data, as shown in Figure 6.16. ☐

The code templates (7.17) and (7.18) assumed static storage allocation. They must be modified to take account of stack storage allocation.

Example 7.15
Although Mini-Δ has no procedures, let us anticipate their introduction – just in order to study the code generator's treatment of local variables.

The code templates for *fetch* (7.17) and *assign* (7.18) would be generalized as follows:

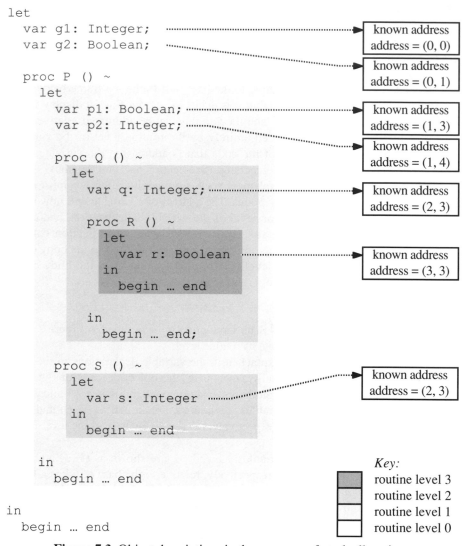

Figure 7.3 Object descriptions in the presence of stack allocation.

fetch $[\![I]\!]$ =   (7.22)
      LOAD (s) $d[r]$ where s = *size*(type of I),
                                                (l, d) = address of I,
                                                l' = current routine level,
                                                r = *display-register*(l', l)

assign $[\![I]\!]$ =   (7.23)
      STORE (s) $d[r]$ where s = *size*(type of I),
                                                (l, d) = address of I,
                                                l' = current routine level,
                                                r = *display-register*(l', l)

The *current routine level* is the routine level of the code that is addressing the variable.

The auxiliary function *display-register*(*l'*, *l*) selects the display register that will enable code at routine level *l'* to address a variable declared at routine level *l*:

display-register(*l'*, 0)	= SB		(7.24a)
display-register(*l*, *l*)	= LB	(*l* > 0)	(7.24b)
display-register(*l*+1, *l*)	= L1	(*l* > 0)	(7.24c)
display-register(*l*+2, *l*)	= L2	(*l* > 0)	(7.24d)

...

Note that the special-case code template (7.20) is unaffected. ☐

In order to implement (7.22) and (7.23), the code generator must know the routine level of each command, expression, and so on. We can communicate this information by giving each encoding procedure a parameter indicating the routine level where the phrase occurs.

Example 7.16

In the Mini-Δ code generator, we enhance the encoding procedures as follows:

```
procedure encodeExecute
                (command: AST;
                 currentLevel: Natural;
                 frameSize: Natural);
    ...;      {Generate code as specified by 'execute command'.
              currentLevel is the routine level of command.
              frameSize is the amount of frame space already in use.}

procedure encodeEvaluate
                (expression: AST;
                 currentLevel: Natural;
                 frameSize: Natural;
                 var valSize: Natural);
    ...;      {Generate code as specified by 'evaluate expression'.
              currentLevel is the routine level of expression.
              frameSize is the amount of frame space already in use.
              Set valSize to the size of the result.}

procedure encodeFetch
                (vname: AST;
                 currentLevel: Natural);
    ...;      {Generate code as specified by 'fetch vname'.
              currentLevel is the routine level of vname.}

procedure encodeAssign
                (vname: AST;
                 currentLevel: Natural);
    ...;      {Generate code as specified by 'assign vname'.
              currentLevel is the routine level of vname.}
```

```
procedure encodeElaborate
                (declaration: AST;
                 currentLevel: Natural;
                 frameSize: Natural;
                 var extraSize: Natural);
...     {Generate code as specified by 'elaborate declaration'.
        currentLevel is the routine level of declaration.
        frameSize is the amount of frame space already in use.
        Set extraSize to the increase in frame size.}
```

The following procedure implements code templates (7.20) and (7.22):

```
procedure encodeFetch
                (vname: AST;
                 currentLevel: Natural);
    begin
    with vname^ do
        case tag of

            I:
                with decl^.obj^ do
                        {... object description bound to I}
                    case kind of
                        knownValue:      { fetch [[I]] =              }
                            emit(LOADLop,   { LOADL d             }
                                    null, null,
                                    value);
                        unknownValue,
                        knownAddress:    { fetch [[I]] =              }
                            emit(LOADop,     { LOAD (s) d[r]       }
                                    typeSize(type of I),
                                    displayReg(currentLevel,
                                            address.level),
                                    address.displacement)
                    end{case}

        end{case}
    end{encodeFetch}
```

The following procedure implements code template (7.23):

```
procedure encodeAssign
                (vname: AST;
                 currentLevel: Natural);
    begin
    with vname^ do
        case tag of

            I:
```

```
        with decl^.obj^ do
              {object description of variable I}
            case kind of
              knownAddress:  { assign [[I]] =              }
                    emit(STOREop,   { STORE (s) d[r]   }
                          typeSize (type of I),
                          displayReg(currentLevel,
                                address.level),
                          address.displacement)
            end{case}

        end{case}
    end{encodeAssign}
```

The auxiliary function `displayReg` implements equations (7.24):

```
    function displayReg (curLevel, objLevel: Natural)
                  : RegisterNumber;   ...
```

The above procedures assume that the object descriptions are generalized:

```
    type ObjectKind =
              (knownValue,    unknownValue,
               knownAddress, unknownAddress,
               knownRoutine, unknownRoutine);
        ObjectAddress =
              record
                 level: Natural
                 displacement: Integer
              end;
        ObjectDescription =
              record
                 size: Natural;
                 case kind: ObjectKind of
                    knownValue:
                        ( value: Integer );
                    unknownValue,
                    knownAddress, unknownAddress,
                    knownRoutine, unknownRoutine:
                        ( address: ObjectAddress )
              end
```

The following procedure shows how the object descriptions are now set up:

```
    procedure encodeElaborate
                    (declaration: AST;
                     currentLevel: Natural;
                     frameSize: Natural;
                     var extraSize: Natural);
```

```
var valSize, extraSize1, extraSize2: Natural;
begin
with declaration^ do
   case tag of
      constIisE:
         begin
         if child[2]^.tag = IL then
            begin
            new(obj);
            obj^.kind := knownValue;
            obj^.size := 1;
            obj^.value :=
                  valuation(child[2]^.spelling);
            extraSize := 0
            end
         else
            begin
            encodeEvaluate(child[2],
                  currentLevel, frameSize,
                  valSize);
            new(obj);
            obj^.kind := unknownValue;
            obj^.size := valSize;
            obj^.address.level := currentLevel;
            obj^.address.displacement :=
                  frameSize;
            extraSize := valSize
            end
         end;

      varIcolonT:
         begin
         extraSize := typeSize(child[2]);
         emit(PUSHop, null, null, extraSize);
         new(obj);
         obj^.kind := knownAddress;
         obj^.size := 1;
         obj^.address.level := currentLevel;
         obj^.address.displacement := frameSize
         end;

      procIisC:
         begin
         ...;
         emit(JUMPop, ...);
         new(obj);
```

```
          obj^.kind := knownRoutine;
          ...;
          encodeExecute(child[2],
                  currentLevel + 1, 3);
          emit(RETURNop, 0, null, 0);
          ...;
          extraSize := 0
          end;

    DsemicolonD:
          begin
          encodeElaborate(child[1], currentLevel,
                  frameSize, extraSize1);
          encodeElaborate(child[2], currentLevel,
                  frameSize + extraSize1,
                  extraSize2);
          extraSize := extraSize1 + extraSize2
          end

        end{case}
    end{encodeElaborate}
```

Note that, when `encodeExecute` is called to translate the body of a procedure, the level parameter is `currentLevel + 1`.

Finally, procedure `encodeRun` starts off with a level parameter of 0 and with no storage allocated:

```
    procedure encodeRun (program: AST);
        begin
        startCodeGeneration;
        encodeExecute(program, 0, 0);
        emit(HALTop, null, null, null)
        end{encodeRun}
```

$\square$

7.4 Procedures and functions

In this section we study how the code generator handles procedure and function declarations, procedure and function calls, and the association between actual and formal parameters. We start by looking at global procedures and functions. Then we consider nested procedures and functions. Finally we examine the implementation of parameter mechanisms.

A procedure declaration binds an identifier to a procedure, and a function declaration binds an identifier to a function. The run-time object representing a procedure or function is a *routine*. At its simplest, a routine is just code with a designated entry address.

7.4.1   Global procedures and functions

Consider a programming language (such as Fortran or C) in which all procedures are declared globally. In the implementation of such a language, a routine is completely characterized by its *entry address* (i.e., the address of its first instruction). The routine is called by a CALL instruction that designates the entry address. This instruction will pass control to the routine, where control will remain until a RETURN instruction is executed.

From the above, we see that the code generator should treat a procedure declaration as follows. It should create an object description for a known routine, containing the routine's entry address, and bind that object description to the procedure identifier. At an applied occurrence of this identifier, in a procedure call, the code generator should retrieve the corresponding routine's entry address, and generate a CALL instruction designating that entry address.

Example 7.17

Consider again the language Mini-Δ, for which code templates were given in Example 7.2. Let us now extend Mini-Δ with parameterless procedures. The syntactic changes, for procedure declarations and procedure calls, are as follows:

Declaration ::= ...
              | **proc** Identifier **( )** ~ Command   (7.25)

Command   ::= ...
              | Identifier **( )**   (7.26)

We shall assume that all procedure declarations are global, i.e., not nested.

The code template specifying translation of a procedure declaration to TAM code would be:

$$elaborate\ [\![\mathbf{proc}\ I\ (\ )\ \sim\ C]\!] =$$ (7.27)
$$\text{JUMP}\ g$$
$$e:\quad execute\ C$$
$$\text{RETURN(0)}\ \ 0$$
$$g:$$

The generated routine body consists simply of the object code '*execute C*' followed by a RETURN instruction. The two zeros in the RETURN instruction indicate that the routine has no result and no arguments. Of course, we do not want the routine body to be executed at the point where the procedure is *declared*, only where the procedure is *called*. So we also generate a jump round the routine body. The routine's entry address, e, must be bound to I for future reference.

The code template specifying translation of a procedure call would be:

$$execute\ [\![I\ (\ )]\!] =$$ (7.28)
$$\text{CALL(SB)}\ \ e\text{where}\ e = \text{entry address of routine}\ I$$

This is straightforward. The net effect of executing this CALL instruction will be simply to execute the body of the routine denoted by I. □

Example 7.18
The following extended Mini-Δ program illustrates a procedure declaration and call:

```
let
    var n: Integer;
    proc p () ~
        n := n * 2
in
    begin
    n := 1;
    p()
    end
```

The corresponding object program illustrates code templates (7.27) and (7.28):

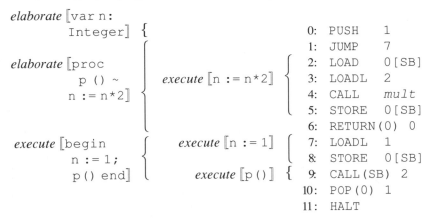

The corresponding decorated AST and object descriptions are shown in Figure 7.4.   □

A function is translated in much the same way as a procedure. The only essential difference is in the code that returns the function result.

Example 7.19
Suppose that Mini-Δ is to be extended with parameterless functions. The syntactic changes are as follows:

Declaration ::= ...
           | **func** Identifier **( )** : Type-denoter   (7.29)
                    ~ Expression

Expression ::= ...
           | Identifier **( )**   (7.30)

As in Example 7.17, we shall assume that all function declarations are global.

The code template specifying translation of a function declaration to TAM code would be:

$$elaborate\; \llbracket\textbf{func}\, I\; (\;)\; :\; T \sim E \rrbracket =$$ (7.31)

JUMP *g*

e :   *evaluate E*

RETURN (*n*)   0   where *n* = *size T*

g :

This RETURN instruction returns a result of size *n*, that result being the value of *E*.

The code template specifying translation of a function call to TAM code would be:

$$evaluate\; \llbracket I\; (\;)\; \rrbracket =$$ (7.32)

CALL (SB) *e*   where *e* = entry address of routine *I*

which is similar to (7.28).   □

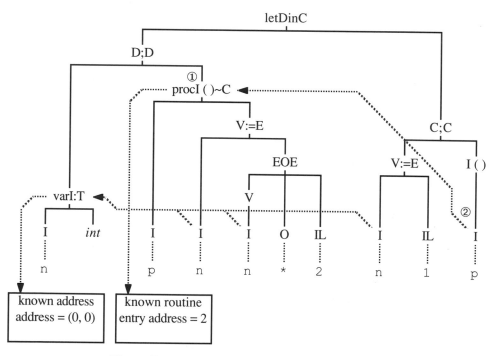

Figure 7.4 Object description for a known routine.

7.4.2   Nested procedures and functions

Now consider a source language that allows procedure and functions to be nested, and allows them to access nonlocal variables. In this case the implementation needs static links, as explained in Section 6.4.2. The call instruction (or instruction sequence) must designate not only the entry address of the called routine but also an appropriate static link.

Suppose that a procedure is represented by a routine R in the object code. R's entry address is known to the code generator, as we have already seen. The appropriate static link for a call to R will be the base address of a frame somewhere in the stack. This base address is not known to the code generator. But the code generator does know which display register will contain that static link, at the time when R is called. Which register will be determined entirely by the routine level of R's declaration and the routine level of the code that calls R.

To implement this, we modify the form of routine addresses in object descriptions. The address of routine R will now be held as a pair (l, e), where l is the routine level of R's declaration (with global routines at level 0), and e is R's entry address.

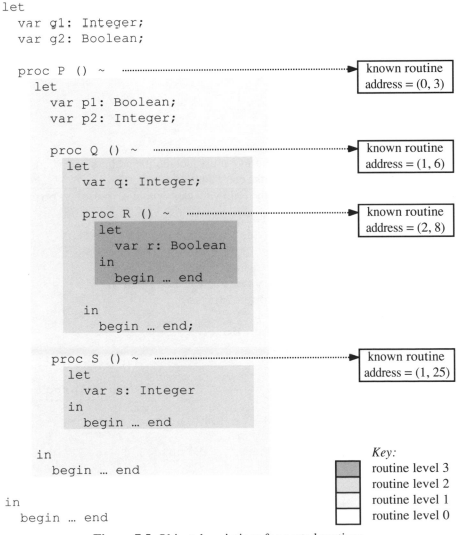

Figure 7.5 Object descriptions for nested routines.

Example 7.20

The Δ program outline of Figure 7.3 is reproduced in Figure 7.5, with object descriptions shown attached to the procedure declarations.

The object description for procedure P describes it as a known routine with address (0, 3), signifying that P was declared at level 0, and its entry address is 3. The object description for procedure Q describes it as a known routine with address (1, 6), signifying that P was declared at level 1, and its entry address is 6. And so on. □

The code template (7.28) in Example 7.17 assumed global procedures only. It must be modified to take account of nested procedures.

Example 7.21

Consider again the language Mini-Δ extended with parameterless procedures. The syntax is unchanged from Example 7.17, but now we shall allow nested procedure declarations.

The code template for a procedure declaration would be unchanged:

$$elaborate\ \mathbf{[proc}\ I\ (\ )\ \sim C\mathbf{]} =$$ (7.33)
```
        JUMP  g
   e:   execute C
        RETURN(0)  0
   g:
```

but now the object description bound to *I* must include the address pair (l, e), where *l* is the current routine level, and *e* is the entry address.

This would be implemented by the following case within encodeElaborate:

```
procedure  encodeElaborate
                      (declaration: AST;
                       currentLevel: Natural;
                       frameSize: Natural;
                       var extraSize: Natural);
     var jumpAddr: CodeAddress;
     begin
     with declaration^ do
       case tag of
          ...;

             procIisC:                      { elaborate [proc I ()   }
                begin                    {            ~ C] =       }
                jumpAddr := nextInstrAddr; {                       }
                emit(JUMPop,                { JUMP  g               }
                      null, CBr, null);    {                       }
                new(obj);                    {                       }
                obj^.kind := knownRoutine; {                       }
                obj^.size := 2;            {                       }
                obj^.address.level :=      {                       }
                      currentLevel;          {                       }
                obj^.address.displacement :={                       }
```

```
                        nextInstrAddr;        { e:              }
              encodeExecute(child[2],         { execute C       }
                        currentLevel + 1, 3);{                  }
              emit(RETURNop,                   { RETURN(0)   0}
                        0, null, 0);          {                  }
              patch(jumpAddr,                  {                  }
                        nextInstrAddr);       { g:              }
              extraSize := 0
            end

      end{case}
   end{encodeElaborate}
```

The code template specifying translation of a procedure call to TAM code would be:

$$execute \; \llbracket I \; (\;) \rrbracket = \qquad\qquad\qquad\qquad\qquad\qquad (7.34)$$
$$\text{CALL} \; (r) \quad e \qquad\qquad \text{where } (l, e) = \text{address of routine } I,$$
$$l' = \text{current routine level},$$
$$r = display\text{-}register(l', l)$$

The net effect of executing this CALL instruction will be to execute the command C that is the body of the procedure denoted by I, using the content of register r as the static link. The latter is determined using the auxiliary function *display-register*, which was defined in (7.24).

This would be implemented by the following case within encodeExecute:

```
      procedure encodeExecute
                    (command: AST;
                     globalSize: Natural);
         ...;
      begin
      with command^ do
         case tag of
            ...;
            Ilprp:                      { execute ⟦I ( )⟧ =      }
               begin                    {                        }
               emit(CALLop,             { CALL (r)  e      }
                     displayReg(
                           currentLevel,
                           address.level),
                     CBr,
                     address.displacement)
               end

         end{case}
      end{encodeExecute}
```

7.4.3   Parameters

Now let us consider how the code generator implements parameter passing. Every source language has one or more *parameter mechanisms*, the means by which arguments are associated with the corresponding formal parameters.

As explained in Section 6.5.1, a parameter passing protocol is needed to ensure that the calling code deposits the arguments in a place where the called routine expects to find them. If the operating system does not impose a standard protocol, the compiler writer must design one, taking account of the source language's parameter mechanisms and the target machine architecture.

The parameter passing protocol adopted in TAM is for the calling code to deposit the arguments at the stack top immediately before the call. Thus the called routine can address its own arguments using negative displacements relative to its own frame base. The code generator can represent the address of each argument in the usual way by a pair (l, d), where l is the routine level of the routine's body and d is the negative displacement.

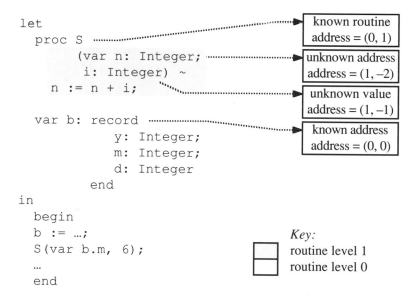

Figure 7.6 Object descriptions for constant and variable parameters.

Example 7.22
Recall the Δ program of Example 6.23, whose run-time behavior was shown in Figure 6.21. The same program is reproduced in Figure 7.6, with appropriate object descriptions attached to the declarations and formal parameters.

The constant parameter i will be bound to an argument *value* whenever procedure S is called. Therefore its object description is that of an unknown value, stored at address $(1, -1)$.

The variable parameter n, on the other hand, will be bound to an argument *address*. Therefore its object description is that of an unknown address, which is itself stored at address (1, –2). This object description implies that each applied occurrence of n must be implemented by indirect addressing.

In TAM, indirect addressing is supported by the instructions LOADI (load indirect) and STOREI (store indirect). These were illustrated in Example 6.23. □

Now we have encountered all combinations of known and unknown values, and known and unknown addresses, in object descriptions. We must therefore generalize our code templates for value-or-variable-names accordingly.

Example 7.23
Consider Mini-Δ extended with procedures, and constant and variable parameters. For simplicity we shall assume that each procedure has a single formal parameter. The syntactic changes, for procedure declarations and procedure calls, are as follows:

Declaration	::=	...	
		| **proc** Identifier (Formal-Parameter) ~ Command	(7.35)
Formal-Parameter	::=	Identifier : Type-denoter	(7.36a)
		| **var** Identifier : Type-denoter	(7.36b)
Command	::=	...	
		| Identifier (Actual-Parameter)	(7.37)
Actual-Parameter	::=	Expression	(7.38a)
		| **var** V-name	(7.38b)

Production rules (7.36a) and (7.38a) are concerned with constant parameters; production rules (7.36b) and (7.38b) are concerned with variable parameters.

The code template for a procedure declaration is now:

$$elaborate \; [\![\mathbf{proc} \; I \; (\; FP \;) \; \sim C]\!] = \qquad\qquad (7.39)$$

```
        JUMP  g
  e:    execute C
        RETURN(0)  d        where d = size of formal parameter FP
  g:
```

Since the TAM protocol requires the *caller* to push the argument on to the stack, the routine body itself contains no code corresponding to the formal parameter *FP*.

The code template specifying translation of a procedure call to TAM code is now:

$$execute \; [\![I \; (\; AP \;)]\!] = \qquad\qquad (7.40)$$

```
        give-argument AP
        CALL(r)  e          where (l, e) = address of routine I,
                                  l' = current routine level,
                                  r = display-register(l', l)
```

The code templates for actual parameters are:

$$give\text{-}argument \ [\![E]\!] = \tag{7.41a}$$
$$evaluate \ E$$

$$give\text{-}argument \ [\![\mathbf{var} \ V]\!] = \tag{7.41b}$$
$$fetch\text{-}address \ V$$

Code template (7.41b) uses a new code function for value-or-variable-names:

$$fetch\text{-}address : \text{V-name} \rightarrow \text{Instruction*} \tag{7.42}$$

where '*fetch-address V*' is code that will push the address of the variable *V* on to the stack top.

The code templates for value-or-variable-names are generalized as follows:

$$fetch \ [\![I]\!] = \tag{7.43}$$

    (i) if *I* denotes a known value:

        LOADL *d*   where d = value of *I*

   (ii) if *I* denotes an unknown value or known address:

        LOAD (*s*) *d* [*r*]   where $s = size$(type of *I*),
                                         (l, d) = address of *I*,
                                         l' = current routine level,
                                         $r = display\text{-}register(l', l)$

  (iii) if *I* denotes an unknown address:

        LOAD (1) *d* [*r*]
        LOADI (*s*)   where $s = size$(type of *I*),
                                           (l, d) = address of *I*,
                                         l' = current routine level,
                                         $r = display\text{-}register(l', l)$

$$assign \ [\![I]\!] = \tag{7.44}$$

    (i) if *I* denotes a known address:

        STORE (*s*) *d* [*r*]   where $s = size$(type of *I*),
                                         (l, d) = address of *I*,
                                       l' = current routine level,
                                       $r = display\text{-}register(l', l)$

   (ii) if *I* denotes an unknown address:

        LOAD (1) *d* [*r*]
        STOREI (*s*)   where $s = size$(type of *I*),
                                         (l, d) = address of *I*,
                                       l' = current routine level,
                                       $r = display\text{-}register(l', l)$

$$fetch\text{-}address \ [\![I]\!] = \tag{7.45}$$

    (i) if *I* denotes a known address:

        LOADA *d* [*r*]   where (l, d) = address of *I*,
                                         l' = current routine level,
                                     $r = display\text{-}register(l', l)$

(ii) if *I* denotes an unknown address:

LOAD (1) *d*[*r*] where (*l, d*) = address of *I*,

l' = current routine level,

r = *display-register*(l', *l*)

□

7.5 Semantics and code generation

The translation of source programs to object code must be consistent with the semantic specification of the source language. The semantic specification allows us to predict the behavior of each source program, i.e., what effect the program should have when run. The source program must be translated to object code that has exactly that effect when run.

In Section 1.3.3 we briefly looked at action semantics, which is one method of formally specifying the semantics of a programming language. In action semantics each phrase has a meaning, or *denotation*, which is expressed in action notation. For each phrase class in the language there is a *semantic function*, which maps all phrases of that class to their denotations. Each semantic function is defined by a group of *semantic equations*, one for each form of phrase in the class.

The code specifications introduced in Section 7.1.1 can be viewed in a similar light. Each element of an action semantic specification has its counterpart in a code specification, as shown in Table 7.1. In particular, the code templates are the counterparts of the semantic equations.

Table 7.1 Code specifications and action semantics.

Code specification	*Action semantics*
target machine language	action notation
object code	denotation (usually an action)
code function	semantic function
code template	semantic equation

Example 7.24

Let us compare the action semantics of Mini-Δ, given in Example 1.8, with the Mini-Δ-to-TAM code specification of Example 7.2.

The Mini-Δ code functions and semantic functions are shown side by side in Table 7.2.

The code templates and semantic equations for Mini-Δ expressions are shown side by side in Table 7.3. The code templates and semantic equations for Mini-Δ commands are shown side by side in Table 7.4. To facilitate comparison, the while-command code template shown here is different from (7.10e). (See Exercise 7.1 for discussion.)   □

Table 7.2 Code functions and semantic functions for Mini-Δ.

Code function			Semantic function		
run	: Program	→ Instruction*	run _	:: Program	→ Action
execute	: Command	→ Instruction*	execute _	:: Command	→ Action
evaluate	: Expression	→ Instruction*	evaluate _	:: Expression	→ Action
apply-unary	: Operator	→ Instruction*	apply-unary _	:: Operator	→ Action
apply-binary	: Operator	→ Instruction*	apply-binary _	:: Operator	→ Action
fetch	: V-name	→ Instruction*	fetch _	:: V-name	→ Action
assign	: V-name	→ Instruction*	assign _	:: V-name	→ Action
elaborate	: Declaration	→ Instruction*	elaborate _	:: Declaration	→ Action

Table 7.3 Code templates and semantic equations for Mini-Δ expressions.

Code template	Semantic equation

evaluate $[\![IL]\!]$ =
     LOADL *d*
          where *d* = *valuation IL*
	evaluate $[\![IL]\!]$ =
	     give valuation *IL*

evaluate $[\![V]\!]$ =
     fetch V
	evaluate $[\![V]\!]$ =
	     fetch *V*

evaluate $[\![O\ E]\!]$ =
     evaluate E
     apply-unary O
	evaluate $[\![O\ E]\!]$ =
	     evaluate *E* then
	     apply-unary *O*

evaluate $[\![E_1\ O\ E_2]\!]$ =
     evaluate E_1
     evaluate E_2
 	
     apply-binary O
	evaluate $[\![E_1\ O\ E_2]\!]$ =
	     │ evaluate E_1 and
	     │ evaluate E_2
	     then
	     │ apply-binary *O*

Table 7.4 Code templates and semantic equations for Mini-Δ commands.

Code template	*Semantic equation*

execute $[\![V := E]\!]$ =
   evaluate E
   assign V
	execute $[\![V := E]\!]$ =
	   evaluate E then
	   assign V

execute $[\![I\ (\ E\ )]\!]$ =
   evaluate E
   CALL d[PB]
      where d = address of
      primitive routine I
      relative to PB
	execute $[\![I\ (\ E\ )]\!]$ =
	   evaluate E then
	   enact application of (the procedure bound to I)
	      to the given value

execute $[\![C_1\ ;\ C_2]\!]$ =
   execute C_1
   execute C_2
	execute $[\![C_1\ ;\ C_2]\!]$ =
	   execute C_1 and then
	   execute C_2

execute $[\![\mathbf{if}\ E\ \mathbf{then}\ C_1$
         $\mathbf{else}\ C_2]\!]$ =
   evaluate E
 	
   JUMPIF(0) g
   execute C_1
   JUMP h
 g:
 	
   execute C_2
 h:
	execute $[\![\mathbf{if}\ E\ \mathbf{then}\ C_1$
	         $\mathbf{else}\ C_2]\!]$ =
	 | evaluate E
	 then
	   | check (the given value is true) and then
	   | execute C_1
	
	   or
	   | check (the given value is false) and then
	   | execute C_2

execute $[\![\mathbf{while}\ E\ \mathbf{do}\ C]\!]$ =
 g:
   evaluate E
 	
   JUMPIF(0) h
   execute C
   JUMP g
 h:
	execute $[\![\mathbf{while}\ E\ \mathbf{do}\ C]\!]$ =
	 unfolding
	   | evaluate E
	   then
	     | check (the given value is true) and then
	     | execute C and then
	     | unfold
	   or
	     | check (the given value is false) and then
	     | complete

(continued)

Table 7.4 Code templates and semantic equations for Mini-Δ commands.
(continued)

Code template	Semantic equation
execute $[\![\mathtt{let}\ D\ \mathtt{in}\ C]\!]$ = 　　*elaborate D* 　　*execute C* 　　POP(0) *s* 　　　if *s* > 0 　　　where *s* = amount of 　　　　storage allocated by *D*	execute $[\![\mathtt{let}\ D\ \mathtt{in}\ C]\!]$ = 　│ rebind moreover elaborate *D* 　hence 　│ execute *C*

The structural similarity of the semantic specification and the code specification should be clear. The semantic functions and code functions are in one-to-one correspondence. The semantic equations and code templates are structurally similar. Each semantic equation specifies the semantics of a phrase of a particular form, in terms of the semantics of its subphrases. The corresponding code template specifies the translation of the same phrase into object code, in terms of the translation of its subphrases. Of course, there are differences in detail: the semantic equations are expressed in terms of action notation, whereas the code templates are expressed in terms of the target machine language.

The action semantics of the source language in effect specifies its translation into action notation. A code specification specifies a translation from the source language into the target machine language. In either case, the translation of a source-language phrase is composed from the translations of its subphrases.

We could even view a code specification as a kind of semantic specification. In principle, by studying the code specification we could learn the source language's semantics, as well as its implementation. But this is possible only if the target machine is already familiar. Even if it is a simple abstract machine, the details of its architecture and instruction set are likely to impede our understanding of the source language's semantics. For example, the semantics of a procedure call are rather obscured in code template (7.10b) by the details of the CALL instruction. If the target machine is a real machine, the machine details are likely be be quite overwhelming! In any case, our understanding of a high-level language such as Pascal or ML should not depend on our understanding of any machine, however abstract. So a code specification is unlikely to be a satisfactory means of specifying semantics.

The purpose of a programming language specification is to communicate a common understanding of the language among the language designer, implementors of language processors, and programmers. It should not contain implementation details, because such details are not of (direct) concern to the language designer nor to programmers. The language specification should, however, guide the implementor's work. We saw in Chapter 4 how the syntactic specification can be used systematically to develop a syntactic analyzer. Similarly, the semantic specification should be used as systematically as possible to guide development of the code generator.

To recapitulate, the implementor should:

(1) Develop a code specification, using the source language's semantic specification as a guide. (An informal specification is also a possible guide, though less reliable.) A specification of the target machine language is also necessary, of course.

(2) Use the code specification to develop a code generator, as shown in Section 7.2.2.

7.6 Case study: code generation in the Δ compiler

The Δ code generator is listed in Section E.6. It adopts methods similar to those described in this chapter, but with some extensions where necessary to deal with particular features of Δ. Here we briefly discuss some of the extensions.

7.6.1 Object descriptions

The Δ code generator deals with a wide variety of run-time objects and object descriptions, some of which we have not yet met. The different kinds of object description are as follows:

• *Known value.* This describes a value bound in a constant declaration whose right-hand side is a literal, e.g.:

```
const daysPerWeek ~ 7;
const currency    ~ '$'
```

• *Unknown value.* This describes a value bound in a constant declaration, if obtained by evaluating an expression at run-time, e.g.:

```
const area ~ length * breadth;
const nul  ~ chr(0)
```

It also describes an argument value bound to a constant parameter, e.g., to n in:

```
func odd (n: Integer) : Boolean ~ ...
```

(*Note:* In principle, `nul` in the above example could be treated as bound to a known value, since 'chr(0)' although not a literal could be evaluated at compile-time. The code generator would have to be enhanced to perform such compile-time evaluation, which is called *constant folding.*)

• *Known address.* This describes an address allocated and bound in a variable declaration. The code generator represents addresses by (level, displacement) pairs, as described in Section 7.3.3.

- *Unknown address*. This describes an argument address bound to a variable parameter, e.g., the argument address bound to n in:

```
proc inc (var n: Integer) ~ ...
```

- *Known routine*. This describes a routine bound in a procedure or function declaration, e.g., the routines bound to inc and odd in the above examples.

- *Unknown routine*. This describes an argument routine bound to a procedural or functional parameter, e.g., the argument routine bound to f in:

```
proc integrate (func f (x: Integer): Integer; ...) ~
    ...
```

- *Primitive routine*. This describes a primitive routine provided by the abstract machine. Primitive routines are bound in the standard environment to operators and identifiers, e.g., to '+', '<', eof, and get.

- *Equality routine*. This describes one of the primitive routines provided by the abstract machine for testing (in)equality of two values. Equality routines are generic, in that the values can be of any size. Equality routines are bound to the operators '=' and '\='.

- *Field*. This describes a field of a record type. Every record field has a known offset relative to the base of the record (see Section 6.1.2), and the field's object description includes this offset.

- *Type representation*. This describes a type. Every type has a known size, which is constant for all values of the type (see Section 6.1), and the type's object description includes that size.

7.6.2 Constants and variables

A value-or-variable-name in the Δ program identifies a constant or variable. Either a constant or a variable may be used as an expression operand, but only a variable may be used on the left-hand side of an assignment command. These two usages give rise to two different code functions on value-or-variable-names:

fetch : V-name → Instruction*
assign : V-name → Instruction*

In the little language Mini-Δ used as a running example in this chapter, a value-or-variable-name was just an identifier (declared in a constant or variable declaration). Accordingly, *fetch* was defined by a single code template (plus a special case), and *assign* by a single code template.

More realistic programming languages have composite types, and operations to select components of composite values and variables. In Δ, a record value-or-variable-name can be subjected to field selection, and an array value-or-variable-name can be indexed.

Example 7.25

Consider the following △ declarations:

```
type   Name        = array 15 of Char;
       TelNumber = array 10 of Char;
       Entry       = record
                         name: Name;
                         num:   TelNumber
                      end;
       Directory = record
                         count: Integer;
                         entry: array 100 of Entry
                      end
```

Now, if `dir` is a variable (or constant) of type `Directory`, the following are all value-or-variable-names (as well as `dir` itself):

```
dir.count
dir.entry
dir.entry[i]
dir.entry[i].num
dir.entry[i].name
dir.entry[i].name[j]
```

The code generator will compute the following type sizes:

size[Name]	$= 15 \times 1$	$= 15$ words
size[TelNumber]	$= 10 \times 1$	$= 10$ words
size[Entry]	$= 15 + 10$	$= 25$ words
size[array 100 of Entry]	$= 100 \times 25$	$= 2500$ words
size[Directory]	$= 2500 + 1$	$= 2501$ words

It will also compute the offsets of the fields of record type `Entry`:

offset of name	$= 0$ words
offset of num	$= 15$ words

and those of record type `Directory`:

offset of count	$= 0$ words
offset of entry	$= 1$ word

As in Section 6.1, we use the notation *address v* for the address of variable (or constant) *v*. For the various components of `dir` we find:

$$address[\texttt{dir.count}] = address[\texttt{dir}] + 0$$

$$address[\texttt{dir.entry}] = address[\texttt{dir}] + 1$$

$$address[\texttt{dir.entry[i]}] = address[\texttt{dir}] + 1 + 25i$$

$$address[\texttt{dir.entry[i].num}] = address[\texttt{dir}] + 1 + 25i + 15$$
$$= address[\texttt{dir}] + 16 + 25i$$

$$address[\texttt{dir.entry[i].name}] \quad = address[\texttt{dir}] + 1 + 25i + 0$$
$$= address[\texttt{dir}] + 1 + 25i$$

$$address[\texttt{dir.entry[i].name[j]}] = address[\texttt{dir}] + 1 + 25i + j$$
$$= address[\texttt{dir}] + 1 + (25i + j)$$

where i and j are the values of $\texttt{i}$ and $\texttt{j}$.

In each case the address formula contains some constant terms. These constant terms are accumulated by the code generator, simplifying the address formula to the sum of three terms: the address of the entire variable (or constant), plus a known offset, plus an unknown value. The known offset is obtained by adding together the offsets of any record fields. The unknown value is determined by evaluating array indices at run-time.

The following instruction sequences illustrate how the Δ code generator uses this information. Let us assume that $address[\texttt{dir}] = (0, 100)$:

fetch $[\texttt{dir.count}]$ {   LOAD(1)   100[SB]

fetch $[\texttt{dir.entry[i]}]$
$\begin{cases} \textit{evaluate } [\texttt{i}] \ \{ & \text{LOAD(1)} \quad \textit{i} \\ & \text{LOADL} \quad\ \ 25 \\ & \text{CALL} \quad\ \ \textit{mult} \\ & \text{LOADA} \quad 101[SB] \\ & \text{CALL} \quad\ \ \textit{add} \\ & \text{LOADI(25)} \end{cases}$

fetch $[\texttt{dir.entry[i].num}]$
$\begin{cases} \textit{evaluate } [\texttt{i}] \ \{ & \text{LOAD(1)} \quad \textit{i} \\ & \text{LOADL} \quad\ \ 25 \\ & \text{CALL} \quad\ \ \textit{mult} \\ & \text{LOADA} \quad 116[SB] \\ & \text{CALL} \quad\ \ \textit{add} \\ & \text{LOADI(10)} \end{cases}$

In each case, the known offset is added into the displacement part of $address[\texttt{dir}]$. Thus the address arithmetic implied by field selection can be done entirely at compile-time. Only indexing must be deferred until run-time.   □

7.7 Further reading

The target machine architecture strongly influences the structure of a code generator. But equally, there is every reason why the problems of code generation should influence the design of new machine architectures. Once upon a time, machines were designed by engineers with no knowledge of code generation. Such machines often had cunning features that could be exploited by skilled assembly language programmers, but were very difficult for code generators to exploit. But now nearly all programs – even operating systems – are written in high-level languages. So it makes more sense for the machine to support the code generator, for example, by providing a simple regular instruction set. A lucid discussion of the interaction between code generation and machine design may be found in Wirth (1986).

Almost all real machines have general-purpose and/or special-purpose registers; some have a stack as well. The number of registers is usually small and always limited. It is quite hard to generate object code that makes effective use of registers. Code generation for register machines is therefore beyond the scope of this introductory textbook. For a thorough treatment, see Chapter 9 of Aho *et al.* (1985).

The code generator described in this chapter works in the context of a multipass compiler: it traverses an AST that represents the entire source program. In the context of a one-pass compiler, on the other hand, the code generator would be structured rather differently: it would be a collection of procedures, which can be called by the syntactic analyzer to generate code 'on the fly' as the source program is parsed. For a clear account of how to organize code generation in a one-pass compiler, see Welsh and McKeag (1980).

The sheer diversity of machine architectures is a problem for implementors. A common practice among software vendors is to construct a family of compilers, translating a single source language to several different target machine languages. These compilers can have a common syntactic analyzer and contextual analyzer. But a distinct code generator might have to be written for each target machine, because a code generator suitable for one target machine might be difficult or impossible to adapt to a dissimilar target machine. *Code generation by pattern matching* is an attractive way to reduce the amount of work to be done. In this method the semantics of each machine instruction is expressed in terms of low-level operations. Each source-program command is translated to a combination of these low-level operations; code generation then consists of finding an instruction sequence that corresponds to the same combination of operations. A survey of code generation by pattern matching may be found in Ganapathi *et al.* (1982). See Graham (1984) for a detailed account of one particular way of implementing code generation by pattern matching.

Exercises 7

Exercises for Section 7.1

7.1   The Δ compiler uses the while-command code template (7.10e), but most compilers use the alternative code template of Table 7.4. Apply the code template of Table 7.4 to determine the object code of:

execute ⟦while n > 0 do n := n - 2⟧

Compare with Example 7.3. Convince yourself that the code template of Table 7.4 is semantically equivalent to (7.10e), but the object code is less efficient. Why, do you think, is this code template commonly used?

7.2*   Suppose that Mini-Δ is to be extended with the following commands:

(a) $V_1 , V_2 := E_1 , E_2$
(b) C_1 , C_2
(c) `if` E `then` C
(d) `repeat` C `until` E
(e) `repeat` C_1 `while` E `do` C_2

Command (a) is a simultaneous assignment: both E_1 and E_2 are to be evaluated, and then their values assigned to the variables V_1 and V_2, respectively. Command (b) is a collateral command: the subcommands C_1 and C_2 are to be executed in any order. Commands (c) and (d) are similar to Pascal's. Command (e) is a loop in which the continuation condition E is tested in the middle of each iteration, after executing C_1 but before executing C_2.

   Write code templates for all these commands.

7.3* Suppose that Mini-Δ is to be extended with the following expressions:
(a) `if` E_1 `then` E_2 `else` E_3
(b) `let` D `in` E
(c) `begin` C `;` `yield` E `end`

Expression (a) is a conditional expression, in which the alternatives E_2 and E_3 must be of the same type. Expression (b) is a block expression: the declaration D is local to the evaluation of the subexpression E. In expression (c), the command C is executed (possibly making side effects), and then the subexpression E is evaluated.

   Write code templates for all these expressions.

Exercises for Section 7.2

7.4* Extend the encoding procedure `encodeEvaluate` (Example 7.8) to implement the expressions of Exercise 7.3.

7.5* Extend the encoding procedure `encodeExecute` (Example 7.8) to implement the commands of Exercise 7.2. Use the method illustrated in Example 7.9 for generating jump instructions.

Exercises for Section 7.3

7.6 (a) Consider Pascal's constant, variable, and procedure declarations, and its value, variable, and procedural parameters. Classify them according to whether they bind identifiers to known or unknown values, variables, or procedures.
(b) Consider ML's value and function declarations, and its parameters. Classify them in the same way.

7.7* Suppose that Mini-Δ is to be extended with a for-command of the form 'for I `from` E_1 `to` E_2 `do` C', with the following semantics. First, the expressions E_1 and E_2 are evaluated, yielding the integers m and n, respectively. Then the subcommand C is executed repeatedly, with I bound to the integers $m, m+1, ..., n$ in successive iterations. If $m > n$, C is not executed at all. The scope of *I* is *C*, which may fetch *I* but may not assign to it.

(a) Write a code template for the for-command.

(b) Extend the encoding procedure `encodeExecute` (Example 7.13) to implement it.

7.8* Suppose that Mini-Δ is to be extended with array types, as found in Δ itself. The relevant extensions to the Mini-Δ grammar are:

> V-name   ::=   ...
> | V-name **[** Expression **]**
>
> Type-denoter   ::=   ...
> | **array** Integer-Literal **of** Type-denoter

(a) Modify the Mini-Δ code specification accordingly.

(b) Modify the Mini-Δ code generator accordingly.

Exercises for Section 7.4

7.9* Modify the Mini-Δ code generator to deal with parameterized procedures, using the code templates of Example 7.23.

7.10* A hypothetical programming language's function declaration has the form '`func` *I* (*FP*) : *T* ~ *C*', i.e., its body is a command. Within a function body, there may be one or more subcommands of the form '`result` *E*'. Such a command evaluates expression *E*, and stores its value in an anonymous variable associated with the function. On return from the function, the *latest* value stored in this way is returned as the function's result.

(a) Modify the Mini-Δ code specification as if Mini-Δ were extended with functions of this form.

(b) Modify the Mini-Δ code generator accordingly.

Exercise for Section 7.5

7.11 Example 7.24 compared the code templates for Mini-Δ commands and expressions with the corresponding semantic equations from Example 1.8. Extend this comparison to value-or-variable-names and declarations.

CHAPTER EIGHT

Interpretation

An interpreter for a given source language takes a source program, expressed in that language, and executes it immediately. Immediacy is the key characteristic of interpretation; there is no prior time-consuming translation of the source program.

In an interactive environment, immediacy is highly advantageous. For example, the user of a system command language (or database query language) expects an immediate answer to each command (or query); it would be unreasonable to expect the user to enter an entire sequence of commands (or queries) before seeing the response from the first one. In this mode of working, the 'program' is used once and thrown away.

The user of a programming language, on the other hand, is much more likely to retain the program for further use, and possibly further development. Even so, translation from the programming language to an intermediate language followed by interpretation of the intermediate language (i.e., interpretive compilation) is a good alternative to full compilation, especially during the early stages of program development.

In this chapter we study two kinds of interpretation:

* iterative interpretation
* recursive interpretation.

Iterative interpretation is suitable when the source language's instructions are all primitive. The instructions of the source program are fetched, analyzed, and executed one after another. Iterative interpretation is suitable for real and abstract machine codes, for some very simple programming languages, and for the simpler system command languages.

Recursive interpretation is necessary if the source language has composite instructions. (In this context, 'instructions' could be commands, expressions, and declarations.) Interpretation of one instruction may trigger interpretation of its component instructions. For most high-level programming languages, interpretation would have to be recursive. The greater complexity of this scheme is one reason why compilation (or at least translation to a lower-level intermediate language) is preferable for most high-level languages.

8.1 Iterative interpretation

Conventional interpreters are iterative: they work in a fetch–analyze–execute cycle. This is captured by the following *iterative interpretation scheme*:

```
begin
    initialize;
repeat
    fetch the next instruction;
    analyze this instruction;
    execute this instruction
until  execution is terminated
end
```

Each instruction is fetched from storage, or in some cases entered directly by the user. The instruction is then analyzed into its component parts, and executed. Generally the source language has several forms of instruction, so execution of an instruction decomposes into several cases, one case for each form of instruction.

In the following subsections we apply this scheme to the interpretation of machine code, of simple high-level languages, and of simple system command languages.

8.1.1 Iterative interpretation of machine code

A machine-code instruction is essentially a packed record, consisting of an operation field (usually called the *op-code*) and some other fields. Instruction analysis (or *decoding*) consists of unpacking these fields, and is therefore simple and fast. Instruction execution is controlled by the op-code.

It is worth recalling here that a real machine *M* is functionally equivalent to an interpreter (or *emulator*) for *M*'s machine code. The only difference is that the real machine uses electronic (and perhaps parallel) hardware to fetch, decode, and execute instructions, and is therefore much faster than the emulator. (Refer back to Section 2.3 for a fuller discussion of this point.)

To implement an emulator, we employ the following simple techniques:

- We represent the machine's storage by a global array. If storage is partitioned, for example into separate stores for code and data, then we can represent each store by a separate global array.

- We implement the machine's registers by global variables. This applies equally to the visible and hidden registers (i.e., those that can be accessed directly by the assembly-language programmer, and those that cannot). One register, the *code pointer*, will contain the address of the next instruction to be executed. Another, the *status register*, will be used to control program termination.

- Fetching an instruction is straightforward.

- To analyze an instruction, we isolate its op-code and other fields.

- To execute an instruction, we use a case-command, with one case for each possible value of the op-code. In each case we obtain the instruction's intended effect by updating storage and/or registers.

Table 8.1 Instruction set of the hypothetical machine HYP.

Op-code	Instruction	Meaning
0	STORE *d*	word at address *d* ← acc
1	LOAD *d*	acc ← word at address *d*
2	LOADL *d*	acc ← *d*
3	ADD *d*	acc ← acc + word at address *d*
4	SUB *d*	acc ← acc − word at address *d*
5	JUMP *d*	CP ← *d*
6	JUMPZ *d*	CP ← *d*, if acc = 0
7	HALT	stop execution

Example 8.1

Consider the hypothetical machine, *HYP*, summarized in Table 8.1.

HYP has a 4096-word code store that contains the instructions of the program. The first instruction to be executed must be located at address 0. An instruction consists of a 4-bit operation field *op* and a 12-bit operand field *d*. Details of the instructions are given in Table 8.1. The code pointer, CP, contains the address of the next instruction to be executed.

HYP also has a 4096-word data store and a 1-word accumulator, *acc*. Each word consists of 16 bits. Data may be placed anywhere in the data store.

Figure 8.1 illustrates the HYP code store and data store. It shows a program occupying the first 14 words of code store. (This particular program finds two integers at addresses 0 and 1, and leaves their product at address 2. For greater readability, the program is also shown with mnemonic op-codes.)

Figure 8.2 illustrates how the machine's state – data store, accumulator, and code pointer – would change during the first few execution steps of the stored program.

We now present an interpreter for HYP. Instructions are represented as follows:

```
const
        STOREop = 0;    LOADop  = 0;
        LOADLop = 2;    ADDop   = 3;
        SUBop   = 4;    JUMPop  = 5;
        JUMPZop = 6;    HALTop  = 7;

type  Address = 0..4095;
      OpCode  = 0..15;
```

The code store is represented by a global array of instructions:

```
type  Instruction =
          packed record op: OpCode; d: Address end;

var   code: array [Address] of Instruction;

procedure loadProgram;
      ...     {Load the program into code store, starting at address 0.}
```

The data store is represented by a global array of 16-bit words:

```
type  Word = -32768..+32767;

var   data: array [Address] of Word
```

The various registers are represented by global variables:

```
var   status: (running, halted, failed);
      CP:      Address;       {address of next instruction}
      instr:   Instruction;   {next instruction to be executed}
      op:      OpCode;        {operation field of next instruction}
      d:       Address;       {operand field of next instruction}
      acc:     Word
```

The interpreter's control structure is a case-command within a loop, preceded by loading of the program and initialization of the registers:

```
begin
{initialize ...}
loadProgram;
status := running;
CP := 0;

repeat

    {fetch the next instruction ...}
    instr := code[CP];
    CP := CP + 1;

    {analyze this instruction ...}
    op := instr.op;
    d  := instr.d;

    {execute this instruction ...}
    case op of

        STOREop:
            data[d] := acc;

        LOADop:
            acc := data[d];

        LOADLop:
            acc := d;
```

```
ADDop:
    acc := acc + data[d];

SUBop:
    acc := acc - data[d];

JUMPop:
    CP := d;

JUMPZop:
    if acc = 0 then CP := d;

HALTop:
    status := halted

end{case}

until status <> running    {... execution is terminated}
end
```

This interpreter has been kept as simple as possible, for the sake of clarity. But it will behave unpredictably if it fetches an instruction with an invalid op-code, or if an ADD or SUB instruction overflows. A more robust version would set status to failed if any such condition arose. (See Exercise 8.1.) □

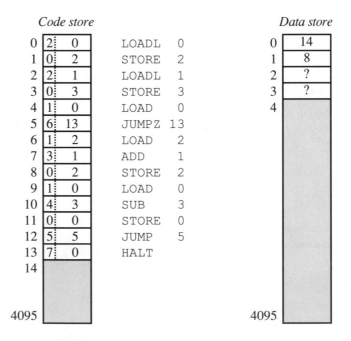

	Code store				*Data store*	
0	2	0	LOADL	0	0	14
1	0	2	STORE	2	1	8
2	2	1	LOADL	1	2	?
3	0	3	STORE	3	3	?
4	1	0	LOAD	0	4	
5	6	13	JUMPZ	13		
6	1	2	LOAD	2		
7	3	1	ADD	1		
8	0	2	STORE	2		
9	1	0	LOAD	0		
10	4	3	SUB	3		
11	0	0	STORE	0		
12	5	5	JUMP	5		
13	7	0	HALT			
14						
4095					4095	

Figure 8.1 HYP: code store and data store.

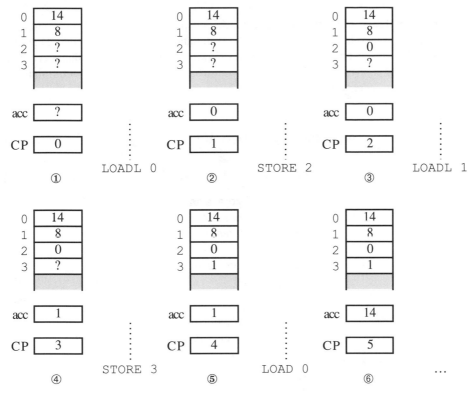

Figure 8.2 HYP: state changes.

When we write an interpreter like that of Example 8.1, it makes no difference whether we are interpreting a real machine code or an abstract machine code. For an abstract machine code, the interpreter will be the only implementation. For a real machine code, a hardware interpreter (processor) will be available as well as a software interpreter (emulator). Of these, the processor will be much the faster. But an emulator is much more flexible than a processor: it can be adapted cheaply for a variety of purposes. An emulator can be used for experimentation before the processor is ever constructed. An emulator can also easily be extended for diagnostic purposes. (Exercises 8.2 and 8.3 suggest some of the possibilities.) So, even when a processor is available, an emulator for the same machine code complements it nicely.

8.1.2 Iterative interpretation of simple high-level languages

Iterative interpretation is possible also for certain high-level languages, provided that the source program is essentially a sequence of primitive commands. The source language must not include any composite commands, i.e., commands that contain subcommands.

In the iterative interpretation scheme, the 'instructions' are taken to be the commands of the source language. Analysis of a command consists of syntactic and perhaps contextual analysis. This makes analysis far slower and more complex than decoding a machine-code instruction. Execution is controlled by the form of command, as determined by its analysis.

Example 8.2

Consider a simple programming language, *Mini-Basic*, with the following syntax (expressed in EBNF):

Program	::=	Command*	(8.1)
Command	::=	Variable = Expression	(8.2a)
	|	**read** Variable	(8.2b)
	|	**write** Variable	(8.2c)
	|	**go** Label	(8.2d)
	|	**if** Expression Relational-Op Expression	(8.2e)
	|	**go** Label	(8.2f)
	|	**stop**	(8.2g)
Expression	::=	primary-Expression	(8.3a)
	|	Expression Arithmetic-Op primary-Expression	(8.3b)
primary-Expression	::=		
		Numeral	(8.4a)
	|	Variable	(8.4b)
	|	(Expression)	(8.4c)
Arithmetic-Op	::=	+ | – | * | /	(8.5a–d)
Relational-Op	::=	= | ≠ | < | ≤ | ≥ | >	(8.6a–f)
Variable	::=	**a** | **b** | **c** | ... | **z**	(8.7a–z)

A Mini-Basic program is just a sequence of commands. The commands are implicitly labeled 0, 1, 2, etc., and these labels may be referenced in **go** and **if** commands. The program may use up to twenty-six variables, which are predeclared.

The semantics of Mini-Basic programs should be intuitively clear. All values are real numbers. The program shown in Figure 8.3 reads a number (into variable a), computes its square root to two decimal places of accuracy (in variable b), and writes the square root.

It is easy to imagine a *Mini-Basic abstract machine*. The Mini-Basic program is loaded into a code store, with successive commands at addresses 0, 1, 2, etc. The code pointer, CP, contains the address of the command due to be executed next.

The program's data are held in a data store of 26 cells, one cell for each variable. Figure 8.3 illustrates the code store and data store. Figure 8.4 shows how the abstract machine's state – data store and code pointer – would change during the first few execution steps of the square-root program, assuming that the number read is 10.0.

We represent the data store by an array indexed by variables:

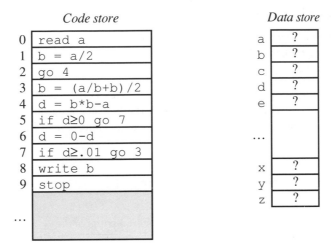

Code store

0	read a
1	b = a/2
2	go 4
3	b = (a/b+b)/2
4	d = b*b-a
5	if d≥0 go 7
6	d = 0-d
7	if d≥.01 go 3
8	write b
9	stop

Data store

a	?
b	?
c	?
d	?
e	?
...	
x	?
y	?
z	?

Figure 8.3 Mini-Basic abstract machine: code store and data store.

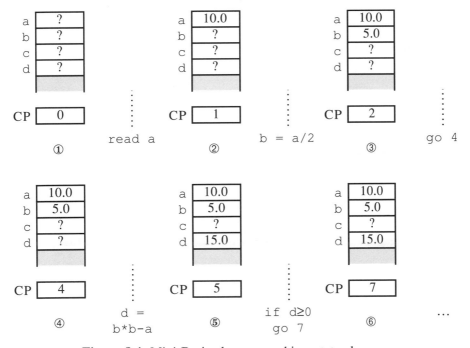

Figure 8.4 Mini-Basic abstract machine: state changes.

```
type Variable = 'a'..'z';
var  data: array [Variable] of Real
```

We must decide how to represent each command in storage. The choices are:

- as source text (exactly as shown in Figure 8.3)
- as a sequence of tokens
- as an AST

The first choice implies scanning and parsing of every command fetched during interpretation: a large overhead. The third choice implies scanning and parsing of every
command as it is loaded into storage. As a reasonable compromise, we adopt the second
choice:

```
type Token = ...;
     StoredCommand = array [1..12] of Token
```

(See also Exercise 8.5.)

We represent the code store by an array of stored commands:

```
type CodeAddress = 0..maxCodeAddress;

var  code: array [CodeAddress] of StoredCommand
```

Analysis of a command should transform it from a token sequence into a form
more convenient for execution. For Mini-Basic, parsing will suffice for this purpose.
All variables are predeclared, so there is no need to check for undeclared variables; and
there is only one data type, so there is no need for type checking.

```
type Expression = ...;
     CommandKind =
         (VeqE, readV, writeV, goL, ifEREgoL, stop);
     Command =
       record
         case kind: CommandKind of
           VeqE:
               ( lhs: Variable;
                 rhs: Expression );
           readV, writeV:
               ( ioVar: Variable );
           goL:
               ( destination: CodeAddress );
           ifEREgoL:
               ( relop: Token;
                 expr1, expr2: Expression;
                 ifDestination: CodeAddress );
           stop:
               ( )
       end;

procedure analyze (storedCom: StoredCommand;
                   var com: Command);
   ...     {Analyze the given stored command.}
```

As usual, we represent registers by global variables:

```
var   status:    (running, halted, failed);
      CP:         CodeAddress;
      storedCom: StoredCommand;
      com:        Command
```

We will use the following auxiliary functions (for details see Exercise 8.6):

```
function evaluate (expr: Expression) : Real;
    ...;
function compare (relop: Token; num1, num2: Real)
            : Boolean;

    ...
```

Now we are ready to present the interpreter proper. We assume that the source program has already been stored (by a separate loader), and perhaps edited. The interpreter just fetches, analyzes, and executes the commands, one after another:

```
begin
{initialize ...}
status := running;
CP := 0;

repeat

    {fetch the next instruction ...}
    storedCom := code[CP];
    CP := CP + 1;

    {analyze this instruction ...}
    analyze(storedCom, com);

    {execute this instruction ...}
    case com.kind of

        VeqE:
            data[com.lhs] := evaluate(com.rhs);

        readV:
            readln(data[com.ioVar]);

        writeV:
            writeln(data[com.ioVar]);

        goL:
            CP := com.destination;

        ifEREgoL:
            if compare(com.relop,
                    evaluate(com.expr1),
                    evaluate(com.expr2)) then
                CP := com.ifDestination;
```

```
        stop:
            status := halted

        end{case}

until status <> running    {... execution is terminated}
end
```

□

8.1.3 Iterative interpretation of command languages

System command languages (such as the Unix *shell* language) are relatively simple languages. In normal usage, the user enters a sequence of commands, and expects an immediate response to each command. Each command will be executed just once. These factors suggest interpretation of each command as soon as it is entered. In fact, command languages are specifically designed to be interpreted. Below we illustrate interpretation of a simple command language.

Example 8.3

Consider a simple system command language, *Mini-Shell*, that allows us to enter commands such as:

```
delete f1 f2 f3
create f3 1000
listfiles
edit f3
sort f3
quit
```

The above is an example of a *script*, which is just a sequence of commands. Each command is to be executed as soon as it is entered.

Mini-Shell provides several built-in commands. In addition, any executable program (such as `sort`) can be run simply by giving the name of the file containing it. A command can be passed at most eight arguments, which may be file-names or literals.

The syntax of a script is as follows:

Script	::=	Command*	(8.8)
Command	::=	Command-Name Argument* end-of-line	(8.9)
Argument	::=	File-Name	(8.10a)
	|	Literal	(8.10b)
Command-Name	::=	**create**	(8.11a)
	|	**delete**	(8.11b)
	|	**edit**	(8.11c)
	|	**listfiles**	(8.11d)
	|	**quit**	(8.11e)
	|	File-Name	(8.11f)

Production rules for File-Name and Literal have been omitted here.

In the Mini-Shell interpreter, we can represent commands as follows:

```
type Token = packed array [1..10] of Char;
     TokenSequence = array [1..8] of Token;
     Command =
          record
               name: Token;
               args: TokenSequence
          end
```

Note that each command is to be executed only once, as soon as it is entered. Thus there is no need to store the complete script.

It will be convenient to combine fetching and analysis of commands:

```
procedure fetchAndAnalyze (var com: Command);
     ...        {Read and analyze the next command.}
```

The commands operate on the file store. We shall encapsulate these operations in the following procedures, hiding the details of the file store itself:

```
procedure create (fname, size: Token);
     ...;      {Create a file with the given name and size.}

procedure delete (fnames: TokenSequence);
     ...;      {Delete the named files.}

procedure edit (fname: Token);
     ...;      {Edit the named file.}

procedure listFiles;
     ...;      {List names of all files owned by the current user.}

procedure run (name: Token;
                args: TokenSequence);
     ...;      {Execute the machine-code program contained in the named file,
               with the given arguments.}
```

We represent the 'registers' as usual by global variables:

```
var   status: (running, halted, failed);
      com:    Command
```

The interpreter just fetches, analyzes, and executes the commands, one after another:

```
begin
{initialize ...}
status := running;

repeat
     {fetch and analyze the next instruction ...}
     fetchAndAnalyze(com);
```

```
{execute this instruction ...}
if com.name = 'create   ' then
    create(com.args[1], com.args[2])

else if com.name = 'delete   ' then
    delete(com.args)

else if com.name = 'edit     ' then
    edit(com.args[1])

else if com.name = 'listfiles ' then
    listFiles

else if com.name = 'quit     ' then
    status := halted

else   {executable program}
    run(com.name, com.args)
until status <> running    {... execution is terminated}
end
```

☐

Similar observations can be made about database query languages and the like. The user enters a query, and expects an immediate response. The query will be evaluated just once. However, queries tend to be more complex than system commands, so we shall not explore this territory here.

8.2   Recursive interpretation

Modern programming languages are higher-level than the simple language of Example 8.2. In particular, commands may be composite, i.e., they may contain subcommands. A higher-level programming language is usually implemented by compilation, or by translation to a low-level intermediate language.

Nevertheless, even a higher-level programming language can be interpreted. The iterative interpretation scheme is inadequate for such a language. Instead, we need a *recursive interpretation scheme*, whereby execution of a composite command may trigger execution of its subcommand(s).

To be more concrete, consider an imperative language in which a program is a composite command C. This contains subcommands, which in turn contain sub-subcommands, and so on. The program would be interpreted as follows:

```
begin
fetch and analyze C;
execute C
end
```

where '*execute C*' recursively executes *C*'s subcommands. If *C* is supplied in source form, '*fetch and analyze C*' must perform syntactic and contextual analysis of *C*, which entails syntactic and contextual analysis of *C*'s subcommands. Thus '*execute C*' will operate on a parsed and checked representation of *C*. In other words, we are driven inexorably to a two-stage process, whereby the entire source program is analyzed before interpretation proper can begin. A suitable representation for the analyzed program is an AST.

Example 8.4

Consider a recursive interpreter for the programming language Mini-Δ of Examples 1.3 and 1.8. Assume that the analyzed program is to be represented by a decorated AST. The source program will be subjected to syntactic and contextual analysis, and also storage allocation, before execution commences.

We must choose a representation of Mini-Δ values. These include not only truth values and integers, but also *undefined* (which is a possible content of a variable). We can represent each value by a variant record:

```
type ValueType = (bool, int, undefined);
     Value     = record
                    case typ: ValueType of
                        bool: ( b: Boolean );
                        int:  ( i: Integer );
                        undefined: ( )
                 end
```

We represent the data store, as usual, by a global array:

```
type DataAddress = 0..maxAddress;

var  data: array [DataAddress] of Value
```

The 'code store' is just the decorated AST representing the source program:

```
var  program: AST
```

We shall use the definition of type AST given in Example 4.7.

We shall use the following auxiliary function and procedure:

```
function valuation (intLit: TokenString) : Integer;
   ...;      {Return the value of integer-literal intLit.}

procedure callStandardProc (id: AST; arg: Value);
   ...        {Call the standard procedure with identifier id, passing arg
              as its argument.}
```

The interpreter will consist of the following mutually recursive *interpreting procedures*, each of which interprets a particular class of ASTs:

```
procedure run (program: AST);
   ...;      {Run program.}
```

```
procedure execute (command: AST);
   ...;       {Execute command.}

procedure evaluate (expression: AST;
                        var val: Value);
   ...;       {Evaluate expression, yielding val.}

procedure applyUnary (operator: AST;
                        val1: Value;
                        var val: Value);
   ...;       {Apply operator to val1, yielding val.}

procedure applyBinary (operator: TokenString;
                        val1, val2: Value;
                        var val: Value);
   ...;       {Apply operator to val1 and val2, yielding val.}

procedure fetch (vname: AST; var val: Value);
   ...;       {Fetch the value of the constant/variable vname into val.}

procedure assign (vname: AST; val: Value);
   ...;       {Assign val to the variable vname.}

procedure elaborate (declaration: AST);
   ...        {Elaborate declaration.}
```

These interpreting procedures are written as follows:

```
procedure execute (command: AST);
   label 1;  var val: Value;
   begin
   with command^ do
     case tag of

         VbecomesE:
            begin
            evaluate(child[2], val);
            assign(child[1], val)
            end;

         IlpErp:
            begin
            evaluate(child[2], val);
            callStandardProc(child[1], val)
            end;

         CsemicolonC:
            begin
            execute(child[1]);
            execute(child[2])
            end;
```

```
      ifEthenCelseC:
        begin
        evaluate(child[1], val);
        if val.b then      {... val is assumed to be bool}
            execute(child[2])
        else
            execute(child[3])
        end;

      whileEdoC:
        begin
        1:
        evaluate(child[1], val);
        if val.b then      {... val is assumed to be bool}
            begin
            execute(child[2]); goto 1
            end   {else do nothing}
        end;

      letDinC:
        begin
        elaborate(child[1]);
        execute(child[2])
        end

      end{case}
  end{execute};

procedure evaluate (expression: AST;
                    var val: Value);
  var val1, val2: Value;
  begin
  with expression^ do
    case tag of

      IL:
        begin
        val.typ := int;
        val.i := valuation(spelling)
        end;

      V:
          fetch(child[1], val);

      OE:
        begin
        evaluate(child[2], val2);
        applyUnary(child[1], val2, val)
        end;
```

```
            EOE:
                begin
                evaluate(child[1], val1);
                evaluate(child[3], val2);
                applyBinary(child[2], val1, val2, val)
                end

            end{case}
    end{evaluate};

procedure fetch (vname: AST; var val: Value);
    begin
    with vname^ do
        case tag of

            I:
                with binding^.obj^ do
                    {... object description bound to var/const I}
                    val := data[address]

            end{case}
    end{fetch};

procedure assign (vname: AST; val: Value);
    begin
    with vname^ do
        case tag of

            I:
                with binding^.obj^ do
                    {... object description bound to variable I}
                    data[address] := val

            end{case}
    end{assign};

procedure elaborate (declaration: AST);
    begin
    with declaration^ do
        case tag of

            constIisE:
                with obj^ do
                    evaluate(child[2], data[address]);

            varIcolonT:
                with obj^ do
                    data[address].typ := undefined;

            DsemicolonD:
                begin
```

```
        elaborate(child[1]);
        elaborate(child[2])
    end

  end{case}
end{elaborate}
```

To run a program, we simply execute it as a command:

```
procedure run (program: AST);
  begin
    execute(program)
  end{run}
```

Assuming appropriate procedures for parsing and checking the source program, the interpreter's top level would look like this:

```
begin
parseProgram(program);
checkProgram(program);
run(program)
end
```

□

The kind of interpreter we have just illustrated analyzes the entire source program before execution commences. Thus it foregoes one of the usual advantages of interpretation, that is immediacy. This, together with the complexity of the method, explains why recursive interpretation is not generally popular. A better alternative is compilation of source programs to a simple intermediate language, followed by (iterative) interpretation of the intermediate language, as outlined in Section 2.4.

8.3   Semantics and interpretation

The interpretation of a source program must respect the source language's semantic specification. The semantic specification allows us to predict the source program's behavior, i.e., what effect the program should have when run with given input data. Interpretation of the source program must produce exactly the same effect.

An example of a semantic specification was given in Example 1.8. Although a semantic specification's main purpose is to convey a precise understanding of the specified language's semantics, it may also be viewed as a kind of interpreter: it suggests how to execute each command, how to evaluate each expression, and so on. The following example illustrates this point by comparing an interpreter with a semantic specification of the same language.

Example 8.5

Parts of the Mini-Δ interpreter of Example 8.4 are reproduced below. The corresponding semantic equations from the Mini-Δ action semantics of Example 1.8 are reproduced alongside, in the form of comments.

First, here is the interpreting procedure for commands, together with semantic equations (1.30a–f) defining semantic function 'execute':

```
procedure execute (command: AST);
    label 1;
    var val: Value;
    begin
    with command^ do
      case tag of

        VbecomesE:                      { execute [[V := E]] =         }
            begin
            evaluate(child[2], val);    { evaluate E then              }
            assign(child[1], val)       { assign V                     }
            end;

        IlpErp:                         { execute [[I ( E )]] =        }
            begin
            evaluate(child[2], val);    { evaluate E then              }
            callStandardProc(child[1],  { enact application of (the    }
                 val)                   {    procedure bound to I)     }
                                        {    to the given value        }
            end;

        CsemicolonC:                    { execute [[C₁ ; C₂]] =        }
            begin
            execute(child[1]);          { execute C₁ and then          }
            execute(child[2])           { execute C₂                   }
            end;

        ifEthenCelseC:                  { execute [[if E then C₁       }
            begin                       {          else C₂]] =         }
            evaluate(child[1], val);    {    evaluate E                }
                                        { then                         }
            if val.b then               {    check (the given         }
                                        {       value is true)         }
                                        {    and then                  }
                execute(child[2])       {       execute C₁             }
            else                        {    or                        }
                                        {       check (the given       }
                                        {          value is false)     }
                                        {       and then               }
                execute(child[3])       {       execute C₂             }
            end;
```

```
whileEdoC:                    { execute ⟦while E        }
   begin                      {          do C⟧ =        }
   1:                         { unfolding               }
   evaluate(child[1], val);   {      evaluate E         }
                              {      then              }
   if val.b then              {        check (the given }
                              {           value is true) }
      begin                   {        and then         }
      execute(child[2]);      {        execute C        }
                              {        and then         }
      goto 1                  {        unfold           }
      end                     {                         }
   {else}                     {      or                 }
                              {        check (the given }
                              {           value is false) }
                              {        and then         }
      {do nothing}            {        complete         }
   end;

letDinC:                      { execute ⟦let D in C⟧ =  }
   begin
                              {    rebind moreover      }
   elaborate(child[1]);       {    elaborate D          }
                              { hence                   }
   execute(child[2])          {    execute C            }
   end

   end{case}
end{execute}
```

Now, here is the interpreting procedure for expressions, together with semantic equations (1.31a–d) defining semantic function 'evaluate':

```
procedure evaluate (expression: AST; var val: Value);
   var val1, val2: Value;
   begin
   with expression^ do
      case tag of
         IL:                        { evaluate ⟦IL⟧ =          }
            begin
            val.typ := int;
            val.i :=                { give valuation IL         }
                  valuation(spelling)
            end;

         V:                         { evaluate ⟦V⟧ =           }
            fetch(child[1], val);   { fetch V                  }
```

```
     OE:                              { evaluate [[O E]] =          }
        begin
        evaluate(child[2], val2);    { evaluate E then           }
        applyUnary(child[1],         { apply-unary O             }
             val2, val)
        end;

     EOE:                             { evaluate [[E₁ O E₂]] =      }
        begin
        evaluate(child[1], val1);    {   evaluate E₁ and        }
        evaluate(child[3], val2);    {   evaluate E₂            }
                                     { then                      }
        applyBinary(child[2],        {   apply-binary O          }
             val1, val2, val)
        end
     end{case}
  end{evaluate}
```

(See also Exercise 8.10.)   ☐

It should be clear that the Mini-Δ interpreter and the Mini-Δ action semantics are structurally similar:

- The action semantics is structured as a semantic function for each phrase class. The interpreter is structured as an interpreting procedure for each phrase class.
- Each semantic function is defined by several semantic equations. Each interpreting procedure's body consist of several cases.
- Each semantic equation tells us how to execute a particular form of command, how to evaluate a particular form of expression, or whatever, and is expressed in action notation. Each case in an interpreting procedure does likewise, but is expressed in an implementation language such as Pascal.

8.4 Case study: the TAM interpreter

The abstract machine TAM was outlined in Section 6.7, and is fully described in Appendix C. It is the target machine of the Δ compiler.

TAM is implemented by an interpreter, which is listed in Appendix D. The TAM interpreter is in most respects similar to other machine-code interpreters, such as that of Example 8.1. But of course it is more sophisticated, since TAM directly supports many features of high-level languages.

TAM instructions (Figure C.5) are represented by packed records, as shown in Example 7.7:

```
     type OpCode = ...;  ...;  Operand = ...;
```

```
Instruction =
      packed record
            op:  OpCode;
            n:   Length;
            r:   RegisterNumber;
            d:   Operand
      end
```

The registers are represented by global variables – except that registers whose contents are fixed are represented by constants:

```
const
      CB = 0;   ...;
      SB = 0;   HB = 0;

var   CP:          CodeAddress;
      ST, HT, LB: DataAddress;
      status:      (running, halted, ...);
      instr:       Instruction
```

The code store and data store are represented by global arrays:

```
var   code: array [CodeAddress] of Instruction;
      data: array [DataAddress] of Word
```

The interpreter proper is a case-command within a loop, preceded by initialization. There is one case for each of the fifteen operation codes:

```
begin
{ initialize ...}
loadProgram;
status := running;
CP := CB;
ST := SB; HT := HB;

repeat

      {fetch the next instruction ...}
      instr := code[CP];
      CP := CP + 1;

      {analyze this instruction ...}
      op := instr.op;  n := instr.n;
      r := instr.r;    d := instr.d;

      {execute this instruction ...}
      case op of

      LOADop:       ...;

      LOADAop:      ...;

      LOADIop:      ...;
```

```
       LOADLop:      ...;

       STOREop:      ...;

       STOREIop:     ...;

       CALLop:       ...;

       CALLIop:      ...;

       RETURNop:     ...;

       PUSHop:       ...;

       POPop:        ...;

       JUMPop:       ...;

       JUMPIop:      ...;

       JUMPIFop:     ...;

       HALTop:       status := halted

    end{case}
```

until status <> running   {... *execution is terminated*}
end

The fact that TAM is a stack machine gives rise to many differences in detail from an interpreter for a register machine. A LOAD, LOADL, LOADA, or LOADI instruction pushes a value or address on to the stack (rather than loading it into a register). A STORE or STOREI instruction stores a value popped off the stack (rather than storing it from a register). For example, LOADL is interpreted as follows:

```
LOADLop:
    begin
    data[ST] := d;
    ST := ST + 1
    end
```

(Register ST points to the word immediately *above* the stack top.)

Further differences arise from the special design features of TAM, which were outlined in Section 6.7.

Addressing and registers

The operand of a LOAD, LOADA, or STORE instruction is of the form '$d[r]$', where r is usually a display register, and d is a constant displacement. The displacement d is added to the current content of register r.

The display registers allow addressing of global variables (using SB), local variables (using LB), and nonlocal variables (using L1, L2, ...). The latter registers are related to LB by the invariants L1 = *content*(LB), L2 = *content*(*content*(LB)), and so on.

As explained in Section 6.7, it is not really worthwhile to have separate registers for access to nonlocal variables. The cost of updating them (on every routine call and return) outweighs the benefit of having them immediately available to compute the addresses of nonlocal variables. In the TAM interpreter, therefore, L1, L2, ... are only *pseudo-registers*: they have no separate existence, and their values are computed only when needed, using the above invariants. This is captured by the following function in the interpreter:

```
function relative (d: Operand; r: RegisterNumber)
                : Word;
    {Return the address defined by displacement d relative to register r.}
    begin
    case r of
        ...;
        SBr:  relative := d + SB;
        LBr:  relative := d + LB;
        L1r:  relative := d + data[LB];
        L2r:  relative := d + data[data[LB]];
        ...
        end{case}
    end{relative}
```

For example, simplified forms of LOAD and STORE would be interpreted as follows:

```
LOADop:
    begin
    data[ST] := data[relative(d, r)];
    ST := ST + 1
    end

STOREop:
    begin
    ST := ST - 1;
    data[relative(d, r)] := data[ST]
    end
```

The operand of a CALL, JUMP, or JUMPIF instruction is also of the form '*d*[*r*]', where *r* is generally CB or PB, and *d* is a constant displacement. As usual, the displacement *d* is added to the content of register *r*. The function relative also handles these cases.

Primitive routines

Each primitive routine (such as *add*, *mult*, *lt*, or *not*) has a designated address within the code store's primitives segment, which is delimited by registers PB and PT. (See Figure C.1.) Thus the interpreter traps any call to an address within the primitives segment:

```
CALLop:
    begin
    addr := relative(d, r);
```

```
if addr >= PB then
        call the primitive routine at address addr
else
        call the code routine at address addr
end
```

Then the interpreter performs the appropriate primitive operation directly. For example, *mult* is interpreted as follows:

```
begin
ST := ST - 1;
data[ST-1] := data[ST-1] * data[ST]
end
```

thus replacing two integers at the stack top by their product.

8.5   Further reading

Basic is one of the few 'high-level' programming languages for which interpretation is the norm. A typical Basic programming system allows programs to be entered, edited, and executed incrementally. Such a system can run in a microcomputer with very limited storage, which probably explains its popularity. But this is possible only because the language is very primitive indeed. Its control structures are more typical of a low-level language, making it unattractive for serious programmers. More recently, 'structured' dialects of Basic have become more popular, and compilation has become an alternative to interpretation.

Recursive interpretation as described in Section 8.2 is less common. However, this form of interpretation has long been associated with Lisp (McCarthy *et al.* 1965). A Lisp program is not just represented by a tree: it *is* a tree! Several features of the language – dynamic binding, dynamic typing, and the possibility of manufacturing extra program code at run-time – make interpretation of Lisp much more suitable than compilation. A description of a Lisp interpreter may be found in McCarthy *et al.* (1965). Lisp has always had a devoted band of followers, but not all are prepared to tolerate slow execution. A recent successful dialect, Scheme (Rees and Clinger 1986), has discarded Lisp's problematic features in order to make compilation feasible.

It is noteworthy that two popular programming languages, Basic and Lisp, both suitable for interpretation but otherwise utterly different, have evolved along somewhat parallel lines, spawning structured dialects suitable for compilation!

The similarity of an action-semantic specification to an interpreter can be exploited to build a prototype implementation of a programming language directly from its specification. For details see Section 8.4 of the companion textbook by Watt (1991).

Exercises 8

8.1   Make the HYP interpreter of Example 8.1 detect the following exceptional condition, and set the status register accordingly: (a) overflow.

      Now suppose that a low-end-of-range model of HYP has less than 4096 words of code store and data store. This makes other exceptional conditions possible: (b) invalid instruction address; (c) invalid data address. Modify the HYP interpreter accordingly.

8.2   Make the HYP interpreter of Example 8.1 display a summary of the machine state after executing each instruction. Display the contents of the accumulator and CP, the instruction just executed, and a selected portion of the data store.

8.3*   Make the HYP interpreter of Example 8.1 into an interactive debugger. Provide the following facilities: (a) execute the next instruction only (*single-step*); (b) set or remove a breakpoint at a given instruction; (c) execute instructions until the next breakpoint; (d) display the contents of the accumulator and CP; (e) display the contents of the data store; (f) terminate execution.

8.4**   Write an emulator for a real machine with which you are familiar.

8.5   The Mini-Basic interpreter of Example 8.2 represents each stored command as a sequence of tokens.

(a) Discuss in detail the advantages and disadvantages of this choice of representation, and of the other possible choices. Bear in mind the context of a Basic language processor, in which commands may be loaded, edited, and executed by the user.

(b) How does the choice of representation influence procedure `analyze`? the procedure that stores a command entered by the user? the procedure that edits a stored command?

8.6*   Fill in the missing details of the Mini-Basic interpreter of Example 8.2.

8.7*   Extend the Mini-Basic interpreter of Example 8.2 to deal with the following extensions (which actually come from Cobol rather than Basic!):

> Command ::=   ...
> | **perform** Label **to** Label
> | **while** Expression Relational-Op Expression
> | **do** Command

      The effect of '`perform` L_1 `to` L_2' is to execute the commands labeled L_1 through L_2 (where L_1 may not follow L_2). This is a kind of parameter-less procedure call.

      The effect of '`while` E_1 R E_2 `do` C' is to repeat the subcommand C

as long as the comparison '$E_1 \, R \, E_2$' yields *true*. C is restricted to be a primitive command (i.e., it may not itself be a while-command).

Do these extensions lead you to reconsider the choice of representation for a stored command (Exercise 8.5)?

8.8   Extend the Mini-Shell interpreter of Example 8.3 to deal with a new command, `call`. This takes a single argument, a file-name. The named file is expected to contain a sequence of Mini-Shell commands, all of which are to be executed immediately.

8.9*   Suppose that Mini-Basic (Example 8.2) is to be replaced by a structured dialect with similar expressive power. The syntax of commands is to become:

```
Command ::=   Variable = Expression
          |   read Variable
          |   write Variable
          |   if Expression Relational-Op Expression
          |       then Command* else Command* end
          |   while Expression Relational-Op Expression
          |       do Command* end
          |   stop
```

Expressions, operators, and variables are unchanged. Write a recursive interpreter for this structured dialect.

8.10   Complete the comparison, begun in Example 8.5, of the Mini-Δ interpreter with the Mini-Δ action semantics.

CHAPTER NINE

Conclusion

The subject of this book is implementation of programming languages. As we study this subject, we should remember that implementation is only part of the *programming language life cycle*, where it takes its place along with design and specification of the programming language. In Section 9.1 we discuss the programming language life cycle, emphasizing the interactions among design, specification, and implementation. We also distinguish between cheap low-quality implementations (*prototypes*) and high-quality implementations.

This naturally leads to a discussion of quality issues in implementation. In previous chapters we have concentrated on introducing the basic methods of compilation and interpretation, and relating these to the source language's specification. Correctness of the implementation, with respect to the language specification, has been our primary consideration. Quality of the implementation is a secondary consideration, although still very important. The key quality issues are *error reporting* and *efficiency*. Sections 9.2 and 9.3 discuss these issues, as they arise both at compile-time and at run-time.

9.1 The programming language life cycle

Every programming language has a life cycle, which is quite similar to the well-known software life cycle. The language is *designed* to meet some requirement. A formal or informal *specification* of the language is written in order to communicate the design to other people. The language is then implemented by means of language processors. As a first step, a *prototype* implementation might be developed so that programmers can try out the language quickly. Later, *compilers* will be developed so that realistic application programming can be undertaken. (There are other phases of the programming language life cycle, such as preparation of manuals and textbooks, but we shall not consider them here.)

As the term suggests, the programming language life cycle is an iterative process. Language design is a highly creative and challenging endeavor, and no designer makes a perfect job at the first attempt. The experience of specifying or implementing a new language tends to expose irregularities in the design. Implementors and programmers might discover flaws in the specification, such as ambiguity, incompleteness, or inconsistency. They might also discover unpleasant features of the language itself, features that make the language unduly hard to implement or unsatisfactory for programming.

In any case, the language might have to be redesigned, respecified, and reimplemented, perhaps several times. This is bound to be costly, i.e., time-consuming and expensive. It is necessary, therefore, to plan the life cycle in such as way as to minimize costs.

Figure 9.1 illustrates a life cycle model that has much to recommend it. Specification immediately follows design. (This is more or less inevitable, since otherwise how could the design be communicated to other people such as implementors and programmers?) Development of a prototype follows, and development of compilers comes last of all. Specification, prototyping, and compiler development are successively more costly, so it makes sense to order them in this way. The designer gets the fastest possible feedback, and costly compiler development is deferred until the language design has more or less stabilized.

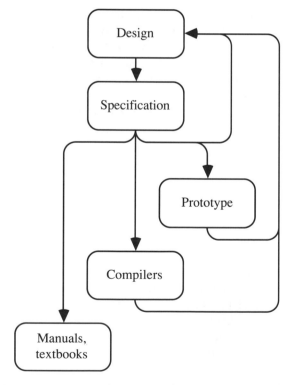

Figure 9.1 A programming language life cycle model.

9.1.1   Design

The essence of programming language design is selecting concepts and deciding how to combine them. A variety of concepts have found their way into programming languages: basic concepts such as values and types, storage, bindings, and abstraction; and more advanced concepts such as encapsulation, polymorphism, exceptions, and concurrency. A single language that supports all these concepts is likely to be very large and complex indeed (and its implementations will be large, complex, and costly). Therefore a judicious selection of concepts is necessary.

The designer should strive for simplicity and regularity. Simplicity implies that the language should support only the concepts essential to the applications for which the language is intended. Regularity implies that the language should combine these concepts in a systematic way, avoiding restrictions that might surprise programmers or make their task more difficult. (Language irregularities also tend to make implementation more difficult.)

A number of principles have been discovered that provide useful guidance to the designer:

- The *type completeness principle* suggests that no operation should be arbitrarily restricted in the types of its operands. For instance, operations like assignment and parameter passing should, ideally, be applicable to all types in the language.

- The *abstraction principle* suggests that, for each phrase that specifies some kind of computation, there should be a way of abstracting that phrase and parameterizing it with respect to the entities on which it operates. For instance, it should be possible to abstract any expression to make a function, or (in an imperative language) to abstract any command to make a procedure.

- The *correspondence principle* suggests that, for each form of declaration, there should be a corresponding parameter mechanism. For instance, it should be possible to take a block with a constant definition and transform it into a procedure (or function) with a constant parameter.

These are principles, not dogma. Designers often have to make compromises (for example to avoid constructions that would be unduly difficult to implement). But at least the principles help the designer to make the hard design decisions rationally and fully conscious of their consequences.

The main purpose of this brief discussion has been to give an insight into why language design is so difficult. Pointers to more extensive discussions of language design may be found in Section 9.4.

9.1.2   Specification

A new language design exists only in the mind of the designer until it is communicated to other people. For this purpose a precise specification of the language's syntax and semantics must be written. The specification may be informal, formal, or (most commonly) a hybrid.

Nearly all language designers specify their syntax formally, using BNF or one of its variants (EBNF or syntax diagrams). These formalisms are widely understood and easy to use. Some older languages, such as Fortran and Cobol, did not have their syntax formalized, and it is noteworthy that their syntax is clumsy and irregular. Formal specification of syntax tends to encourage syntactic simplicity and regularity, as illustrated by Algol (the language for which BNF was invented) and its many successors. For example, the earlier versions of Fortran had several different classes of expression, permissible in different contexts (assignment, array indexing, loop parameters); whereas Algol from the start had just one class of expression, permissible in all contexts.

Similarly, formal specification of semantics tends to encourage semantic simplicity and regularity. Unfortunately, few language designers yet attempt this. Semantic formalisms are much more difficult to master than BNF. Even then, writing a semantic specification of a real programming language (as opposed to a toy language) is a substantial task. Worst of all, the designer has to specify, not a stable well-understood language, but one that is gradually being designed and redesigned. Most semantic formalisms are ill-suited to meet the language designer's requirements, so it is not surprising that almost all designers content themselves with writing informal semantic specifications.

The advantages of formality and the disadvantages of informality should not be underestimated, however. Informal specifications have a strong tendency to be inconsistent or incomplete or both. Such specification errors lead to confusion when the language designer seeks feedback from colleagues, when the new language is implemented, and when programmers try to learn the new language. Of course, with sufficient investment of effort, most specification errors can be detected and corrected, but an informal specification will probably never be completely error-free. The same amount of effort could well produce a formal specification that is at least guaranteed to be precise.

The very act of writing a specification tends to focus the designer's mind on aspects of the design that are incomplete or inconsistent. Thus the specification exercise provides valuable and timely feedback to the designer. Once the design is completed, the specification (whether formal or informal) will be used to guide subsequent implementations of the new language.

9.1.3   Prototypes

A prototype is a cheap but low-quality implementation of a new programming language. Development of a prototype helps to highlight any features of the language that are hard to implement. The prototype also gives programmers an early opportunity to try out the language. Thus the language designer gains further valuable feedback. Moreover, since a prototype can be developed relatively quickly, the feedback is timely enough to make a language revision feasible. A prototype might be lacking in speed and good error reporting; but these qualities are deliberately sacrificed for the sake of rapid implementation.

For a suitable programming language, an interpreter might well be a useful prototype. An interpreter is very much easier and quicker to implement than a compiler for the same language. The drawback of an interpreter is that an interpreted program will run perhaps 100 times more slowly than an equivalent machine-code program. Programmers will quickly tire of this enormous inefficiency, once they pass the stage of trying out the language and start to use it to build real applications.

A more durable form of prototype is an interpretive compiler. This consists of a translator from the programming language to some suitable abstract machine code, together with an interpreter for the abstract machine. The interpreted object program will run 'only' about 10 times more slowly than a machine-code object program. Developing the compiler and interpreter together is still much less costly than developing a compiler that translates the programming language to real machine code. (Better still, a suitable abstract machine might be available 'off the shelf', saving the cost of writing the interpreter.)

Development of the prototype must be guided by the language specification, whether the specification is formal or informal. In Section 8.3 we saw that an interpreter bears a strong structural similarity to an (operational) formal specification of the source language's semantics, so this kind of specification is particularly useful as a guide to the implementor. An informal specification is less reliable as a guide.

9.1.4   Compilers

A prototype is not suitable for use over an extended period by a large number of programmers building real applications. When it has served its purpose of allowing programmers to try out the new language and provide feedback to the language designer, the prototype should be superseded by a higher-quality implementation. This is invariably a compiler – or, more likely, a family of compilers, generating object code for a number of target machines.

Once again, development of these compilers must be guided by the language specification. And once again, a suitable formal specification may prove to be a particularly useful guide to the implementor. In Sections 4.3 and 4.5 we saw that a parser and scanner can be developed systematically from the source language's syntactic specification. A formal specification of the source language's scope rules and type rules would strongly guide the development of a contextual analyzer (although we have not pursued this possibility in this book). Finally, in Section 7.5 we saw that a code specification bears a strong structural similarity to an (operational) formal specification of the source language's semantics; and in turn the code specification can be used to develop a code generator systematically.

In practice, contextual constraints and semantics are rarely specified formally. If we compare separately-developed compilers for the same language, we often find that they are consistent with respect to syntax, but inconsistent with respect to contextual constraints and semantics. This is no accident, because syntax is usually specified formally, and therefore precisely, and everything else informally, leading inevitably to misunderstanding.

9.2   Error reporting

All programmers make errors – frequently. A high-quality language processor assists the programmer to locate and correct these errors. Here we examine detection and reporting of both compile-time and run-time errors.

9.2.1   Compile-time error reporting

The language specification defines a set of well-formed programs. A minimal view of a compiler's function is that it simply rejects any ill-formed program. But a good-quality compiler should be more helpful.

As well as rejecting an ill-formed program, the compiler should report the location of each error, together with some explanation. It should at least distinguish between the major categories of compile-time error:

- *Syntactic error:* missing or unexpected characters or tokens. The error report might indicate what characters or tokens *were* expected.
- *Scope error:* a violation of the language's scope rules. The error report should indicate which identifier violated the rules and how (e.g., undeclared, or declared twice).
- *Type error:* a violation of the language's type rules. The error report should indicate which type rule was violated, and/or what type was expected.

Ideally the error report should be self-explanatory. If this is not feasible, it should at least refer to the appropriate section of the language specification.

If the compiler forms part of an integrated language processor, and thus the programmer can switch very easily between editing and compiling, it is acceptable for the compiler to halt on detecting the first error. The compiler should highlight the erroneous phrase and pass control immediately to the editor. The programmer can then correct the error and reinvoke the compiler.

On the other hand, a 'batch' or 'software tool' compiler – one intended to compile the entire source program without interaction with the programmer – should detect and report as many errors as it can find. This allows the programmer to correct several errors after each compilation. This requirement has a significant impact on the compiler's internal organization. After detecting and reporting an error, the compiler must attempt *error recovery*. This means that the compiler must try to get itself into a state where analysis of the source program can continue as normally as possible. Error recovery is often quite difficult.

Example 9.1
The following Δ program fragment contains scope and type errors:

```
let
    var phonenum: Integer;
    var local: Boolean
in
```

```
      begin
      ...;
①    if phonenum[0] = '0' then
②       locale := false
      else
          ...
      end
```

These errors should be detected during contextual analysis.

Consider the expression at ①. The phrase 'phonenum[0]' clearly violates the indexing operation's type rule, since phonenum is not of array type. But what error recovery is appropriate? It is not at all obvious what type should be ascribed to 'phonenum[0]', to allow type checking to continue. If the type checker ascribes the type *int*, for example, then at the next step it will find that the operands of '=' appear to violate that operator's type rule (one operand being *int* and the other *char*), and it will generate a second error report, which is really spurious. Fortunately, the result type of '=' does not depend on the types of its operands, so the type checker should obviously ascribe the type *bool* to the expression 'phonenum[0] = '0''. At the next step the type checker will find that this expression satisfies the if-command's type rule.

At ②, there is an applied occurrence of an identifier, locale, that has not been declared, in violation of a scope rule. Again, what error recovery is appropriate? Suppose that the type checker arbitrarily chooses *int* as the type of locale. Then at the next step the type checker will find that the assignment command's type rule appears to be violated (one side being *int* and the other *bool*), and again it will generate a spurious error report. □

To facilitate error recovery during type checking, it is useful for the type checker to ascribe a special improper type, *error-type*, to any ill-typed expression. The type checker can then turn a blind eye to *error-type* whenever it is subsequently encountered. This technique would avoid both the spurious error reports mentioned in Example 9.1.

Example 9.2
The following Δ program fragment contains some common syntactic errors:

```
      let
          var score: Integer;
          var grade: Char
①       var pass:  Boolean
      in
          begin
          ...;
②       if 50 <= score /\ score < 60 then
③          grade := 'C';
④          pass = true
⑤       else
              ...
          end
```

These errors should be detected during parsing.

At ①, the token 'var' is encountered unexpectedly. Clearly, the error is a missing semicolon between the declarations, and the best error recovery is to continue parsing as if the semicolon had been there.

After the assignment command at ③, a semicolon is encountered where 'else' was expected. Here error recovery is more difficult. (Recall that the parser works in a single pass through the source program, and has not yet seen the tokens after the semicolon.) There are two reasonable ways in which the parser might attempt to recover at this point:

(a) The parser might assume that the else-part of the if-command is missing, and continue as if the if-command had been completely parsed. Given the above source program, this error recovery would turn out badly: eventually the parser would unexpectedly encounter the token 'else' at ⑤, and would spuriously report a syntactic error at that point.

(b) Alternatively, the parser might skip tokens in the hope of finding the expected 'else'. Given the above source program, this error recovery would turn out reasonably well: the parser would find the token 'else' at ④, and would then resume parsing the if-command. The only drawback is that the parser would skip the tokens 'pass = true', and thus would overlook the syntactic error there.

By way of contrast, given a different program where the 'else' was actually missing, error recovery (a) would turn out well, but (b) would turn out badly.

The expression at ② illustrates another problem with error reporting. This expression is syntactically well-formed, but the Δ parser will treat this expression as equivalent to '((50 <= score) /\ score) < 60' – not at all what the programmer intended! Consequently, contextual analysis will report type errors in connection with the operators '/\' and '<'. The programmer's actual mistake, however, was the syntactic mistake of failing to parenthesize the expression properly.   □

As these examples illustrate, it is easy for a compiler to discover that the source program is ill-formed, and to generate error reports. But it is difficult to ensure that the compiler never generates misleading error reports. There is a genuine tension between the task of compiling well-formed source programs and the need to make some sense of ill-formed programs. A compiler is structured primarily to deal with well-formed source programs, so it must be enhanced with special error recovery algorithms to make it deal reasonably with ill-formed programs.

Syntactic error recovery is particularly difficult. At one extreme, an over-ambitious error recovery algorithm might induce an avalanche of spurious error reports. At the opposite extreme, an over-cautious error recovery algorithm might skip a large part of the source program and fail to detect genuine syntactic errors.

9.2.2 Run-time error reporting

Run-time error reporting is a completely different but equally important problem. Among the more common run-time errors are:

- arithmetic overflow
- division by zero
- out-of-range array indexing

These errors can be detected only at run-time, because they depend on values computed at run-time. (If the language is dynamically typed, i.e., a variable can take values of different types at different times, then type errors also are run-time errors. However, we do not consider dynamically typed languages here.)

Some run-time errors are detected by the target machine. For example, overflow usually results in a machine interrupt. But in some machines the only effect of overflow is to set a bit in the condition code register, and the object program must explicitly test this bit whenever there is a risk of overflow.

Other run-time errors are not detected by the machine at all, but instead must be detected by tests in the object program. For example, out-of-range array indexing might result in computing the address of a word that is not actually part of the array. This is usually not detected by the machine unless the computed address is actually invalid (e.g., a negative number).

These examples illustrate only typical machine behavior. Real machines range from one extreme, where *no* run-time errors are detected automatically, to the opposite extreme, where all the more common run-time errors are detected automatically. The typical situation is that some run-time errors are detected by hardware, leaving others to be detected by software.

Where a particular run-time error is *not* detected by hardware, the compiler should generate code to test for the error explicitly. In array indexing, for example, the compiler should generate code not only to evaluate the index but also to check whether it lies within the array's index range.

Example 9.3
The following Δ program fragment illustrates array indexing:

```
    let
        var name: array 6 of Char;
        var i: Integer
    in
        begin
        ...;
①     name[i] := ' ';
        ...
        end
```

Assume that characters and integers occupy one word each, and that the addresses of global variables `name` and `i` are 200 and 206, respectively. Thus `name` occupies words 200 through 205; and the address of `name [i]` is $200 + i$, provided that $0 \le i \le 5$.

The Δ compiler does not currently generate index checks. The assignment command at ① will be translated to object code like this (omitting some minor details):

```
    LOADL    48          – fetch the blank character
    LOAD     206         – fetch the value of i
```

```
LOADL   200              – fetch the address of name[0]
CALL    add              – compute the address of name[i]
STOREI                   – store the blank character at that address
```

This code is dangerous. If the value of i is out of range, the blank character will not be stored in an element of name, but in some other variable – possibly of a different type. (If the value of i happens to be 6, then i itself will be corrupted in this way!)

We could correct this deficiency by making the compiler generate object code with index checks, like this:

```
LOADL   48               – fetch the blank character
LOAD    206              – fetch the value of i
LOADL   0                – fetch the lower bound of name
LOADL   5                – fetch the upper bound of name
CALL    indexcheck       – check that the index is within range
LOADL   200              – fetch the address of name[0]
CALL    add              – compute the address of name[i]
STOREI                   – store the blank character at that address
```

The index check is italicized for emphasis. The auxiliary routine *indexcheck*, when called with arguments i, m, and n, is supposed to return i if $m \leq i \leq n$, or to fail otherwise. The space cost of the index check is three instructions, and the time cost is three instructions plus the time taken by *indexcheck* itself.   □

Software run-time checks are expensive in terms of object-program size and speed. Without them, however, the object program might continue to run, eventually failing somewhere else, or terminating with meaningless results. And, let it be emphasized, if a compiler generates object programs whose behavior differs from the language specification, it is simply incorrect. The compiler should, at the very least, allow the programmer the option of including or suppressing run-time checks. Then a program's unpredictable behavior would be the responsibility of the programmer who opts to suppress run-time checks.

Whether the run-time check is performed by hardware or software, there remains the problem of generating a suitable error report. This should not only describe the nature of the error (e.g., 'arithmetic overflow' or 'index out of range'), but should also locate it in the source program. An error report stating that overflow occurred at instruction address 1234 (say) would be unhelpful to a programmer who is trying to debug a high-level language program. A better error report would locate the error at a particular line in the *source program*.

The general principle here is that error reports should relate to the source program, not to the object program. Another example of this principle is a facility to display the current values of variables during or after the running of the program. A simple storage dump is of little value: the programmer cannot understand it without a detailed knowledge of the run-time organization assumed by the compiler (data representation, storage allocation, layout of stack frames, layout of the heap, etc.). Better is a symbolic dump that displays each variable's source-program identifier, together with its current value in source-language syntax.

Example 9.4

Consider the Δ program fragment of Example 9.3. Suppose that an out-of-range index is detected at ①. The following error report and storage dump are expressed largely in object-program terms:

```
Array indexing error at instruction address 1234.

Storage dump at this point:
      address   content
         ...       ...
         200        79
         201        96
         202       114
         203        98
         204        96
         205       107
         206        10
         ...       ...
```

This information is hard to understand, to put it mildly. It is not clear which array indexing operation failed. There is no indication that some of the words in the store constitute an array. There is no distinction between different types of data such as integers and characters.

The following error report and dump are expressed more helpfully in source-program terms:

```
Array indexing error at line 45.

Symbolic dump at this point:
      name = ['P', 'a', 's', 'c', 'a', 'l']
      i    = 10
```

Here the programmer can tell at a glance what went wrong.   □

But how can the source-program line number be determined at run-time? One possible method is this. We dedicate a register (or storage cell) that will contain the current line number. The compiler generates code to update this register whenever control passes from one source-program line to another. Clearly, however, this method is costly in terms of extra instructions in the object program.

An alternative method is as follows. The compiler generates a table relating line numbers to instruction addresses. If the object program stops, the code pointer is used to search the table and determine the corresponding line number. This method has the great advantage of imposing no time or space overheads on the object program. (The line-number table can be stored separately from the object program.)

To generate a symbolic dump requires more sophisticated techniques. The compiler must generate a 'symbol table' containing the identifier, type, and address of each variable in the source program, and the identifier and entry address of each procedure and function. If the object program stops, using the symbol table each (live) variable can be located in the store. The variable's identifier can be printed along with its current value, formatted according to its type. If one or more procedures are active at the time when the program stops, the store will contain one or more stack frames. To allow the symbolic dump to cover local variables, the symbol table must record which variables are local to which procedures, and the procedure to which each frame belongs must be identified in some way. (See Exercise 9.4.)

9.3   Efficiency

When we consider efficiency in the context of a compiler, we must carefully distinguish between compile-time efficiency and run-time efficiency. They are not the same thing at all; indeed, there is often a tradeoff between the two. The more a compiler strives to generate efficient (compact and fast) object code, the less efficient (bulkier and slower) the compiler itself tends to become.

The most efficient compilers are those that generate abstract machine code, where the abstract machine has been designed specifically to support the operations of the source language. Compilation is simple and fast because there is a straightforward translation from the source language to the target language, with few special cases to worry about. Such a compiler is the Δ compiler used as a case study in this book. Of course, the object code has to be interpreted, imposing a significant speed penalty at run-time.

Compilers that generate code for real machines are generally less efficient. They must solve a variety of awkward problems. There is often a mismatch between the operations of the source language and the operations provided by the target machine. The target-machine operations are often irregular, complicating the translation. There might be many ways of translating the same source program into object code, forcing the compiler writer to implement lots of special cases in an attempt to generate the best possible object code.

9.3.1   Compile-time efficiency

Let us examine a compiler from the point of view of algorithmic complexity. Ideally, we would like the compiler to run in $O(n)$ time[1], where n is some measure of the source program's size (for example, the number of tokens). In other words, a 10-fold increase in the size of the source program should result in a 10-fold increase in

---

[1] The O-notation is a way of estimating the efficiency of a program. Let n be the size of the program's input. If we state that the program's running time is $O(n)$, we mean that its running time is proportional to n. (We are not concerned whether the actual running time is $100n$ or $0.01n$.) Similarly, $O(n \log n)$ time means time proportional to $n \log n$, $O(n^2)$ time means time proportional to n^2, and so on. In estimates of algorithmic complexity, the constants of proportionality are generally less important than the difference between, for example, $O(n)$ and $O(n^2)$.

compilation time. A compiler that runs in $O(n^2)$ time would be completely unacceptable: a 10-fold increase in the size of the source program would result in a 100-fold increase in compilation time! In practice, $O(n \log n)$ might be an acceptable compromise.

If all phases of a compiler run in $O(n)$ time, then the compiler as a whole will run in $O(n)$ time.[2] But if just one of the phases runs in $O(n^2)$ time, then the compiler as a whole will run in $O(n^2)$ time.[3] In general, compilation time is dominated by the phase with the worst time complexity!

The parsing, type checking, and code generation algorithms described in Chapters 4, 5, and 7 do in fact run in $O(n)$ time. However, a common weak link is identification.

Assume that the number of applied occurrences of identifiers in the source program is $O(n)$, and that the average number of entries in the identification table is $O(n)$. If linear search is used, each identification will take $O(n)$ time, so total identification time will be $O(n^2)$. If instead some kind of binary search is used, each identification will take $O(\log n)$ time, so total identification time will be $O(n \log n)$. With clever use of hashing it is possible to bring each identification down to almost constant time, so total identification time will be $O(n)$, the ideal.

There are other weak links in some compilers. The polymorphic type inference algorithm needed in an ML compiler runs in $O(2^n)$ time in the worst case, which is enormously slow. Fortunately the worst case never arises in practice; but type inference is still very slow! Some code transformation algorithms run in $O(n^2)$ time, as we shall see in the next subsection.

9.3.2 Run-time efficiency

Let us now consider the efficiency of object programs, and in particular programs that run on real machines. Perhaps the most problematic single feature of real machines is the fact that they provide general-purpose registers. Computer architects provide registers because they speed up object programs. But compilers have to work harder to generate object programs that make effective use of the registers!

Example 9.5
The following Δ command:

```
a := (b*c) - (d + (e*f))
```

would be translated to the following TAM code:

---

[2] Suppose that phase A runs in time an, and phase B in time bn (where a and b are constants). Then the combination of these phases will run in time $an + bn = (a + b)n$, which is still $O(n)$.

[3] Suppose that phase A runs in time an, and phase B in time bn^2 (where a and b are constants). Then the combination of these phases will run in time $an + bn^2$. Even if a is much greater than b, the second term will increasingly dominate as n increases.

```
LOAD    b
LOAD    c
CALL    mult
LOAD    d
LOAD    e
LOAD    f
CALL    mult
CALL    add
CALL    sub
STORE   a
```

As we saw in Chapter 7, a simple efficient code generator can easily perform this translation. The code generator has no registers to worry about.

Now suppose that the target machine has a pool of registers and a typical one-address instruction set. Now the command would be translated to object code like this:

```
LOAD    R1 b
MULT    R1 c
LOAD    R2 d
LOAD    R3 e
MULT    R3 f
ADD     R2 R3
SUB     R1 R2
STORE   R1 a
```

Although this is comparatively straightforward, some complications are already evident. The code generator must allocate a register for the result of each operation. It must ensure that the register is not reused until that result has been used. (Thus R1 cannot be used during the evaluation of 'd + (e*f)', because at that time it contains the unused result of evaluating 'b*c'.) Furthermore, when the right operand of an operator is a simple variable, the code generator should avoid a redundant load by generating, for example, 'MULT R1 c' rather than 'LOAD R2 c' followed by 'MULT R1 R2'.

The above is not the only possible object code, nor even the best. One improvement is to evaluate 'd + (e*f)' *before* 'b*c'. A further improvement is to evaluate '(e*f) + d' instead of 'd + (e*f)', exploiting the commutativity of '+'. The combined effect of these improvements is to save an instruction and a register:

```
LOAD    R1 e
MULT    R1 f
ADD     R1 d
LOAD    R2 b
MULT    R2 c
SUB     R2 R1
STORE   R2 a
```

But that is not all. The compiler might decide to allocate registers to selected variables throughout their lifetimes. Supposing that registers R6 and R7 are thus allocated to variables a and d, the object code could be further improved as follows:

```
LOAD    R1  e
MULT    R1  f
ADD     R1  R7
LOAD    R6  b
MULT    R6  c
SUB     R6  R1
```

                                                                  □

Several factors make code generation for a register machine rather complicated. Register allocation is one factor. Another is that compilers must in practice achieve code improvements of the kind illustrated above – programmers demand nothing less.

But even a compiler that achieves such improvements will still generate rather mediocre object code (typically four times slower than hand-written assembly code). A variety of algorithms have been developed that allow a compiler to generate much more efficient object code (typically twice as slow as hand-written assembly code). These are called *code transformation* algorithms. (A more widely used term is *code optimization*, but this is inappropriate because it is infeasible for a compiler to generate truly optimal object code.) Some of the more common code transformations are:

- *Constant folding.* If an expression depends only on known values, it can be evaluated at compile-time rather than run-time.

- *Common subexpression elimination.* If the same expression occurs in two different places, and is guaranteed to yield the same result in both places, it might be possible to save the result of the first evaluation and reuse it later.

- *Code movement.* If a piece of code executed inside a loop always has the same effect, it might be possible to move that code out of the loop, where it will be executed fewer times.

Example 9.6
Consider the following Pascal program fragment:

```
const pi = 3.1416
...
volume := 4/3 * pi * r * r * r
```

The compiler could replace the subexpression '4/3 * pi' by 4.1888. This constant folding saves a run-time division and multiplication. The programmer could have written '4.1888 * r * r * r' in the first place, of course, but only at the expense of making the program less readable.

Now consider the following Δ program fragment:

```
type Date = record
                y: Integer, m: Integer, d: Integer
            end;
var hol: array 6 of Date
...
hol[2].m := 12
```

The relevant addressing formula is:

$$\begin{aligned}
address[\text{hol[2].m}] &= address[\text{hol[2]}] + 1 \\
&= address[\text{hol}] + 2 \times 3 + 1 \\
&= address[\text{hol}] + 7
\end{aligned}$$

(assuming that each integer occupies one word). Furthermore, if the compiler decides that $address[\text{hol}] = 20$ (relative to SB), then $address[\text{hol[2].m}]$ can be folded to the constant address 27. This is shown in the following object code:

```
LOADL 12
STORE 27[SB]
```

Address folding makes field selection into a compile-time operation. It even makes indexing of a static array by a literal into a compile-time operation.   □

Example 9.7
Consider the following Δ program fragment:

```
var x: Integer;  var y: Integer;  var z: Integer
...
... (x-y) * (x-y+z) ...
```

Here the subexpression 'x-y' is a common subexpression. If the compiler takes no special action, the two occurrences of this subexpression will be translated into two separate instruction sequences, as in object code (a) below. But their results are guaranteed to be equal, so it would be more efficient to compute the result once and then copy it when required, as in object code (b) below.

```
(a)  LOAD   x          (b)  LOAD   x
     LOAD   y               LOAD   y
     CALL   sub             CALL   sub
     LOAD   x
     LOAD   y
     CALL   sub             LOAD   -1[ST]   (copies the value of x-y)
     LOAD   z               LOAD   z
     CALL   add             CALL   add
     CALL   mult            CALL   mult
```

Now consider the following Δ program fragment:

```
type T = ...;
var a: array 10 of T;  var b: array 20 of T
...
a[i] := b[i]
```

Here there is another, less obvious, example of a common subexpression. It is revealed in the addressing formulas for a[i] and b[i]:

$$\begin{aligned}
address[\text{a[i]}] &= address[\text{a}] + (i \times 4) \\
address[\text{b[i]}] &= address[\text{b}] + (i \times 4)
\end{aligned}$$

where to be concrete we have assumed that each value of type T occupies four words.

The common subexpression 'x-y' could have been eliminated by modifying the source program. But the common subexpression '$i \times 4$' can be eliminated only by the compiler, because it exists only at the target machine level.   □

Example 9.8
Consider the following Δ program fragment:

```
var name: array 3 of array 10 of Char
...
i := 0;
while i < 3 do
   begin
   j := 0;
   while j < 10 do
      begin name[i][j] := ' '; j := j + 1 end;
   i := i + 1
   end
```

The addressing formula for name [*i*] [*j*] is:

$$address[\text{name}[i][j]] = address[\text{name}] + (i \times 10) + j$$

(assuming that each character occupies one word). A straightforward translation of this program fragment will generate code to evaluate $address[\text{name}] + (i \times 10)$ inside the inner loop. But this code will yield the same address in every iteration of the inner loop, since the variable i is not updated by the inner loop.

The object program would be more efficient if this code were moved out of the inner loop. (It cannot be moved out of the outer loop, of course, because the variable i is updated by the outer loop.)   □

Constant folding is a relatively straightforward transformation, requiring only local analysis, and is performed even by simple compilers. For example, the Δ compiler performs constant folding on address formulas.

Other code transformations such as common subexpression elimination and code movement, on the other hand, require nontrivial analysis of large parts of the source program, to discover which transformations are feasible and safe. To ensure that common subexpression elimination is safe, the relevant part of the program must be analyzed to ensure that no variable in the subexpression has been updated between the first and second evaluations of the subexpression. To ensure that code can be safely moved out of a loop, the whole loop must be analyzed to ensure that the movement does not change the program's behavior.

Code transformation algorithms always slow down the compiler, in an absolute sense, even when they run in $O(n)$ time. But some of these algorithms, especially ones that require analysis of the entire source program, may consume as much as $O(n^2)$ time.

Code transformations are only occasionally justified. During program development, when the program is compiled and recompiled almost as often as it is run, fast compilation is more important than generating very efficient object code. It is only when the program is ready for production use, when it will be run many times without recompilation, that it pays to use the more time-consuming code transformation algorithms.

For a production compiler, a sensible compromise is to provide *optional* code transformation algorithms. The programmer (who is the best person to judge) can then compile the program without code transformations during the development phase, and can decide when the program has stabilized sufficiently to justify compiling it with code transformations.

9.4 Further reading

More detailed discussions of the major issues in programming language design and specification, and their interaction, may be found in the concluding chapters of the companion textbooks by Watt (1990, 1991).

A formal specification of a programming language makes a more reliable guide to the implementor than an informal specification. More radically, it might well be feasible to use a suitable formal specification of a programming language to *generate* an implementation automatically. A system that does this is called a *compiler generator*. Development of compiler generators has long been a major goal of programming languages research.

Good-quality compiler generators are not yet available, but useful progress has been made. From a syntactic specification we can generate a scanner and parser, as described in Chapters 3 and 4 of Aho *et al.* (1985). The idea of generating an interpreter from a semantic specification is explored in Sections 4.4 and 8.4 of Watt (1991). Generating compilers from semantic specifications is the hardest problem. Lee (1989) surveys past efforts in this direction, which have succeeded in generating only poor-quality compilers. Brown *et al.* (1992) describe a current project to generate much better-quality compilers from action-semantic specifications.

A large variety of syntactic error recovery methods have been proposed and used in practice. One method, which is particularly suitable for use in conjunction with a recursive-descent parser, is described in Welsh and McKeag (1980).

An extensive source-language diagnostic system for Pascal programs is described in Watt and Findlay (1981). This system includes a post-mortem symbolic dump, which displays the local variables of all active procedures and functions, and which displays not only primitive values but also sets, arrays, records, and file buffers. A later version of this system is part of the model Pascal implementation presented in Welsh and Hay (1986).

Code transformation is a major topic in compilers. A detailed account is beyond the scope of this textbook. Instead, see the very extensive account in Chapter 10 of Aho *et al.* (1985). Although code transformation is now regarded as an advanced topic, surprisingly it was one of the first topics to engage the attention of compiler writers. In the 1950s, the writers of the first Fortran compiler went to extraordinary lengths to generate efficient object code, perceiving that this was the only way to attract hard-bitten assembly-language programmers to Fortran. The resulting compiler was noteworthy both for its Byzantine compiling algorithms and for its remarkably good object code!

Fortunately, our understanding of compiling algorithms – and of programming language design and specification – has developed a long way since those early days. In this textbook, and in its two companions, I have tried to convey this understanding to a wide readership. I hope I have succeeded!

Exercises 9

9.1 Obtain a sample of ill-formed programs. (A first programming course should be a good source of such programs!) Compile them, and study the error reports. Does the compiler detect every error, and report it accurately? Does the compiler generate any spurious error reports?

9.2 Write a critical account of your favorite language processor's reporting of run-time errors and its diagnostic facilities. Does it detect every run-time error? Does it report errors in source-program terms? Does it provide a symbolic diagnostic facility?

9.3 Obtain a sample of working programs, with a variety of sizes. Using your favorite compiler, measure and plot compilation time against source program size (n). Do you think that the compiler takes $O(n)$ time, $O(n \log n)$ time, or worse?

9.4 Obtain a sample of working programs. Using a compiler with a code transformation option, measure these programs' running time with and without code transformation. (If the compiler has several 'levels' of transformation, try them all.)

9.5* Consider the following Δ program fragment:

```
var a: array ... of Integer
...
i := m - 1; j := n; pivot := a[n];
repeat
    repeat i := i + 1 until a[i] >= pivot;
    repeat j := j - 1 until a[j] <= pivot;
    if not (i >= j) then
        begin
        t := a[i]; a[i] := a[j]; a[j] := t
        end
```

```
until i >= j;
t := a[i]; a[i] := a[n]; a[n] := t
```

(a) Find out the object code that would be generated by the Δ compiler.

(b) Write down the object code that would be generated by a Δ compiler that performs code transformations such as constant folding, common subexpression elimination, and code movement.

Projects with the Δ language processor

All of the following projects involve modifications to the Δ language processor, which is listed in Appendices D and E. To undertake these projects you will need to obtain a copy of the Δ language processor. (See the Preface for instructions.)

Nearly every project involves a modification to the language. Rather than plunging straight into implementation, you should first *specify* the language extension. Do this by modifying the informal specification of Δ in Appendix B, following the same style. You might even like to modify one of the formal specifications of Δ's semantics, which you will find in Appendices D and E of Watt (1991).

9.6* (a) Extend Δ with a repeat-command of the form:

```
repeat C until E
```

Its semantics and type rule are similar to Pascal's.

(b) Extend Δ with a for-command of the form:

```
for I from E₁ to E₂ do C
```

This command is executed as follows. First, the expressions E_1 and E_2 are evaluated, yielding the integers m and n (say), respectively. Then the sub-command C is executed repeatedly, with identifier I bound in successive iterations to each integer in the range m through n. If $m > n$, C is not executed at all. (The scope of I is C, which may use the value of I but may not update it. The types of E_1 and E_2 must be `Integer`.) Example:

```
for n from 2 to m do
    if prime(n) then
        putint(n)
```

9.7* Extend Δ with a case-command of the form:

```
case E of
    IL₁:    C₁;
    ...;
    ILₙ:    Cₙ;
    else: C₀
```

This command is executed as follows. First E is evaluated; then if the value of E matches the integer-literal IL_i, the corresponding subcommand C_i is executed. If the value of E matches none of the integer-literals, the subcommand C_0 is executed. (The expression E must be of type `Integer`, and the integer-literals must all be distinct.) Example:

```
case today.m of
    2:   days := if leap then 29 else 28;
    4:   days := 30;
    6:   days := 30;
    9:   days := 30;
   11:   days := 30;
  else: days := 31
```

9.8**   Extend Δ with an initializing variable declaration of the form:

```
var I := E
```

This declaration is elaborated by binding I to a newly created variable. The variable's initial value is obtained by evaluating E. The variable exists only during the activation of the enclosing block. (The type of I will be the type of E.)

9.9**   Extend Δ with unary and binary operator declarations of the form:

$$\text{func } O \ (I_1 \colon T_1) \ : \ T \ \sim \ E$$

$$\text{func } O \ (I_1 \colon T_1, \ I_2 \colon T_2) \ : \ T \ \sim \ E$$

Operators are to be treated like functions. A unary operator application '$O\ E$' is to be treated like a function call '$O\ (E)$', and a binary operator application '$E_1\ O\ E_2$' is to be treated like a function call '$O\ (E_1,\ E_2)$'. Examples:

```
func -- (i: Integer) : Integer ~
   0 - n;

func ** (b: Integer, n: Integer) : Integer ~
   if n = 0 then
      1
   else   ! assume that n > 0
      n * (b ** (n-1))
```

(*Notes:* The Δ lexicon, Section B.8, already provides a whole class of operators from which the programmer may choose. The Δ standard environment, Section B.9, already treats the standard operators '+', '-', '*', etc., like predeclared functions.)

9.10**   Replace Δ's constant and variable parameters by value and result parameters. Design your own syntax.

9.11** Extend Δ with enumeration types. Provide a special enumeration type declaration of the form:

$$\text{enum type } I \sim (I_1, \ldots, I_n)$$

which creates a new and distinct primitive type with n values, and respectively binds the identifiers I_1, ..., and I_n to these values. Make the generic operations of assignment, '=', and '\=' applicable to enumeration types. (They are applicable to all Δ types.) Provide new operations of the form 'succ E' (successor) and 'pred E' (predecessor), where succ and pred are keywords.

9.12** Extend Δ with a new family of types, string n, whose values are strings of exactly n characters ($n \geq 1$). Provide string-literals of the form "$c_1 \ldots c_n$". Make the generic operations of assignment, '=', and '\=' applicable to strings. Provide a new binary operator '<<' (lexicographic comparison). Finally, provide an array-like string indexing operation of the form '$V [E]$', where V names a string value or variable. (*Hint:* Represent a string in the same way as a static array.)

Or:

Extend Δ with a new type, String, whose values are character strings of any length (including the empty string). Provide string-literals of the form "$c_1 \ldots c_n$" ($n \geq 0$). Make the generic operations of assignment, '=', and '\=' applicable to strings. Provide new binary operators '<<' (lexicographic comparison) and '++' (concatenation). Finally, provide an array-like string indexing operation of the form '$V [E]$', and a substring operation of the form '$V [E_1 : E_2]$', where V names a string value or variable. But do not permit string variables to be selectively updated. (*Hint:* Use an indirect representation for strings. The handle should consist of a length field and a pointer to an array of characters stored in the heap. In the absence of selective updating, string assignment can be implemented simply by copying the handle.)

9.13** Extend Δ with recursive types. Provide a special recursive type declaration of the form:

$$\text{rec type } I \sim T$$

where the type-denoter T may contain applied occurrences of I. (Typically, T will be a record type containing one or more fields of type I.) Every recursive type is to include a special empty value, denoted by the keyword nil. Do not permit variables of recursive types to be selectively updated. Example:

```
rec type IntList ~
        record head: Integer, tail: IntList end;

func cons (n: Integer, ns: IntList): IntList ~
    {head ~ n, tail ~ ns};
```

```
proc putints (ns: IntList) ~
   if ns \= nil then
      begin
      putint(ns.head); put(' ');
      putints(ns.tail)
      end;

var primes: IntList
...
primes := cons(2, cons(3, cons(5,
            cons(7, cons(11, nil)))));
putInts(primes)
```

(*Hint:* See Section 6.1.6 for a suggested indirect representation of recursive types. In the absence of selective updating, assignment can be implemented simply by copying the handle.)

9.14** (a) Extend Δ with package declarations of the form:

```
package I ~ D end
```

This declaration is elaborated as follows. *I* is bound to a package of entities declared in *D*. The packaged entities may be constants, variables, types, procedures, functions, or any mixture of these. A packaged entity declared with identifier *I'* is named *I$I'* outside the package declaration. Example:

```
package Graphics ~

   type Point ~
         record h: Integer, v: Integer end;

   func cart (x: Integer, y: Integer): Point ~
      {h ~ x, v ~ y};

   proc movex (dist: Integer, var p: Point) ~
      p.h := p.h + dist

end;

var z: Graphics$Point
...
z := Graphics$cart(3, 4);
Graphics$movex(7, z)
```

(b) Further extend Δ with package declarations of the form:

```
package I ~ D₁ where D₂ end
```

A declaration of this form supports information hiding. Only the entities declared in D_1 are visible outside the package. The entities declared in D_2 are visible only in D_1.

9.15** Modify the Δ language processor to perform run-time index checks, wherever necessary. (*Hint:* Add a new primitive routine `indexcheck` to TAM, as suggested in Example 9.3.)

9.16** Modify the Δ language processor to produce run-time error reports and symbolic dumps along the lines illustrated in Example 9.4. You will have to modify both the compiler and the interpreter. (*Hint:* First, restrict your attention to global variables of primitive type. Then deal with procedures and local variables. Finally, deal with variables of composite type.)

9.17** Modify the Δ compiler to perform constant folding wherever possible.

9.18** Modify the Δ compiler to perform code movement in the following circumstances. Suppose that in the following loop:

```
while ... do ... E ...
```

the (sub)expression *E* is *invariant*, i.e., it does not use the value of any variable that is updated anywhere in the loop. Then transform the loop to:

```
let const I ~ E
in
    while ... do ... I ...
```

where *I* is some identifier not used elsewhere in the loop. (*Hint:* Implement this by a transformation of the decorated AST representing the source program.)

Answers to Selected Exercises

Specimen answers to about half of the exercises are given here. Some of the answers are given only in outline.

Answers 1

1.1   Other kinds of language processor: syntax checkers, cross-referencers, high-level translators, program transformers, symbolic debuggers, etc.

1.4   AST:

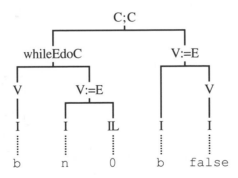

1.5   Mini-Δ expressions: (a) and (e) only. (Mini-Δ has no functions, no unary operators, and no operator '>='.)

        Commands: (f) and (j) only. (Mini-Δ procedures have exactly one parameter cach, and there is no if-command without an else-part.)

        Declarations: (l), (m), and (o). (Mini-Δ has no real-literals, and no multiple variable declarations.)

1.6   The value written is 10, i.e., product (sum (2, 3), 2).

Answers 2

2.2   (a) Compiling and (b) running a Δ program:

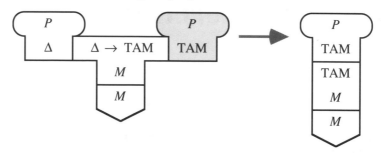

(c) Disassembling the object program:

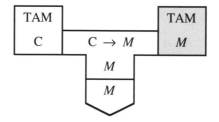

The purpose of the disassembler is to allow the programmer to read the compiler's object code.

2.4   (a) Compiling the TAM interpreter:

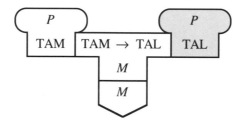

(b) Compiling the Algol compiler:

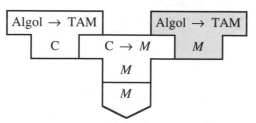

(c) Compiling and running an Algol program:

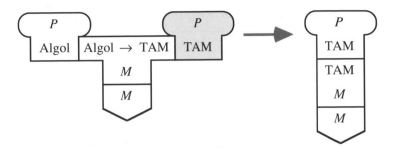

2.7   *Strategy 1*. Extend the Pascal-into-P-code translator to become an XP-into-P-code translator, and compile it. Composed with the P-code-into-*M* translator, this gives a two-stage XP compiler (similar to the given Pascal compiler):

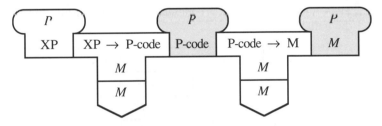

Strategy 2. Write an XP-into-Pascal translator (a *preprocessor*) in Pascal, and compile it. Composed with the two-stage Pascal-into-*M* compiler, this gives a three-stage XP compiler:

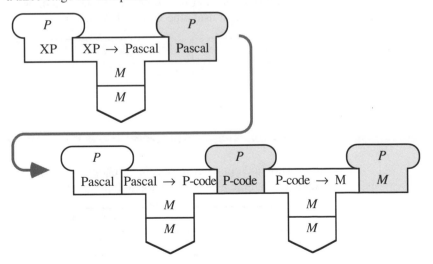

Strategy 2 requires more work, because the preprocessor must not only analyze the XP source program, but also generate a Pascal object program (requiring good layout if intended to be readable). Moreover the resulting compiler will be slower, being three-stage rather than two-stage. The advantage of strategy 2 is that the resulting compiler will be more modular:

any improvements in the Pascal-into-P-code translator will benefit the XP compiler as well as the Pascal compiler.

2.10   Write an initial version of the Utopia-1 compiler in C, and compile it using the C compiler:

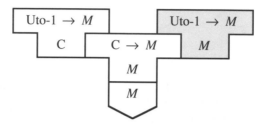

Then rewrite the Utopia-1 compiler in Utopia-1 itself, and compile it using the initial version:

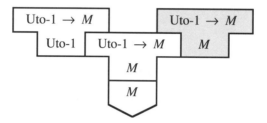

Extend the Utopia-1 compiler to become a Utopia-2 compiler, still expressed in Utopia-1. Compile it using the Utopia-1 compiler:

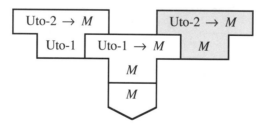

Extend the Utopia-2 compiler to become a Utopia-3 compiler, still expressed in Utopia-1. Compile it using the Utopia-1 compiler:

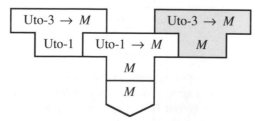

(Alternatively, the Utopia-3 compiler could be written in Utopia-2.)

Answers 3

3.3   The contextual errors are (i) 'Logical' is not declared; (ii) the expression of the if-command is not of type *bool*; and (iii) 'yes' is not declared:

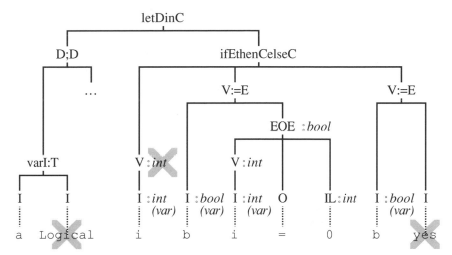

3.5   In brief, compile the subprograms one at a time. After parsing a subprogram and constructing its AST, perform contextual analysis and code generation on the AST. Then prune the AST: replace the subprogram's body by a stub, and retain only the part(s) of the AST that will be needed to compile subsequent calls to the subprogram (i.e., its identifier, formal parameters, and result type if any).

   The maximum space requirement will be for the largest subprogram's AST, plus the pruned ASTs of all the subprograms.

3.6   This restructuring would be feasible. It would be roughly similar to Answer 3.5, although the interleaving of syntactic analysis, contextual analysis, and code generation would be more complicated.

Answers 4

4.6   AST traversal procedure:

```
procedure displayAST (theAST: AST);
  var i: 1..3;
  begin
  with theAST^ do
```

```
case tag of
    {Nonterminal nodes ...}
    VbecomesE, IlpErp, CsemicolonC,
    ifEthenCelseC, whileEdoC, letDinC,
    V, OE, EOE,
    constIisE, varIcolonT, DsemicolonD:
        begin
        display tag;
        for i := 1 to arity do
            displayAST(child[i])
        end;
    {Terminal nodes ...}
    I, IL, O:
        display spelling
    end{case}
end
```

4.7   (a) AST definition, distinguishing among unary, binary, and ternary nodes:

```
type AST = ^ ASTNode;

    ASTNode =
        record
            case tag: ASTTag of
                {Unary node ...}
                V:
                    ( childI: AST );
                {Binary nodes ...}
                VbecomesE, IlpErp, CsemicolonC,
                whileEdoC, letDinC, OE,
                constIisE, varIcolonT,
                DsemicolonD:
                    ( childII:
                        array [1..2] of AST );
                {Ternary nodes ...}
                ifEthenCelseC, EOE:
                    ( childIII:
                        array [1..3] of AST );
                {Terminal nodes ...}
                I, IL, O:
                    ( spelling: TokenString )
        end
```

The constructor functions `leafAST`, `unaryAST`, etc., would be similar to those of Example 4.7.

The traversal procedure `displayAST` would have separate cases for unary, binary, and ternary nodes.

(b) AST definition, distinguishing among syntactic classes:

```
type ComTag =
        (VbecomesE, IlpErp, CsemicolonC,
         ifEthenCelseC, whileEdoC, letDinC);
     ExprTag =
        (V, OE, EOE);
     ...;

     Com   = ^ ComNode;
     Expr  = ^ ExprNode;
     Vname = ^ VnameNode;
     Decl  = ^ DeclNode;
     Leaf  = ^ TokenSpelling;

     ComNode =
        record
          case tag: ComTag of
            VbecomesE:
                ( lhs: Vname; rhs: Expr );
            IlpErp:
                ( proc: Leaf; arg: Expr );
            CsemicolonC:
                ( com1, com2: Com );
            whileEdoC:
                ( loopcond: Expr;
                  loopbody: Com );
            ifEthenCelseC:
                ( ifcond: Expr;
                  thencom, elsecom: Com );
            letDinC:
                ( local: Decl;
                  blockbody: Com )
        end;
     ExprNode =
        record
          case tag: ExprTag of
            V:
                ( name: Vname );
            OE:
                ( unaryop: Leaf;
                  arg: Expr );
            EOE:
                ( binaryop: Leaf;
                  arg1, arg2: Expr )
        end;
     ...
```

There would have to be a separate constructor function for every tag, e.g.:

```
function newVbecomesE
            (lhs: Vname; rhs: Expr): Com;
    ...;

function newOE
            (unaryop: Leaf; arg: Expr): Expr;
    ...
```

The traversal procedure `displayAST` would have to be replaced by a group of mutually recursive procedures: `displayCom`, `displayExpr`, etc. Each of these procedures would have a separate case for each tag.

4.11   (a) Refine '*parse E | F*' (using a common Pascal extension) to:

```
case currentToken.class of
    starters⟦E⟧:    parse E;
    starters⟦F⟧:    parse F;
    otherwise  report a syntactic error
    end{case}
```

This is correct if and only if *starters*⟦*E*⟧ and *starters*⟦*F*⟧ are disjoint.
(b) Refine '*parse E | ε*' to:

```
if currentToken.class in starters⟦E⟧ then
    parse E
```

This is correct if and only if *starters*⟦*E*⟧ is disjoint from the set of tokens that can follow *E | ε* in this particular context.
(c) Refine '*parse E E**' to:

```
repeat
    parse E
until not (currentToken.class in starters⟦E⟧)
```

This is correct if and only if *starters*⟦*E*⟧ is disjoint from the set of tokens that can follow *E E** in this particular context.

4.12   Parsing procedure when left recursion has not been eliminated:

```
procedure parseCommand;
    begin
    if currentToken.class
            in [identifierToken, ifToken,
                whileToken, letToken, beginToken]
    then
        begin
        parseCommand;
        accept(semicolonToken);
        parseSingleCommand
```

```
        end
   else
   if currentToken.class
         in [identifierToken, ifToken,
              whileToken, letToken, beginToken]
   then
      parseSingleCommand
   else
      report a syntactic error
   end{parseCommand}
```

This procedure will forever call itself recursively!

4.13   Factorized production rule:

single-Command ::= ...
                  | **if** Expression **then** single-Command
                       (**else** single-Command | ε)
                  | ...

The tokens that can follow a single-command are {else, end}. This set is not disjoint from *starters*⟦**else** single-Command⟧ = {else}, so the grammar is not LL(1). (In fact, no ambiguous grammar is LL(1).)

The parsing procedure would be:

```
procedure parseSingleCommand;
   begin
   if currentToken.class
         = identifierToken then
      ...
   else
   if currentToken.class = ifToken then
      begin
      acceptIt;
      parseExpression;
      accept(thenToken);
      parseSingleCommand;
      if currentToken.class = elseToken then
         begin
         acceptIt;
         parseSingleCommand
         end
      else if currentToken.class
            in [elseToken, endToken] then
         {skip}
      end
   else
      ...
```

```
        else
            report a syntactic error
        end
```

Given (4.31) as input, `parseSingleCommand` would accept 'if E_1 then', and then call itself recursively. The recursive activation of `parseSingleCommand` would accept 'if E_2 then C_1 else C_2', and then return. The original activation would then also return.

This behavior is exactly what Pascal specifies.

4.15   EBNF production rules:

```
Expression ::= secondary-Expression
                   (add-Operator secondary-Expression)*

secondary-Expression ::= primary-Expression
                   (mult-Operator primary-Expression)*
```

Parsing procedures (with AST enhancements in italics):

```
procedure parseExpression
               (var exprAST: AST);
    var e1AST, e2AST, opAST: AST;
    begin
    parseSecondaryExpression(e1AST);
    while currentToken.class = addOpToken do
        begin
        parseAddOperator(opAST);
        parseSecondaryExpression(e2AST);
        e1AST := binaryAST(EOE, e1AST, e2AST)
        end;
    exprAST := e1AST
    end{parseExpression};

procedure parseSecondaryExpression
               (var exprAST: AST);
    var e1AST, e2AST, opAST: AST;
    begin
    parsePrimaryExpression(e1AST);
    while currentToken.class = multOpToken do
        begin
        parseMultOperator(opAST);
        parsePrimaryExpression(e2AST);
        e1AST := binaryAST(EOE, e1AST, e2AST)
        end;
    exprAST := e1AST
    end{parseSecondaryExpression}
```

Procedure `parsePrimaryExpression` would be unchanged.

4.17 This lexical grammar is ambiguous. The scanning procedure would turn out as follows:

```
procedure scanToken;
  begin
  start;
  if currentChar in ['a'..'z'] then
    scanIdentifier
  else
  if currentChar in ['0'..'9'] then
    scanIntegerLiteral
  else
  if currentChar in ... then
    scanOperator
  else
  if currentChar = 'i' then
    begin
    takeIt; take('f');
    finish(ifToken)
    end
  else
  if currentChar = 't' then
    begin
    takeIt; take('h'); take('e'); take('n');
    finish(thenToken)
    end
  else
    ...
  else
    report a lexical error
  end
```

(where take is analogous to accept). This scanner is incorrect: keywords will be treated as identifiers.

There is no reasonable way to fix this scanner. If we reordered the alternatives to try keywords before identifiers, the scanner would still be incorrect: identifiers starting with 'i', 't', etc., would not be recognized at all.

Answers 5

5.3 One possibility would be a pair of subtables, one for globals and one for locals. (Each subtable could be an ordered binary tree or a hash table.) There would also be a variable, the *current level*, set to either *global* or *local*. Procedure startIdentification would set the current level to *global*, and would empty both subtables. Procedure `enter` would add the new entry to the global or local subtable, according to the current level. Procedure `retrieve` would search the local subtable first, and if unsuccessful would search the global subtable second. Procedures `openScope` would change the current level to *local*. Procedure `closeScope` would change it to *global*, and would also empty the local subtable.

5.4   Procedure `startIdentification` would make the stack contain a single empty binary tree. Procedure `enter` would add the new entry to the topmost binary tree. Procedure `retrieve` would search the binary trees in turn, starting with the topmost, and stopping as soon as it finds a match. Procedure `openScope` would push an empty binary tree on to the stack. Procedure `closeScope` would pop the topmost binary tree.

This implementation would be more efficient than the simple stack implementation, because it would replace linear search by binary search. In terms of time complexity, retrieval would be $O(\log n)$ rather than $O(n)$.

5.5   Procedure `startIdentification` would make the table contain a single (empty) column. Procedure `enter` would add the new entry to the leftmost column, and to the row indexed by the given identifier. Procedure `retrieve` would access the first entry in the row indexed by the given identifier. Procedure `openScope` would insert a new leftmost (empty) column. Procedure `closeScope` would remove the leftmost column.

This implementation would be more efficient than the simple stack implementation or the stack of binary trees, because retrieval would be essentially a constant-time operation. In terms of time complexity, retrieval would be $O(1)$ rather than $O(n)$ or $O(\log n)$. (This assumes that identifiers are hashed to index the table rows efficiently.)

5.7   Since each type is represented by a *pointer* to a tree, simply compare pointers:

```
function equivalent (type1, type2: Type)
              : Boolean;
    begin
    equivalent := (type1 = type2)
    end
```

5.9   Undecorated AST:

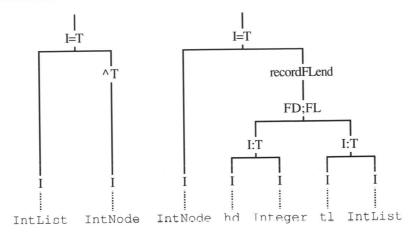

After elimination of type identifiers:

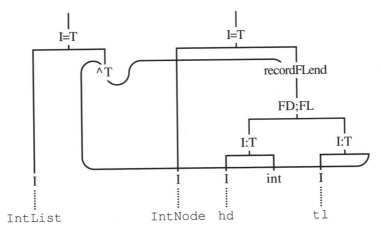

The AST has been transformed to a directed graph, with the mutually recursive types giving rise to a cycle.

The complication is that function `equivalent` must be able to compare two (possibly cyclic) graphs for structural equivalence. It must be implemented carefully to avoid nontermination.

5.10   Consider the function call 'I (E)'. Check that I has been declared by a function declaration, say '**func** I $(I': T')$: $T \sim E$'. Check that the type of the actual parameter E is equivalent to the formal parameter type T'. Infer that the type of the function call is T.

Answers 6

6.3   Advantage of single-word representation:

- It is economical in storage.

Advantages of double-word representation:

- It is closer to the mathematical (unbounded) set of integers.
- Overflow is less likely.

A Pascal compiler should adopt the double-word representation for `Int-eger`, and the single-word representation for sufficiently-small subranges of `Integer`. This combines all the above advantages.

6.5   (a)

freq['a']	9
freq['b']	3
freq['c']	4
...	...
freq['z']	0

pixel[red]	1
pixel[orange]	15
pixel[yellow]	3
pixel[green]	0
pixel[blue]	0

(b) Every T_{index} has a minimum value, $min\ T_{index}$; a maximum value, $max\ T_{index}$; and an *ord* function that maps the values of the type to consecutive integers. Thus:

$$size\ T = (u - l + 1) \times size\ T_{elem}$$
$$origin\ a = address\ a - (l \times size\ T_{elem})$$
$$address[\![a[i]]\!] = origin\ a + (ord\ i \times size\ T_{elem})$$

where $l = ord(min\ T_{index})$ and $u = ord(max\ T_{index})$.

6.6

$$size\ T = m \times n \times size\ T_{elem}$$
$$address[\![a[i][j]]\!]$$
$$= address\ a + (i \times (n \times size\ T_{elem})) + (j \times size\ T_{elem})$$

6.8   Make the handle contain the lower and upper bounds in both dimensions, as well as a pointer to the elements. Store the elements themselves row by row (as in Example 6.6). If l, u, l', and u' are the values of E_1, E_2, E_3, and E_4, respectively, then we get:

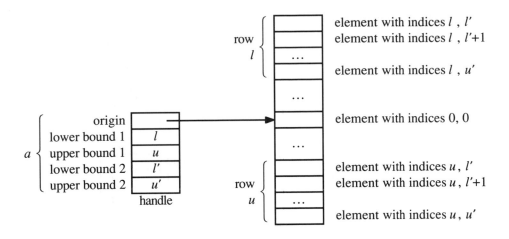

6.10   (a) Evaluate subexpression '1 - (c * 2)' before 'a * b':

```
LOAD  R1  c
MULT  R1  #2
LOAD  R2  #1
SUB   R2  R1
LOAD  R1  a
MULT  R1  b
ADD   R1  R2
```

(b) Save the accumulator's contents to a temporary location (say *temp*) whenever the accumulator is needed to evaluate something else:

```
LOAD   c
MULT   #2
STORE  temp
LOAD   #1
SUB    temp
STORE  temp
LOAD   a
MULT   b
ADD    temp
```

(In general, more than one temporary location might be needed.)

6.12   Address of global variable v_i is:

$$address\ v_i\ =\ size\ T_1 + ... + size\ T_{i-1}$$

Only the addresses allocated to the variables are affected by the order of the variable declarations. The *net* behavior of the object program is not affected.

6.15   Let each frame consist of a static part and a dynamic part. The static part accommodates variables of primitive type, and the handles of dynamic arrays.

The dynamic part expands as necessary to accommodate elements of dynamic arrays. The frame containing v would look like this:

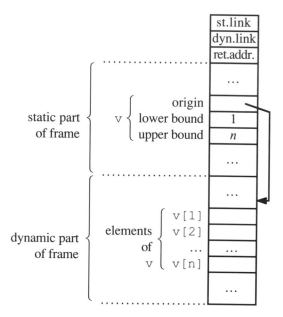

Since everything in the static part is of constant size, the compiler can determine each variable's address relative to the frame base. This is not true for the dynamic part, but the array elements there are always addressed indirectly through the handles.

6.16 There are three cases of interest. If $n = m+1$, R is local to the caller. If $n = m$, R is at the same level as the caller. If $n < m$, R encloses the caller.

(a) On call, push R's frame on to the stack. In all cases, set Dn to point to the base of the new frame. (*Note:* If $n < m$, D$(n+1)$, ..., and Dm become undefined.)

(b) On return, pop R's frame off the stack. If $n \leq m$, reset Dm to point to the base of the (now) topmost frame. If $n < m$, reset other display registers using the static links: D$(m-1) \leftarrow content$ (Dm); ...; D$n \leftarrow content$ (D$(n+1)$). (*Note:* If $n = m+1$, Dn becomes undefined.)

There is no need to change D0, D1, ..., D$(n-1)$ at either the call or the return, since these registers point to the same frames before, during, and after the activation of R.

Advantages and disadvantages (on the assumption that D0, D1, etc., are all true registers):

- Nonlocal variables can be accessed as efficiently as local or global variables.
- The display registers must be updated at every call and return.
- The caller must reset the display registers after return, since R does not know where it was called from, i.e., it does not know m.

- Complications arise when *R* is an unknown routine (e.g., an argument), because then the caller does not know *n*.

6.18 (a)

Stack machine code	*Register machine code*
LOAD *a*	LOAD R1 *a*
LOAD *b*	LOAD R2 *b*
LOAD *c*	LOAD R3 *c*
CALL *f*	CALL *f*

(b)

LOAD *a*	LOAD R1 *a*
CALL *g*	CALL *g*
	STORE R0 *temp*
LOAD *b*	LOAD R1 *b*
LOAD *c*	LOAD R2 *c*
CALL *h*	CALL *h*
	LOAD R2 R0
LOAD *d*	LOAD R3 *d*
	LOAD R1 *temp*
CALL *f*	CALL *f*

6.22 The following algorithm uses an address translation table, in which each entry (*a*, *a'*) consists of a heap variable's old address *a* together with its new address *a'* after compaction.

```
begin
newAddr := HB;
for each heap variable hv, in order of distance from HB do
    begin
    newAddr := newAddr - size of hv;
    add an entry (address of hv, newAddr) to the table
    end;
for each heap variable hv, in order of distance from HB do
    begin
    for each pointer p in hv do
        begin
        find an entry (p, q) in the table;
        replace p by q
        end;
    find an entry (address of hv, q) in the table;
    copy hv to address q
    end;
HT := newAddr;
for each pointer p in the stack do
    begin
    find an entry (p, q) in the table;
    replace p by q
```

end
end

This algorithm assumes that the heap variables are linked (by hidden link fields), in order of increasing distance from HB.

Answers 7

7.1   Code template (7.10e) gives rise to object code in which one jump instruction is executed per iteration. The code template of Table 7.4 gives rise to object code in which two jump instructions are executed per iteration, which is slower.

The code template of Table 7.4 is commonly used because it is more suitable for one-pass compilation.

7.2   (a)

$$execute \; [\![V_1 \, , \; V_2 := E_1 \, , \; E_2]\!] =$$
$$evaluate \; E_1$$
$$evaluate \; E_2$$
$$assign \; V_2$$
$$assign \; V_1$$

(b)

$$execute \; [\![C_1 \, , \; C_2]\!] =$$
$$execute \; C_1$$
$$execute \; C_2$$

(c)

$$execute \; [\![\textbf{if} \; E \; \textbf{then} \; C]\!] =$$
$$evaluate \; E$$
$$\text{JUMPIF(0)} \; g$$
$$execute \; C$$
$$g:$$

(d)

$$execute \; [\![\textbf{repeat} \; C \; \textbf{until} \; E]\!] =$$
$$g: \quad execute \; C$$
$$evaluate \; E$$
$$\text{JUMPIF(0)} \; g$$

(e)

$$execute \; [\![\textbf{repeat} \; C_1 \; \textbf{while} \; E \; \textbf{do} \; C_2]\!] =$$
$$\text{JUMP} \; h$$
$$g: \quad execute \; C_2$$
$$h: \quad execute \; C_1$$

> *evaluate E*
> JUMPIF(1) *g*

7.3   (a)

> *evaluate* $\llbracket$**if** E_1 **then** E_2 **else** $E_3\rrbracket$ =
> *evaluate* E_1
> JUMPIF(0) *g*
> *evaluate* E_2
> JUMP *h*
> *g*: *evaluate* E_3
> *h*:

(b)

> *evaluate* $\llbracket$**let** D **in** $E\rrbracket$ =
> *elaborate D*
> *evaluate E*
> POP(n) s if $s > 0$
>   where s = amount of storage allocated by D
> n = *size* (type of E)

(c)

> *evaluate* $\llbracket$**begin** C ; **yield** E **end**$\rrbracket$ =
> *execute C*
> *evaluate E*

7.5   Parts (a), (c), and (d):

```
procedure encodeExecute (command: AST);
  var jumpifAddr, loopAddr: CodeAddress;
  begin
  with command^ do
    case tag of

        ...

        VcommaVbecomesEcommaE:
          begin
          encodeEvaluate(child[3]);
          encodeEvaluate(child[4]);
          encodeAssign(child[2]);
          encodeAssign(child[1])
          end;

      ifEthenC:
          begin
          encodeEvaluate(child[1]);
          jumpifAddr := nextInstrAddr;
          emit(JUMPIFop, 0, CBr, null);
          encodeExecute(child[2]);
```

```
                    patch(jumpifAddr, nextInstrAddr)
                  end;

            repeatCuntilE:
                  begin
                  loopAddr := nextInstrAddr;
                  encodeExecute(child[1]);
                  encodeEvaluate(child[2]);
                  emit(JUMPIFop, 0, CBr, loopAddr)
                  end;

                  ...

                  end{case}
            end{encodeExecute}
```

7.7   (a) The most efficient solution is:

$execute \; [\![\mathbf{for} \; I \; \mathbf{from} \; E_1 \; \mathbf{to} \; E_2 \; \mathbf{do} \; C]\!] =$

	evaluate E_2	– compute final value
	evaluate E_1	– compute initial value of I
	JUMP *h*	
g:	*execute C*	
	CALL *succ*	– increment current value of I
h:	LOAD –1ST	– fetch current value of I
	LOAD –2ST	– fetch final value
	CALL *le*	– test current value ≤ final value
	JUMPIF(1) *g*	– if so, repeat
	POP(0) 2	– discard current and final values

At *g* and at *h*, the current value of *I* is at the stack top (at address –1ST), and the final value is immediately underlying (at address –2ST).

(b)

```
          procedure encodeExecute
                         (command: AST;
                          globalSize: Natural);
            var jumpAddr, loopAddr: CodeAddress;
                valSize: Natural;
            begin
            with command^ do
               case tag of

                   ...

               forIfromEtoEdoC:
                  begin
                  new(obj);   {object description to be bound
                                 to the control variable I}
                  obj^.kind := unknownValue;
```

```
obj^.size := 1;
obj^.address := globalSize + 1;
encodeEvaluate(child[3],
        globalSize, valSize);
encodeEvaluate(child[2],
        globalSize + 1, valSize);
jumpAddr := nextInstrAddr;
emit(JUMPop, 0, CBr, null)
loopAddr := nextInstrAddr;
encodeExecute(child[4],
        globalSize + 2);
emit(CALLop, SBr, PBr, succAddr);
patch(jumpAddr, nextInstrAddr);
emit(LOADop, 1, STr, -1);
emit(LOADop, 1, STr, -2);
emit(CALLop, SBr, PBr, leAddr);
emit(JUMPIFop, 1, CBr, loopAddr);
emit(POPop, 0, null, 2)
end;

    ...

            end{case}
    end{encodeExecute}
```

The for-command case first creates an object description for the control variable *I*, and attaches it to the for-command. Provided that the contextual analyzer has linked each applied occurrence of the control variable to the for-command itself, the loop body *C* will be able to fetch (but not assign to) the control variable.

7.10   (a) Reserve space for the result variable just above the link data in the function's frame (at address 3 [LB]):

$$\textit{elaborate} \; [\textbf{func} \; I \; (\; FP \;) : T \sim C] =$$

```
        JUMP  g
    e:  PUSH  n              where n = size T
        execute C
        RETURN (n)  d        where d = size of FP
    g:
```

$$\textit{execute} \; [\textbf{result} \; E] =$$

```
        evaluate E
        STORE (n)  3[LB]     where n = size (type of E)
```

(b)

```
procedure  encodeElaborate
                (declaration: AST;
                 currentLevel: Natural;
```

```
                                    frameSize: Natural;
                                var extraSize: Natural);
            var jumpAddr: CodeAddress;
                paramSize, resultSize: Natural;
            begin
            with declaration^ do
                case tag of

                    ...;

                    funcIlpFPrpcolonTisC:
                        begin
                        jumpAddr := nextInstrAddr;
                        emit(JUMPop, null, CBr, null);
                        new(obj);
                        obj^.kind := knownRoutine;
                        obj^.size := 2;
                        obj^.address.level :=
                            currentLevel;
                        obj^.address.displacement :=
                            nextInstrAddr;
                        encodeParam(child[2], paramSize);
                        {... creates an object description for the formal
                          parameter, and sets paramSize to the size of
                          the parameter}
                        resultSize := typeSize(child[3]);
                        emit(PUSHop, null, null,
                            resultSize);
                        encodeExecute(child[4],
                            currentLevel + 1,
                            3 + resultSize);
                        emit(RETURNop, resultSize, null,
                            paramSize);
                        patch(jumpAddr, nextInstrAddr);
                        extraSize := 0
                        end;

                    ...

                end{case}
            end{encodeElaborate};

        procedure encodeExecute
                    (command: AST;
                     currentLevel: Natural;
                     frameSize: Natural);
            var valSize: Natural;
            begin
```

```
with command^ do
   case tag of

      ...;

      resultE:
         begin
         encodeEvaluate(child[1],
                 currentLevel, frameSize,
                 valSize);
         emit(STOREop, valSize, LBr, 3)
         end;

      ...

      end{case}
   end{encodeExecute}
```

Answers 8

8.3   In outline:

```
type CommandKind =
        (singleStep, flipBreakpoint,
         runToBreakpoint, peekRegisters,
         peekDataStore, terminate);
     UserCommand =
        record
          case kind: CommandKind of
             singleStep,
             runToBreakpoint, peekRegisters,
             peekDataStore, terminate:
                 ( );
             flipBreakpoint:
                 ( point: CodeAddress )
        end;
var break: array [Address] of Boolean;
    command: UserCommand;

procedure clearBreakpoints;
   begin
   for d := 0 to 4095 do break[d] := false
   end{clearBreakpoints};

procedure interact (var com: UserCommand);
   ...;     {Obtain a command from the user.}
```

```
procedure step;
    begin
    {fetch the next instruction ...}
    instr := code[CP];
    CP := CP + 1;
    {analyze this instruction ...}
    ...;
    {execute this instruction ...}
    ...
    end{step};

begin
loadProgram; clearBreakpoints;
status := running; CP := 0;
repeat
    interact(command);
    case command.kind of
       singleStep:
          step;
       flipBreakpoint:
          break[command.point] :=
                not break[command.point]
       runToBreakpoint:
          repeat
             step
          until break[CP]
                or (status <> running);
       peekRegisters:
          ...;
       peekDataStore:
          ...;
       terminate:
          status := halted
       end{case}
    until status <> running
    end
```

8.5   (a) Advantages and disadvantages of storing commands as *text*:

  • Loading and editing are easy.
  • Commands have to be scanned and parsed whenever fetched for execution, which is slow.

Advantages and disadvantages of storing commands as *tokens*:

  • Loading and editing are fairly easy.
  • Commands have to be parsed whenever fetched for execution, which is moderately slow.

Advantages and disadvantages of storing commands as *ASTs*:

- Commands have to be scanned and parsed when loaded.
- Editing is awkward.
- Commands are immediately ready for execution.

(b) Answer implied by the above.

8.8   In outline:

```
procedure fetchAndAnalyze
                (var source: Text;
                 var com: Command);
    ...     {Read and analyze the next command from file
            source.}

procedure execute (com: Command);
    var script: Text; subCom: Command;
    begin
    if com.name = 'create    ' then
        ...

    ...

    else if com.name = 'call      ' then
        begin
        open(com.args[1], script);
        while (status = running)
                    and not eof(script) do
            begin
            fetchAndAnalyze(script, subCom);
            execute(subCom)
            end;
        close(script)
        end

    else    {executable program}
        run(com.name, com.args)
    end{execute};

begin
{initialize ...}
status := running;
repeat
    {fetch and analyze the next instruction ...}
    fetchAndAnalyze(input, com);
    {execute this instruction ...}
    execute (com)
until status <> running   {... execution is terminated}
end
```

Answers 9

9.5   In outline:

At the points marked ① below, 'i >= j' is a common subexpression. At the points marked ②, the *address* of a[i] is a common subexpression. At the points marked ③, the *address* of a[j] is a common subexpression.

```
i := m - 1; j := n; pivot := a[n];
repeat
    repeat i := i + 1 until a[i]② >= pivot;
    repeat j := j - 1 until a[j]③ <= pivot;
    if not (i >= j①) then
        begin
        t := a[i]②; a[i]② := a[j]③; a[j]③ := t
        end
until i >= j①;
t := a[i]②; a[i]② := a[n]; a[n] := t
```

Informal Specification of the Programming Language Δ

B.1 Introduction

Δ is a regularized extensible subset of Pascal. It has been designed as a model language to assist in the study of the concepts, formal specification, and implementation of programming languages.

The following sorts of entity can be declared and used in Δ:

- A *value* is a truth value, integer, character, record, or array.
- A *variable* is an entity that may contain a value and that can be updated. Each variable has a well-defined lifetime.
- A *procedure* is an entity whose body may be executed in order to update variables. A procedure may have constant, variable, procedural, and functional parameters.
- A *function* is an entity whose body may be evaluated in order to yield a value. A function may have constant, variable, procedural, and functional parameters.
- A *type* is an entity that determines a set of values. Each value, variable, and function has a specific type.

Each of the following sections specifies part of the language. The subsection headed **Syntax** specifies its grammar in BNF (except for Section B.8 which uses EBNF). The subsection headed **Semantics** informally specifies the semantics (and contextual constraints) of each syntactic form. Finally, the subsection headed **Examples** illustrates typical usage.

B.2 Commands

A command is executed in order to update variables. (This includes input–output.)

Syntax

A single-command is a restricted form of command. (A command must be enclosed between **begin** ... **end** brackets in places where only a single-command is allowed.)

```
Command          ::=   single-Command
                 |  Command ; single-Command

single-Command ::=
                 |  V-name := Expression
                 |  Identifier ( Actual-Parameter-Sequence )
                 |  begin Command end
                 |  let Declaration in single-Command
                 |  if Expression then single-Command
                        else single-Command
                 |  while Expression do single-Command
```

(The first form of single-command is empty.)

Semantics

- The skip command ' ' has no effect when executed.
- The assignment command '$V := E$' is executed as follows. The expression E is evaluated to yield a value; then the variable identified by V is updated with this value. (The types of V and E must be equivalent.)
- The procedure calling command 'I (*APS*)' is executed as follows. The actual-parameter-sequence *APS* is evaluated to yield an argument list; then the procedure bound to I is called with that argument list. (I must be bound to a procedure. *APS* must be compatible with that procedure's formal-parameter-sequence.)
- The sequential command 'C_1; C_2' is executed as follows. C_1 is executed first; then C_2 is executed.
- The bracketed command '**begin** C **end**' is executed simply by executing C.
- The block command '**let** D **in** C' is executed as follows. The declaration D is elaborated; then C is executed, in the environment of the block command overlaid by the bindings produced by D. The bindings produced by D have no effect outside the block command.
- The if-command '**if** E **then** C_1 **else** C_2' is executed as follows. The expression E is evaluated; if its value is true, then C_1 is executed; if its value is false, then C_2 is executed. (The type of E must be Boolean.)
- The while-command '**while** E **do** C' is executed as follows. The expression E is evaluated; if its value is true, then C is executed, and then the while-command is executed again; if its value is false, then execution of the while-command is completed. (The type of E must be Boolean.)

Examples

The following examples assume the standard environment (Section B.9), and also the following declarations:

```
var i: Integer;
var s: array 8 of Char;
```

```
      var t: array 8 of Char;
      proc sort (var a: array 8 of Char) ~
            ...
```

(a) `s[i] := '*'; t := s`

(b) `getint (var i); putint (i); puteol ()`

(c) `sort (var s)`

(d)
```
if s[i] > s[i+1] then
    let var c : Char
    in
        begin
        c := s[i]; s[i] := s[i+1]; s[i+1] := c
        end
else  ! skip
```

(e)
```
i := 7;
while (i > 0) /\ (s[i] = ' ') do
    i := i - 1
```

B.3   Expressions

An expression is evaluated to yield a value. A record-aggregate is evaluated to construct a record value from its component values. An array-aggregate is evaluated to construct an array value from its component values.

Syntax
A secondary-expression and a primary-expression are progressively more restricted forms of expression. (An expression must be enclosed between parentheses in places where only a primary-expression is allowed.)

```
Expression        ::=  secondary-Expression
                  |  let Declaration in Expression
                  |  if Expression then Expression else Expression

secondary-Expression
                  ::=  primary-Expression
                  |  secondary-Expression Operator primary-Expression

primary-Expression
                  ::=  Integer-Literal
                  |  Character-Literal
                  |  V-name
                  |  Identifier ( Actual-Parameter-Sequence )
                  |  Operator primary-Expression
```

```
                              |   ( Expression )
                              |   { Record-Aggregate }
                              |   [ Array-Aggregate ]

Record-Aggregate
                    ::=   Identifier ~ Expression
                     |    Identifier ~ Expression , Record-Aggregate

Array-Aggregate    ::=   Expression
                     |    Expression , Array-Aggregate
```

Semantics

- The expression '*IL*' yields the value of the integer-literal *IL*. (The type of the expression is `Integer`.)
- The expression '*CL*' yields the value of the character-literal *CL*. (The type of the expression is `Char`.)
- The expression '*V*', where *V* is a value-or-variable-name, yields the value identified by *V*, or the current value of the variable identified by *V*. (The type of the expression is the type of *V*.)
- The function calling expression '*I* (*APS*)' is evaluated as follows. The actual-parameter-sequence *APS* is evaluated to yield an argument list; then the function bound to *I* is called with that argument list. (*I* must be bound to a function. *APS* must be compatible with that function's formal-parameter-sequence. The type of the expression is the result type of that function.)
- The expression '*O E*' is, in effect, equivalent to a function call '*O* (*E*)'.
- The expression '$E_1 O E_2$' is, in effect, equivalent to a function call '*O* (E_1, E_2)'.
- The expression '(*E*)' yields just the value yielded by *E*.
- The block expression '**let** *D* **in** *E*' is evaluated as follows. The declaration *D* is elaborated; then *E* is evaluated, in the environment of the block expression over-laid by the bindings produced by *D*. The bindings produced by *D* have no effect outside the block expression. (The type of the expression is the type of *E*.)
- The if-expression '**if** E_1 **then** E_2 **else** E_3' is evaluated as follows. The expression E_1 is evaluated; if its value is true, then E_2 is evaluated; if its value is false, then E_3 is evaluated. (The type of E_1 must be `Boolean`. The type of the expression is the same as the types of E_2 and E_3, which must be equivalent.)
- The expression '{*RA*}' yields just the value yielded by the record-aggregate *RA*. (The type of '{I_1 ~ E_1, ..., I_n ~ E_n}' is '**record** I_1: T_1, ..., I_n: T_n **end**', where the type of each E_i is T_i. The identifiers I_1, ..., I_n must all be distinct.)
- The expression '[*AA*]' yields just the value yielded by the array-aggregate *AA*. (The type of '[E_1, ..., E_n]' is '**array** *n* **of** *T*', where the type of every E_i is *T*.)
- The record-aggregate '*I* ~ *E*' yields a record value, whose only field has the identifier *I* and the value yielded by *E*.

- The record-aggregate '*I* ~ *E*, *RA*' yields a record value, whose first field has the identifier *I* and the value yielded by *E*, and whose remaining fields are those of the record value yielded by *RA*.
- The array-aggregate '*E*' yields an array value, whose only component (with index 0) is the value yielded by *E*.
- The array-aggregate '*E*, *AA*' yields an array value, whose first component (with index 0) is the value yielded by *E*, and whose remaining components (with indices 1, 2, ...) are the components of the array value yielded by *AA*.

Examples

The following examples assume the standard environment (Section B.9), and also the following declarations:

```
func multiple (m: Integer,
               n: Integer) : Boolean ~
       (m // n) = 0;

var current: Char;

type Date ~
        record
           y: Integer, m: Integer, d: Integer
        end;
var today: Date;
func leap (yr: Integer): Boolean ~
        ...
```

(a)   `{y ~ today.y + 1, m ~ 1, d ~ 1}`

(b)   `[31, if leap (today.y) then 29 else 28,`
       `31, 30, 31, 30, 31, 31, 30, 31, 30, 31]`

(c)   `eof ()`

(d)   `(multiple (yr, 4) /\ \ multiple (yr, 100))`
       `\/ multiple (yr, 400)`

(e)   `let`
       `const shift ~ ord ('a') - ord ('A');`
       `func capital (ch : Char) : Boolean ~`
           `(ord ('A') <= ord (ch))`
             `/\ (ord (ch) <= ord ('Z'))`
  `in`
       `if capital (current)`
       `then chr (ord (current) + shift)`
       `else current`

B.4 Names

A value-or-variable-name identifies a value or variable.

Syntax

> V-name ::= Identifier
> | V-name . Identifier
> | V-name **[** Expression **]**

Semantics
- The simple value-or-variable-name '*I*' identifies the value or variable bound to *I*. (*I* must be bound to a value or variable. The type of the value-or-variable-name is the type of that value or variable.)
- The qualified value-or-variable-name '*V.I*' identifies the field *I* of the record value or variable identified by *V*. (The type of *V* must be a record type with a field *I*. The type of the value-or-variable-name is the type of that field.)
- The indexed value-or-variable-name '*V*[*E*]' identifies that component, of the array value or variable identified by *V*, whose index is the value yielded by the expression *E*. If the array has no such index, the program fails. (The type of *E* must be Integer, and the type of *V* must be an array type. The type of the value-or-variable-name is the component type of that array type.)

Examples
The following examples assume the standard environment (Section B.9), and also the following declarations:

```
type Date ~
        record
            m : Integer, d : Integer
        end;
const xmas ~ {m ~ 12, d ~ 25};
var easter : Date;
var holiday : array 10 of Date
```

(a) easter

(b) xmas

(c) xmas.m

(d) holiday

(e) holiday[7]

(f) holiday[2].m

B.5 Declarations

A declaration is elaborated to produce bindings. Elaborating a declaration may also have the side effect of creating and updating variables.

Syntax
A single-declaration is just a restricted form of declaration.

Declaration	::=	single-Declaration
	|	Declaration **;** single-Declaration

single-Declaration	::=	**const** Identifier ~ Expression
	|	**var** Identifier **:** Type-denoter
	|	**proc** Identifier **(** Formal-Parameter-Sequence **)** ~
		single-Command
	|	**func** Identifier **(** Formal-Parameter-Sequence **)**
		: Type-denoter ~ Expression
	|	**type** Identifier ~ Type-denoter

Semantics
- The constant declaration '**const** I ~ E' is elaborated by binding I to the value yielded by the expression E. (The type of I will be the type of E.)
- The variable declaration '**var** I : T' is elaborated by binding I to a newly created variable of type T. The variable's current value is initially undefined. The variable exists only during the activation of the block that caused the variable declaration to be elaborated.
- The procedure declaration '**proc** I (FPS) ~ C' is elaborated by binding I to a procedure whose formal-parameter-sequence is FPS and whose body is the command C. The effect of calling that procedure with an argument list is determined as follows: FPS is associated with the argument list; then C is executed, in the environment of the procedure declaration overlaid by the bindings of the formal-parameters.
- The function declaration '**func** I (FPS) : T ~ E' is elaborated by binding I to a function whose formal-parameter-sequence is FPS and whose body is the expression E. The effect of calling that function with an argument list is determined as follows: FPS is associated with the argument list; then E is evaluated to yield a value, in the environment of the function declaration overlaid by the bindings of the formal-parameters. (The type of E must be equivalent to the type denoted by T.)
- The type declaration '**type** I ~ T' is elaborated by binding I to the type denoted by T.
- The sequential declaration 'D_1 **;** D_2' is elaborated by elaborating D_1 followed by D_2, and combining the bindings they produce. D_2 is elaborated in the environment of the sequential declaration, overlaid by the bindings produced by D_1. (D_1 and D_2 must not produce bindings for the same identifier.)

Examples

The following examples assume the standard environment (Section B.9):

(a) **const** minchar ~ chr (0)

(b) **var** name: **array** 20 **of** Char;
    var initial: Char

(c) **proc** inc (**var** n: Integer) ~
           n := n + 1

(d) **func** odd (n: Integer): Boolean ~
           (n // 2) \= 0

(e) **func** power (a: Integer,
               n: Integer): Integer ~
           if n = 0
           then 1
           else a * power (a, n - 1)

(f) **type** Rational ~
           record num: Integer, den: Integer **end**

B.6 Parameters

Formal-parameters are used to parameterize a procedure or function with respect to (some of) the free identifiers in its body. On calling a procedure or function, the formal-parameters are associated with the corresponding arguments, which may be values, variables, procedures, or functions. These arguments are yielded by actual-parameters.

Syntax

```
Formal-Parameter-Sequence
        ::=
        |  proper-Formal-Parameter-Sequence

proper-Formal-Parameter-Sequence
            ::=  Formal-Parameter
            |  Formal-Parameter ,
                  proper-Formal-Parameter-Sequence

Formal-Parameter ::=  Identifier : Type-denoter
                 |  var Identifier : Type-denoter
                 |  proc Identifier ( Formal-Parameter-Sequence )
                 |  func Identifier ( Formal-Parameter-Sequence )
                     : Type-denoter
```

Actual-Parameter-Sequence

   ::=

    | proper-Actual-Parameter-Sequence

proper-Actual-Parameter-Sequence

    ::= Actual-Parameter

    | Actual-Parameter ,

       proper-Actual-Parameter-Sequence

Actual-Parameter ::= Expression

    | **var** V-name

    | **proc** Identifier

    | **func** Identifier

(The first form of actual-parameter-sequence and the first form of formal-parameter-sequence are empty.)

Semantics

- A formal-parameter-sequence 'FP_1, ..., FP_n' is associated with a list of arguments, by associating each FP_i with the ith argument. The corresponding actual-parameter-sequence 'AP_1, ..., AP_n' yields a list of arguments, with each AP_i yielding the ith argument. (The number of actual parameters must equal the number of actual parameters, and the corresponding actual and formal parameters must be compatible. Both the formal-parameter-sequence and the actual-parameter-sequence may be empty.)
- The formal-parameter '$I : T$' is associated with an argument value by binding I to that argument. The corresponding actual-parameter must be of the form 'E', and the argument value is obtained by evaluating E. (The type of E must be equivalent to the type denoted by T.)
- The formal-parameter '**var** $I : T$' is associated with an argument variable by binding I to that argument. The corresponding actual-parameter must be of the form '**var** V', and the argument variable is the one identified by V. (The type of V must be equivalent to the type denoted by T.)
- The formal-parameter '**proc** I (FPS)' is associated with an argument procedure by binding I to that argument. The corresponding actual-parameter must be of the form '**proc** I', and the argument procedure is the one bound to I. (I must be bound to a procedure, and that procedure must have a formal-parameter-sequence equivalent to FPS.)
- The formal-parameter '**func** I (FPS) : T' is associated with an argument function by binding I to that argument. The corresponding actual-parameter must be of the form '**func** I', and the argument function is the one bound to I. (I must be bound to a function, and that function must have a formal-parameter-sequence equivalent to FPS and a result type equivalent to the type denoted by T.)

Examples

The following examples assume the standard environment (Section B.9):

(a)
```
while \ eol () do
   begin get (var ch); put (ch) end;
geteol (); puteol ()
```

(b)
```
proc increment (var count: Integer) ~
        count := count + 1
...
increment (var freq[n])
```

(c)
```
func uppercase (letter: Char): Char ~
        if (ord('a') <= ord(letter))
           /\ (ord(letter) <= ord('z'))
        then chr (ord(letter)-ord('a')+ord('A'))
        else letter
...
if uppercase (request) = 'Q' then quit
```

(d)
```
type Point ~ record x: Integer, y: Integer end;

proc shiftright (var pt: Point, xshift: Integer) ~
        pt.x := pt.x + xshift
...
shiftright (var penposition, 10)
```

(e)
```
proc iteratively (proc p (n: Integer),
                    var a: array 10 of Integer) ~
        let var i: Integer
        in
           begin
           i := 0;
           while i < 10 do
              begin p (a[i]); i := i + 1 end
           end;

var v : array 10 of Integer
...
iteratively (proc putint, var v)
```

B.7   Type-denoters

A type-denoter denotes a data type. Every value, constant, variable, and function has a specified type.

A record-type-denoter denotes the structure of a record type.

Syntax

> Type-denoter ::= Identifier
> | **array** Integer-Literal **of** Type-denoter
> | **record** Record-Type-denoter **end**
>
> Record-Type-denoter
> ::= Identifier : Type-denoter
> | Identifier : Type-denoter , Record-Type-denoter

Semantics

- The type-denoter '*I*' denotes the type bound to *I*.
- The type-denoter '**array** *IL* **of** *T*' denotes a type whose values are arrays. Each array value of this type has an index range whose lower bound is zero and whose upper bound is one less than the integer-literal *IL*. Each array value has one component of type *T* for each value in its index range.
- The type-denoter '**record** *RT* **end**' denotes a type whose values are records. Each record value of this type has the record structure denoted by *RT*.
- The record-type-denoter '*I* : *T*' denotes a record structure whose only field has the identifier *I* and the type *T*.
- The record-type-denoter '*I* : *T*, *RT*' denotes a record structure whose first field has the identifier *I* and the type *T*, and whose remaining fields are determined by the record structure denoted by *RT*. *I* must not be a field identifier of *RT*.

   (Type equivalence is structural:

- Two primitive types are equivalent if and only if they are the same type.
- The type **record** ..., I_i: T_i, ... **end** is equivalent to **record** ..., I_i': T_i', ... **end** if and only if each I_i is the same as I_i' and each T_i is equivalent to T_i'.
- The type **array** n **of** T is equivalent to **array** n' **of** T' if and only $n = n'$ and T is equivalent to T'.)

Examples

   (a) `Boolean`

   (b) **`array`** `80` **`of`** `Char`

   (c) **`record`** `y: Integer, m: Month, d: Integer` **`end`**

   (d) **`record`**
```
     size: Integer,
     entry: array 100 of
             record
                 name: array 20 of Char,
                 number: Integer
             end
     end
```

B.8   Lexicon

At the lexical level, the program text consists of tokens, comments, and blank space.

The tokens are literals, identifiers, operators, various reserved words, and various punctuation marks. No reserved word may be chosen as an identifier.

Comments and blank space have no significance, but may be used freely to improve the readability of the program text. However, two consecutive tokens that would otherwise be confused must be separated by comments and/or blank space.

Syntax

Program	::=	(Token I Comment I Blank)*
Token	::=	Integer-Literal I Character-Literal I Identifier I Operator I **array** I **begin** I **const** I **do** I **else** I **end** I **func** I **if** I **in** I **let** I **of** I **proc** I **record** I **then** I **type** I **var** I **while** I . I : I ; I , I := I ~ I (I) I [I] I { I }
Integer-Literal	::=	Digit Digit*
Character-Literal	::=	'Graphic'
Identifier	::=	Letter (Letter I Digit)*
Operator	::=	Op-character Op-character*
Comment	::=	! Graphic* end-of-line
Blank	::=	space I tab I end-of-line
Graphic	::=	Letter | Digit | Op-character | space | tab | . | : | ; | , | ~ I (I) I [I] I { I } I _ I | I ! I ' I ` I " I # I $
Letter	::=	a I b I c I d I e I f I g I h I i I j I k I l I m I n I o I p I q I r I s I t I u I v I w I x I y I z I A I B I C I D I E I F I G I H I I I J I K I L I M I N I O I P I Q I R I S I T I U I V I W I X I Y I Z
Digit	::=	0 I 1 I 2 I 3 I 4 I 5 I 6 I 7 I 8 I 9
Op-character	::=	+ I - I * I / I = I < I > I \ I & I @ I % I ^ I ?

(*Note:* The symbols space, tab, and end-of-line stand for individual characters that cannot stand for themselves in the syntactic rules.)

Semantics
- The value of the integer-literal $d_n...d_1d_0$ is $d_n \times 10^n + ... + d_1 \times 10 + d_0$.
- The value of the character-literal 'c' is the graphic character c.
- Every character in an identifier is significant. The cases of the letters in an identifier are also significant.

- Every character in an operator is significant. Operators are, in effect, a subclass of identifiers (but they are bound only in the standard environment, to unary and binary functions).

Examples

(a) Integer-literals: 0   1987

(b) Character-literals: '%'   'Z'   '''

(c) Identifiers: x   pi   v101   Integer   get   gasFlowRate

(d) Operators: +   *   <=   \=   \/

B.9 Programs

A program communicates with the user by performing input–output.

Syntax

Program   ::=   Command

Semantics
- The program '*C*' is run by executing the command *C* in the standard environment.

Example

```
let
   type Line ~ record
                  length: Integer,
                  content: array 80 of Char
               end;

   proc getline (var l: Line) ~
            begin
            l.length := 0;
            while \ eol () do
               begin
               get (var l.content[l.length]);
               l.length := l.length + 1
               end;
            geteol ()
            end;

   proc putreversedline (l: Line) ~
            let var i : Integer
            in
```

```
              begin
              i := l.length;
              while i > 0 do
                 begin
                 i := i - 1;
                 put (l.content[i])
                 end;
              puteol ()
              end;

     var currentline: Line

in
   while \ eof () do
      begin
      getline (var currentline);
      putreversedline (currentline)
      end
```

Standard environment

The standard environment includes the following constant, type, procedure, and function declarations:

```
type Boolean ~ ...;    ! truth values false and true
const false ~ ...;     ! the truth value false
const true  ~ ...;     ! the truth value true
func \   (b: Boolean): Boolean ~
         ...;    ! not b, i.e., logical negation
func /\  (b1: Boolean, b2: Boolean): Boolean ~
         ...;    ! b1 and b2, i.e., logical conjunction
func \/  (b1: Boolean, b2: Boolean): Boolean ~
         ...;    ! b1 or b2, i.e., logical disjunction

type Integer ~ ...;    ! integers up to maxint in magnitude
const maxint ~ ...;    ! implementation-defined maximum integer
func +   (i1: Integer, i2: Integer): Integer ~
         ...;    ! i1 plus i2
                 ! failing if the result exceeds maxint in magnitude
func -   (i1: Integer, i2: Integer): Integer ~
         ...;    ! i1 minus i2
                 ! failing if the result exceeds maxint in magnitude
func *   (i1: Integer, i2: Integer): Integer ~
         ...;    ! i1 times i2
                 ! failing if the result exceeds maxint in magnitude
func /   (i1: Integer, i2: Integer): Integer ~
         ...;    ! i1 divided by i2, truncated towards zero
                 ! failing if i2 is zero
```

```
func //  (i1: Integer, i2: Integer): Integer ~
         ...;    ! i1 modulo i2
                 ! failing unless i2 is positive
func <   (i1: Integer, i2: Integer): Boolean ~
         ...;    ! true iff i1 is less than i2
func <=  (i1: Integer, i2: Integer): Boolean ~
         ...;    ! true iff i1 is less than or equal to i2
func >   (i1: Integer, i2: Integer): Boolean ~
         ...;    ! true iff i1 is greater than i2
func >=  (i1: Integer, i2: Integer): Boolean ~
         ...;    ! true iff i1 is greater than or equal to i2

type Char ~ ...;    ! implementation-defined character set
func chr (i: Integer): Char ~
         ...;    ! character whose internal code is i
                 ! failing if no such character exists
func ord (c: Char): Integer ~
         ...;    ! internal code of c

func eof (): Boolean ~
         ...;    ! true iff end-of-file has been reached in input
func eol (): Boolean ~
         ...;    ! true iff end-of-line has been reached in input
proc get (var c: Char) ~
         ...;    ! read the next character from input and assign it to c
                 ! failing if end-of-file already reached
proc put (c: Char) ~
         ...;    ! write character c to output
proc getint (var i: Integer) ~
         ...;    ! read an integer literal from input and assign its value
                 ! to i
                 ! failing if the value exceeds maxint in magnitude
                 ! failing if end-of-file already reached
proc putint (i: Integer) ~
         ...;    ! write to output the integer literal whose value is i
proc geteol () ~
         ...;    ! skip past the next end-of-line in input
                 ! failing if end-of-file already reached
proc puteol () ~
         ...;    ! write an end-of-line to output
```

In addition, the following functions are available for every type T:

```
func =   (val1: T, val2: T): Boolean ~
         ...;    ! true iff val1 is equal to val2
func \=  (val1: T, val2: T): Boolean ~
         ...     ! true iff val1 is not equal to val2
```

Description of the Abstract Machine TAM

TAM is an abstract machine whose design makes it especially suitable for executing programs compiled from a block-structured language (such as Algol, Pascal, or Δ). All evaluation takes place on a stack. Primitive arithmetic, logical, and other operations are treated uniformly with programmed functions and procedures.

C.1 Storage and registers

TAM has two separate stores:

- *Code Store*, consisting of 32-bit instruction words (read only).
- *Data Store*, consisting of 16-bit data words (read–write).

The layouts of both stores are illustrated in Figure C.1.

Each store is divided into *segments*, whose boundaries are pointed to by dedicated registers. Data and instructions are always addressed relative to one of these registers.

While a program is running, the segmentation of Code Store is fixed, as follows:

- The *code segment* contains the program's instructions. Registers CB and CT point to the base and top of the code segment. Register CP points to the next instruction to be executed, and is initially equal to CB (i.e., the program's first instruction is at the base of the code segment).
- The *primitive segment* contains 'microcode' for elementary arithmetic, logical, input–output, heap, and general-purpose operations. Registers PB and PT point to the base and top of the primitive segment.

While a program is running, the segmentation of Data Store may vary:

- The *stack* grows from the low-address end of Data Store. Registers SB and ST point to the base and top of the stack, and ST is initially equal to SB.
- The *heap* grows from the high-address end of Data Store. Registers HB and HT point to the base and top of the heap, and HT is initially equal to HB.

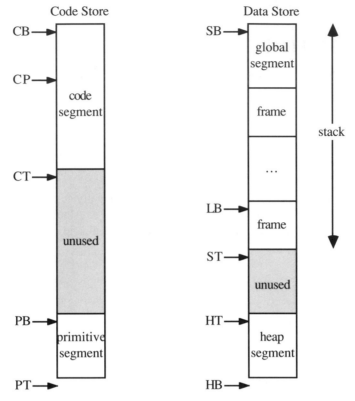

Figure C.1 Layout of the TAM Code Store and Data Store.

Both stack and heap can expand and contract. Storage exhaustion arises when ST and HT attempt to cross over.

The stack itself consists of one or more segments:

- The *global segment* is always at the base of the stack, and contains global data used by the program.
- The stack may contain any number of other segments, known as *frames*. Each frame contains data local to an activation of some routine. Calling a routine causes a new frame to be pushed on to the stack; return from a routine causes the topmost frame to be popped. The topmost frame may expand and contract, but the underlying frames are (temporarily) fixed in size. Register LB points to the base of the topmost frame.

Figure C.2 shows the outline of a source program in some block-structured language. Figure C.3 shows successive stack snapshots while this program is running:

(a) The main program has called procedure P. Register LB points to the topmost frame, associated with P.
(b) Procedure P has called procedure S. Register LB points to the topmost frame, associated with S; register L1 points to a frame associated with P.

(c) Procedure S has called procedure Q. Register LB points to the topmost frame, associated with Q; register L1 still points to a frame associated with P.

(d) Procedure Q has called procedure R. Register LB points to the topmost frame, associated with R; register L1 now points to a frame associated with Q; register L2 points to a frame associated with P.

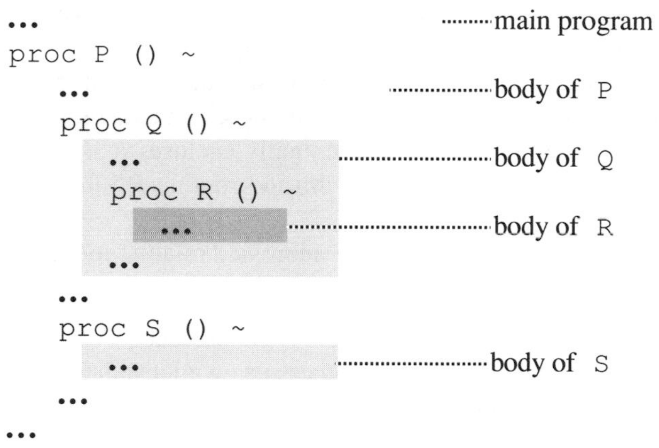

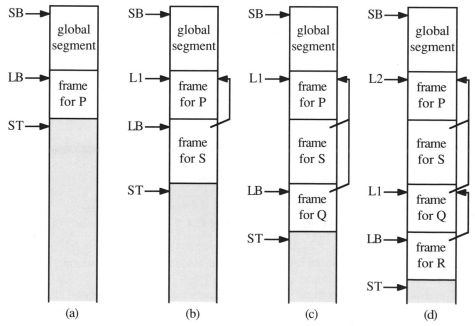

Figure C.2 Outline of a source program.

Figure C.3 Snapshots of the TAM stack. (Dynamic links, and static links pointing to the global segment, are not shown.)

Global, local, and nonlocal data can be accessed as follows:

LOAD (*n*)	*d*[SB]	– for any procedure to load global data
LOAD (*n*)	*d*[LB]	– for any procedure to load its own local data
LOAD (*n*)	*d*[L1]	– for procedure Q or S to load data local to P
LOAD (*n*)	*d*[L1]	– for procedure R to load data local to Q
LOAD (*n*)	*d*[L2]	– for procedure R to load data local to P

In each case an *n*-word object is loaded from address *d* relative to the base of the appropriate segment. Storing is analogous to loading.

In general, register LB points to the topmost frame, which is always associated with the routine *R* whose code is currently being executed; register L1 points to a frame associated with the routine *R'* that textually encloses *R* in the source program; register L2 points to a frame associated with the routine *R''* that textually encloses *R'*; and so on.

All accessible data in the stack may be addressed relative to registers SB, LB, L1, L2, etc., as follows:

d[SB]	– for any routine to access global data
d[LB]	– for any routine to access its own local data
d[L1]	– for routine *R* to access data local to *R'*
d[L2]	– for routine *R* to access data local to *R''*

In each case an object is accessed at address *d* relative to the base of the appropriate segment. (In practice, registers L1, L2, etc., are used far less often than LB and SB.)

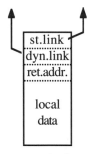

Figure C.4 Layout of a frame in TAM.

The layout of a frame is illustrated in Figure C.4. Consider a frame associated with routine *R*:

• The *static link* points to an underlying frame associated with the routine that textually encloses *R* in the source program.
• The *dynamic link* points to the frame immediately underlying this one in the stack.
• The *return address* is the address of the instruction immediately following the call instruction that activated *R*.

There are sixteen registers, summarized in Table C.1. Every register is dedicated to a particular purpose. (No instructions use registers to operate on data.) Some of the registers are constant.

Note that L1, L2, etc., are only pseudo-registers – whenever needed for addressing nonlocal data, they are dynamically evaluated from LB using the invariants L1 = *content*(LB), L2 = *content*(*content*(LB)), etc., where *content*(*a*) means the word contained at address *a*. This works because LB points to the first word of a frame, which contains its static link, which in turn points to the first word of an underlying frame, and so on.

Table C.1 Summary of TAM registers.

Register number	*Register mnemonic*	*Register name*	*Behavior*
0	CB	Code Base	constant
1	CT	Code Top	constant
2	PB	Primitives Base	constant
3	PT	Primitives Top	constant
4	SB	Stack Base	constant
5	ST	Stack Top	changed by most instructions
6	HB	Heap Base	constant
7	HT	Heap Top	changed by heap routines
8	LB	Local Base	changed by call and return instructions
9	L1	Local base 1	$L1 = content(\text{LB})$
10	L2	Local base 2	$L2 = content(content(\text{LB}))$
11	L3	Local base 3	$L3 = content(content(content(\text{LB})))$
12	L4	Local base 4	$L4 = content(content(content(\\ content(\text{LB}))))$
13	L5	Local base 5	$L5 = content(content(content(\\ content(content(\text{LB})))))$
14	L6	Local base 6	$L6 = content(content(content(\\ content(content(content(\text{LB}))))))$
15	CP	Code Pointer	changed by all instructions

C.2 Instructions

All TAM instructions have a common format, illustrated in Figure C.5. The *op* field contains the operation code. The *r* field contains a register number, and the *d* field usually contains an address displacement (possibly negative); together these define the operand's address (*d* + register *r*). The *n* field usually contains the size of the operand. The TAM instruction set is summarized in Table C.2 (page 376).

op	*r*	*n*	*d*
4 bits	4 bits	8 bits	16 bits (signed)

Figure C.5 TAM instruction format.

C.3   Routines

Every TAM routine must strictly respect the protocol illustrated in Figure C.6. Assume that routine R accepts d words of arguments and returns an n-word result. Immediately before R is called, its arguments must be at the stack top. (If R takes no arguments, d will be zero.) On return from R, its arguments must be replaced at the stack top by its result. (If R does not return a result, n will be zero.)

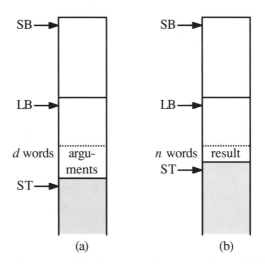

Figure C.6 Stack layout (a) before, and (b) after calling a TAM routine.

There are two kinds of routine in TAM:

- code routines
- primitive routines

A *code routine* consists of a sequence of instructions stored in the code segment. Control is transferred to the first instruction of that sequence by a CALL or CALLI instruction, and subsequently transferred back by a RETURN instruction. Figure C.7 illustrates the layout of the stack during a call to a code routine R.

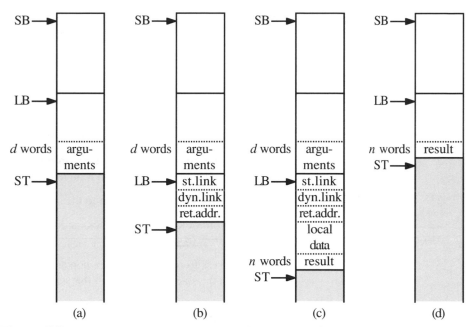

Figure C.7 Stack layout (a) before, (b–c) during, and (d) after calling a code routine.

(a) Immediately before the call, *R*'s arguments (if any) must be at the stack top.

(b) The call instruction pushes a new frame on top of the arguments. The frame's static link is supplied by the call instruction. (The instruction 'CALL (*n*) ...' takes the address in register *n* as the static link. The instruction 'CALLI' takes the static link from the closure at the stack top.) The frame's dynamic link is the address formerly in register LB. The frame's return address is the address of the instruction immediately following the call instruction. At this stage the new frame contains only these three words.

(c) The instructions of *R* may expand the topmost frame, e.g., by allocating space for local data. Immediately before the return, *R* must place any result at the stack top.

(d) The return instruction 'RETURN (*n*) *d*' pops the topmost frame and replaces the *d* words of arguments by the *n*-word result. LB is reset using the dynamic link, and control is transferred to the instruction at the return address.

Since *R*'s arguments lie immediately below its frame, *R* can access the arguments using negative displacements relative to LB. For example:

```
LOAD(1) -d[LB]     – for R to load its first argument (1 word)
LOAD(1) -1[LB]     – for R to load its last argument (1 word)
```

A *primitive routine* is one that performs an elementary arithmetic, logical, input–output, heap, or general-purpose operation. The primitive routines are summarized in Table C.3. Each primitive routine has a fixed address in the primitive segment. TAM traps every call to an address in that segment, and performs the corresponding operation directly.

Table C.2 Summary of TAM instructions.

Op-code	Instruction mnemonic	Effect
0	LOAD (n) $d[r]$	Fetch an n-word object from the data address (d + register r), and push it on to the stack.
1	LOADA $d[r]$	Push the data address (d + register r) on to the stack.
2	LOADI (n)	Pop a data address from the stack, fetch an n-word object from that address, and push it on to the stack.
3	LOADL d	Push the 1-word literal value d on to the stack.
4	STORE (n) $d[r]$	Pop an n-word object from the stack, and store it at the data address (d + register r).
5	STOREI (n)	Pop an address from the stack, then pop an n-word object from the stack and store it at that address.
6	CALL (n) $d[r]$	Call the routine at code address (d + register r), using the address in register n as the static link.
7	CALLI	Pop a closure (static link and code address) from the stack, then call the routine at that code address.
8	RETURN (n) d	Return from the current routine: pop an n-word result from the stack, then pop the topmost frame, then pop d words of arguments, then push the result back on to the stack.
9	–	(unused)
10	PUSH d	Push d words (uninitialized) on to the stack.
11	POP (n) d	Pop an n-word result from the stack, then pop d more words, then push the result back on to the stack.
12	JUMP $d[r]$	Jump to code address (d + register r).
13	JUMPI	Pop a code address from the stack, then jump to that address.
14	JUMPIF (n) $d[r]$	Pop a 1-word value from the stack, then jump to code address (d + register r) if and only if that value equals n.
15	HALT	Stop execution of the program.

Table C.3 Summary of TAM primitive routines.

Address	Mnemonic	Arguments	Result	Effect
PB + 1	id	w	w'	Set $w' = w$.
PB + 2	not	t	t'	Set $t' = \neg\, t$.
PB + 3	and	t_1, t_2	t'	Set $t' = t_1 \wedge t_2$.
PB + 4	or	t_1, t_2	t'	Set $t' = t_1 \vee t_2$.
PB + 5	succ	i	i'	Set $i' = i + 1$.
PB + 6	pred	i	i'	Set $i' = i - 1$.
PB + 7	neg	i	i'	Set $i' = -i$.
PB + 8	add	i_1, i_2	i'	Set $i' = i_1 + i_2$.
PB + 9	sub	i_1, i_2	i'	Set $i' = i_1 - i_2$.
PB + 10	mult	i_1, i_2	i'	Set $i' = i_1 \times i_2$.
PB + 11	div	i_1, i_2	i'	Set $i' = i_1 / i_2$ (truncated).
PB + 12	mod	i_1, i_2	i'	Set $i' = i_1$ modulo i_2.
PB + 13	lt	i_1, i_2	t'	Set $t' = true$ iff $i_1 < i_2$.
PB + 14	le	i_1, i_2	t'	Set $t' = true$ iff $i_1 \leq i_2$.
PB + 15	ge	i_1, i_2	t'	Set $t' = true$ iff $i_1 \geq i_2$.
PB + 16	gt	i_1, i_2	t'	Set $t' = true$ iff $i_1 > i_2$.
PB + 17	eq	v_1, v_2, i	t'	Set $t' = true$ iff $v_1 = v_2$.
PB + 18	ne	v_1, v_2, i	t'	Set $t' = true$ iff $v_1 \neq v_2$. (v_1 and v_2 are i-word values.)
PB + 19	eol	–	t'	Set $t' = true$ iff the next character to be read is an end-of-line.
PB + 20	eof	–	t'	Set $t' = true$ iff there are no more characters to be read (end of file).
PB + 21	get	a	–	Read a character, and store it at address a.
PB + 22	put	c	–	Write the character c.
PB + 23	geteol	–	–	Read characters up to and including the next end-of-line.
PB + 24	puteol	–	–	Write an end-of-line.
PB + 25	getint	a	–	Read an integer-literal (optionally preceded by blanks and/or signed), and store its value at address a.
PB + 26	putint	i	–	Write the integer-literal i.
PB + 27	new	i	a'	Set $a' =$ address of a newly allocated i-word object in the heap.
PB + 28	dispose	i, a	–	Deallocate the i-word object at address a in the heap.

Notes for Table C.3
- *a* denotes a data address
- *c* denotes a character
- *i* denotes an integer
- *t* denotes a truth value (0 for *false* or 1 for *true*)
- *v* denotes a value of any type
- *w* denotes any 1-word value

The TAM Interpreter

This appendix lists an interpreter for the abstract machine TAM, which is described in Appendix C. The interpreter is written as two THINK Pascal units. (See the notes on THINK Pascal at the start of Appendix E.)

D.1   Run-time organization

```
unit RuntimeOrganization;

interface

{WORDS AND ADDRESSES}

  type
    Word = -32767..+32767;    {16 bits signed}
    CodeAddress = 0..+32767;  {15 bits unsigned}
    DataAddress = 0..+32767;  {15 bits unsigned}


{INSTRUCTIONS}

  const
    LOADop = 0;     LOADAop = 1;   LOADIop = 2;   LOADLop = 3;
    STOREop = 4;    STOREIop = 5;  CALLop = 6;    CALLIop = 7;
    RETURNop = 8;                  PUSHop = 10;   POPop = 11;
    JUMPop = 12;    JUMPIop = 13;  JUMPIFop = 14; HALTop = 15;
    {Operation codes}

  type
    OpCode = 0..15;               {4 bits unsigned}
    Length = 0..255;              {8 bits unsigned}
    RegisterNumber = 0..15;       {4 bits unsigned}
    Operand = -32767..+32767;     {16 bits signed}

    Instruction = packed record
        op: OpCode;
        r: RegisterNumber;
        n: Length;
        d: Operand
      end;
      {Represents TAM instructions.}
```

```
{CODE STORE}

  var
    code: array[0..1023] of Instruction;


{CODE STORE REGISTERS}

  const
    CB = 0;
    PB = 1024; {= upper bound of code + 1}
    PT = 1052; {= PB + 28}
  var
    CT, CP: Word;


{REGISTER NUMBERS}

  const
    CBr = 0;    CTr = 1;    PBr = 2;    PTr = 3;
    SBr = 4;    STr = 5;    HBr = 6;    HTr = 7;
    LBr = 8;    L1r = 9;    L2r = 10;   L3r = 11;
    L4r = 12;   L5r = 13;   L6r = 14;   CPr = 15;
    {L1r = LBr+1, L2r = LBr+2, etc.}


{DATA REPRESENTATION}

  const
    booleanSize = 1;
    characterSize = 1;
    integerSize = 1;
    addressSize = 1;
    closureSize = 2;  {= 2 * addressSize}

    linkDataSize = 3; {= 3 * addressSize}

    falseRep = 0;
    trueRep = 1;
    maxintRep = 32767;


{ADDRESSES OF PRIMITIVE ROUTINES}

  const
    idDisplacement = 1;       otDisplacement = 2;
    andDisplacement = 3;      orDisplacement = 4;
    succDisplacement = 5;     predDisplacement = 6;
    negDisplacement = 7;      addDisplacement = 8;
    subDisplacement = 9;      multDisplacement = 10;
    divDisplacement = 11;     modDisplacement = 12;
    ltDisplacement = 13;      leDisplacement = 14;
    geDisplacement = 15;      gtDisplacement = 16;
    eqDisplacement = 17;      neDisplacement = 18;
    eolDisplacement = 19;     eofDisplacement = 20;
    getDisplacement = 21;     putDisplacement = 22;
    geteolDisplacement = 23;  puteolDisplacement = 24;
    getintDisplacement = 25;  putintDisplacement = 26;
    newDisplacement = 27;     disposeDisplacement = 28;

{================================================================================}

implementation

      {Nothing to implement!}

end. {RuntimeOrganization}
```

D.2 Interpretation

```
unit Interpreter;

interface

  uses
    RuntimeOrganization;

  procedure runProgram;
      {Runs the object program in Code Store.}

{================================================================================}

implementation

  type
    Natural = 0..maxInt;


{DATA STORE}

  var
    data: array[0..1023] of Word;


{DATA STORE REGISTERS AND OTHER REGISTERS}

  const
    SB = 0;
    HB = 1024;  {= upper bound of data array + 1}
  var
    ST, HT, LB: Word;
    status: (running, halted, failedDataStoreFull, failedInvalidCodeAddress,
        failedInvalidInstruction, failedOverflow, failedZeroDivide);
    accumulator: LongInt;

  function relative (d: Operand;
                     r: RegisterNumber): Word;
      {Returns the address d relative to register r, even if r is one of the
       pseudo-registers L1..L6.}
  begin
    case r of
      CBr:  relative := d + CB;
      CTr:  relative := d + CT;
      PBr:  relative := d + PB;
      PTr:  relative := d + PT;
      SBr:  relative := d + SB;
      STr:  relative := d + ST;
      HBr:  relative := d + HB;
      HTr:  relative := d + HT;
      LBr:  relative := d + LB;
      L1r:  relative := d + data[LB];
      L2r:  relative := d + data[data[LB]];
      L3r:  relative := d + data[data[data[LB]]];
      L4r:  relative := d + data[data[data[data[LB]]]];
      L5r:  relative := d + data[data[data[data[data[LB]]]]];
      L6r:  relative := d + data[data[data[data[data[data[LB]]]]]];
      CPr:  relative := d + CP
    end {case}
  end; {relative}
```

```
{PROGRAM STATUS}

  procedure dump;
    ...; {Writes a summary of the machine state.}

  procedure showStatus;
      {Writes an indication of whether and why the program has terminated.}
  begin
    ...;
    if status <> halted then dump
  end; {showStatus}

{INTERPRETATION}

  procedure checkSpace (spaceNeeded: Natural);
      {Checks whether there is enough space to expand the stack or heap by
       spaceNeeded. Fail if there is not enough space.}
  begin
    if HT - ST < spaceNeeded then status := failedDataStoreFull
  end; {checkSpace}

  procedure callPrimitive (primitiveDisplacement: Operand);
      {Invokes the given primitive routine.}
    var
      addr: DataAddress;
      size: Natural;
      ch: Char;

    function isTrue (datum: Word): Boolean;
    begin
      isTrue := (datum = trueRep)
    end; {isTrue}

    function equal (size: Natural;
                      addr1, addr2: DataAddress): Boolean;
      var
        eq: Boolean;
        index: Natural;
    begin
      eq := true;   index := 0;
      while eq and (index < size) do
        if data[addr1 + index] = data[addr2 + index] then
          index := index + 1
        else
          eq := false;
      equal := eq
    end; {equal}

    function overflowChecked (datum: LongInt): Word;
    begin
      if (-maxIntRep <= datum) and (datum <= maxIntRep) then
        overflowChecked := datum
      else
        begin
          status := failedOverflow;  overflowChecked := 0
        end
    end; {overflowChecked}

  begin {callPrimitive}
    case primitiveDisplacement of
      idDisplacement:
        ; {nothing to be done}
      notDisplacement:
        data[ST - 1] := ord(not isTrue(data[ST - 1]));
      andDisplacement:
        begin
          ST := ST - 1;
          data[ST - 1] := ord(isTrue(data[ST - 1]) and isTrue(data[ST]))
        end;
```

```
orDisplacement:
  begin
    ST := ST - 1;
    data[ST - 1] := ord(isTrue(data[ST - 1]) or isTrue(data[ST]))
  end;
succDisplacement:
  data[ST - 1] := overflowChecked(succ(data[ST - 1]));
predDisplacement:
  data[ST - 1] := overflowChecked(pred(data[ST - 1]));
negDisplacement:
  data[ST - 1] := -data[ST - 1];
addDisplacement:
  begin
    ST := ST - 1;  accumulator := data[ST - 1];
    data[ST - 1] := overflowChecked(accumulator + data[ST])
  end;
subDisplacement:
  begin
    ST := ST - 1;  accumulator := data[ST - 1];
    data[ST - 1] := overflowChecked(accumulator - data[ST])
  end;
multDisplacement:
  begin
    ST := ST - 1;  accumulator := data[ST - 1];
    data[ST - 1] := overflowChecked(accumulator * data[ST])
  end;
divDisplacement:
  begin
    ST := ST - 1;  accumulator := data[ST - 1];
    if data[ST] <> 0 then
      data[ST - 1] := accumulator div data[ST]
    else
      status := failedZeroDivide
  end;
modDisplacement:
  begin
    ST := ST - 1;  accumulator := data[ST - 1];
    if data[ST] <> 0 then
      data[ST - 1] := accumulator mod data[ST]
    else
      status := failedZeroDivide
  end;
ltDisplacement:
  begin
    ST := ST - 1;
    data[ST - 1] := ord(data[ST - 1] < data[ST])
  end;
leDisplacement:
  begin
    ST := ST - 1;
    data[ST - 1] := ord(data[ST - 1] <= data[ST])
  end;
geDisplacement:
  begin
    ST := ST - 1;
    data[ST - 1] := ord(data[ST - 1] >= data[ST])
  end;
gtDisplacement:
  begin
    ST := ST - 1;
    data[ST - 1] := ord(data[ST - 1] > data[ST])
  end;
eqDisplacement:
  begin
    size := data[ST - 1]; {size of each comparand}
    ST := ST - 2 * size;
    data[ST - 1] := ord(equal(size, ST - 1, ST - 1 + size))
  end;
neDisplacement:
```

```
          begin
            size := data[ST - 1]; {size of each comparand}
            ST := ST - 2 * size;
            data[ST - 1] := ord(not equal(size, ST - 1, ST - 1 + size))
          end;
        eolDisplacement:
          begin
            data[ST] := ord(eoln);  ST := ST + 1
          end;
        eofDisplacement:
          begin
            data[ST] := ord(eof);  ST := ST + 1
          end;
        getDisplacement:
          begin
            ST := ST - 1;  addr := data[ST];
            read(ch);  data[addr] := ord(ch)
          end;
        putDisplacement:
          begin
            ST := ST - 1;  ch := chr(data[ST]);
            write(ch)
          end;
        geteolDisplacement:
          readLn;
        puteolDisplacement:
          writeLn;
        getintDisplacement:
          begin
            ST := ST - 1;  addr := data[ST];
            read(accumulator);  data[addr] := accumulator
          end;
        putintDisplacement:
          begin
            ST := ST - 1;  accumulator := data[ST];
            write(accumulator : 1)
          end;
        newDisplacement:
          begin
            size := data[ST - 1];
            checkSpace(size);
            HT := HT - size;
            data[ST - 1] := HT
          end;
        disposeDisplacement:
          begin
            ST := ST - 1 {no action taken at present}
          end
    end {case}
end; {callPrimitive}

procedure interpretProgram;
    {Actually runs the program.}
  var
    currentInstr: Instruction;
    op: OpCode;
    r: RegisterNumber;
    n: Length;
    d: Operand;
    addr, index: Word;
begin
  {Initialize registers ...}
  ST := SB;  HT := HB;  LB := SB;  CP := CB;
  status := running;
  repeat
  {Fetch instruction ...}
    currentInstr := code[CP];
  {Decode instruction ...}
    op := currentInstr.op;  r := currentInstr.r;
```

```
    n := currentInstr.n;   d := currentInstr.d;
{Execute instruction ...}
  case op of
    LOADop:
      begin
        addr := relative(d, r);   checkSpace(n);
        for index := 0 to n - 1 do
          data[ST + index] := data[addr + index];
        ST := ST + n;   CP := CP + 1
      end;
    LOADAop:
      begin
        addr := relative(d, r);   checkSpace(1);
        data[ST] := addr;   ST := ST + 1;   CP := CP + 1
      end;
    LOADIop:
      begin
        ST := ST - 1;   addr := data[ST];   checkSpace(n);
        for index := 0 to n - 1 do
          data[ST + index] := data[addr + index];
        ST := ST + n;   CP := CP + 1
      end;
    LOADLop:
      begin
        checkSpace(1);   data[ST] := d;   ST := ST + 1;   CP := CP + 1
      end;
    STOREop:
      begin
        addr := relative(d, r);   ST := ST - n;
        for index := 0 to n - 1 do
          data[addr + index] := data[ST + index];
        CP := CP + 1
      end;
    STOREIop:
      begin
        ST := ST - 1;   addr := data[ST];   ST := ST - n;
        for index := 0 to n - 1 do
          data[addr + index] := data[ST + index];
        CP := CP + 1
      end;
    CALLop:
      begin
        addr := relative(d, r);
        if addr >= PB then
          begin
            callPrimitive(addr - PB);   CP := CP + 1
          end
        else
          begin
            checkSpace(3);
            if n in [0..15] then
              data[ST] := relative(0, n)   {static link}
            else
              status := failedInvalidInstruction;
            data[ST + 1] := LB;              {dynamic link}
            data[ST + 2] := CP + 1;         {return address}
            LB := ST;   ST := ST + 3;   CP := addr
          end
      end;
    CALLIop:
      begin
        ST := ST - 2;   addr := data[ST + 1];
        if addr >= PB then
          begin
            callPrimitive(addr - PB);   CP := CP + 1
          end
        else
          begin                          {static link in place already}
            data[ST + 1] := LB;      {dynamic link}
```

```
                    data[ST + 2] := CP + 1; {return address}
                  LB := ST;   ST := ST + 3;   CP := addr
              end
        end;
      RETURNop:
        begin
          addr := LB - d;   CP := data[LB + 2];
          LB := data[LB + 1];   ST := ST - n;
          for index := 0 to n - 1 do
            data[addr + index] := data[ST + index];
          ST := addr + n
        end;
      PUSHop:
        begin
          checkSpace(d);   ST := ST + d;   CP := CP + 1
        end;
      POPop:
        begin
          addr := ST - n - d;   ST := ST - n;
          for index := 0 to n - 1 do
            data[addr + index] := data[ST + index];
          ST := addr + n;   CP := CP + 1
        end;
      JUMPop:
        CP := relative(d, r);
      JUMPIop:
        begin
          ST := ST - 1;   CP := data[ST]
        end;
      JUMPIFop:
        begin
          ST := ST - 1;
          if data[ST] = n then
            CP := relative(d, r)
          else
            CP := CP + 1
        end;
      HALTop:
        status := halted
    end; {case}
    if (CP < CB) or (CP >= CT) then
      status := failedInvalidCodeAddress
  until status <> running
end; {interpretProgram}


{RUNNING}

  procedure runProgram;
  begin
    writeLn;
    writeLn('********** TAM Interpreter (version 1) **********');
    interpretProgram;
    showStatus
  end; {runProgram}

end. {Interpreter}
```

The Δ Compiler

This appendix lists a compiler for the programming language Δ. The compiler is written as a number of THINK Pascal units. Its structure is shown in Figure 3.10.

Notes on THINK Pascal
The THINK Pascal language extends Standard Pascal in a number of ways. To make the Δ compiler as portable as possible, only the following extensions have actually been used:

- Declarations may be in any order. (They need not follow the usual rigid order of constants before types before variables before procedures and functions.)

- A program may be decomposed into *units*, each unit being of the form:

> **unit** *unit-identifier;*
>
> **interface**
>
>> **uses** *unit-identifiers;*
>>
>> *declarations of exported constants, types, and variables, and headings of exported procedures and functions;*
>
> **implementation**
>
>> *complete declarations of exported procedures and functions, and declarations of private constants, types, variables, procedures, and functions;*
>
> **end.**

A unit is a kind of module, and is compiled separately from other units.

The *interface part* of unit *U* specifies *U*'s interface to other units. It first lists the identifiers of all other units on which *U* depends. *U* may refer to the exports of these listed units only.

The interface part of *U* also declares *U*'s exports, which are constants, types, variables, procedures, and functions intended to be visible outside *U*. The bodies of exported procedures and functions are omitted, and only their headings appear here.

(This is enough to specify their parameter types, and their result types in the case of functions.)

The *implementation part* of unit *U* contains all private implementation detail. It completes the declarations of any exported procedures and functions whose headings appeared in the interface part of *U*. It also declares any private constants, types, variables, procedures, and functions; these may be used inside *U*'s implementation part, but are not visible to any other units.

These extensions make large programs such as the Δ compiler significantly easier to understand. But they do imply that the Δ compiler must be adapted to work under different Pascal language processors. To adapt the Δ compiler to Standard Pascal, proceed as follows:

• Make any procedure or function headings (in interface parts) into forward-declarations.

• Collect the constant definitions from all units, in the same order as they appear in this appendix. Similarly collect all the type definitions; all the variable declarations; and all the procedure and function declarations.

E.1   Compiler globals

```
unit CompilerGlobals;

interface

  type
    Natural = 0..maxint;
    Positive = 1..maxint;


{SOURCE TEXT}

  {The source program is read from the source window.}

  {The following constant and type definitions are system-dependent.}

  const
    eot = …;   eol = …;   tab = …;   {ordinal numbers of blank characters}

  type
    SourceFile = …;

    SourcePosition = record
        start, finish: Integer
      end;
      {Represents the position of a token or phrase in the source program.}

  procedure openSource (var source: SourceFile);
      {Prepares to read the first character of the source program.}

  procedure getSource (var nextChar: Char);
      {Reads the next character (perhaps eot/eol/tab) from the source program.}

  function currentSourcePoint: Integer;
      {Returns the position of the next character in the source program.}
```

```
{TOKENS}

  const
    tokenSize = 10;

  type
    TokenString = packed array[1..tokenSize] of Char;
      {Represents the spelling of a token in the source program.}

  function integerValuation (integerLiteral: TokenString): Natural;
      {Returns the value of integerLiteral.}

  procedure spellInteger (number: Natural;
                    var integerLiteral: TokenString);
      {Sets integerLiteral to the literal whose value is the given number.}


{ERROR REPORTING}

  const
    messageSize = 40;

  type
    MessageString = packed array[1..messageSize] of Char;
      {Represents a message, e.g., one describing a compile-time error.}

  var
    noErrors: Boolean;
      {True iff the source program is well-formed so far.}

  procedure startErrorReporting;
      {Initializes the reporting of compile-time errors.}

  procedure reportError (messageTemplate: MessageString;
                    tokenQuoted: TokenString;
                    errorPosition: SourcePosition);
      {Reports a compile-time error. The error message is messageTemplate. If the
       character '%' is present in messageTemplate, it is replaced by tokenQuoted.}

  procedure reportRestriction (message: MessageString);
      {Reports that the source program cannot be compiled, because of some
       limitation of the compiler itself.}


{RUN-TIME OBJECTS}

{Should really be in RuntimeOrganization, but needed to define type AST in
 AbstactSyntaxTrees.}

  const
    maxRoutineLevel = 7;

  type
    RoutineLevel = 0..maxRoutineLevel;
      {Standard environment and globals are at routine level 0.}

    ObjectKind = (knownValue, unknownValue, knownAddress, unknownAddress,
          knownRoutine, unknownRoutine, primitiveRoutine, equalityRoutine,
          typeRepresentation, field);
    ObjectAddress = record
          level: RoutineLevel;
          displacement: Integer
        end;
    ObjectPointer = ^ObjectDescription;
    ObjectDescription = record
          size: Natural;
          case kind : ObjectKind of
            knownValue: (
                value: Integer
```

```
                        );
                    unknownValue, knownAddress, unknownAddress, knownRoutine,
                    unknownRoutine: (
                        address: ObjectAddress
                    );
                    primitiveRoutine, equalityRoutine: (
                        displacement: Natural
                    );
                    field: (
                        fieldOffset: Natural
                    );
                    typeRepresentation: (
                    )
                end;
                {Describes a value, variable, routine, or type in the object program.}

{==============================================================================}

implementation

{SOURCE TEXT}

    {The implementation is system-dependent.}

    ...;

    procedure openSource (var source: SourceFile);
        ...;

    procedure getSource (var nextChar: Char);
        ...;

    function currentSourcePoint: Integer;
        ...;


{TOKENS}

    function integerValuation (integerLiteral: TokenString): Natural;
        ...;

    procedure spellInteger (number: Natural;
                            var integerLiteral: TokenString);
        ...;


{ERROR REPORTING}

    procedure composeMessage (template: MessageString;
                              quote: TokenString;
                              var message: MessageString);
        {Sets message to a copy of template; except if the latter contains the
         character '%', in which case that character is replaced by quote.}
        ...;

    procedure startErrorReporting;
    begin
        noErrors := true
    end; {startErrorReporting}

    procedure reportError (messageTemplate: MessageString;
                           tokenQuoted: TokenString;
                           errorPosition: SourcePosition);
        var
            message: MessageString;
    begin
        composeMessage(messageTemplate, tokenQuoted, message);
        writeLn(output, 'ERROR at ', errorPosition.start : 1, '..',
            errorPosition.finish : 1, ':  ', message);
```

```
      noErrors := false
   end; {reportError}

   procedure reportRestriction (message: MessageString);
   begin
      writeLn(output, 'RESTRICTION:  ', message);
      noErrors := false
   end; {reportRestriction}

end. {CompilerGlobals}
```

E.2 Abstract syntax trees

```
unit AbstractSyntaxTrees;

interface

   uses
      CompilerGlobals;


{ABSTRACT SYNTAX TREE STRUCTURE}

   const
      maxASTarity = 4;
         {Maximum no. of subtrees of any nonterminal AST node.}

   type
      ASTTag = (
            any, bool, charr, empty, int,                        {nullary}
            E, funcI, lbAArb, lcRArc, procI, recordRTend, V, varV, {unary}
            APcommaAPS, arrayILofT, constIisE, CsemicolonC, DsemicolonD,
            EcommaAA, FPcommaFPS, IcolonT, IisE, IlpAPSrp, letDinC,
            letDinE, OE, procIlpFPSrp, typeIisT, varIcolonT, VbecomesE,
            VdotI, VlbErb, whileEdoC,                            {binary}
            EOE, funcIlpFPSrpcolonT, IcolonTcommaRT, ifEthenCelseC,
            ifEthenEelseE, IisEcommaRA, opOcolonTtoT, procIlpFPSrpisC, {ternary}
            funcIlpFPSrpcolonTisE, opOcolonTxTtoT,               {quaternary}
            CL, I, IL, O);                                       {leafs}
         {Defines the possible tags on abstract syntax tree nodes. Some of these tags
          are used only in the representation of the standard environment.}

      AST = ^ASTNode;
      ASTNode = record
            position: SourcePosition; {used for diagnostics}
            refcount: Natural; {used for garbage collection}
            typ: AST; {type of expression or value-or-variable-name}
            case tag : ASTTag of
               any, bool, charr, empty, int,                     {nullary}
               E, funcI, lbAArb, lcRArc, procI, recordRTend, V, varV, {unary}
               APcommaAPS, arrayILofT, constIisE, CsemicolonC, DsemicolonD,
               EcommaAA, FPcommaFPS, IcolonT, IisE, IlpAPSrp, letDinC,
               letDinE, OE, procIlpFPSrp, typeIisT, varIcolonT, VbecomesE,
               VdotI, VlbErb, whileEdoC,                         {binary}
               EOE, funcIlpFPSrpcolonT, IcolonTcommaRT, ifEthenCelseC,
               ifEthenEelseE, IisEcommaRA, procIlpFPSrpisC,      {ternary}
               funcIlpFPSrpcolonTisE:                            {quaternary}
                  (
                     child: array[1..maxASTarity] of AST;
                     arity: Natural;
                     obj: ObjectPointer {object description attached to declaration node}
                  );
               CL, I, IL, O: (
```

```
                    spelling: TokenString;
                    decl: AST {link from id or op node to corresponding declaration}
            )
        end;
    {An AST is a pointer to an abstract syntax tree node. Each terminal (leaf)
    node contains a literal, identifier, or operator. Each nonterminal node has
    up to maxArity subtrees. Every node has a tag, and the source position of
    the represented construct.
        In a decorated AST, the following additional fields are used. Any node
    may be decorated by a type (which is itself represented by a small AST). An
    identifier or operator node may be linked to the corresponding declaration.
    A declaration node may have an attached run-time object description.}

function leafAST (givenTag: ASTTag;
                  givenSpelling: TokenString;
                  givenPosition: SourcePosition): AST;
    {Constructs a terminal node containing the given token details.}

function nullaryAST (givenTag: ASTTag;
                     givenPosition: SourcePosition): AST;
    {Constructs a nonterminal node with the given tag and no subtrees.}

function unaryAST (givenTag: ASTTag;
                   child1: AST;
                   givenPosition: SourcePosition): AST;
    {Constructs a nonterminal node with the given tag and one subtree.}

function binaryAST (givenTag: ASTTag;
                    child1, child2: AST;
                    givenPosition: SourcePosition): AST;
    {Constructs a nonterminal node with the given tag and two subtrees.}

function ternaryAST (givenTag: ASTTag;
                     child1, child2, child3: AST;
                     givenPosition: SourcePosition): AST;
    {Constructs a nonterminal node with the given tag and three subtrees.}

function quaternaryAST (givenTag: ASTTag;
                        child1, child2, child3, child4: AST;
                        givenPosition: SourcePosition): AST;
    {Constructs a nonterminal node with the given tag and four subtrees.}

function isLeaf (subtree: AST): Boolean;
    {Tests whether the given node is terminal.}

procedure shareAST (var oldtree: AST;
                    newtree: AST);
    {Makes oldtree point to newtree instead.}

procedure disposeAST (oldtree: AST);
    {Reclaims space occupied by oldtree and its descendants.}


{STANDARD ENVIRONMENT}

    var
        booleanType, charType, integerType, anyType, errorType: AST;
        {These are small ASTs representing standard types.}

        falseDecl, trueDecl, maxintDecl: AST;
        notDecl, andDecl, orDecl,
        addDecl, subtractDecl, multiplyDecl, divideDecl, moduloDecl,
        equalDecl, unequalDecl, lessDecl, notlessDecl, greaterDecl, notgreaterDecl,
        chrDecl, ordDecl, eolDecl, eofDecl,
        getDecl, putDecl, getintDecl, putintDecl, geteolDecl, puteolDecl: AST;
        {These are small ASTs representing "declarations" of standard entities.}

    procedure disposeStdEnvironment;
        {Reclaims space occupied by "declarations" of standard entities.}
```

```
{DRAWING ABSTRACT SYNTAX TREES}

  procedure drawAST (wholeAST: AST);
      {Displays the given AST on the screen.}

{=============================================================================}

implementation

{ABSTRACT SYNTAX TREE STRUCTURE}

  function leafAST (givenTag: ASTTag;
                    givenSpelling: TokenString;
                    givenPosition: SourcePosition): AST;
    var
      tree: AST;
  begin
    new(tree);
    with tree^ do
      begin
        tag := givenTag;
        spelling := givenSpelling;  position := givenPosition;
        refcount := 1;  typ := nil;  decl := nil
      end;
    leafAST := tree
  end; {leafAST}

  function newAST (givenTag: ASTTag;
                   givenArity: Natural;
                   child1, child2, child3, child4: AST;
                   givenPosition: SourcePosition): AST;
    var
      tree: AST;
  begin
    new(tree);
    with tree^ do
      begin
        tag := givenTag;
        child[1] := child1;  child[2] := child2;
        child[3] := child3;  child[4] := child4;
        arity := givenArity;  position := givenPosition;
        refcount := 1;  typ := nil;  obj := nil
      end;
    newAST := tree
  end; {newAST}

  function nullaryAST (givenTag: ASTTag;
                       givenPosition: SourcePosition): AST;
  begin
    nullaryAST := newAST(givenTag, 0, nil, nil, nil, nil, givenPosition)
  end; {nullaryAST}

  function unaryAST (givenTag: ASTTag;
                     child1: AST;
                     givenPosition: SourcePosition): AST;
  begin
    unaryAST := newAST(givenTag, 1, child1, nil, nil, nil, givenPosition)
  end; {unaryAST}

  function binaryAST (givenTag: ASTTag;
                      child1, child2: AST;
                      givenPosition: SourcePosition): AST;
  begin
    binaryAST := newAST(givenTag, 2, child1, child2, nil, nil, givenPosition)
  end; {binaryAST}

  function ternaryAST (givenTag: ASTTag;
                       child1, child2, child3: AST;
                       givenPosition: SourcePosition): AST;
```

```
  begin
    ternaryAST := newAST(givenTag, 3, child1, child2, child3, nil, givenPosition)
  end; {ternaryAST}

  function quaternaryAST (givenTag: ASTTag;
                  child1, child2, child3, child4: AST;
                  givenPosition: SourcePosition): AST;
  begin
    quaternaryAST := newAST(givenTag, 4, child1, child2, child3, child4,
          givenPosition)
  end; {quaternaryAST}

  function isLeaf (subtree: AST): Boolean;
  begin
    isLeaf := subtree^.tag in [CL, I, IL, O]
  end; {isLeaf}

  procedure shareAST (var oldtree: AST;
                  newtree: AST);
  begin
    disposeAST(oldtree);  oldtree := newtree;
    newtree^.refcount := newtree^.refcount + 1
  end; {share}

  procedure disposeAST (oldtree: AST);
    ...;


{STANDARD ENVIRONMENT}

  procedure disposeStdEnvironment;
  begin
    disposeAST(falseDecl);      disposeAST(trueDecl);      disposeAST(maxintDecl);
    disposeAST(notDecl);        disposeAST(andDecl);       disposeAST(orDecl);
    disposeAST(addDecl);        disposeAST(subtractDecl);  disposeAST(multiplyDecl);
    disposeAST(divideDecl);     disposeAST(moduloDecl);    disposeAST(equalDecl);
    disposeAST(unequalDecl);    disposeAST(lessDecl);      disposeAST(notlessDecl);
    disposeAST(greaterDecl);    disposeAST(notgreaterDecl); disposeAST(chrDecl);
    disposeAST(ordDecl);        disposeAST(eolDecl);       disposeAST(eofDecl);
    disposeAST(getDecl);        disposeAST(putDecl);       disposeAST(getintDecl);
    disposeAST(putintDecl);     disposeAST(geteolDecl);    disposeAST(puteolDecl)
  end; {disposeStdEnvironment}


{DRAWING ABSTRACT SYNTAX TREES}

  procedure drawAST (wholeAST: AST);
    ...;

end. {AbstractSyntaxTrees}
```

E.3   Lexical analysis

```
unit LexicalAnalyser;

interface

  uses
    CompilerGlobals;

  type
    TokenClass = (
        intliteral, charliteral, identifier, operator,    {literals, idents, ops}
```

```
                  arrayToken, beginToken, constToken, doToken,
                  elseToken, endToken, funcToken, ifToken, inToken,
                  letToken, ofToken, procToken, recordToken,
                  thenToken, typeToken, varToken, whileToken,        {reserved words - must be
                                                                      in alphabetical order}

                  dotToken, colonToken, semicolonToken, commaToken,
                  becomesToken, isToken,                             {punctuation}
                  lparenToken, rparenToken, lbracketToken,
                  rbracketToken, lcurlyToken, rcurlyToken,           {brackets}
                  eotToken, errorToken);
         Token = record
                  class: TokenClass;
                  spelling: TokenString;
                  position: SourcePosition;
                  separationStart: Integer {needed to compute phrase positions.}
                end;
                {Represents a single token of the source program.}

      procedure startLexicalAnalysis;
          {Prepares to scan the source program.}

      procedure scan (var nextToken: Token);
          {Sets nextToken to the next token from the source program.}

      procedure spell (class: TokenClass;
                        var spelling: TokenString);
          {Determines the spelling of a token of the given class.}

{================================================================================}

implementation

   {Implementation notes:
    Words are classified as identifiers or reserved words by searching tokenTable.
    The search method (linear search) is simple but crude.}

   var
     currentChar: Char;
     letters, digits, opchars, blanks: set of Char;
     tokenTable: array[TokenClass] of TokenString;

   procedure startLexicalAnalysis;
   begin
     letters := ['a'..'z', 'A'..'Z'];  digits := ['0'..'9'];
     opchars := ['+', '-', '*', '/', '=', '<', '>', '\', '&', '@', '%', '^', '?'];
     blanks := [' ', chr(tab), chr(eol)];
     tokenTable[intliteral] := '<int>      ';
     tokenTable[charliteral] := '''<char>'' ';
     tokenTable[identifier] := '<id>       ';
     tokenTable[operator] := '<op>      ';
     tokenTable[arrayToken] := 'array     ';
     tokenTable[beginToken] := 'begin     ';
     tokenTable[constToken] := 'const     ';
     tokenTable[doToken] := 'do        ';
     tokenTable[elseToken] := 'else      ';
     tokenTable[endToken] := 'end       ';
     tokenTable[funcToken] := 'func      ';
     tokenTable[ifToken] := 'if        ';
     tokenTable[inToken] := 'in        ';
     tokenTable[letToken] := 'let       ';
     tokenTable[ofToken] := 'of        ';
     tokenTable[procToken] := 'proc      ';
     tokenTable[recordToken] := 'record    ';
     tokenTable[thenToken] := 'then      ';
     tokenTable[typeToken] := 'type      ';
     tokenTable[varToken] := 'var       ';
     tokenTable[whileToken] := 'while     ';
     tokenTable[dotToken] := '.         ';
     tokenTable[colonToken] := ':         ';
```

```
    tokenTable[semicolonToken] := ';            ';
    tokenTable[commaToken] := ',            ';
    tokenTable[becomesToken] := ':=          ';
    tokenTable[isToken] := '~             ';
    tokenTable[lparenToken] := '(            ';
    tokenTable[rparenToken] := ')            ';
    tokenTable[lbracketToken] := '[            ';
    tokenTable[rbracketToken] := ']            ';
    tokenTable[lcurlyToken] := '{            ';
    tokenTable[rcurlyToken] := '}            ';
    tokenTable[eotToken] := '            ';
    tokenTable[errorToken] := '<error>   ';

  getSource(currentChar)
end; {startLexicalAnalysis}

procedure scan (var nextToken: Token);
  var
    sizeSoFar: Natural;

  procedure start;
  begin
    sizeSoFar := 0;  nextToken.spelling := '          ';
    nextToken.position.start := currentSourcePoint
  end; {start}

  procedure takeIt;
  begin
    sizeSoFar := sizeSoFar + 1;
    if sizeSoFar <= tokenSize then
      nextToken.spelling[sizeSoFar] := currentChar;
    {otherwise truncate the spelling}
    getSource(currentChar)
  end; {takeIt}

  procedure finish (class: TokenClass);
  begin
    nextToken.class := class;
    nextToken.position.finish := currentSourcePoint - 1
  end; {finish}

  procedure takeItAndFinish (class: TokenClass);
  begin
    takeIt;  finish(class)
  end; {takeItAndFinish}

  procedure screen;
    const
      firstReservedWord = arrayToken;
      lastReservedWord = whileToken;
    var
      reserved: (yes, no, maybe);
      class: TokenClass;
  begin
    reserved := maybe;  class := firstReservedWord;
    repeat
      if tokenTable[class] = nextToken.spelling then
        begin
          finish(class);  reserved := yes
        end
      else if (class = lastReservedWord)
          or (tokenTable[class] > nextToken.spelling) then
        begin
          finish(identifier);  reserved := no
        end
      else
        class := succ(class)
    until reserved <> maybe
  end; {screen}
```

```
      procedure scanSeparator;
      begin
        if currentChar = '!' then
          begin {comment}
            repeat getSource(currentChar) until currentChar = chr(eol);
            getSource(currentChar)
          end
        else {currentChar in blanks}
          getSource(currentChar)
      end; {scanSeparator}

begin {scan}
  nextToken.separationStart := currentSourcePoint;
  while currentChar in blanks + ['!'] do scanSeparator;
  start;

  if currentChar = chr(eot) then
    finish(eotToken)

  else if currentChar in digits then
    begin {integer literal}
      repeat takeIt until not (currentChar in digits);
      finish(intliteral)
    end

  else if currentChar = '''' then
    begin {character literal}
      takeIt;  takeIt; {the quoted character}
      if currentChar = '''' then
        takeItAndfinish(charliteral)
      else
        finish(errorToken)
    end

  else if currentChar in letters then
    begin {identifier or reserved word}
      repeat takeIt until not (currentChar in letters + digits);
      screen
    end

  else if currentChar in opchars then
    begin {operator}
      repeat takeIt until not (currentChar in opchars);
      finish(operator)
    end

  else if currentChar = '.' then
    takeItAndFinish(dotToken)

  else if currentChar = ':' then
    begin
      takeIt;
      if currentChar = '=' then
        takeItAndFinish(becomesToken)
      else
        finish(colonToken)
    end

  else if currentChar = ';' then
    takeItAndFinish(semicolonToken)

  else if currentChar = ',' then
    takeItAndFinish(commaToken)

  else if currentChar = '~' then
    takeItAndFinish(isToken)

  else if currentChar = '(' then
    takeItAndFinish(lparenToken)
```

```
      else if currentChar = ')' then
        takeItAndFinish(rparenToken)

      else if currentChar = '[' then
        takeItAndFinish(lbracketToken)

      else if currentChar = ']' then
        takeItAndFinish(rbracketToken)

      else if currentChar = '{' then
        takeItAndFinish(lcurlyToken)

      else if currentChar = '}' then
        takeItAndFinish(rcurlyToken)

      else
        takeItAndFinish(errorToken)
  end; {scan}

  procedure spell (class: TokenClass;
                      var spelling: TokenString);
  begin
    spelling := tokenTable[class]
  end; {spell}

end. {LexicalAnalyser}
```

E.4   Syntactic analysis

```
unit SyntacticAnalyser;

interface

  uses
    CompilerGlobals, AbstractSyntaxTrees, LexicalAnalyser;

  procedure parseProgram (var programAST: AST);
      {Parses the source program, and constructs programAST to represent its
       phrase structure.}

{================================================================================}

implementation

  {Implementation notes:
   The parsing algorithm is recursive descent. There is no error recovery: parsing
   stops at the first syntactic error.}

  procedure parseProgram (var programAST: AST);

    label
      999; {exit from parser}

    var
      currentToken: Token;

    procedure syntacticError (messageTemplate: MessageString;
                      tokenQuoted: TokenString);
    begin
      reportError(messageTemplate, tokenQuoted, currentToken.position);
      goto 999 {exit from parser}
    end; {syntacticError}
```

```
procedure accept (tokenExpected: TokenClass);
  var
    spelling: TokenString;
begin
  if currentToken.class = tokenExpected then
    scan(currentToken)
  else
    begin
      spell(tokenExpected, spelling);
      syntacticError('"%" expected here                  ', spelling)
    end
end; {accept}

procedure acceptIt;
begin
  scan(currentToken)
end; {acceptIt}

procedure start (var position: SourcePosition);
begin
  position.start := currentToken.position.start;
end; {start}

procedure finish (var position: SourcePosition);
begin
  position.finish := currentToken.separationStart - 1;
end; {start}

procedure parseCommand (var commandAST: AST);
forward;
procedure parseSingleCommand (var commandAST: AST);
forward;

procedure parseExpression (var expressionAST: AST);
forward;
procedure parseSecondaryExpression (var expressionAST: AST);
forward;
procedure parsePrimaryExpression (var expressionAST: AST);
forward;
procedure parseRecordAggregate (var aggregateAST: AST);
forward;
procedure parseArrayAggregate (var aggregateAST: AST);
forward;

procedure parseVname (var vnameAST: AST);
forward;
procedure parseRestOfVname (identifierAST: AST;
                var vnameAST: AST);
forward;

procedure parseDeclaration (var declarationAST: AST);
forward;
procedure parseSingleDeclaration (var declarationAST: AST);
forward;

procedure parseFormalParameterSequence (var formalsAST: AST);
forward;
procedure parseProperFormalParameterSequence (var formalsAST: AST);
forward;
procedure parseFormalParameter (var formalAST: AST);
forward;

procedure parseActualParameterSequence (var actualsAST: AST);
forward;
procedure parseProperActualParameterSequence (var actualsAST: AST);
forward;
procedure parseActualParameter (var actualAST: AST);
forward;
```

```
procedure parseTypedenoter (var typeAST: AST);
forward;
procedure parseRecordTypedenoter (var recordtypeAST: AST);
forward;

{Literals, identifiers, and operators}

procedure parseIntegerLiteral (var literalAST: AST);
begin
   if currentToken.class = intliteral then
      begin
        literalAST := leafAST(IL, currentToken.spelling, currentToken.position);
        scan(currentToken)
      end
   else
      begin
        literalAST := nil;
        syntacticError('integer literal expected here          ', '          ')
      end
end; {parseIntegerLiteral}

procedure parseCharacterLiteral (var literalAST: AST);
begin
   if currentToken.class = charliteral then
      begin
        literalAST := leafAST(CL, currentToken.spelling, currentToken.position);
        scan(currentToken)
      end
   else
      begin
        literalAST := nil;
        syntacticError('character literal expected here          ', '          ')
      end
end; {parseCharacterLiteral}

procedure parseIdentifier (var identifierAST: AST);
begin
   if currentToken.class = identifier then
      begin
        identifierAST := leafAST(I, currentToken.spelling,
            currentToken.position);
        scan(currentToken)
      end
   else
      begin
        identifierAST := nil;
        syntacticError('identifier expected here          ', '          ')
      end
end; {parseIdentifier}

procedure parseOperator (var operatorAST: AST);
begin
   if currentToken.class = operator then
      begin
        operatorAST := leafAST(O, currentToken.spelling, currentToken.position);
        scan(currentToken)
      end
   else
      begin
        operatorAST := nil;
        syntacticError('operator expected here          ', '          ')
      end
end; {parseOperator}

{Commands}

procedure parseCommand (var commandAST: AST);
  var
    c2AST: AST;
```

```
      commandPos: SourcePosition;
begin
  commandAST := nil; {in case there's a syntactic error}
  start(commandPos);  parseSingleCommand(commandAST);
  while currentToken.class = semicolonToken do
    begin
      acceptIt;  parseSingleCommand(c2AST);  finish(commandPos);
      commandAST := binaryAST(CsemicolonC, commandAST, c2AST, commandPos)
    end
end; {parseCommand}

procedure parseSingleCommand (var commandAST: AST);
  var
    iAST, c1AST, c2AST, eAST, vAST, dAST, apsAST: AST;
    commandPos: SourcePosition;
begin
  commandAST := nil; {in case there's a syntactic error}
  start(commandPos);

  if currentToken.class = identifier then
    begin
      parseIdentifier(iAST);
      if currentToken.class = lparenToken then
        begin
          acceptIt;  parseActualParameterSequence(apsAST);
          accept(rparenToken);  finish(commandPos);
          commandAST := binaryAST(IlpAPSrp, iAST, apsAST, commandPos)
        end
      else
        begin
          parseRestOfVname(iAST, vAST);  accept(becomesToken);
          parseExpression(eAST);  finish(commandPos);
          commandAST := binaryAST(VbecomesE, vAST, eAST, commandPos)
        end
    end

  else if currentToken.class = beginToken then
    begin
      acceptIt;  parseCommand(commandAST);  accept(endToken)
    end

  else if currentToken.class = letToken then
    begin
      acceptIt;  parseDeclaration(dAST);  accept(inToken);
      parseSingleCommand(c1AST);  finish(commandPos);
      commandAST := binaryAST(letDinC, dAST, c1AST, commandPos)
    end

  else if currentToken.class = ifToken then
    begin
      acceptIt;  parseExpression(eAST);  accept(thenToken);
      parseSingleCommand(c1AST);  accept(elseToken);
      parseSingleCommand(c2AST);  finish(commandPos);
      commandAST := ternaryAST(ifEthenCelseC, eAST, c1AST, c2AST, commandPos)
    end

  else if currentToken.class = whileToken then
    begin
      acceptIt;  parseExpression(eAST);  accept(doToken);
      parseSingleCommand(c1AST);  finish(commandPos);
      commandAST := binaryAST(whileEdoC, eAST, c1AST, commandPos)
    end

  else if currentToken.class in [semicolonToken, endToken, elseToken, inToken,
      eotToken] then
    begin
      finish(commandPos);
      commandAST := nullaryAST(empty, commandPos)
    end
```

```
        else
          syntacticError('"%" cannot start a command              ',
              currentToken.spelling)
    end; {parseSingleCommand}

    {Expressions}

    procedure parseExpression (var expressionAST: AST);
      var
        dAST, e1AST, e2AST, e3AST: AST;
        expressionPos: SourcePosition;
    begin
      expressionAST := nil; {in case there's a syntactic error}
      start(expressionPos);

      if currentToken.class = letToken then
        begin
          acceptIt;  parseDeclaration(dAST);  accept(inToken);
          parseExpression(e1AST);  finish(expressionPos);
          expressionAST := binaryAST(letDinE, dAST, e1AST, expressionPos)
        end

      else if currentToken.class = ifToken then
        begin
          acceptIt;  parseExpression(e1AST);  accept(thenToken);
          parseExpression(e2AST);  accept(elseToken);
          parseExpression(e3AST);  finish(expressionPos);
          expressionAST := ternaryAST(ifEthenEelseE, e1AST, e2AST, e3AST,
              expressionPos)
        end

      else
        parseSecondaryExpression(expressionAST)
    end; {parseExpression}

    procedure parseSecondaryExpression (var expressionAST: AST);
      var
        e2AST, opAST: AST;
        expressionPos: SourcePosition;
    begin
      expressionAST := nil; {in case there's a syntactic error}
      start(expressionPos);  parsePrimaryExpression(expressionAST);
      while currentToken.class = operator do
        begin
          parseOperator(opAST);  parsePrimaryExpression(e2AST);
          finish(expressionPos);
          expressionAST := ternaryAST(EOE, expressionAST, opAST, e2AST,
              expressionPos)
        end
    end; {parseSecondaryExpression}

    procedure parsePrimaryExpression (var expressionAST: AST);
      var
        iAST, vAST, apsAST, opAST, e1AST: AST;
        expressionPos: SourcePosition;
    begin
      expressionAST := nil; {in case there's a syntactic error}
      start(expressionPos);

      if currentToken.class = intliteral then
        parseIntegerLiteral(expressionAST)

      else if currentToken.class = charliteral then
        parseCharacterLiteral(expressionAST)

      else if currentToken.class = lbracketToken then
        begin
          acceptIt;  parseArrayAggregate(e1AST);
          accept(rbracketToken);  finish(expressionPos);
```

```
              expressionAST := unaryAST(lbAArb, e1AST, expressionPos)
          end

    else if currentToken.class = lcurlyToken then
      begin
        acceptIt;  parseRecordAggregate(e1AST);
        accept(rcurlyToken);  finish(expressionPos);
        expressionAST := unaryAST(lcRArc, e1AST, expressionPos)
      end

    else if currentToken.class = identifier then
      begin
        parseIdentifier(iAST);
        if currentToken.class = lparenToken then
          begin
            acceptIt;  parseActualParameterSequence(apsAST);
            accept(rparenToken); finish(expressionPos);
            expressionAST := binaryAST(IlpAPSrp, iAST, apsAST, expressionPos)
          end
        else
          begin
            parseRestOfVname(iAST, vAST);  finish(expressionPos);
            expressionAST := unaryAST(V, vAST, expressionPos)
          end
      end

    else if currentToken.class = operator then
      begin
        parseOperator(opAST);  parsePrimaryExpression(e1AST);
        finish(expressionPos);
        expressionAST := binaryAST(OE, opAST, e1AST, expressionPos)
      end

    else if currentToken.class = lparenToken then
      begin
        acceptIt;  parseExpression(expressionAST);  accept(rparenToken)
      end

    else
      syntacticError('"%" cannot start an expression         ',
          currentToken.spelling)
end; {parsePrimaryExpression}

procedure parseRecordAggregate (var aggregateAST: AST);
  var
    iAST, eAST, aAST: AST;
    aggregatePos: SourcePosition;
begin
  aggregateAST := nil; {in case there's a syntactic error}
  start(aggregatePos);  parseIdentifier(iAST);
  accept(isToken);  parseExpression(eAST);
  if currentToken.class = commaToken then
    begin
      acceptIt;  parseRecordAggregate(aAST);  finish(aggregatePos);
      aggregateAST := ternaryAST(IisEcommaRA, iAST, eAST, aAST, aggregatePos)
    end
  else
    begin
      finish(aggregatePos);
      aggregateAST := binaryAST(IisE, iAST, eAST, aggregatePos)
    end
end; {parseRecordAggregate}

procedure parseArrayAggregate (var aggregateAST: AST);
  var
    eAST, aAST: AST;
    aggregatePos: SourcePosition;
begin
  aggregateAST := nil; {in case there's a syntactic error}
```

```
      start(aggregatePos);   parseExpression(eAST);
      if currentToken.class = commaToken then
        begin
          acceptIt;   parseArrayAggregate(aAST);   finish(aggregatePos);
          aggregateAST := binaryAST(EcommaAA, eAST, aAST, aggregatePos)
        end
      else
        begin
          finish(aggregatePos);
          aggregateAST := unaryAST(E, eAST, aggregatePos)
        end
end; {parseArrayAggregate}

{Value-or-variable-names}

procedure parseVname (var vnameAST: AST);
  var
    iAST: AST;
begin
  vnameAST := nil; {in case there's a syntactic error}
  parseIdentifier(iAST);   parseRestOfVname(iAST, vnameAST)
end; {parseVname}

procedure parseRestOfVname (identifierAST: AST;
                  var vnameAST: AST);
  var
    vAST, iAST, eAST: AST;
    vnamePos: SourcePosition;
begin
  vAST := identifierAST;   vnamePos := identifierAST^.position;
  while currentToken.class in [dotToken, lbracketToken] do
    if currentToken.class = dotToken then
      begin
        acceptIt;   parseIdentifier(iAST);   finish(vnamePos);
        vAST := binaryAST(VdotI, vAST, iAST, vnamePos)
      end
    else
      begin
        accept(lbracketToken);   parseExpression(eAST);
        accept(rbracketToken);   finish(vnamePos);
        vAST := binaryAST(VlbErb, vAST, eAST, vnamePos)
      end;
  vnameAST := vAST
end; {parseRestOfVname}

{Declarations}

procedure parseDeclaration (var declarationAST: AST);
  var
    d2AST: AST;
    declarationPos: SourcePosition;
begin
  declarationAST := nil; {in case there's a syntactic error}
  start(declarationPos);   parseSingleDeclaration(declarationAST);
  while currentToken.class = semicolonToken do
    begin
      acceptIt;   parseSingleDeclaration(d2AST);   finish(declarationPos);
      declarationAST := binaryAST(DsemicolonD, declarationAST, d2AST,
          declarationPos)
    end
end; {parseDeclaration}

procedure parseSingleDeclaration (var declarationAST: AST);
  var
    iAST, eAST, cAST, fpsAST, tAST: AST;
    declarationPos: SourcePosition;
begin
  declarationAST := nil; {in case there's a syntactic error}
  start(declarationPos);
```

```
      if currentToken.class = constToken then
        begin
          acceptIt;  parseIdentifier(iAST);  accept(isToken);
          parseExpression(eAST);  finish(declarationPos);
          declarationAST := binaryAST(constIisE, iAST, eAST, declarationPos)
        end

    else if currentToken.class = varToken then
      begin
        acceptIt;  parseIdentifier(iAST);
        accept(colonToken);  parseTypedenoter(tAST);  finish(declarationPos);
        declarationAST := binaryAST(varIcolonT, iAST, tAST, declarationPos)
      end

    else if currentToken.class = procToken then
      begin
        acceptIt;  parseIdentifier(iAST);  accept(lparenToken);
        parseFormalParameterSequence(fpsAST);  accept(rparenToken);
        accept(isToken);  parseSingleCommand(cAST);  finish(declarationPos);
        declarationAST := ternaryAST(procIlpFPSrpisC, iAST, fpsAST, cAST,
            declarationPos)
      end

    else if currentToken.class = funcToken then
      begin
        acceptIt;  parseIdentifier(iAST);  accept(lparenToken);
        parseFormalParameterSequence(fpsAST);  accept(rparenToken);
        accept(colonToken);  parseTypedenoter(tAST);  accept(isToken);
        parseExpression(eAST);  finish(declarationPos);
        declarationAST := quaternaryAST(funcIlpFPSrpcolonTisE, iAST, fpsAST,
            tAST, eAST, declarationPos)
      end

    else if currentToken.class = typeToken then
      begin
        acceptIt;  parseIdentifier(iAST);  accept(isToken);
        parseTypedenoter(tAST);  finish(declarationPos);
        declarationAST := binaryAST(typeIisT, iAST, tAST, declarationPos)
      end

    else
      syntacticError('"%" cannot start a declaration            ',
          currentToken.spelling)
  end; {parseSingleDeclaration}

{Parameters}

procedure parseFormalParameterSequence (var formalsAST: AST);
  var
    formalsPos: SourcePosition;
begin
  start(formalsPos);
  if currentToken.class = rparenToken then
    begin
      finish(formalsPos);
      formalsAST := nullaryAST(empty, formalsPos)
    end
  else
    parseProperFormalParameterSequence(formalsAST)
end; {parseFormalParameterSequence}

procedure parseProperFormalParameterSequence (var formalsAST: AST);
  var
    fpAST, fpsAST: AST;
    formalsPos: SourcePosition;
begin
  formalsAST := nil; {in case there's a syntactic error}
  start(formalsPos);  parseFormalParameter(fpAST);
  if currentToken.class = commaToken then
```

```
      begin
        acceptIt;   parseProperFormalParameterSequence(fpsAST);
        finish(formalsPos);
        formalsAST := binaryAST(FPcommaFPS, fpAST, fpsAST, formalsPos)
      end
    else
      formalsAST := fpAST
end; {parseProperFormalParameterSequence}

procedure parseFormalParameter (var formalAST: AST);
    var
      iAST, tAST, fpsAST: AST;
      formalPos: SourcePosition;
begin
    formalAST := nil; {in case there's a syntactic error}
    start(formalPos);

    if currentToken.class = identifier then
      begin
        parseIdentifier(iAST);   accept(colonToken);
        parseTypedenoter(tAST);   finish(formalPos);
        formalAST := binaryAST(IcolonT, iAST, tAST, formalPos)
      end

    else if currentToken.class = varToken then
      begin
        acceptIt;   parseIdentifier(iAST);   accept(colonToken);
        parseTypedenoter(tAST);   finish(formalPos);
        formalAST := binaryAST(varIcolonT, iAST, tAST, formalPos)
      end

    else if currentToken.class = procToken then
      begin
        acceptIt;   parseIdentifier(iAST);   accept(lparenToken);
        parseFormalParameterSequence(fpsAST);   accept(rparenToken);
        finish(formalPos);
        formalAST := binaryAST(procIlpFPSrp, iAST, fpsAST, formalPos)
      end

    else if currentToken.class = funcToken then
      begin
        acceptIt;   parseIdentifier(iAST);   accept(lparenToken);
        parseFormalParameterSequence(fpsAST);   accept(rparenToken);
        accept(colonToken);   parseTypedenoter(tAST);   finish(formalPos);
        formalAST := ternaryAST(funcIlpFPSrpcolonT, iAST, fpsAST, tAST,
            formalPos)
      end

    else
      syntacticError('"%" cannot start a formal param.        ',
          currentToken.spelling)
end; {parseFormalParameter}

procedure parseActualParameterSequence (var actualsAST: AST);
    var
      actualsPos: SourcePosition;
begin
    start(actualsPos);
    if currentToken.class = rparenToken then
      begin
        finish(actualsPos);
        actualsAST := nullaryAST(empty, actualsPos)
      end
    else
      parseProperActualParameterSequence(actualsAST)
end; {parseActualParameterSequence}

procedure parseProperActualParameterSequence (var actualsAST: AST);
    var
```

```
    apAST, apsAST: AST;
    actualsPos: SourcePosition;
begin
  actualsAST := nil; {in case there's a syntactic error}
  start(actualsPos);  parseActualParameter(apAST);
  if currentToken.class = commaToken then
    begin
      acceptIt;  parseProperActualParameterSequence(apsAST);
      finish(actualsPos);
      actualsAST := binaryAST(ApcommaAPS, apAST, apsAST, actualsPos)
    end
  else
    actualsAST := apAST
end; {parseProperActualParameterSequence}

procedure parseActualParameter (var actualAST: AST);
  var
    eAST, vAST, iAST: AST;
    actualPos: SourcePosition;
begin
  actualAST := nil; {in case there's a syntactic error}
  start(actualPos);

  if currentToken.class in [identifier, intliteral, charliteral, operator,
      letToken, ifToken, lparenToken, lbracketToken, lcurlyToken] then
    begin
      parseExpression(eAST);  finish(actualPos);
      actualAST := unaryAST(E, eAST, actualPos)
    end

  else if currentToken.class = varToken then
    begin
      acceptIt;  parseVname(vAST);  finish(actualPos);
      actualAST := unaryAST(varV, vAST, actualPos)
    end

  else if currentToken.class = procToken then
    begin
      acceptIt;  parseIdentifier(iAST);  finish(actualPos);
      actualAST := unaryAST(procI, iAST, actualPos)
    end

  else if currentToken.class = funcToken then
    begin
      acceptIt;  parseIdentifier(iAST);  finish(actualPos);
      actualAST := unaryAST(funcI, iAST, actualPos)
    end

  else
    syntacticError('"%" cannot start an actual param        ',
        currentToken.spelling)
end; {parseActualParameter}

{Type-denoters}

procedure parseTypedenoter (var typeAST: AST);
  var
    iAST, ilAST, tAST, rtAST: AST;
    typePos: SourcePosition;
begin
  typeAST := nil; {in case there's a syntactic error}
  start(typePos);

  if currentToken.class = identifier then
    begin
      parseIdentifier(iAST);  typeAST := iAST
    end

  else if currentToken.class = arrayToken then
```

```
          begin
            acceptIt;  parseIntegerLiteral(ilAST);  accept(ofToken);
            parseTypedenoter(tAST);  finish(typePos);
            typeAST := binaryAST(arrayILofT, ilAST, tAST, typePos)
          end

      else if currentToken.class = recordToken then
          begin
            acceptIt;  parseRecordTypedenoter(rtAST);
            accept(endToken);  finish(typePos);
            typeAST := unaryAST(recordRTend, rtAST, typePos)
          end

      else
          syntacticError('"%" cannot start a type denoter          ',
              currentToken.spelling)
    end; {parseTypedenoter}

  procedure parseRecordTypedenoter (var recordtypeAST: AST);
    var
      iAST, tAST, rtAST: AST;
      recordtypePos: SourcePosition;
    begin
      recordtypeAST := nil; {in case there's a syntactic error}
      start(recordtypePos);  parseIdentifier(iAST);
      accept(colonToken);  parseTypedenoter(tAST);
      if currentToken.class = commaToken then
        begin
          acceptIt;  parseRecordTypedenoter(rtAST);  finish(recordtypePos);
          recordtypeAST := ternaryAST(IcolonTcommaRT, iAST, tAST, rtAST,
              recordtypePos)
        end
      else
        begin
          finish(recordtypePos);
          recordtypeAST := binaryAST(IcolonT, iAST, tAST, recordtypePos)
        end
    end; {parseRecordTypedenoter}

  {Programs}

  begin {parseProgram}
    startLexicalAnalysis;
    scan(currentToken);
    parseCommand(programAST);
    if currentToken.class <> eotToken then
      syntacticError('"%" not expected after end of program   ',
          currentToken.spelling);
999: {exit from parser}
  end; {parseProgram}

end. {SyntacticAnalyser}
```

E.5   Contextual analysis

```
unit ContextualAnalyser;

interface

  uses
    CompilerGlobals, AbstractSyntaxTrees;

  procedure establishStdEnvironment;
```

```
     {Creates a collection of small ASTs to represent standard types, and also the
     "declarations" of standard constants, types, procedures, and functions.}

  procedure checkProgram (programAST: AST);
     {Checks whether the source program represented by programAST satisfies the
     language's scope rules and type rules. Also decorates programAST as follows:
        (a) Each applied occurrence of an identifier or operator is linked to the
            corresponding declaration.
        (b) Each expression and value-or-variable-name is decorated by its type.
        (c) Each type identifier is replaced by the type it denotes.
     Types are represented by small ASTs.}

{================================================================================}

implementation

  var
     dummyPos: SourcePosition;


{IDENTIFICATION}

  {Implementation notes:
   Each entry in the identification table is an (identifier, attribute, level)
   triple, where the attribute is a pointer to the identifier's declaration in the
   AST. These entries are organized in a stack. The search method (linear search)
   is simple but crude.}

  type
     ScopeLevel = Natural;
     IdEntryPtr = ^IdEntryNode;
     IdEntryNode = record
         id: TokenString;
         attr: AST;
         level: ScopeLevel;
         previous: IdEntryPtr
       end;

  var
     idTable: record
         level: ScopeLevel;
         latest: IdEntryPtr
       end;

  procedure startIdentification;
  begin
     idTable.level := 0;   idTable.latest := nil
  end; {startIdentification}

  procedure openScope;
  begin
     idTable.level := idTable.level + 1
  end; {openInnerScope}

  procedure closeScope;
     var
        this, local: IdEntryPtr;
  begin
     {Presumably, idTable.level > 0.}
     this := idTable.latest;
     while this^.level = idTable.level do
       begin
          local := this;   this := local^.previous;   dispose(local)
       end;
     idTable.level := idTable.level - 1;   idTable.latest := this
  end; {closeInnerScope}

  procedure enter (id: TokenString;
                   attr: AST);
```

```
    var
      this: IdEntryPtr;
  begin
    new(this);   this^.id := id;   this^.attr := attr;
    this^.level := idTable.level;   this^.previous := idTable.latest;
    idTable.latest := this
  end; {enter}

  procedure retrieve (id: TokenString;
                      var found: Boolean;
                      var attr: AST);
    var
      this: IdEntryPtr;
      searching: Boolean;
  begin
    this := idTable.latest;   searching := true;
    repeat
      if this = nil then
        begin
          searching := false;   found := false
        end
      else if this^.id = id then
        begin
          searching := false;   found := true;   attr := this^.attr
        end
      else
        this := this^.previous
    until not searching
  end; {lookup}


{STANDARD ENVIRONMENT}

  procedure establishStdEnvironment;
    var
      dummyI: AST;

    procedure declareStdType (id: TokenString;
                      typedenoter: AST);
      var
        binding: AST;
    begin
      binding := binaryAST(typeIisT, leafAST(I, id, dummyPos), typedenoter,
          dummyPos);
      enter(id, binding)
    end; {declareStdType}

    procedure declareStdConst (id: TokenString;
                      constType: AST;
                      var binding: AST);
      var
        constExpr: AST;
    begin
      constExpr := leafAST(IL, '           ', dummyPos);
      {… used only as a placeholder for constType}
      constExpr^.typ := constType;
      binding := binaryAST(constIisE, leafAST(I, id, dummyPos), constExpr,
          dummyPos);
      enter(id, binding)
    end; {declareStdConst}

    procedure declareStdProc (id: TokenString;
                      fps: AST;
                      var binding: AST);
    begin
      binding := ternaryAST(procIlpFPSrpisC, leafAST(I, id, dummyPos), fps,
          nullaryAST(empty, dummyPos), dummyPos);
      enter(id, binding)
    end; {declareStdProc}
```

```
    procedure declareStdFunc (id: TokenString;
                    fps, resultType: AST;
                    var binding: AST);
    begin
      binding := quaternaryAST(funcIlpFPSrpcolonTisE, leafAST(I, id, dummyPos),
          fps, resultType, nullaryAST(empty, dummyPos), dummyPos);
      enter(id, binding)
    end; {declareStdFunc}

    procedure declareStdUnaryOp (op: TokenString;
                    argType, resultType: AST;
                    var binding: AST);
    begin
      binding := ternaryAST(opOcolonTtoT, leafAST(O, op, dummyPos), argType,
          resultType, dummyPos);
      enter(op, binding)
    end; {declareStdUnaryOp}

    procedure declareStdBinaryOp (op: TokenString;
                    arg1Type, arg2Type, resultType: AST;
                    var binding: AST);
    begin
      binding := quaternaryAST(opOcolonTxTtoT, leafAST(O, op, dummyPos), arg1Type,
          arg2Type, resultType, dummyPos);
      enter(op, binding)
    end; {declareStdBinaryOp}

begin {establishStdEnvironment}
    startIdentification;
    dummyI := leafAST(I, '            ', dummyPos);
    booleanType := nullaryAST(bool, dummyPos);
    integerType := nullaryAST(int, dummyPos);
    charType := nullaryAST(charr, dummyPos);
    anyType := nullaryAST(any, dummyPos);
    errorType := nullaryAST(empty, dummyPos);
    declareStdType('Boolean    ', booleanType);
    declareStdConst('false      ', booleanType, falseDecl);
    declareStdConst('true       ', booleanType, trueDecl);
    declareStdUnaryOp('\         ', booleanType, booleanType, notDecl);
    declareStdBinaryOp('/\       ', booleanType, booleanType, booleanType,
        andDecl);
    declareStdBinaryOp('\/       ', booleanType, booleanType, booleanType,
        orDecl);
    declareStdType('Integer    ', integerType);
    declareStdConst('maxint     ', integerType, maxintDecl);
    declareStdBinaryOp('+        ', integerType, integerType, integerType,
        addDecl);
    declareStdBinaryOp('-        ', integerType, integerType, integerType,
        subtractDecl);
    declareStdBinaryOp('*        ', integerType, integerType, integerType,
        multiplyDecl);
    declareStdBinaryOp('/        ', integerType, integerType, integerType,
        divideDecl);
    declareStdBinaryOp('//       ', integerType, integerType, integerType,
        moduloDecl);
    declareStdBinaryOp('<        ', integerType, integerType, booleanType,
        lessDecl);
    declareStdBinaryOp('<=       ', integerType, integerType, booleanType,
        notgreaterDecl);
    declareStdBinaryOp('>        ', integerType, integerType, booleanType,
        greaterDecl);
    declareStdBinaryOp('>=       ', integerType, integerType, booleanType,
        notlessDecl);
    declareStdType('Char       ', charType);
    declareStdFunc('chr        ', binaryAST(IcolonT, dummyI, integerType, dummyPos),
        charType, chrDecl);
    declareStdFunc('ord        ', binaryAST(IcolonT, dummyI, charType, dummyPos),
        integerType, ordDecl);
    declareStdFunc('eof        ', nullaryAST(empty, dummyPos), booleanType,
```

```
            eofDecl);
     declareStdFunc('eol        ', nullaryAST(empty, dummyPos), booleanType,
            eolDecl);
     declareStdProc('get        ', binaryAST(varIcolonT, dummyI, charType, dummyPos),
            getDecl);
     declareStdProc('put        ', binaryAST(IcolonT, dummyI, charType, dummyPos),
            putDecl);
     declareStdProc('getint     ', binaryAST(varIcolonT, dummyI, integerType,
            dummyPos), getintDecl);
     declareStdProc('putint     ', binaryAST(IcolonT, dummyI, integerType, dummyPos),
            putintDecl);
     declareStdProc('geteol     ', nullaryAST(empty, dummyPos), geteolDecl);
     declareStdProc('puteol     ', nullaryAST(empty, dummyPos), puteolDecl);
     declareStdBinaryOp('=       ', anyType, anyType, booleanType, equalDecl);
     declareStdBinaryOp('\=      ', anyType, anyType, booleanType, unequalDecl)
   end; {establishStdEnvironment}


{TYPE CHECKING}

   function equivalent (type1, type2: AST): Boolean;

     function equivalentRecord (rectype1, rectype2: AST): Boolean;
     begin
       if rectype1^.tag = rectype2^.tag then
         case rectype1^.tag of
           IcolonT:
             equivalentRecord :=
                 (rectype1^.child[1]^.spelling = rectype2^.child[1]^.spelling)
                  and equivalent(rectype1^.child[2], rectype2^.child[2]);
           IcolonTcommaRT:
             equivalentRecord :=
                 (rectype1^.child[1]^.spelling = rectype2^.child[1]^.spelling)
                 and equivalent(rectype1^.child[2], rectype2^.child[2])
                 and equivalentRecord(rectype1^.child[3], rectype2^.child[3])
         end
       else
         equivalentRecord := false
     end; {equivalentRecord}

   begin {equivalent}
     if (type1 = errorType) or (type2 = errorType) then
       equivalent := true
     else if type1^.tag = type2^.tag then
       case type1^.tag of
         bool, charr, int:
           equivalent := true;
         arrayILofT:
           if integerValuation(type1^.child[1]^.spelling)
               = integerValuation(type2^.child[1]^.spelling) then
             equivalent := equivalent(type1^.child[2], type2^.child[2])
           else
             equivalent := false;
         recordRTend:
           equivalent := equivalentRecord(type1^.child[1], type2^.child[1])
       end {case}
     else
       equivalent := false
   end; {equivalent}

   function equivalentFormals (formals1, formals2: AST): Boolean;
   begin
     if formals1^.tag = formals2^.tag then
       case formals1^.tag of
         empty:
           equivalentFormals := true;
         FPcommaFPS:
           equivalentFormals :=
               equivalentFormals(formals1^.child[1], formals2^.child[1])
```

```
                and equivalentFormals(formals1^.child[2], formals2^.child[2]);
        IcolonT:
          equivalentFormals := equivalent(formals1^.child[2], formals2^.child[2]);
        varIcolonT:
          equivalentFormals := equivalent(formals1^.child[2], formals2^.child[2]);
        procIlpFPSrp:
          equivalentFormals :=
              equivalentFormals(formals1^.child[2], formals2^.child[2]);
        funcIlpFPSrpcolonT:
          equivalentFormals :=
              equivalentFormals(formals1^.child[2], formals2^.child[2])
              and equivalent(formals1^.child[3], formals2^.child[3])
      end {case}
    else
      equivalentFormals := false
  end; {equivalentFormals}


{CHECKING THE ABSTRACT SYNTAX TREE}

  procedure reportUndeclared (leaf: AST);
  begin
    reportError('"%" is not declared                    ', leaf^.spelling,
        leaf^.position)
  end; {reportUndeclared}

  procedure checkIdentifier (id: AST;
                    var declared: Boolean;
                    var binding: AST);
  begin
    retrieve(id^.spelling, declared, binding);
    if declared then
      id^.decl := binding
    {otherwise id^.decl remains nil}
  end; {checkIdentifier}

  procedure checkFieldIdentifier (fieldid: AST;
                    recordTypedenoter: AST;
                    var fieldType: AST);
  begin
    with recordTypedenoter^ do
      case tag of
        IcolonT:
          if child[1]^.spelling = fieldid^.spelling then
            begin
              fieldType := child[2];  fieldid^.decl := recordTypedenoter
            end
          else
            fieldType := errorType;
        IcolonTcommaRT:
          if child[1]^.spelling = fieldid^.spelling then
            begin
              fieldType := child[2];  fieldid^.decl := recordTypedenoter
            end
          else
            checkFieldIdentifier(fieldid, child[3], fieldType)
      end {case}
  end; {checkFieldIdentifier}

  procedure checkCommand (command: AST);
  forward;

  procedure checkExpression (expression: AST;
                    var expressionType: AST);
  forward;
  procedure checkRecordAggregate (aggregate: AST;
                    var aggregateType: AST);
  forward;
  procedure checkArrayAggregate (aggregate: AST;
```

```
                    var elemCount: Positive;
                    var elemType: AST);
    forward;

procedure checkVname (vname: AST;
                    var vnameType: AST;
                    var variable: Boolean);
    forward;

procedure checkDeclaration (declaration: AST);
    forward;

procedure checkFormalParameters (formals: AST);
    forward;
procedure checkActualParameters (actuals: AST;
                    formals: AST);
    forward;

procedure checkTypeDenoter (var typedenoter: AST);
    forward;
procedure checkRecordTypeDenoter (recordTypedenoter: AST);
    forward;

{Commands}

procedure checkCommand (command: AST);
    var
      eType, vType: AST;
      declared, variable: Boolean;
      binding: AST;
begin
  with command^ do
      case tag of
        empty:
            ;
        VbecomesE:
          begin
            checkVname(child[1], vType, variable);
            checkExpression(child[2], eType);
            if not variable then
              reportError('LHS of assignment is not a variable     ',
                    '            ', child[1]^.position);
            if not equivalent(eType, vType) then
              reportError('assignment incompatibility             ',
                    '              ', position)
          end;
        IlpAPSrp:
          begin
            checkIdentifier(child[1], declared, binding);
            if not declared then
              reportUndeclared(child[1])
            else if not (binding^.tag in [procIlpFPSrpisC, procIlpFPSrp]) then
              reportError('"%" is not a procedure identifier      ',
                    child[1]^.spelling, child[1]^.position)
            else
              checkActualParameters(child[2], binding^.child[2])
          end;
        CsemicolonC:
          begin
            checkCommand(child[1]);
            checkCommand(child[2])
          end;
        letDinC:
          begin
            openScope;
            checkDeclaration(child[1]);
            checkCommand(child[2]);
            closeScope
          end;
```

```
        ifEthenCelseC:
          begin
            checkExpression(child[1], eType);
            if not equivalent(eType, booleanType) then
              reportError('Boolean expression expected here        ',
                     '       ', child[1]^.position);
            checkCommand(child[2]);
            checkCommand(child[3])
          end;
        whileEdoC:
          begin
            checkExpression(child[1], eType);
            if not equivalent(eType, booleanType) then
              reportError('Boolean expression expected here        ',
                     '           ', child[1]^.position);
            checkCommand(child[2])
          end
      end {case}
end; {checkCommand}

{Expressions}

procedure checkExpression (expression: AST;
                  var expressionType: AST);
   var
     e1Type, e2Type, e3Type, vType, rType: AST;
     binding: AST;
     declared, variable: Boolean;
     elemCount: Positive;
     elemCountSpelling: TokenString;
begin
   expressionType := errorType; {to be overridden if the expression is well-typed}
   with expression^ do
     begin
       case tag of
         IL:
           expressionType := integerType;
         CL:
           expressionType := charType;
         V:
           checkVname(child[1], expressionType, variable);
         IlpAPSrp:
           begin
             checkIdentifier(child[1], declared, binding);
             if not declared then
               reportUndeclared(child[1])
             else if not (binding^.tag in [funcIlpFPSrpcolonTisE,
                 funcIlpFPSrpcolonT]) then
               reportError('"%" is not a function identifier        ',
                   child[1]^.spelling, child[1]^.position)
             else
               begin
                 checkActualParameters(child[2], binding^.child[2]);
                 expressionType := binding^.child[3]
               end
           end;
         OE:
           begin
             checkExpression(child[2], e1Type);
             checkIdentifier(child[1], declared, binding);
             {… treating operators like identifiers}
             if not declared then
               reportUndeclared(child[1])
             else
               begin
                 if binding^.tag <> opOcolonTtoT then
                   reportError('"%" is not a unary operator          ',
                       child[1]^.spelling, child[1]^.position)
                 else
```

```
                  begin
                    if not equivalent(e1Type, binding^.child[2]) then
                      reportError('wrong argument type for "%"            ',
                            child[1]^.spelling, child[2]^.position);
                    expressionType := binding^.child[3]
                  end
            end
    end;
EOE:
  begin
    checkExpression(child[1], e1Type);
    checkExpression(child[3], e2Type);
    checkIdentifier(child[2], declared, binding);
    {… treating operators like identifiers}
    if not declared then
      reportUndeclared(child[2])
    else
      begin
        if binding^.tag <> opOcolonTxTtoT then
          reportError('"%" is not a binary operator            ',
                child[2]^.spelling, child[2]^.position)
        else
          begin
            if binding^.child[2]^.tag = any then {must be "=" or "\="}
              begin
                if not equivalent(e1Type, e2Type) then
                  reportError(
                      'incompatible argument types for "%"       ',
                      child[2]^.spelling, position)
              end
            else if not equivalent(e1Type, binding^.child[2]) then
              reportError('wrong argument type for "%"            ',
                  child[2]^.spelling, child[1]^.position)
            else if not equivalent(e2Type, binding^.child[3]) then
              reportError('wrong argument type for "%"            ',
                  child[2]^.spelling, child[3]^.position);
            expressionType := binding^.child[4]
          end
      end
  end;
letDinE:
  begin
    openScope;
    checkDeclaration(child[1]);
    checkExpression(child[2], expressionType);
    closeScope
  end;
ifEthenEelseE:
  begin
    checkExpression(child[1], e1Type);
    if not equivalent(e1Type, booleanType) then
      reportError('Boolean expression expected here          ',
          '             ', child[1]^.position);
    checkExpression(child[2], e2Type);
    checkExpression(child[3], e3Type);
    if not equivalent(e2Type, e3Type) then
      reportError('incompatible limbs in if-expression     ',
          '               ', position);
    expressionType := e2Type
  end;
lcRArc:
  begin
    checkRecordAggregate(child[1], rType);
    expressionType := unaryAST(recordRTend, rType, dummyPos)
  end;
lbAArb:
  begin
    checkArrayAggregate(child[1], elemCount, e1Type);
    spellInteger(elemCount, elemCountSpelling);
```

```
                    expressionType := binaryAST(arrayILofT,
                        leafAST(IL, elemCountSpelling, dummyPos), e1Type, dummyPos)
                end
            end; {case}
            typ := expressionType
        end
end; {checkExpression}

procedure checkRecordAggregate (aggregate: AST;
                    var aggregateType: AST);
    var
        eType, rType, fType: AST;
begin
    with aggregate^ do
        begin
            case tag of
                IisE:
                    begin
                        checkExpression(child[2], eType);
                        aggregateType := binaryAST(IcolonT, child[1], eType, dummyPos)
                    end;
                IisEcommaRA:
                    begin
                        checkExpression(child[2], eType);
                        checkRecordAggregate(child[3], rType);
                        checkFieldIdentifier(child[1], rType, fType);
                        if fType <> errorType then
                            reportError('duplicate field "%" in record            ',
                                child[1]^.spelling, child[1]^.position);
                        aggregateType := ternaryAST(IcolonTcommaRT, child[1], eType, rType,
                            dummyPos)
                    end
            end; {case}
            typ := aggregateType
        end
end; {checkRecordAggregate}

procedure checkArrayAggregate (aggregate: AST;
                    var elemCount: Positive;
                    var elemType: AST);
    var
        eType: AST;
begin
    with aggregate^ do
        case tag of
            E:
                begin
                    checkExpression(child[1], elemType);
                    elemCount := 1
                end;
            EcommaAA:
                begin
                    checkExpression(child[1], eType);
                    checkArrayAggregate(child[2], elemCount, elemType);
                    elemCount := elemCount + 1;
                    if not equivalent(eType, elemType) then
                        reportError('incompatible array-aggregate element    ',
                            '                ', child[1]^.position)
                end
        end {case}
end; {checkArrayAggregate}

{Value-or-variable-names}

procedure checkVname (vname: AST;
                    var vnameType: AST;
                    var variable: Boolean);
    var
        eType, vType: AST;
```

```
     binding: AST;
     declared: Boolean;
begin
   variable := false;
   vnameType := errorType; {to be overridden if the v-name is well-typed}
   with vname^ do
     begin
       case tag of
         I:
           begin
             checkIdentifier(vname, declared, binding);
             if not declared then
               reportUndeclared(vname)
             else
               with binding^ do
                 if not (binding^.tag in [constIisE, IcolonT, varIcolonT]) then
                   reportError('"%" is not a const or var identifier   ',
                       spelling, position)
                 else
                   case tag of
                     constIisE:
                       begin
                         vnameType := child[2]^.typ;  variable := false
                       end;
                     IcolonT:
                       begin
                         vnameType := child[2];  variable := false
                       end;
                     varIcolonT:
                       begin
                         vnameType := child[2];  variable := true
                       end
                   end {case}
           end;
         VdotI:
           begin
             checkVname(child[1], vType, variable);
             if vType <> errorType then
               begin
                 if vType^.tag <> recordRTend then
                   reportError('record expected here                  ',
                       '                 ', child[1]^.position)
                 else
                   begin
                     checkFieldIdentifier(child[2], vType^.child[1], vnameType);
                     if vnameType = errorType then
                       reportError('no field "%" in this record type       ',
                           child[2]^.spelling, child[2]^.position)
                   end
               end
           end;
         VlbErb:
           begin
             checkVname(child[1], vType, variable);
             checkExpression(child[2], eType);
             if vType <> errorType then
               begin
                 if vType^.tag <> arrayILofT then
                   reportError('array expected here                  ',
                       '                 ', child[1]^.position)
                 else
                   begin
                     if not equivalent(eType, integerType) then
                       reportError('Integer expression expected here       ',
                           '                 ', child[2]^.position);
                     vnameType := vType^.child[2]
                   end
               end
           end
     end
```

```
            end; {case}
            typ := vnameType
         end
end; {checkVname}

{Declarations}

procedure checkDeclaration (declaration: AST);
   var
      eType: AST;
begin
   with declaration^ do
      case tag of
         constIisE:
            begin
               checkExpression(child[2], eType);
               enter(child[1]^.spelling, declaration)
            end;
         varIcolonT:
            begin
               checkTypeDenoter(child[2]);
               enter(child[1]^.spelling, declaration)
            end;
         procIlpFPSrpisC:
            begin
               enter(child[1]^.spelling, declaration); {permits recursion}
               openScope;
               checkFormalParameters(child[2]);
               checkCommand(child[3]);
               closeScope
            end;
         funcIlpFPSrpcolonTisE:
            begin
               checkTypeDenoter(child[3]);
               enter(child[1]^.spelling, declaration); {permits recursion}
               openScope;
               checkFormalParameters(child[2]);
               checkExpression(child[4], eType);
               closeScope;
               if not equivalent(eType, child[3]) then
                  reportError('body of function "%" has wrong type      ',
                        child[1]^.spelling, child[2]^.position)
            end;
         typeIisT:
            begin
               checkTypeDenoter(child[2]);
               enter(child[1]^.spelling, declaration)
            end;
         DsemicolonD:
            begin
               checkDeclaration(child[1]);
               checkDeclaration(child[2])
            end
      end {case}
end; {checkDeclaration}

{Parameters}

procedure checkFormalParameters (formals: AST);
begin
   with formals^ do
      case tag of
         empty:
            ;
         FPcommaFPS:
            begin
               checkFormalParameters(child[1]);
               checkFormalParameters(child[2])
            end;
```

```
            IcolonT:
              begin
                checkTypeDenoter(child[2]);
                enter(child[1]^.spelling, formals)
              end;
            varIcolonT:
              begin
                checkTypeDenoter(child[2]);
                enter(child[1]^.spelling, formals)
              end;
            procIlpFPSrp:
              begin
                openScope;
                checkFormalParameters(child[2]);
                closeScope;
                enter(child[1]^.spelling, formals)
              end;
            funcIlpFPSrpcolonT:
              begin
                openScope;
                checkFormalParameters(child[2]);
                closeScope;
                checkTypeDenoter(child[3]);
                enter(child[1]^.spelling, formals)
              end
        end {case}
end; {checkFormalParameters}

procedure checkActualParameters (actuals: AST;
                  formals: AST);
  var
    apType: AST;
    declared, variable: Boolean;
    binding: AST;
begin
  with actuals^ do
    case tag of
      empty:
        if formals^.tag <> empty then
          reportError('too few actual parameters              ', '           ',
              position);
      APcommaAPS:
        if formals^.tag <> FPcommaFPS then
          reportError('too many actual parameters             ', '           ',
              position)
        else
          begin
            checkActualParameters(child[1], formals^.child[1]);
            checkActualParameters(child[2], formals^.child[2])
          end;
      E:
        begin
          checkExpression(child[1], apType);
          if formals^.tag <> IcolonT then
            reportError('const actual parameter not expected here',
                '            ', position)
          else if not equivalent(apType, formals^.child[2]) then
            reportError('wrong type for const actual parameter   ',
                '            ', child[1]^.position)
        end;
      varV:
        begin
          checkVname(child[1], apType, variable);
          if not variable then
            reportError('actual parameter is not a variable      ',
                '            ', child[1]^.position)
          else if formals^.tag <> varIcolonT then
            reportError('var actual parameter not expected here  ',
                '            ', position)
```

```
               else if not equivalent(apType, formals^.child[2]) then
                 reportError('wrong type for var actual parameter   ',
                     '            ', child[1]^.position)
           end;
         procI:
           begin
             checkIdentifier(child[1], declared, binding);
             if not declared then
               reportUndeclared(child[1])
             else if not (binding^.tag in [procIlpFPSrpisC, procIlpFPSrp]) then
                 reportError('"%" is not a procedure identifier      ',
                     child[1]^.spelling, child[1]^.position)
             else if formals^.tag <> procIlpFPSrp then
                 reportError('proc actual parameter not expected here ',
                     '           ', position)
             else if not equivalentFormals(binding^.child[2],
                 formals^.child[2]) then
                 reportError('wrong signature for procedure "%"       ',
                     child[1]^.spelling, child[1]^.position)
           end;
         funcI:
           begin
             checkIdentifier(child[1], declared, binding);
             if not declared then
               reportUndeclared(child[1])
             else if not (binding^.tag in
                 [funcIlpFPSrpcolonTisE, funcIlpFPSrpcolonT]) then
                 reportError('"%" is not a function identifier        ',
                     child[1]^.spelling, child[1]^.position)
             else if formals^.tag <> funcIlpFPSrpcolonT then
                 reportError('func actual parameter not expected here ',
                     '           ', position)
             else if not equivalentFormals(binding^.child[2],
                 formals^.child[2]) then
                 reportError('wrong signature for function "%"         ',
                     child[1]^.spelling, child[1]^.position)
             else if not equivalent(binding^.child[3], formals^.child[3]) then
                 reportError('wrong type for function "%"             ',
                     child[1]^.spelling, child[1]^.position)
           end
       end {case}
end; {checkActualParameters}

{Type-denoters}

procedure checkTypeDenoter (var typedenoter: AST);
   var
     newTypedenoter: AST;
     binding: AST;
     declared: Boolean;
begin
   with typedenoter^ do
     case tag of
       I:
           begin
             checkIdentifier(typedenoter, declared, binding);
             if not declared then
               begin
                 reportUndeclared(typedenoter);
                 shareAST(typedenoter, errorType)
               end
             else if binding^.tag <> typeIisT then
               begin
                 reportError('"%" is not a type identifier             ',
                     spelling, position);
                 shareAST(typedenoter, errorType)
               end
             else
               shareAST(typedenoter, binding^.child[2])
```

```
                    {… replace the type identifier by the denoted type}
              end;
          arrayILofT:
            begin
              checkTypeDenoter(child[2]);
              if integerValuation(child[1]^.spelling) = 0 then
                reportError('arrays must not be empty                ',
                  '              ', child[1]^.position)
            end;
          recordRTend:
            begin
              checkRecordTypeDenoter(child[1])
            end
        end {case}
  end; {checkTypeDenoter}

  procedure checkRecordTypeDenoter (recordTypedenoter: AST);
  begin
    with recordTypedenoter^ do
      case tag of
        IcolonT:
          begin
            checkTypeDenoter(child[2])
          end;
        IcolonTcommaRT:
          begin
            checkTypeDenoter(child[2]);
            checkRecordTypeDenoter(child[3])
          end
      end {case}
  end; {checkRecordTypeDenoter}

  {Programs}

  procedure checkProgram (programAST: AST);
  begin
    dummyPos.start := -1;
    dummyPos.finish := -1;
    checkCommand(programAST)
  end; {checkProgram}

end. {ContextualAnalyser}
```

E.6   Code generation

```
unit CodeGenerator;

interface

  uses
    CompilerGlobals, AbstractSyntaxTrees, RuntimeOrganization;

  procedure elaborateStdEnvironment;
    {Decides run-time representation of entities in the standard environment.}

  procedure encodeRun (programAST: AST;
                   showingTable: Boolean);
    {Translates the program represented by programAST into TAM code. If
     showingTable is true, displays run-time representation of all declared
     entities.}

{================================================================================}
```

```
implementation

{OBJECT CODE}

  {Implementation notes:
   Object code is generated directly into the TAM Code Store, starting at CB. The
   address of the next instruction is held in nextInstrAddr.}

  const
    null = 0;  {for placing in unused fields of instructions}

  var
    nextInstrAddr: CodeAddress;

  procedure startCodeGeneration;
  begin
    nextInstrAddr := CB
  end; {startCodeGeneration}

  procedure finishCodeGeneration;
  begin
    CT := nextInstrAddr
  end; {finishCodeGeneration}

  procedure emit (op: OpCode;
                  n: Natural;
                  r: RegisterNumber;
                  d: Operand);
     var
        nextInstr: Instruction;
  begin
    if n > 255 then
      begin
        reportRestriction('length of operand can''t exceed 255 words');
        n := 255 {to allow code generation to continue}
      end;
    nextInstr.op := op;  nextInstr.n := n;
    nextInstr.r := r;  nextInstr.d := d;
    if nextInstrAddr = PB then
      reportRestriction('too many instructions for code segment  ')
    else
      begin
        code[nextInstrAddr] := nextInstr;  nextInstrAddr := nextInstrAddr + 1
      end
  end; {emit}

  procedure patch (addr: CodeAddress;
                   d: Operand);
  begin
    code[addr].d := d
  end; {patch}


{OBJECT DESCRIPTIONS}

  {An object description describes a value, variable, routine, or type in the
   object program. For definitions, see unit CompilerGlobals.}

  var
    tableDetailsReqd: Boolean;

  procedure writeTableDetails (declaration: AST);
     {Writes a summary of an object description for the user's benefit.}
    …;

  procedure attach (var newObject: ObjectPointer;
                    newKind: ObjectKind);
     {Attaches a new object description, of the given kind, to the pointer field
      newObject.}
```

```
begin
  new(newObject);  newObject^.kind := newKind
end; {attach}


{DATA REPRESENTATION}

  function characterValuation (spelling: TokenString): Word;
      {Returns the machine representation of the given character literal.}
  begin
    characterValuation := ord(spelling[2])
  end; {characterValuation}

  function typeSize (typedenoter: AST): Natural;
      {Returns the no. of words occupied by each value of the given type.}
    var
      size: Natural;

    function recordTypeSize (recordTypedenoter: AST;
                    offset: Natural): Natural;
      var
        fieldSize, recordSize: Natural;
    begin
      with recordTypedenoter^ do
        begin
          case tag of
            IcolonT:
              begin
                fieldSize := typeSize(child[2]);
                recordTypeSize := fieldSize
              end;
            IcolonTcommaRT:
              begin
                fieldSize := typeSize(child[2]);
                recordSize := recordTypeSize(child[3], offset + fieldSize);
                recordTypeSize := fieldSize + recordSize
              end
          end; {case}
          attach(obj, field);
          obj^.size := fieldSize;  obj^.fieldOffset := offset;
          writeTableDetails(recordTypedenoter)
        end
    end; {recordTypeSize}

  begin {typeSize}
    with typedenoter^ do
      if obj <> nil then {this type's representation has already been determined}
        typeSize := obj^.size
      else
        begin
          case tag of
            bool:
              size := booleanSize;
            charr:
              size := characterSize;
            int:
              size := integerSize;
            arrayILofT:
              size := integerValuation(child[1]^.spelling) * typeSize(child[2]);
            recordRTend:
              size := recordTypeSize(child[1], 0)
          end; {case}
          attach(obj, typeRepresentation);  obj^.size := size;
          typeSize := size;
          writeTableDetails(typedenoter)
        end
  end; {typeSize}
```

```
{STANDARD ENVIRONMENT}

  procedure elaborateStdEnvironment;

    procedure elaborateStdConst (constDeclaration: AST;
                       value: Integer);
    begin
      with constDeclaration^ do
        begin
          attach(obj, knownValue);
          obj^.value := value;  obj^.size := typeSize(child[2]^.typ);
          writeTableDetails(constDeclaration)
        end
    end; {elaborateStdType}

    procedure elaborateStdRoutine (routineDeclaration: AST;
                       routineOffset: Integer;
                       routineKind: ObjectKind);
    begin
      with routineDeclaration^ do
        begin
          attach(obj, routineKind);  obj^.size := closureSize;
          case routineKind of
            primitiveRoutine, equalityRoutine:
              obj^.displacement := routineOffset;
            knownRoutine:
              begin
                obj^.address.level := 0;
                obj^.address.displacement := routineOffset
              end
          end; {case}
          writeTableDetails(routineDeclaration)
        end
    end; {elaborateStdRoutine}

  begin
    tableDetailsReqd := false;
    elaborateStdConst(falseDecl, falseRep);  elaborateStdConst(trueDecl, trueRep);
    elaborateStdRoutine(notDecl, notDisplacement, primitiveRoutine);
    elaborateStdRoutine(andDecl, andDisplacement, primitiveRoutine);
    elaborateStdRoutine(orDecl, orDisplacement, primitiveRoutine);
    elaborateStdConst(maxintDecl, maxintRep);
    elaborateStdRoutine(addDecl, addDisplacement, primitiveRoutine);
    elaborateStdRoutine(subtractDecl, subDisplacement, primitiveRoutine);
    elaborateStdRoutine(multiplyDecl, multDisplacement, primitiveRoutine);
    elaborateStdRoutine(divideDecl, divDisplacement, primitiveRoutine);
    elaborateStdRoutine(moduloDecl, modDisplacement, primitiveRoutine);
    elaborateStdRoutine(lessDecl, ltDisplacement, primitiveRoutine);
    elaborateStdRoutine(notgreaterDecl, leDisplacement, primitiveRoutine);
    elaborateStdRoutine(greaterDecl, gtDisplacement, primitiveRoutine);
    elaborateStdRoutine(notlessDecl, geDisplacement, primitiveRoutine);
    elaborateStdRoutine(chrDecl, idDisplacement, primitiveRoutine);
    elaborateStdRoutine(ordDecl, idDisplacement, primitiveRoutine);
    elaborateStdRoutine(eolDecl, eolDisplacement, primitiveRoutine);
    elaborateStdRoutine(eofDecl, eofDisplacement, primitiveRoutine);
    elaborateStdRoutine(getDecl, getDisplacement, primitiveRoutine);
    elaborateStdRoutine(putDecl, putDisplacement, primitiveRoutine);
    elaborateStdRoutine(getintDecl, getintDisplacement, primitiveRoutine);
    elaborateStdRoutine(putintDecl, putintDisplacement, primitiveRoutine);
    elaborateStdRoutine(geteolDecl, geteolDisplacement, primitiveRoutine);
    elaborateStdRoutine(puteolDecl, puteolDisplacement, primitiveRoutine);
    elaborateStdRoutine(equalDecl, eqDisplacement, equalityRoutine);
    elaborateStdRoutine(unequalDecl, neDisplacement, equalityRoutine)
  end; {elaborateStdEnvironment}


{REGISTERS}

  function displayRegister (currentLevel, objectLevel: Natural): RegisterNumber;
```

```
      {Returns the register number appropriate for addressing a data object at
      objectLevel.}
  begin
    if objectLevel = 0 then
      displayRegister := SBr
    else if currentLevel - objectLevel <= 6 then
      displayRegister := LBr + currentLevel - objectLevel   {LBr or ... or L6r}
    else
      begin
        reportRestriction('can''t access data more than 6 levels out');
        displayRegister := L6r  {to allow code generation to continue}
      end
  end; {displayRegister}


{ENCODING THE ABSTRACT SYNTAX TREE}

  {Implementation notes:
   A run-time object description will be attached to each single-declaration node.
   At an applied occurrence of an identifier or operator, this object description
   can be accessed via the link from the applied occurrence to the declaration.}

  procedure encodeRoutineCall (routineId: AST;
                   currentLevel: RoutineLevel;
                   argsSize: Natural);
  begin
    with routineId^.decl^.obj^ do
      case kind of
        knownRoutine:
          emit(CALLop, displayRegister(currentLevel, address.level), CBr,
            address.displacement);
        unknownRoutine:
          begin
            emit(LOADop, closureSize, displayRegister(currentLevel,
              address.level), address.displacement);
            emit(CALLIop, null, null, null)
          end;
        primitiveRoutine:
          if displacement <> idDisplacement then
            emit(CALLop, SBr, PBr, displacement);
        equalityRoutine:  {"=" or "\="}
          begin
            emit(LOADLop, null, null, argsSize div 2);
            emit(CALLop, SBr, PBr, displacement)
          end
      end {case}
  end; {encodeRoutineCall}

  procedure encodeExecute (command: AST;
                   currentLevel: RoutineLevel;
                   frameSize: Natural);
  forward;

  procedure encodeEvaluate (expression: AST;
                   currentLevel: RoutineLevel;
                   frameSize: Natural;
                   var valSize: Natural);
  forward;
  procedure encodeEvaluateRecord (aggregate: AST;
                   currentLevel: RoutineLevel;
                   frameSize: Natural;
                   var recordSize: Natural);
  forward;
  procedure encodeEvaluateArray (aggregate: AST;
                   currentLevel: RoutineLevel;
                   frameSize: Natural;
                   var arraySize: Natural);
  forward;
```

```
procedure encodeIdentify (vname: AST;
                currentLevel: RoutineLevel;
                frameSize: Natural;
                var baseObject: ObjectPointer;
                var offset: Natural;
                var indexed: Boolean);
forward;
procedure encodeAssign (vname: AST;
                currentLevel: RoutineLevel;
                frameSize, valSize: Natural);
forward;
procedure encodeFetch (vname: AST;
                currentLevel: RoutineLevel;
                frameSize, valSize: Natural);
forward;
procedure encodeFetchAddress (vname: AST;
                currentLevel: RoutineLevel;
                frameSize: Natural);
forward;

procedure encodeElaborate (declaration: AST;
                currentLevel: RoutineLevel;
                frameSize: Natural;
                var extraSize: Natural);
forward;

procedure encodeBindParameters (formals: AST;
                currentLevel: RoutineLevel;
                otherArgsSize: Natural;
                var argsSize: Natural);
forward;
procedure encodeGiveArguments (actuals: AST;
                currentLevel: RoutineLevel;
                frameSize: Natural;
                var argsSize: Natural);
forward;

{Commands}

procedure encodeExecute (command: AST;
                currentLevel: RoutineLevel;
                frameSize: Natural);
   var
     valSize, argsSize, extraSize: Natural;
     jumpAddr, jumpifAddr, loopAddr: CodeAddress;
begin
   with command^ do
     case tag of
       empty:
         ;   {no code to be generated}
       VbecomesE:
         begin
           encodeEvaluate(child[2], currentLevel, frameSize, valSize);
           encodeAssign(child[1], currentLevel, frameSize + valSize, valSize)
         end;
       IlpAPSrp:
         begin
           encodeGiveArguments(child[2], currentLevel, frameSize, argsSize);
           encodeRoutineCall(child[1], currentLevel, argsSize)
         end;
       CsemicolonC:
         begin
           encodeExecute(child[1], currentLevel, frameSize);
           encodeExecute(child[2], currentLevel, frameSize)
         end;
       letDinC:
         begin
           encodeElaborate(child[1], currentLevel, frameSize, extraSize);
           encodeExecute(child[2], currentLevel, frameSize + extraSize);
```

```
              if extraSize > 0 then
                emit(POPop, 0, null, extraSize)
            end;
        ifEthenCelseC:
          begin
            encodeEvaluate(child[1], currentLevel, frameSize, valSize);
            jumpifAddr := nextInstrAddr;
            emit(JUMPIFop, falseRep, CBr, null);
            encodeExecute(child[2], currentLevel, frameSize);
            jumpAddr := nextInstrAddr;
            emit(JUMPop, null, CBr, null);
            patch(jumpifAddr, nextInstrAddr);
            encodeExecute(child[3], currentLevel, frameSize);
            patch(jumpAddr, nextInstrAddr)
          end;
        whileEdoC:
          begin
            jumpAddr := nextInstrAddr;
            emit(JUMPop, null, CBr, null);
            loopAddr := nextInstrAddr;
            encodeExecute(child[2], currentLevel, frameSize);
            patch(jumpAddr, nextInstrAddr);
            encodeEvaluate(child[1], currentLevel, frameSize, valSize);
            emit(JUMPIFop, trueRep, CBr, loopAddr)
          end
      end {case}
end; {encodeExecute}

{Expressions}

procedure encodeEvaluate (expression: AST;
                currentLevel: RoutineLevel;
                frameSize: Natural;
                var valSize: Natural);
  var
    valSize1, valSize2, argsSize, extraSize: Natural;
    jumpAddr, jumpifAddr: CodeAddress;
begin
  with expression^ do
    begin
      valSize := typeSize(typ);
      case tag of
        IL:
          emit(LOADLop, null, null, integerValuation(spelling));
        CL:
          emit(LOADLop, null, null, characterValuation(spelling));
        V:
          encodeFetch(child[1], currentLevel, frameSize, valSize);
        IlpAPSrp:
          begin
            encodeGiveArguments(child[2], currentLevel, frameSize, argsSize);
            encodeRoutineCall(child[1], currentLevel, argsSize)
          end;
        OE:
          begin
            encodeEvaluate(child[2], currentLevel, frameSize, valSize1);
            encodeRoutineCall(child[1], currentLevel, valSize1)
          end;
        EOE:
          begin
            encodeEvaluate(child[1], currentLevel, frameSize, valSize1);
            encodeEvaluate(child[3], currentLevel, frameSize + valSize1,
                valSize2);
            encodeRoutineCall(child[2], currentLevel, valSize1 + valSize2)
          end;
        letDinE:
          begin
            encodeElaborate(child[1], currentLevel, frameSize, extraSize);
            encodeEvaluate(child[2], currentLevel, frameSize + extraSize,
```

```
                            valSize);
                    if extraSize > 0 then
                        emit(POPop, valSize, null, extraSize)
                end;
            ifEthenEelseE:
                begin
                    encodeEvaluate(child[1], currentLevel, frameSize, valSize1);
                    jumpifAddr := nextInstrAddr;
                    emit(JUMPIFop, falseRep, CBr, null);
                    encodeEvaluate(child[2], currentLevel, frameSize, valSize);
                    jumpAddr := nextInstrAddr;
                    emit(JUMPop, null, CBr, null);
                    patch(jumpifAddr, nextInstrAddr);
                    encodeEvaluate(child[3], currentLevel, frameSize, valSize);
                    patch(jumpAddr, nextInstrAddr)
                end;
            lcRArc:
                encodeEvaluateRecord(child[1], currentLevel, frameSize, valSize);
            lbAArb:
                encodeEvaluateArray(child[1], currentLevel, frameSize, valSize)
        end {case}
    end
end; {encodeEvaluate}

procedure encodeEvaluateRecord (aggregate: AST;
                    currentLevel: RoutineLevel;
                    frameSize: Natural;
                    var recordSize: Natural);
    var
        fieldSize: Natural;
begin
    with aggregate^ do
        case tag of
            IisE:
                encodeEvaluate(child[2], currentLevel, frameSize, recordSize);
            IisEcommaRA:
                begin
                    encodeEvaluate(child[2], currentLevel, frameSize, fieldSize);
                    encodeEvaluateRecord(child[3], currentLevel, frameSize + fieldSize,
                        recordSize);
                    recordSize := fieldSize + recordSize
                end
        end {case}
end; {encodeEvaluateRecord}

procedure encodeEvaluateArray (aggregate: AST;
                    currentLevel: RoutineLevel;
                    frameSize: Natural;
                    var arraySize: Natural);
    var
        elemSize: Natural;
begin
    with aggregate^ do
        begin
            case tag of
                E:
                    encodeEvaluate(child[1], currentLevel, frameSize, arraySize);
                EcommaAA:
                    begin
                        encodeEvaluate(child[1], currentLevel, frameSize, elemSize);
                        encodeEvaluateArray(child[2], currentLevel, frameSize + elemSize,
                            arraySize);
                        arraySize := elemSize + arraySize
                    end
            end {case}
        end
end; {encodeEvaluateArray}
```

```
{Value-or-variable-names}

procedure encodeIdentify (vname: AST;
                 currentLevel: RoutineLevel;
                 frameSize: Natural;
                 var baseObject: ObjectPointer;
                 var offset: Natural;
                 var indexed: Boolean);
  var
    elemSize, indexSize: Natural;
begin
  with vname^ do
    case tag of
      I:
        begin
          baseObject := decl^.obj;
          offset := 0;
          indexed := false;
        end;
      VdotI:
        begin
          encodeIdentify(child[1], currentLevel, frameSize, baseObject, offset,
              indexed);
          offset := offset + child[2]^.decl^.obj^.fieldOffset
          {… child[2]^.decl points to the appropriate record field}
        end;
      VlbErb:
        begin
          encodeIdentify(child[1], currentLevel, frameSize, baseObject, offset,
              indexed);
          elemSize := typeSize(typ);
          if child[2]^.tag = IL then
            offset := offset + integerValuation(child[2]^.spelling) * elemSize
          else {v-name is indexed by a proper expression, not a literal}
            begin
              if indexed then
                frameSize := frameSize + integerSize;
              encodeEvaluate(child[2], currentLevel, frameSize, indexSize);
              if elemSize <> 1 then
                begin
                  emit(LOADLop, null, null, elemSize);
                  emit(CALLop, SBr, PBr, multDisplacement)
                end;
              if indexed then
                emit(CALLop, SBr, PBr, addDisplacement)
              else
                indexed := true
            end
        end
    end {case}
end; {encodeIdentify}

procedure encodeAssign (vname: AST;
                 currentLevel: RoutineLevel;
                 frameSize, valSize: Natural);
  var
    baseObject: ObjectPointer;
    offset: Natural;
    indexed: Boolean;
begin
  encodeIdentify(vname, currentLevel, frameSize, baseObject, offset, indexed);
  {If indexed = true, code will have been generated to load an index value.}
  if valSize > 255 then
    begin
      reportRestriction('can''t store values larger than 255 words');
      valSize := 255; {to allow code generation to continue}
    end;
  with baseObject^ do
    case kind of
```

```
            knownAddress:
              if indexed then
                begin
                  emit(LOADAop, null, displayRegister(currentLevel, address.level),
                      address.displacement + offset);
                  emit(CALLop, SBr, PBr, addDisplacement);
                  emit(STOREIop, valSize, null, null)
                end
              else
                emit(STOREop, valSize, displayRegister(currentLevel, address.level),
                    address.displacement + offset);
            unknownAddress:
              begin
                emit(LOADop, addressSize, displayRegister(currentLevel,
                    address.level), address.displacement);
                if indexed then
                  emit(CALLop, SBr, PBr, addDisplacement);
                if offset <> 0 then
                  begin
                    emit(LOADLop, null, null, offset);
                    emit(CALLop, SBr, PBr, addDisplacement)
                  end;
                emit(STOREIop, valSize, null, null)
              end
          end {case}
  end; {encodeAssign}

  procedure encodeFetch (vname: AST;
                    currentLevel: RoutineLevel;
                    frameSize, valSize: Natural);
    var
      baseObject: ObjectPointer;
      offset: Natural;
      indexed: Boolean;
  begin
    encodeIdentify(vname, currentLevel, frameSize, baseObject, offset, indexed);
    {If indexed = true, code will have been generated to load an index value.}
    if valSize > 255 then
      begin
        reportRestriction('can''t load values larger than 255 words ');
        valSize := 255; {to allow code generation to continue}
      end;
    with baseObject^ do
      case kind of
        knownValue:
          {presumably offset = 0 and indexed = false}
            emit(LOADLop, null, null, value);
        unknownValue, knownAddress:
          if indexed then
            begin
              emit(LOADAop, null, displayRegister(currentLevel, address.level),
                  address.displacement + offset);
              emit(CALLop, SBr, PBr, addDisplacement);
              emit(LOADIop, valSize, null, null)
            end
          else
            emit(LOADop, valSize, displayRegister(currentLevel, address.level),
                address.displacement + offset);
        unknownAddress:
          begin
            emit(LOADop, addressSize, displayRegister(currentLevel,
                address.level), address.displacement);
            if indexed then
              emit(CALLop, SBr, PBr, addDisplacement);
            if offset <> 0 then
              begin
                emit(LOADLop, null, null, offset);
                emit(CALLop, SBr, PBr, addDisplacement)
              end;
```

```
                    emit(LOADIop, valSize, null, null)
              end
        end {case}
  end; {encodeFetch}

  procedure encodeFetchAddress (vname: AST;
                    currentLevel: RoutineLevel;
                    frameSize: Natural);
     var
       baseObject: ObjectPointer;
       offset: Natural;
       indexed: Boolean;
  begin
     encodeIdentify(vname, currentLevel, frameSize, baseObject, offset, indexed);
     {If indexed = true, code will have been generated to load an index value.}
     with baseObject^ do
        case kind of
           knownAddress:
             begin
                emit(LOADAop, null, displayRegister(currentLevel, address.level),
                    address.displacement + offset);
                if indexed then
                  emit(CALLop, SBr, PBr, addDisplacement)
             end;
           unknownAddress:
             begin
                emit(LOADop, addressSize, displayRegister(currentLevel,
                    address.level), address.displacement);
                if indexed then
                  emit(CALLop, SBr, PBr, addDisplacement);
                if offset <> 0 then
                  begin
                     emit(LOADLop, null, null, offset);
                     emit(CALLop, SBr, PBr, addDisplacement)
                  end
             end
        end {case}
  end; {encodeFetchAddress}

  {Declarations}

  procedure encodeElaborate (declaration: AST;
                    currentLevel: RoutineLevel;
                    frameSize: Natural;
                    var extraSize: Natural);
     var
       valSize, argsSize, extraSize1, extraSize2: Natural;
       jumpAddr: CodeAddress;
  begin
     with declaration^ do
        case tag of
           constIisE:
             begin
                if child[2]^.tag in [CL, IL] then
                   begin
                      attach(obj, knownValue);
                      case child[2]^.tag of
                        CL:
                           begin
                              obj^.size := characterSize;
                              obj^.value := characterValuation(child[2]^.spelling)
                           end;
                        IL:
                           begin
                              obj^.size := integerSize;
                              obj^.value := integerValuation(child[2]^.spelling)
                           end
                      end; {case}
                      extraSize := 0
```

```
          end
      else
        begin
          encodeEvaluate(child[2], currentLevel, frameSize, valSize);
          attach(obj, unknownValue);
          obj^.size := valSize;
          obj^.address.level := currentLevel;
          obj^.address.displacement := frameSize;
          extraSize := valSize
        end;
      writeTableDetails(declaration)
    end;
varIcolonT:
  begin
    extraSize := typeSize(child[2]);
    emit(PUSHop, null, null, extraSize);
    attach(obj, knownAddress);
    obj^.size := addressSize;
    obj^.address.level := currentLevel;
    obj^.address.displacement := frameSize;
    writeTableDetails(declaration)
  end;
procIlpFPSrpisC:
  begin
    jumpAddr := nextInstrAddr;
    emit(JUMPop, null, CBr, null);
    attach(obj, knownRoutine);
    obj^.size := closureSize;
    obj^.address.level := currentLevel;
    obj^.address.displacement := nextInstrAddr;
    writeTableDetails(declaration);
    if currentLevel = maxRoutineLevel then
      reportRestriction('can''t nest routines so deeply           ')
    else
      begin
        encodeBindParameters(child[2], currentLevel + 1, 0, argsSize);
        encodeExecute(child[3], currentLevel + 1, linkDataSize)
      end;
    emit(RETURNop, 0, null, argsSize);
    patch(jumpAddr, nextInstrAddr);
    extraSize := 0
  end;
funcIlpFPSrpcolonTisE:
  begin
    jumpAddr := nextInstrAddr;
    emit(JUMPop, null, CBr, null);
    attach(obj, knownRoutine);
    obj^.size := closureSize;
    obj^.address.level := currentLevel;
    obj^.address.displacement := nextInstrAddr;
    writeTableDetails(declaration);
    if currentLevel = maxRoutineLevel then
      reportRestriction('can''t nest routines more than 7 deep    ')
    else
      begin
        encodeBindParameters(child[2], currentLevel + 1, 0, argsSize);
        encodeEvaluate(child[4], currentLevel + 1, linkDataSize, valSize)
      end;
    emit(RETURNop, valSize, null, argsSize);
    patch(jumpAddr, nextInstrAddr);
    extraSize := 0
  end;
typeIisT:
  begin
    valSize := typeSize(child[2]);
    {… just to ensure the type's representation is decided}
    extraSize := 0
  end;
DsemicolonD:
```

```
        begin
          encodeElaborate(child[1], currentLevel, frameSize, extraSize1);
          encodeElaborate(child[2], currentLevel, frameSize + extraSize1,
              extraSize2);
          extraSize := extraSize1 + extraSize2
        end
    end {case}
end; {encodeElaborate}

{Parameters}

procedure encodeBindParameters (formals: AST;
                  currentLevel: RoutineLevel;
                  otherArgsSize: Natural;
                  var argsSize: Natural);
  var
    valSize, argsSize1, argsSize2: Natural;
begin
  with formals^ do
    case tag of
      empty:
        argsSize := 0;
      FPcommaFPS:
        begin
          encodeBindParameters(child[2], currentLevel, otherArgsSize,
              argsSize1);
          encodeBindParameters(child[1], currentLevel,
              otherArgsSize + argsSize1, argsSize2);
          argsSize := argsSize1 + argsSize2
        end;
      IcolonT:
        begin
          valSize := typeSize(child[2]);
          argsSize := valSize;
          attach(obj, unknownValue);
          obj^.size := valSize;
          obj^.address.level := currentLevel;
          obj^.address.displacement := -otherArgsSize - argsSize;
          writeTableDetails(formals)
        end;
      varIcolonT:
        begin
          valSize := typeSize(child[2]);
          {… just to ensure the type's representation is decided}
          argsSize := addressSize;
          attach(obj, unknownAddress);
          obj^.size := addressSize;
          obj^.address.level := currentLevel;
          obj^.address.displacement := -otherArgsSize - argsSize;
          writeTableDetails(formals)
        end;
      procIlpFPSrp, funcIlpFPSrpcolonT:
        begin
          argsSize := closureSize;
          attach(obj, unknownRoutine);
          obj^.size := closureSize;
          obj^.address.level := currentLevel;
          obj^.address.displacement := -otherArgsSize - argsSize;
          writeTableDetails(formals)
        end
    end {case}
end; {encodeBindParameters}

procedure encodeGiveArguments (actuals: AST;
                  currentLevel: RoutineLevel;
                  frameSize: Natural;
                  var argsSize: Natural);
  var
    argsSize1, argsSize2: Natural;
```

```
        begin
          with actuals^ do
            case tag of
              empty:
                argsSize := 0;
              APcommaAPS:
                begin
                  encodeGiveArguments(child[1], currentLevel, frameSize, argsSize1);
                  encodeGiveArguments(child[2], currentLevel, frameSize + argsSize1,
                      argsSize2);
                  argsSize := argsSize1 + argsSize2
                end;
              E:
                encodeEvaluate(child[1], currentLevel, frameSize, argsSize);
              varV:
                begin
                  encodeFetchAddress(child[1], currentLevel, frameSize);
                  argsSize := addressSize
                end;
              procI, funcI:
                begin
                  with child[1]^.decl^.obj^ do
                    case kind of
                      knownRoutine:
                        begin
                          emit(LOADAop, null, displayRegister(currentLevel,
                              address.level), 0); {static link}
                          emit(LOADAop, null, CBr, address.displacement) {entry address}
                        end;
                      unknownRoutine:
                        emit(LOADop, closureSize, displayRegister(currentLevel,
                            address.level), address.displacement);
                      primitiveRoutine:
                        begin
                          emit(LOADAop, null, SBr, 0); {static link}
                          emit(LOADAop, null, PBr, displacement) {entry address}
                        end
                    end; {case}
                  argsSize := closureSize
                end
            end {case}
        end; {encodeGiveArguments}

        {Programs}

        procedure encodeRun (programAST: AST;
                        showingTable: Boolean);
        begin
          tableDetailsReqd := showingTable;
          startCodeGeneration;
          encodeExecute(programAST, 0, 0);
          emit(HALTop, null, null, null);
          finishCodeGeneration
        end; {encodeRun}

      end. {CodeGenerator}
```

E.7   Compilation

```
unit Compiler;

interface

  uses
    CompilerGlobals, AbstractSyntaxTrees, LexicalAnalyser, SyntacticAnalyser,
    ContextualAnalyser, RuntimeOrganization, CodeGenerator;

  procedure initCompilation;
    {Make ready for future compilations, by setting up the standard environment.}

  procedure compileProgram (showingAST, showingTable: Boolean;
                      var successful: Boolean);
    {Translate the source program into TAM code, after ensuring that it is
    well-formed.}

{===============================================================================}

implementation

  procedure initCompilation;
  begin
    establishStdEnvironment;
    elaborateStdEnvironment
  end; {initCompilation}

  procedure compileProgram (showingAST, showingTable: Boolean;
                      var successful: Boolean);
      var
        theAST: AST;
  begin
    startErrorReporting;
    ...;
    writeLn('********** Triangle Compiler (version 1.5)**********');
    writeLn('Syntactic analysis ...');
    parseProgram(theAST);                      {... 1st pass}
    if noErrors then
      begin
        writeLn('Contextual analysis ...');
        checkProgram(theAST);                  {... 2nd pass}
        if showingAST then drawAST(theAST);
        if noErrors then
          begin
            writeLn('Code generation ...');
            encodeRun(theAST, showingTable)    {... 3rd pass}
          end
      end;
    disposeAST(theAST);
    successful := noErrors;
    if successful then
      writeLn('Compilation was successful.')
    else
      writeLn('Compilation was unsuccessful.')
  end; {compileProgram}

end. {Compiler}
```

Bibliography

Aho, A.H., Sethi, R., and Ullman, J.D. (1985) *Compilers – Principles, Methods, and Tools*, Addison–Wesley, Reading, Massachusetts, United States.

Aho, A.H., and Ullman, J.D. (1972) *The Theory of Parsing, Translation and Compiling*, Vol. I: *Parsing*, Prentice Hall, Englewood Cliffs, New Jersey, United States.

Ammann, U. (1981) The Zürich implementation, in *Pascal – the Language and its Implementation* (ed. Barron, D.W.), Wiley, Chichester, England, pp. 63–82.

Backhouse, R. (1979) *The Syntax of Programming Languages*, Prentice Hall International, Hemel Hempstead, England.

Brown, D.F., Moura, H., and Watt, D.A. (1992) Actress – an action semantics directed compiler generator, in *Compiler Construction – 4th International Conference, CC '92* (ed. Kastens, U., and Pfahler, P.), Springer, Berlin, Germany, pp. 95–109.

Cardelli, L. (1984) Compiling a functional language, in *Eleventh Annual ACM Symposium on Principles of Programming Languages*, ACM Press, New York, United States, pp. 208–17.

DeRemer, F.L., and Jüllig, R. (1980) Tree-affix dendrogrammars for languages and compilers, in *Semantics-Directed Compiler Generation* (ed. Jones, N.D.), Springer, Berlin, Germany, pp. 300–19.

Dijkstra, E.W. (1960) Recursive programming, *Numerische Mathematik* **2**, 312–18; also in *Programming Systems and Languages* (ed. Rosen, S.), McGraw–Hill, New York, United States, pp. 221–7.

Earley, J., and Sturgis, H. (1970) A formalism for translator interactions, *Communications of the ACM* **13**, 607–17.

Ganapathi, M., Fischer, C.N., and Hennessy, J.L. (1982) Retargetable compiler code generation, *Computing Surveys* **14**, 573–92.

Ghezzi, C., and Jazayeri, M. (1987) *Programming Language Concepts*, 2nd edn, Wiley, New York, United States.

Graham, S.L. (1984) Code generation and optimization, in *Methods and Tools for Compiler Construction* (ed. Lorho, B.), Cambridge University Press, Cambridge, England.

Hoare, C.A.R. (1972) Notes on data structuring, in *Structured Programming* (eds. Dahl, O.-J., Dijkstra, E.W., and Hoare, C.A.R.), Academic Press, London, England, pp. 83–174.

Hoare, C.A.R. (1973) Hints on programming language design, in *First Annual ACM Symposium on Principles of Programming Languages*, ACM Press, New York, United States.

Hoare, C.A.R. (1975) Recursive data structures, *International Journal of Computer and Information Sciences* **4**, 105–32.

Lee, P. (1989) *Realistic Compiler Generation*, MIT Press, Cambridge, Massachusetts, United States.

McCarthy, J. (1963) Towards a mathematical science of computation, in *Information Processing 1962*, North-Holland, Amsterdam, Netherlands, pp. 21–8.

McCarthy, J., Abrahams, P.W., Edwards, D.J., *et al.* (1965) *LISP 1.5 Programmer's Manual*, 2nd edn, MIT Press, Cambridge, Massachusetts, United States.

Milner, R. (1978) A theory of type polymorphism in programming, *Journal of Computer and System Science* **17**, 348–75.

Mosses, P.D. (1992) *Action Semantics*, Cambridge University Press, Cambridge, England.

Nori, K.V., Ammann, U., Jensen, K., *et al.* (1981) Pascal-P implementation notes, in *Pascal – the Language and its Implementation* (ed. Barron, D.W.), Wiley, Chichester, England, pp. 125–70.

Rees, J., and Clinger, W. (eds.) (1986) Revised[3] report on the algorithmic language Scheme, *ACM SIGPLAN Notices* **21**, 37–79.

Sethi, R. (1988) *Programming Languages – Concepts and Constructs*, Addison–Wesley, Reading, Massachusetts, United States.

Tennent, R.D. (1981) *Principles of Programming Languages*, Prentice Hall International, Hemel Hempstead, England.

Watt, D.A. (1990) *Programming Language Concepts and Paradigms*, Prentice Hall International, Hemel Hempstead, England.

Watt, D.A. (1991) *Programming Language Syntax and Semantics*, Prentice Hall International, Hemel Hempstead, England.

Watt, D.A., and Findlay, W. (1981) A Pascal diagnostic system, in *Pascal – the Language and its Implementation* (ed. Barron, D.W.), Wiley, Chichester, England, pp. 181–98.

Welsh, J., and Hay, A. (1986) *A Model Implementation of Standard Pascal*, Prentice Hall International, Hemel Hempstead, England.

Welsh, J., and McKeag, M. (1980) *Structured System Programming*, Prentice Hall International, Hemel Hempstead, England.

Welsh, J., and Quinn, C. (1972) A Pascal compiler for ICL 1900 series computers, *Software Practice and Experience* **2**, 73–7.

Wilson, P.R. (1992) Uniprocessor garbage collection techniques, in *Proceedings of International Workshop on Memory Management*, Springer, Berlin, Germany.

Wirth, N. (1971) The design of a Pascal compiler, *Software Practice and Experience* **1**, 309–33.

Wirth, N. (1986) Microprocessor architectures – a comparison based on code generation by compiler, *Communications of the ACM* **29**, 978–90.

Index